CURRIES 500

CURRIES 500

Discover a world of spice in dishes from India, Thailand and South-East Asia, as well as Africa, the Middle East and the Caribbean, shown in 500 sizzling photographs

Consultant Editor: MRIDULA BALJEKAR

HERMES
HOUSE

This edition is published by Hermes House,
an imprint of Anness Publishing Ltd,
Blaby Road,
Wigston, Leicestershire
LE18 4SE

Email: info@anness.com

Web: www.hermeshouse.com; www.annesspublishing.com

If you like the images in this book and would like to investigate
using them for publishing, promotions or advertising, please visit
our website www.practicalpictures.com for more information.

Publisher: Joanna Lorenz
Editor: Joy Wotton
Jacket Design: Nigel Partridge
Copy Editor: Jay Thundercliffe
Production Controller: Mai-Ling Collyer
Editorial Reader: Lauren Taylor
Proofreading Manager: Lindsay Zamponi
Design: SMI

© Anness Publishing Ltd 2010, 2011

ETHICAL TRADING POLICY

At Anness Publishing we believe that business should be
conducted in an ethical and ecologically sustainable way, with
respect for the environment and a proper regard to the
replacement of the natural resources we employ.
As a publisher, we use a lot of wood pulp in high-quality paper for
printing, and that wood commonly comes from spruce trees. We
are therefore currently growing more than 750,000 trees in three
Scottish forest plantations: Berrymoss (130 hectares/320 acres),
West Touxhill (125 hectares/305 acres) and Deveron Forest
(75 hectares/185 acres). The forests we manage contain more
than 3.5 times the number of trees employed each year in
making paper for the books we manufacture.
Because of this ongoing ecological investment programme, you, as
our customer, can have the pleasure and reassurance of knowing
that a tree is being cultivated on your behalf to naturally replace
the materials used to make the book you are holding.
Our forestry programme is run in accordance with the UK
Woodland Assurance Scheme (UKWAS) and will be certified by
the internationally recognized Forest Stewardship Council (FSC).
The FSC is a non-government organization dedicated to
promoting responsible management of the world's forests.
Certification ensures forests are managed in an environmentally
sustainable and socially responsible way. For further information
about this scheme, go to www.annesspublishing.com/trees

A CIP catalogue record for this book is available from
the British Library.

Recipes in this book have previously appeared in other books
published by Lorenz Books.

PUBLISHER'S NOTE

Although the advice and information in this book are believed to
be accurate and true at the time of going to press, neither the
authors nor the publisher can accept any legal responsibility or
liability for any errors or omissions that may have been made nor
for any inaccuracies nor for any harm or injury that comes about
from following instructions or advice in this book.

Notes

Bracketed terms are intended for American readers.
For all recipes, quantities are given in both metric and imperial measures and, where appropriate, in standard
cups and spoons. Follow one set of measures, but not a mixture, because they are not interchangeable.
Standard spoon and cup measures are level. 1 tsp = 5ml, 1 tbsp = 15ml, 1 cup = 250ml/8fl oz. Australian standard tablespoons
are 20ml. Australian readers should use 3 tsp in place of 1 tbsp for measuring small quantities.
American pints are 16fl oz/2 cups. American readers should use 20fl oz/2.5 cups in place of 1 pint when measuring liquids.
Electric oven temperatures in this book are for conventional ovens. When using a fan oven, the temperature will probably need to
be reduced by about 10–20°C/20–40°F. Since ovens vary, you should check with your manufacturer's instruction book for guidance.

The nutritional analysis given for each recipe is calculated per portion (i.e. serving or item), unless otherwise stated.
If the recipe gives a range, such as Serves 4–6, then the nutritional analysis will be for the smaller portion size, i.e. 6 servings.
The analysis does not include optional ingredients, such as salt added to taste.
Medium (US large) eggs are used unless otherwise stated.
Vegetable ghee has been used in the recipes, but ghee made from butter can be used instead.

Main front cover image shows Lahore-style Lamb – for recipe, see page 124

Contents

Introduction

Exotic spiced sauces, or curries, have been used for thousands of years to liven up the daily staples of rice, noodles and bread. Turmeric, cumin, coriander, cardamom, chilli, fenugreek and

many other pungent spices and scented flavourings have been used to contribute magical tastes and aromas to dishes all over the world. It is the careful blending and combining of these various spices, herbs and other aromatics, often into a mixed powder or blended into a paste to which other ingredients are then added, that defines much of the art of creating mouthwatering curries.

India has long been known as the spice bowl of the world, and South-east Asia, too, has its own important place in the international history of the spice trade. The use of spices was an established way of life in these sun-drenched, monsoon-fed lands long before traders and merchants, including Arabs, English, Dutch, Portuguese and Spanish, were lured by the value of these exotic ingredients.

The word curry is generally believed to be an anglicized version of the south Indian word *kaari*, and in India, the word refers to a sauce or gravy used as an accompaniment to moisten

rice or to make bread more enjoyable. Other theories suggest that the word *cury* has existed in English in the context of cooking since the 14th century, and that it was originally derived from the French verb *cuire* (to cook).

Curries are perfect for modern living with their emphasis on fresh ingredients, speedy preparation and exciting flavours. Besides offering fabulous tastes, Indian and South-east Asian cooking can be extremely healthy with their focus on fresh food and good-quality

ingredients – it is even thought that garlic and root ginger, essential ingredients in many curries, contain properties that may help to combat heart diseases and stomach ulcers respectively. Traditionally, curry in India is accompanied by rice or breads, in South-east Asia by rice or noodles. Curried meat and fish are usually served in small quantities, surrounded by inviting little side dishes, such as pickles, chutneys, salads and sambals, flavoured with fresh herbs and chillies, yogurt or soy sauce, and used as seasonings.

Discover how to make over 500 authentic curry dishes in this easy-to-use guide, which offers an incredible range of some of the greatest curries of the world. All the classics are here, from Rogan Josh and Beef Madras to creamy Lamb Korma and Chicken Saag, but there are many unusual contemporary dishes to try too, such as Green Curry Puffs or Sumac Spiced Burgers with Relish. The recipes are divided into accessible chapters on Appetizers and Light Bites; Fish and Shellfish; Chicken and Poultry; Meat and Game; Vegetarian; Biryanis and Rice; Rice Side Dishes and Breads; Side Dishes; and Chutneys, Pickles and Salads.

Many of the spices, herbs and aromatics used in this book are readily available. Cumin, coriander, cardamom, garlic, turmeric, cinnamon, ginger, chilli and peppercorns are available in most stores and supermarkets, both in the form of dried and ground powder, as seeds, or fresh and whole. Some ingredients may be harder to buy – mango powder, asafoetida, galangal and fennel, as well as fresh leaves such as curry leaves, kaffir lime leaves and fenugreek – however, there are many Asian speciality stores where these ingredients can be bought or you can look for them online or through mail order.

Spicy food is universally popular, and you will find here an inspiring range of dishes from many countries around the world including the Indian Subcontinent, Iran, Malaysia, Burma, Thailand, Singapore, Vietnam, Korea and China. With every deliciously tempting curry recipe clearly explained in steps with a photograph of the finished dish, you can be certain to find a curry dish that is perfect for you, whatever your mood or occasion.

Spiced Mango Soup

This delicious dish was invented at Chutney Mary's, the Anglo-Indian restaurant in London. It is best served lightly chilled. Gram flour, also known as besan or chickpea flour, is available from Asian stores.

Serves 4

2 ripe mangoes
15ml/1 tbsp gram flour
120ml/4fl oz/½ cup natural (plain) yogurt
900ml/1½ pints/3¾ cups cold or chilled water
2.5ml/½ tsp grated fresh root ginger
2 fresh red chillies, seeded and finely chopped
30ml/2 tbsp olive oil
2.5ml/½ tsp mustard seeds
2.5ml/½ tsp cumin seeds
8 curry leaves
salt and ground black pepper
fresh mint leaves, shredded, to garnish
natural (plain) yogurt, to serve

1 Peel the mangoes, remove the stones (pits) and cut the flesh into chunks. Purée in a food processor or blender until smooth. Pour the purée into a pan and stir in the gram flour, yogurt, measured water, ginger and chillies.

2 Bring all the ingredients slowly to the boil, stirring them occasionally. Simmer for about 4–5 minutes until thickened slightly, then set aside off the heat.

3 Heat the oil in a frying pan over medium to low heat. Add the mustard seeds, cover the pan, and cook for a few seconds until they begin to pop, then add the cumin seeds.

4 Add the curry leaves to the pan and then cook for about 5 minutes. Stir the spice mixture into the soup, return it to the heat and simmer for 10 minutes.

5 Press through a sieve (strainer), if you like, then season to taste with salt and black pepper. Leave the soup to cool completely, then chill for at least 1 hour.

6 Ladle the soup into chilled serving bowls, and top each with a dollop of natural yogurt. Garnish with the shredded fresh mint leaves and serve immediately.

Forest Curry Soup

This is a thin, soupy curry with lots of fresh green vegetables and robust flavours. It originated in the forested regions of Thailand, where it would be made using wild leaves and roots.

Serves 2

600ml/1 pint/2½ cups water
5ml/1 tsp Thai vegetarian red curry paste
5cm/2in piece fresh galangal or fresh root ginger
90g/3½oz/scant 1 cup green beans
2 kaffir lime leaves, torn
8 baby corn cobs, halved widthways
2 heads Chinese broccoli, chopped
90g/3½oz/generous 3 cups beansprouts
15ml/1 tbsp drained bottled green peppercorns, crushed
10ml/2 tsp sugar
5ml/1 tsp salt

1 Heat the water in a large pan. Add the red curry paste and stir until it has dissolved completely. Bring to the boil.

2 Meanwhile, using a sharp knife, peel and finely chop the fresh galangal or root ginger.

3 Add the galangal or ginger, green beans, lime leaves, baby corn cobs, broccoli and beansprouts to the pan. Stir in the crushed peppercorns, sugar and salt. Bring back to the boil, then reduce the heat to low and simmer for 2 minutes. Serve immediately in warmed bowls.

Cook's Tip
You can serve this soup with plain rice or noodles for a simple lunch or a quick and easy supper.

Variation
Garnish the soup with some thinly sliced hard-boiled egg just before serving, or, if you prefer, provide a couple of whole hard-boiled eggs to serve on the side.

Spiced Mango Soup Energy 83kcal/354kJ; Protein 3g; Carbohydrate 14.4g, of which sugars 12.7g; Fat 2g, of which saturates 0.5g; Cholesterol 0mg; Calcium 72mg; Fibre 2g; Sodium 28mg.
Forest Curry Energy 154kcal/643kJ; Protein 14.9g; Carbohydrate 14.1g, of which sugars 11.8g; Fat 4.5g, of which saturates 0.8g, Cholesterol 0mg; Calcium 173mg; Fibre 9.1g; Sodium 678mg.

Potato Soup with Garlic Samosas

Soup and samosas are the ideal partners. Bought samosas are given an easy, but clever, flavour lift in this simple recipe.

Serves 4
60ml/4 tbsp sunflower oil
10ml/2 tsp black
   mustard seeds
1 large onion, chopped
1 fresh red chilli, seeded
   and chopped
2.5ml/½ tsp ground turmeric
1.5ml/¼ tsp cayenne pepper
900g/2lb potatoes, cut into cubes

4 fresh curry leaves
750ml/1¼ pint/3 cups
   vegetable stock
225g/8oz spinach leaves, torn
   if large
400ml/14fl oz/1⅔ cups
   coconut milk
handful of fresh coriander
   (cilantro) leaves
salt and black pepper

For the garlic samosas
1 large garlic clove, crushed
25g/1oz/2 tbsp butter
6 vegetable samosas

1 Heat the oil in a large pan. Add the mustard seeds, cover and cook until they begin to pop. Add the onion and chilli and cook for 5–6 minutes, until softened.

2 Stir the turmeric, cayenne, potatoes, curry leaves and stock into the pan. Bring to the boil, reduce the heat and cover the pan. Simmer for about 15 minutes, stirring occasionally, until the potatoes are just tender.

3 Meanwhile, prepare the samosas. Preheat the oven to 180°C/350°F/Gas 4. Melt the garlic with the butter in a small pan, stirring and crushing the garlic into the butter.

4 Place the samosas on an ovenproof dish – a gratin dish or quiche dish is ideal. Brush them lightly with the butter, turn them over and brush with the remaining butter. Heat through in the oven for about 5 minutes, until piping hot.

5 Add the spinach to the soup and cook for 5 minutes. Stir in the coconut milk and cook for a further 5 minutes.

6 Season and add the coriander leaves before ladling the soup into bowls. Serve with the garlic samosas.

Curried Parsnip Soup

The mild sweetness of parsnips and mango chutney is given an exciting lift with a blend of spices in this simple soup.

Serves 4
30ml/2 tbsp olive oil
1 onion, chopped
1 garlic clove, crushed
1 small green chilli, seeded and
   finely chopped
15ml/1 tbsp grated fresh
   root ginger
5 large parsnips, diced
5ml/1 tsp cumin seeds

5ml/1 tsp ground coriander
2.5ml/½ tsp ground turmeric
30ml/2 tbsp mango chutney
1.2 litres/2 pints/5 cups water
juice of 1 lime
salt and ground black pepper
60ml/4 tbsp natural (plain) yogurt
   and mango chutney, to serve
chopped fresh coriander (cilantro),
   to garnish (optional)

For the sesame naan croûtons
45ml/3 tbsp olive oil
1 large naan, cut into small dice
15ml/1 tbsp sesame seeds

1 Heat the oil in a large pan and add the onion, garlic, chilli and ginger. Cook for 4–5 minutes, until the onion has softened. Add the parsnips and cook for 2–3 minutes. Sprinkle in the cumin seeds, ground coriander and turmeric, and cook for 1 minute, stirring.

2 Add the chutney and the water. Season well with salt and pepper and bring to the boil. Reduce the heat, cover and simmer for 15 minutes, until the parsnips are soft.

3 Cool the soup slightly, then purée it in a food processor or blender and return it to the pan. Stir in the lime juice.

4 To make the naan croûtons, heat the oil in a large frying pan and cook the diced naan for 3–4 minutes, stirring, until golden all over. Remove from the heat and drain off any excess oil. Add the sesame seeds and return the pan to the heat for no more than 30 seconds, until the seeds are pale golden.

5 Ladle the soup into bowls. Spoon a little yogurt into each portion, then top with a little mango chutney and some of the sesame naan croûtons. Garnish with chopped fresh coriander, if you like.

Curried Parsnip Energy 150kcal/623kJ; Protein 4.7g; Carbohydrate 7.8g, of which sugars 6.8g; Fat 11.4g, of which saturates 7g; Cholesterol 32mg; Calcium 170mg; Fibre 0.8g; Sodium 112mg.
Potato with Samosas Energy 658kcal/2744kJ; Protein 8.8g; Carbohydrate 63.4g, of which sugars 15.5g; Fat 42.8g, of which saturates 5.1g; Cholesterol 13mg; Calcium 184mg; Fibre 5.9g; Sodium 375mg.

Monkfish Soup with Red Thai Spices

This light and creamy coconut soup provides a base for a colourful fusion of red-curried tender monkfish chunks and flat rice noodles.

Serves 4
175g/6oz flat rice noodles
30ml/2 tbsp vegetable oil
2 garlic cloves, chopped
15ml/1 tbsp red curry paste
450g/1lb monkfish fillet, cut into bitesize pieces
300ml/½ pint/1¼ cups coconut cream
750ml/1¼ pints/3 cups hot chicken stock
45ml/3 tbsp Thai fish sauce
15ml/1 tbsp palm sugar (jaggery)
60ml/4 tbsp roasted peanuts, roughly chopped
4 spring onions (scallions), shredded lengthways
50g/2oz/½ cup beansprouts
large handful of fresh Thai basil leaves
salt and ground black pepper
1 fresh red chilli, seeded and cut lengthways into slivers, to garnish

1 Soak the noodles in a bowl of boiling water for 10 minutes, or according to the packet instructions. Drain.

2 Heat the oil in a wok or pan over high heat. Add the garlic and cook for 2 minutes. Stir in the curry paste and cook for 1 minute, until fragrant.

3 Add the monkfish and stir-fry over high heat for about 4–5 minutes, until just tender. Pour the coconut cream and chicken stock into the pan.

4 Stir the fish sauce and sugar into the pan, and bring the mixture just to the boil. Add the drained noodles and cook for 1–2 minutes, until tender.

5 Stir half the peanuts, half the spring onions, half the beansprouts and the Thai basil leaves into the pan. Season with salt and black pepper to taste.

6 Ladle the soup into deep individual soup bowls and sprinkle over the remaining peanuts. Garnish with the remaining spring onions, beansprouts and the slivers of red chilli.

Curried Salmon Soup

A hint of mild curry paste really enhances the flavour of this tasty soup, without making it too spicy. Grated creamed coconut adds a luxury touch, while helping to amalgamate the flavours.

Serves 4
50g/2oz/¼ cup butter
2 onions, roughly chopped
10ml/2 tsp mild curry paste
150ml/¼ pint/⅔ cup white wine
300ml/½ pint/1¼ cups double (heavy) cream
50g/2oz/½ cup creamed coconut, grated or 120ml/4fl oz/½ cup coconut cream
2 potatoes, about 350g/12oz, cubed
450g/1lb salmon fillet, skinned and cut into bitesize pieces
60ml/4 tbsp chopped fresh flat-leaf parsley
salt and ground black pepper

1 Melt the butter in a large pan, add the onions and cook for about 3–4 minutes until beginning to soften. Stir in the curry paste. Cook for 1 minute more.

2 Add 475ml/16fl oz/2 cups water, the wine, cream and creamed coconut or coconut cream, with seasoning. Bring to the boil, stirring until the coconut has dissolved.

3 Add the potatoes and simmer, covered, for about 15 minutes or until they are almost tender. Do not allow them to break down into the liquid.

4 Add the fish and cook gently so as not to break it up for about 2–3 minutes until just cooked. Add the parsley and adjust the seasoning. Serve immediately.

> **Cook's Tip**
> There is a wide choice of curry pastes available. Select a concentrated paste for this recipe, rather than a 'cook-in-sauce' type of product. If you cannot find a suitable paste, cook 5ml/1 tsp curry powder in a pan with a little melted butter over low heat and use that mixture instead.

Red Monkfish Energy 379kcal/1589kJ; Protein 25.5g; Carbohydrate 41.2g, of which sugars 4.7g; Fat 12g, of which saturates 2g; Cholesterol 18mg; Calcium 49mg; Fibre 0.9g; Sodium 111mg.
Curried Salmon Energy 837kcal/3466kJ; Protein 26.3g; Carbohydrate 16.6g, of which sugars 3.6g; Fat 71.8g, of which saturates 41.2g; Cholesterol 186mg; Calcium 74mg; Fibre 0.9g; Sodium 158mg.

Chicken Soup with Curry Paste

This is an example of a distinctly Eurasian dish – a delicious spicy chicken soup made with freshly made curry paste.

Serves 4–6
1 chicken, about 1kg/2¼lb
2 cinnamon sticks
5ml/1 tsp black peppercorns
5ml/1 tsp fennel seeds
5ml/1 tsp cumin seeds
15ml/1 tbsp ghee or vegetable oil with a little butter
15–30ml/1–2 tbsp brown mustard seeds
a handful of fresh curry leaves
salt and ground black pepper
2 limes, quartered, to serve

For the curry paste
40g/1½oz fresh root ginger, peeled and chopped
4 garlic cloves, chopped
4 shallots, chopped
2 lemon grass stalks, trimmed and chopped
4 dried red chillies, soaked to soften, drained, seeded and the pulp scraped out
15–30ml/1–2 tbsp Indian curry powder

1 To make the curry paste, grind the ginger with the garlic, shallots and lemon grass, using a mortar and pestle, food processor or blender. Add the chilli pulp and curry powder, blend again, and set aside.

2 Put the chicken and the chicken feet, if using, in a deep pan with the cinnamon sticks, peppercorns, fennel and cumin seeds. Add enough water to just cover, and bring it to the boil.

3 Reduce the heat and cook gently for about 1 hour, until the chicken is cooked. Remove the chicken from the broth, skin it and shred the meat. Strain the broth, discarding the spices.

4 In a pan or wok, heat the ghee or oil and butter. Stir in the mustard seeds and, once they begin to pop and give off a nutty aroma, add the curry paste. Fry the paste until fragrant, then pour in the strained broth.

5 Bring the broth to the boil and season to taste with salt and pepper. Add the curry leaves and shredded chicken, and ladle the soup into bowls. Serve with wedges of lime to squeeze into the soup.

Aubergine Soup with Beef and Lime

This tasty soup can be made with aubergines, green jackfruit or any of the squash family. The quantity of rice should be greater than the soup, as the soup is meant to moisten and flavour the rice.

Serves 4
30ml/2 tbsp palm, groundnut (peanut) or corn oil
150g/5oz lean beef, cut into thin strips
500ml/17fl oz/generous 2 cups coconut milk
10ml/2 tsp sugar
3–4 Thai aubergines (eggplants) or 1 large aubergine, cut into wedges
3–4 kaffir lime leaves
juice of 1 lime
salt

For the spice paste
4 shallots, chopped
4 red chillies, seeded and chopped
25g/1oz fresh root ginger, chopped
15g/½oz fresh turmeric, chopped or 2.5ml/½ tsp ground turmeric
2 garlic cloves, chopped
5ml/1 tsp coriander seeds
2.5ml/½ tsp cumin seeds
3 candlenuts or macadamia nuts

To serve
cooked rice
1 lime, quartered
chilli sambal

1 To make the spice paste, using a mortar and pestle, grind all the ingredients together to form a textured paste, or process them together in an electric blender or food processor.

2 Heat the oil in a wok or heavy pan, stir in the spice paste and fry until fragrant.

3 Add the beef, stirring to coat it well in the spice paste, then add the coconut milk and sugar. Bring the liquid to the boil, then reduce the heat and simmer gently for 10 minutes.

4 Add the aubergine wedges and kaffir lime leaves to the pan and cook gently for a further 5–10 minutes, until tender but not mushy. Stir in the lime juice and season with salt to taste.

5 Ladle the soup into individual warmed bowls and serve with bowls of cooked rice to spoon the soup over, wedges of lime to squeeze on the top and a chilli sambal.

Chicken Soup Energy 264kcal/1093kJ; Protein 20.7g; Carbohydrate 1.6g, of which sugars 1g; Fat 19.4g, of which saturates 6.3g; Cholesterol 112mg; Calcium 19mg; Fibre 0.5g; Sodium 104mg.
Aubergine Soup Energy 224kcal/938kJ; Protein 12.1g; Carbohydrate 14.6g, of which sugars 12.6g; Fat 13.6g, of which saturates 3.2g; Cholesterol 22mg; Calcium 79mg; Fibre 3g; Sodium 181mg.

Curry Crackers

Crisp curry-flavoured crackers are very good with creamy cheese or yogurt dips and make an unusual nibble with pre-dinner drinks. Add a pinch of cayenne pepper for an extra kick.

Makes about 30
175g/6oz/1½ cups self-raising (self-rising) flour, plus extra for dusting
pinch of salt
10ml/2 tsp garam masala
75g/3oz/6 tbsp butter, diced
5ml/1 tsp finely chopped fresh coriander (cilantro)
1 egg, beaten

For the topping
1 egg, beaten
black onion seeds
garam masala

1 Preheat the oven to 200°C/400°F/Gas 6. Put the flour, salt and garam masala into a bowl. Rub in the butter until the mixture resembles fine breadcrumbs. Stir in the coriander, add the egg and mix to a soft dough.

2 Turn out on to a lightly floured surface and knead gently until smooth. Roll out to a thickness of about 3mm/⅛in.

3 Cut the dough into neat rectangles measuring about 7.5 × 2.5cm/3 × 1in. Brush with a little beaten egg and sprinkle each cracker with a few black onion seeds. Place on non-stick baking sheets and bake in the oven for about 12 minutes, until the crackers are light golden brown all over.

4 Remove from the oven and, using a metal spatula, transfer to a wire rack. Put a little garam masala in a saucer and, using a dry pastry brush, dust each cracker with a little of the spice mixture. Leave to cool before serving.

> **Cook's Tip**
> *Garam masala is a mixture of Indian spices that usually contains a blend of cinnamon, cloves, peppercorns, cardamom seeds and cumin seeds. You can buy it ready-made from supermarkets or Asian stores or make your own.*

Low-fat Curry Thins

These spicy little crackers are low in fat and are ideal as a tasty pre-dinner snack.

Makes 12
50g/2oz/1½ cups plain (all-purpose) flour, plus extra for dusting
pinch of salt
5ml/1 tsp curry powder
1.5ml/¼ tsp chilli powder
15ml/1 tbsp chopped fresh coriander (cilantro)
30ml/2 tbsp water

1 Preheat the oven to 180°C/350°F/Gas 4.

2 Sift the flour and salt into a mixing bowl. Add the curry powder and the chilli powder. Make a well in the centre and add the coriander and water. Gradually incorporate the flour and mix to a firm dough.

3 Turn out the dough on to a lightly floured surface, knead with your hands until the dough is smooth and then set it aside to rest for 5 minutes.

4 Cut the dough into 12 equal pieces and knead each into a small ball. Roll out each ball very thinly to a 10cm/4in round, sprinkling more flour over the dough if necessary to prevent it from sticking to the rolling pin.

5 Arrange the rounds on two ungreased baking sheets, spaced apart, then bake in the preheated oven for 15 minutes. Use a metal spatula to turn the crackers over once during cooking. When very lightly browned, using a metal spatula, carefully transfer the crackers to a wire rack to cool.

> **Cook's Tip**
> *Commercial curry powders vary enormously in flavour and their degree of heat, depending on the specific spices used and their proportions. The best-quality ones tend to be more expensive, but this is not invariably the case. Try different brands until you find one that you like.*

Curry Crackers Energy 39kcal/164kJ; Protein 0.6g; Carbohydrate 4.6g, of which sugars 0.1g; Fat 2.2g, of which saturates 1.3g; Cholesterol 5mg; Calcium 11mg; Fibre 0.3g; Sodium 17mg.
Low-fat Curry Thins Energy 17kcal/73kJ; Protein 0.5g; Carbohydrate 3.6g, of which sugars 0.1g; Fat 0.2g, of which saturates 0g; Cholesterol 0mg; Calcium 14mg; Fibre 0.4g; Sodium 6mg.

Spiced Savoury Biscuits

These biscuits are ideal for serving with drinks. Poppy and onion seeds contribute to the flavour of these crunchy treats.

Makes 20–30

150g/5oz/1¼ cups plain (all-purpose) flour
10ml/2 tsp curry powder
115g/4oz/½ cup butter
75g/3oz/¾ cup grated Cheddar cheese
10ml/2 tsp poppy seeds
5ml/1 tsp black onion seeds
1 egg yolk
cumin seeds, to garnish

1 Grease two large baking sheets. Sift the flour and curry powder into a mixing bowl.

2 Rub in the butter until the mixture resembles breadcrumbs, then stir in the cheese, poppy seeds and black onion seeds.

3 Stir the egg yolk into the mixture and mix with a wooden spoon until a firm dough forms.

4 Wrap the dough in a piece of clear film (plastic wrap) and chill in the refrigerator for 30 minutes.

5 Roll out the dough on a floured surface to a thickness of about 3mm/⅛in. Cut into shapes with a cookie cutter.

6 Arrange the biscuits on the prepared baking sheets and sprinkle with the cumin seeds. Chill them in the refrigerator for about 15 minutes.

7 Preheat the oven to 190°C/375°F/Gas 5. Bake the biscuits for about 20 minutes in the oven until they are crisp and golden. Serve them warm or cold.

Cook's Tip
These savoury biscuits are best eaten when they are freshly baked. The dough can be made in advance and chilled in the refrigerator until it is required.

Peanut Crackers

These tasty little snacks are extremely popular across South-east Asia. They could be considered as the region's version of fried potato crisps, although they are infinitely more tasty and interesting.

Serves 4–5

225g/8oz/2 cups plus 30ml/ 2 tbsp rice flour
5ml/1 tsp baking powder
5ml/1 tsp ground turmeric
5ml/1 tsp ground coriander
300ml/½ pint/1¼ cups coconut milk
115g/4oz/¾ cup unsalted peanuts, coarsely chopped or crushed
2–3 candlenuts or macadamia nuts, ground
2–3 garlic cloves, crushed
corn or groundnut (peanut) oil, for shallow frying
salt and ground black pepper
chilli sambal, for dipping

To season
5ml/1 tsp paprika or fine chilli flakes
salt

1 Put the rice flour, baking powder, ground turmeric and ground coriander into a bowl.

2 Make a well in the centre, pour in the coconut milk and stir to combine. Beat well to make a smooth batter.

3 Add the peanuts, candlenuts or macadamia nuts and garlic to the bowl and mix well together. Season with salt and black pepper and then set the mixture aside for 30 minutes.

4 Meanwhile, in a small bowl, prepare the seasoning by mixing the paprika or fine chilli flakes with a little salt.

5 Heat a thin layer of oil in a wok or large frying pan and drop in a spoonful of batter for each cracker – the crackers can vary in size. Work in batches, flipping the crackers over when the lacy edges become crispy and golden brown. Drain on kitchen paper and transfer them to a basket.

6 Sprinkle the paprika mixture over the crackers and toss them lightly. Serve immediately while still warm and crisp with some chilli sambal for dipping.

Spiced Savoury Biscuits Energy 59kcal/244kJ; Protein 1.3g; Carbohydrate 4g, of which sugars 0.1g; Fat 4.2g, of which saturates 2.7g; Cholesterol 18mg; Calcium 29mg; Fibre 0.2g; Sodium 49mg.
Peanut Crackers Energy 403kcal/1679kJ; Protein 9.7g; Carbohydrate 42.2g, of which sugars 4.6g; Fat 21.3g, of which saturates 3.4g; Cholesterol 0mg; Calcium 44mg; Fibre 2.5g; Sodium 69mg.

Curried Sweet Potato Balls

These sweet potato balls, with roots in Chinese and South-east Asian cooking, are delicious dipped in a fiery red chilli sauce, fried black chilli sauce or hot peanut dipping sauce. They are ideal for serving as a pre-appetizer.

Serves 4

450g/1lb sweet potatoes or taro root, boiled or baked, and peeled
30ml/2 tbsp sugar
15ml/1 tbsp Indian curry powder or spice blend of your choice
25g/1oz fresh root ginger, peeled and grated
150g/5oz/1¼ cups glutinous rice flour or plain (all-purpose) flour
salt
sesame seeds or poppy seeds
vegetable oil, for deep-frying
dipping sauce, to serve

1 In a large bowl, mash the cooked sweet potatoes or taro root. Beat in the sugar, curry powder and ginger.

2 Add the rice or plain flour (sift it if you are using plain flour) and salt to the bowl, and mix well to work into a stiff dough, adding more flour if necessary.

3 Pull off lumps of the dough and mould them into small balls with your hands – you should be able to make roughly 24 balls. Roll the balls on a bed of sesame seeds or poppy seeds until they are completely coated.

4 Heat enough oil for deep-frying in a wok. Fry the sweet potato balls in batches, until golden. Drain on kitchen paper. Serve the balls with wooden skewers to make it easier to dip them into a dipping sauce of your choice.

Variation
Also known as dasheen, taro root is a starchy tuber cultivated in many parts of Asia. If you opt to use it instead of the sweet potato in this recipe, you may need to add more sugar as it has a much more nutty taste when cooked.

Crisp Fried Spicy Aubergine

The spicy gram flour coating on these slices is deliciously crisp, revealing the succulent aubergine beneath. Choose a firm aubergine with a glossy skin.

Serves 4

50g/2oz/½ cup gram flour
15ml/1 tbsp semolina or ground rice
2.5ml/½ tsp onion seeds
5ml/1 tsp cumin seeds
2.5ml/½ tsp fennel seeds or aniseeds
2.5–5ml/½–1 tsp hot chilli powder
2.5ml/½ tsp salt, or to taste
1 large aubergine (eggplant)
vegetable oil, for deep-frying
chutney, to serve

1 Sift the gram flour into a large mixing bowl and add the semolina or ground rice with the onion and cumin seeds, fennel or aniseeds, and the hot chilli powder and salt.

2 Halve the aubergine lengthways and cut each half into 5mm/¼in thick slices. Rinse them and shake off the excess water, but do not pat dry. With some of the water still clinging to the slices, add them to the spiced gram flour mixture. Toss them around until they are evenly coated with the flour. Use a spoon if necessary to ensure that all the flour is used.

3 Heat the oil in a karahi, wok or deep-fryer to a temperature of 190°C/375°F, or until a cube of bread dropped in the oil browns in about 45 seconds. If it floats immediately, the oil has reached the right temperature.

4 Fry the spice-coated aubergine slices in a single layer. Avoid overcrowding the pan as this will lower the temperature, resulting in a soggy texture. Fry until crisp and well browned. Drain on kitchen paper and serve with a chutney.

Cook's Tip
Fennel and aniseeds aid digestion, and many deep-fried Indian recipes use them for this reason.

Crisp Fried Aubergine Energy 226kcal/939kJ; Protein 5g; Carbohydrate 12.2g, of which sugars 2.7g; Fat 17.7g, of which saturates 1.9g; Cholesterol 0mg; Calcium 39mg; Fibre 2.6g; Sodium 9mg.
Sweet Potato Balls Energy 354kcal/1495kJ; Protein 4.9g; Carbohydrate 61g, of which sugars 14.8g; Fat 11.8g, of which saturates 1.5g; Cholesterol 0mg; Calcium 84mg; Fibre 3.9g; Sodium 47mg.

Green Curry Puffs

Shrimp paste and green curry sauce, used judiciously, give these puffs their distinctive spicy, savoury flavour, and the addition of chilli steps up the heat.

Makes 24
24 small wonton wrappers, about 8cm/3¼in square, thawed if frozen
15ml/1 tbsp cornflour (cornstarch), mixed to a paste with 30ml/2 tbsp water
vegetable oil, for deep-frying

For the filling
1 small potato, about 115g/4oz, boiled and mashed
25g/1oz/3 tbsp cooked petits pois (baby peas)
25g/1oz/3 tbsp cooked corn
few sprigs fresh coriander (cilantro), chopped
1 small fresh red chilli, seeded and finely chopped
½ lemon grass stalk, finely chopped
15ml/1 tbsp soy sauce
5ml/1 tsp shrimp paste or fish sauce
5ml/1 tsp Thai green curry paste

1 To make the filling combine the mashed potato, peas, corn, coriander, chilli and lemon grass in a bowl. Stir in the soy sauce, shrimp paste or fish sauce and Thai green curry paste.

2 Lay out one wonton wrapper on a chopping board or clean work surface and place a teaspoon of the filling in the centre of the wrapper. Brush a little of the cornflour paste along two sides of the square wrapper.

3 Fold the other two sides over to meet them, then press together to make a triangular pastry and seal in the filling. Make more pastries in the same way.

4 Heat the oil in a wok to 190°C/375°F or until a cube of bread, added to the oil, browns in about 45 seconds. Add the pastries to the oil, a few at a time, and fry them for about 5 minutes, until golden brown.

5 Remove from the wok and drain on kitchen paper. If you intend serving the puffs hot, place them in a single layer on a serving plate in a low oven while cooking successive batches. The puffs also taste good when served cold.

Fish Cakes with Cucumber Relish

These wonderful, small fish cakes are a very familiar and popular appetizer in Thailand and increasingly throughout South-east Asia.

Makes about 12
8 kaffir lime leaves
300g/11oz cod fillet, cut into chunks
30ml/2 tbsp red curry paste
1 egg
30ml/2 tbsp Thai fish sauce
5ml/1 tsp sugar
30ml/2 tbsp cornflour (cornstarch)

15ml/1 tbsp chopped fresh coriander (cilantro)
50g/2oz/½ cup green beans, thinly sliced
vegetable oil, for deep-frying

For the cucumber relish
60ml/4 tbsp coconut or rice vinegar
50g/2oz/¼ cup sugar
60ml/4 tbsp water
1 head pickled garlic
1cm/½in piece fresh root ginger, chopped
1 cucumber, cut into thin batons
4 shallots, thinly sliced

1 To make the cucumber relish, mix the coconut or rice vinegar, sugar and water in a pan. Heat gently, stirring constantly until the sugar has dissolved. Remove from the heat and leave to cool.

2 Place the garlic and ginger in a mixing bowl. Add the cucumber and shallots. Mix in the vinegar and stir lightly to combine. Cover and set aside.

3 Reserve two or three kaffir lime leaves for the garnish and thinly slice the remaining leaves. Put the fish, curry paste and egg in a food processor and blend to a smooth paste. Transfer to a bowl and stir in the fish sauce, sugar, cornflour, sliced kaffir lime leaves, coriander and green beans. Shape the mixture into thick cakes.

4 Heat the oil in a deep-frying pan or wok to 190°C/375°F or until a cube of bread, added to the oil, browns in about 45 seconds. Fry the fish cakes, a few at a time, for 4–5 minutes, until cooked and evenly brown. Lift out and drain on kitchen paper.

5 Keep each batch hot in a low oven, while frying successive batches. Garnish with the reserved kaffir lime leaves and serve with the cucumber relish.

Green Curry Puffs Energy 69kcal/291kJ; Protein 1.4g; Carbohydrate 9.9g, of which sugars 0.4g; Fat 3g, of which saturates 0.4g; Cholesterol 1mg; Calcium 22mg; Fibre 0.5g; Sodium 58mg.
Fish Cakes Energy 86kcal/361kJ; Protein 6.2g; Carbohydrate 8.1g, of which sugars 5.4g; Fat 3.4g, of which saturates 0.5g; Cholesterol 27mg; Calcium 16mg; Fibre 0.2g; Sodium 2040mg.

Spiced Sweet Potato Turnovers

The lightly spiced sweet potatoes make a great filling for this recipe.

Serves 4
1 sweet potato, about 225g/8oz
30ml/2 tbsp vegetable oil
2 shallots, finely chopped
10ml/2 tsp coriander
   seeds, crushed
5ml/1 tsp ground cumin
5ml/1 tsp garam masala
115g/4oz/1 cup frozen peas
15ml/1 tbsp chopped
   fresh mint

salt and ground black pepper
mint sprigs, to garnish

For the pastry
15ml/1 tbsp olive oil
1 small egg
150ml/1/4 pint/2/3 cup natural
   (plain) yogurt
115g/4oz/8 tbsp butter, melted
275g/10oz/2 1/2 cups plain
   (all-purpose) flour
1.5ml/1/4 tsp bicarbonate of soda
   (baking soda)
10ml/2 tsp paprika
5ml/1 tsp salt

1 Cook the sweet potato in boiling water for 15–20 minutes, until tender. Drain well and leave to cool. When cool enough to handle, peel the potato and cut into 1cm/1/2in cubes.

2 Heat the oil in a frying pan, add the shallots and cook until softened. Add the sweet potato and fry until it browns at the edges. Add the spices and fry for a few seconds. Remove from the heat and add the peas, mint and seasoning. Leave to cool.

3 Preheat the oven to 200°C/400°F/Gas 6. Grease a baking sheet. To make the pastry, whisk together the oil and egg, stir in the yogurt, then add the melted butter. Sift the flour, bicarbonate of soda, paprika and salt into a bowl, then stir into the yogurt mixture to form a soft dough. Turn out the dough, and knead gently. Roll it out, then stamp it out into rounds.

4 Spoon 10ml/2 tsp of the filling on to one side of each round, then fold over and seal the edges. Re-roll the trimmings and stamp out more rounds until the filling has all been used.

5 Arrange the turnovers on the baking sheet and brush the tops with beaten egg. Bake in the oven for about 20 minutes until crisp and golden brown. Serve hot, garnished with the mint.

Vegetable Samosas

Throughout the East, these spicy snacks are sold by street vendors, and eaten at any time of day.

Makes about 20
1 packet 25cm/10in square
   spring roll wrappers, thawed
   if frozen
30ml/2 tbsp plain (all-purpose)
   flour, mixed to a paste with
   a little water
vegetable oil, for deep-frying
coriander (cilantro) leaves,
   to garnish

For the filling
25g/1oz/2 tbsp ghee or
   unsalted butter

1 small onion, finely chopped
1cm/1/2in piece fresh root ginger,
   peeled and chopped
1 garlic clove, crushed
2.5ml/1/2 tsp chilli powder
1 large potato, about 225g/8oz,
   cooked until just tender and
   finely diced
50g/2oz/1/2 cup cauliflower
   florets, lightly cooked, chopped
   into small pieces
50g/2oz/1/2 cup frozen
   peas, thawed
5–10ml/1–2 tsp garam masala
15ml/1 tbsp chopped fresh
   coriander (cilantro) leaves
   and stems
squeeze of lemon juice
salt

1 To make the filling, heat the ghee or butter in a large frying pan and fry the onion, ginger and garlic for 5 minutes until the onion has softened but not browned.

2 Add the chilli powder and cook for 1 minute, then stir in the potato, cauliflower and peas. Sprinkle with garam masala and set aside to cool. Stir in the coriander, lemon juice and salt.

3 Cut the spring roll wrappers into three equal strips (or two for larger samosas). Brush the edges with a little of the flour paste. Place a small spoonful of filling about 2cm/3/4in in from the edge of one strip. Fold one corner over the filling to make a triangle and continue this folding until the entire strip has been used and a triangular pastry has been formed. Seal any open edges with more flour and water paste.

4 Heat the oil for deep-frying to 190°C/375°F and fry the samosas, a few at a time, until golden and crisp. Drain well on kitchen paper and serve hot, garnished with coriander leaves.

Potato Turnovers Energy 660kcal/2760kJ; Protein 13.9g; Carbohydrate 75.8g, of which sugars 9.3g; Fat 35.9g, of which saturates 17g; Cholesterol 105mg; Calcium 216mg; Fibre 5.2g; Sodium 740mg.
Vegetable Samosas Energy 56kcal/235kJ; Protein 1.3g; Carbohydrate 10g, of which sugars 0.8g; Fat 1.4g, of which saturates 0.2g; Cholesterol 0mg; Calcium 16mg; Fibre 0.7g; Sodium 8mg.

Curried Lamb Samosas

Filo pastry is perfect for making samosas. Once you've mastered folding them, you'll be amazed at how quick they are to make. These lamb samosas have a simple filling that is tasty and quick to make – perfect for party fare.

Makes 12
25g/1oz/2 tbsp butter
225g/8oz/1 cup minced
  (ground) lamb
30ml/2 tbsp mild curry paste
12 sheets of filo pastry,
  wrapped in a damp dish towel
salt and ground black pepper

1 Heat a little of the butter in a large heavy pan and add the lamb. Fry for 5–6 minutes, stirring occasionally until the meat is evenly browned all over. Stir in the curry paste and cook for 1–2 minutes. Season and set aside. Preheat the oven to 200°C/400°F/Gas 6.

2 Melt the remaining butter in a pan. Cut the pastry sheets in half lengthways. Brush one strip of pastry with butter, then lay another strip on top and brush with more butter.

3 Place a spoonful of lamb in the corner of the strip and fold over to form a triangle at one end. Keep folding over in the same way to form a triangular shape.

4 Brush with butter and place on a baking sheet. Repeat using the remaining pastry and filling. Bake in the oven for about 10–15 minutes until golden. Serve immediately.

> **Variation**
> For Cashew Nut Samosas, mix together 225g/8oz cooked and mashed potato, 15ml/1 tbsp chopped cashew nuts, 5ml/1 tsp coconut milk powder, ½ chopped green chilli, 5ml/1 tsp mustard seeds, 5ml/1 tsp cumin seeds, 15ml/1 tbsp chopped fresh coriander (cilantro) and 5ml/1 tsp soft light brown sugar. Use this mixture to fill the samosas in place of the lamb filling. If you like, the mustard and cumin seeds can be dry-roasted first.

Thai Curry-spiced Potato Samosas

Most samosas are deep-fried, but these are baked, making them a healthier option. They are also perfect for parties as they are easier to cook.

Makes 25
1 large potato, about
  250g/9oz, diced
15ml/1 tbsp groundnut
  (peanut) oil
2 shallots, finely chopped
1 garlic clove, finely chopped
60ml/4 tbsp coconut milk
5ml/1 tsp Thai red or green
  curry paste
75g/3oz/¾ cup peas
juice of ½ lime
25 samosa wrappers or
  10 x 5cm/4 x 2in strips
  of filo pastry
salt and ground black pepper
vegetable oil, for brushing

1 Preheat the oven to 220°C/425°F/Gas 7. Bring a small pan of water to the boil, add the diced potato, cover and cook for 10–15 minutes, until tender. Drain and set aside.

2 Meanwhile, heat the groundnut oil in a large frying pan and cook the shallots and garlic over medium heat, stirring occasionally, for 4–5 minutes, until softened and golden.

3 Add the drained potato, coconut milk, red or green curry paste, peas and lime juice to the frying pan. Mash coarsely with a wooden spoon. Season to taste with salt and pepper and cook over a low heat for 2–3 minutes, then remove the pan from the heat and set aside until the mixture has cooled a little.

4 Lay a samosa wrapper or filo strip flat on the work surface. Brush with a little oil, then place a generous teaspoonful of the mixture in the middle of one end. Turn one corner diagonally over the filling to meet the long edge.

5 Continue folding over the filling, keeping the triangular shape as you work down the strip. Brush with a little more oil if necessary and place on a baking sheet. Prepare all the other samosas in the same way.

6 Bake for 15 minutes, or until the pastry is golden and crisp. Leave to cool slightly before serving.

Thai Potato Samosas Energy 42kcal/178kJ; Protein 1.2g; Carbohydrate 8.5g, of which sugars 0.6g; Fat 0.6g, of which saturates 0.1g; Cholesterol 0mg; Calcium 14mg; Fibre 0.5g; Sodium 4mg.
Curried Lamb Samosas Energy 101kcal/423kJ; Protein 5g; Carbohydrate 10.4g, of which sugars 0.2g; Fat 4.6g, of which saturates 2.3g; Cholesterol 19mg; Calcium 37mg; Fibre 1g; Sodium 37mg.

Spiced Beef and Potato Puffs

These crisp, golden pillows of pastry filled with spiced beef and potatoes are delicious served straight from the wok. The light pastry puffs up in the hot oil and contrasts enticingly with the fragrant spiced beef.

Serves 4
15ml/1 tbsp sunflower oil
½ small onion, finely chopped
3 garlic cloves, crushed
5ml/1 tsp fresh root ginger, grated
1 red chilli, seeded and chopped
30ml/2 tbsp hot curry powder
75g/3oz minced (ground) beef
115g/4oz mashed potato
60ml/4 tbsp chopped fresh
   coriander (cilantro)
2 sheets ready-rolled, fresh
   puff pastry
1 egg, lightly beaten
vegetable oil, for deep-frying
salt and ground black pepper
fresh coriander (cilantro) leaves,
   to garnish
tomato ketchup, to serve

1 Heat the oil in a wok, then add the onion, garlic, ginger and chilli. Stir-fry over medium heat for 2–3 minutes. Add the curry powder and beef and stir-fry over high heat for 4–5 minutes, or until the beef is browned and just cooked through, then remove from the heat.

2 Transfer the beef mixture to a large bowl and add the mashed potato and chopped fresh coriander. Stir well, then season with salt and pepper and set aside.

3 Lay the pastry sheets on a clean, dry surface and cut out eight rounds, using a 7.5cm/3in pastry (cookie) cutter. Place a large spoonful of the beef mixture in the centre of each pastry round. Brush the edges of the pastry with the beaten egg and fold each round in half to enclose the filling. Press and crimp the edges with the tines of a fork to seal.

4 Fill a wok or large heavy pan one-third full of vegetable oil and heat to 190°C/375°F or until a cube of bread, added to the oil, browns in about 45 seconds.

5 Deep-fry the puffs, in batches, for 2–3 minutes until golden brown. Drain on kitchen paper and garnish with fresh coriander leaves. Serve with tomato ketchup for dipping.

Chickpea Cakes with Tahini

These spicy little cakes are equally good hot or cold. For a more substantial snack, tuck them into pitta bread with salad.

Serves 4
2 x 425g/15oz cans chickpeas
2 garlic cloves, crushed
1 bunch spring onions (scallions),
   white parts only, chopped
10ml/2 tsp ground cumin
10ml/2 tsp ground coriander
1 fresh green chilli, seeded and
   finely chopped
30ml/2 tbsp chopped fresh
   coriander (cilantro)
1 small egg, beaten
30ml/2 tbsp plain
   (all-purpose) flour
seasoned flour, for shaping
vegetable oil, for shallow-frying
salt and ground black pepper
lemon wedges and fresh
   coriander, to garnish

For the tahini and lemon dip
30ml/2 tbsp tahini
juice of 1 lemon
2 garlic cloves, crushed

1 Drain the chickpeas thoroughly. Transfer them into a blender or food processor and process until smooth. Add the garlic, spring onions, cumin and ground coriander. Process again.

2 Scrape the mixture into a bowl and stir in the chilli, fresh coriander, egg and flour. Mix well and season with salt and pepper. If the mixture is very soft add a little more flour. Chill for about 30 minutes to firm the mixture.

3 Make the dip. Mix the tahini, lemon juice and garlic in a bowl, adding a little water if the sauce is too thick. Set aside.

4 Using floured hands, shape the chickpea mixture into 12 cakes. Heat the oil in a frying pan and fry the cakes in batches for about 1 minute on each side, until crisp and golden. Drain well on kitchen paper and serve immediately with the dip and lemon and coriander garnish.

> **Variation**
> Another quick and easy dipping sauce is made by mixing yogurt with a little chopped chilli and fresh mint.

Spiced Beef Puffs Energy 408kcal/1695kJ; Protein 9g; Carbohydrate 24.2g, of which sugars 1.8g; Fat 31.8g, of which saturates 4.2g; Cholesterol 67mg; Calcium 46mg; Fibre 0.5g; Sodium 202mg.
Chickpea Cakes Energy 342kcal/1433kJ; Protein 15.9g; Carbohydrate 28.1g, of which sugars 1.8g; Fat 19.5g, of which saturates 2.6g; Cholesterol 48mg; Calcium 171mg; Fibre 7.9g; Sodium 358mg.

Split Pea or Lentil Fritters

These delicious spicy fritters are an Indian speciality.

Serves 4–6

250g/9oz/generous 1 cup yellow split peas or red lentils, soaked overnight
3–5 garlic cloves, chopped
30ml/2 tbsp roughly chopped fresh root ginger
120ml/4fl oz/½ cup chopped fresh coriander (cilantro) leaves
2.5–5ml/½–1 tsp ground cumin
1.5–2.5ml/¼–½ tsp ground turmeric
large pinch of cayenne pepper or ½–1 fresh green chilli, chopped
2.5ml/½ tsp salt
2.5ml/½ tsp ground black pepper
120ml/4fl oz/½ cup gram flour
5ml/1 tsp baking powder
30ml/2 tbsp couscous
2 large or 3 small onions, chopped
vegetable oil, for frying
lemon wedges and fresh chilli, to serve

1 Drain the split peas or lentils, reserving a little of the soaking water. Put the chopped garlic and ginger in a food processor or blender and process until finely minced (ground). Add the drained peas or lentils, 15–30ml/1–2 tbsp of the reserved soaking water and the coriander, and process to form a paste.

2 Add the cumin, turmeric, cayenne or chilli, the salt and pepper, the gram flour, baking powder and couscous to the mixture and combine. The mixture should form a thick batter. If it seems too thick, add a spoonful of the soaking water. Add a little more flour or couscous if it is too watery. Mix in the onions.

3 Heat the oil in a wide, deep frying pan, to a depth of about 5cm/2in, until it is hot enough to brown a cube of bread in 30 seconds. Using two spoons, form the mixture into two-bitesize balls and slip each one gently into the hot oil. Cook until golden brown on the underside, then turn and cook the second side until golden brown.

4 Remove the fritters from the hot oil with a slotted spoon and drain well on kitchen paper. Transfer the fritters to a baking sheet and keep them warm in a preheated oven until all the mixture is cooked. Serve the fritters hot or at room temperature with lemon wedges and chopped fresh chilli.

Spicy Corn Patties

When it comes to snack food, these spicy fried patties are a must. Serve with chilli sambal on the side to give that extra fiery kick to these tasty snacks.

Serves 4

2 fresh corn on the cob
3 shallots, chopped
2 garlic cloves, chopped
25g/1oz galangal or fresh root ginger, chopped
1–2 chillies, seeded and chopped
2–3 candlenuts or macadamia nuts, ground
5ml/1 tsp ground coriander
5ml/1 tsp ground cumin
15ml/1 tbsp coconut oil
3 eggs
45–60ml/3–4 tbsp grated fresh coconut or desiccated (dry unsweetened shredded) coconut
2–3 spring onions (scallions), white parts only, finely sliced
corn or groundnut (peanut) oil, for shallow frying
1 small bunch fresh coriander (cilantro) leaves, chopped
salt and ground black pepper
1 lime, quartered, for serving
chilli sambal, for dipping

1 Put the corn on the cob into a large pan of water, bring to the boil and boil for about 8 minutes. Drain the cobs and scrape all the corn off the cob and put aside. Discard the cobs.

2 Using a mortar and pestle, grind the shallots, garlic, galangal or ginger, and chillies to a paste. Add the candlenuts or macadamia nuts, ground coriander and cumin and beat well together.

3 Heat the coconut oil in a heavy pan, stir in the spice paste and stir-fry until the paste becomes fragrant and begins to colour. Transfer the paste on to a plate and leave to cool.

4 Beat the eggs in a bowl. Add the coconut and spring onions and beat in the corn and the spice paste. Season to taste.

5 Heat a thin layer of corn oil in a heavy frying pan. Working in batches, drop spoonfuls of the corn mixture into the oil and fry the patties for 2–3 minutes, until golden brown on both sides.

6 Drain the patties on kitchen paper and arrange them on a serving dish on top of the coriander leaves. Serve hot or cool with wedges of lime and a chilli sambal for dipping.

Split Pea Fritters Energy 360kcal/1511kj; Protein 14.1g; Carbohydrate 51.3g, of which sugars 8.3g; Fat 12.3g, of which saturates 1.4g; Cholesterol 0mg; Calcium 119mg; Fibre 5.3g; Sodium 26g.
Corn Patties Energy 368kcal/1531kj; Protein 10.8g; Carbohydrate 18.1g, of which sugars 8.2g; Fat 28.7g, of which saturates 9.7g; Cholesterol 143mg; Calcium 68mg; Fibre 4.1g; Sodium 196mg.

Rice Cakes with Dipping Sauce

These cakes are easy to make and will last for weeks in an airtight container.

Serves 4–6
175g/6oz/1 cup Thai jasmine rice
350ml/12fl oz/1½ cups water
oil, for deep-frying and greasing

For the spicy dipping sauce
6–8 dried chillies
2.5ml/½ tsp salt
2 shallots, chopped
2 garlic cloves, chopped
4 coriander (cilantro) roots

10 white peppercorns
250ml/8fl oz/1 cup coconut milk
5ml/1 tsp shrimp paste
115g/4oz minced (ground) pork
115g/4oz cherry tomatoes, chopped
15ml/1 tbsp Thai fish sauce
15ml/1 tbsp palm sugar
  (jaggery) or light muscovado
  (brown) sugar
30ml/2 tbsp tamarind juice
  (tamarind paste mixed with
  warm water)
30ml/2 tbsp coarsely chopped
  roasted peanuts
2 spring onions (scallions), chopped

1 Make the sauce. Snap off the chilli stems, scrape out the seeds and soak the chillies in warm water for 20 minutes. Drain and put in a mortar. Sprinkle over the salt and crush. Add the shallots, garlic, coriander and peppercorns. Pound to a paste.

2 Pour the coconut milk into a pan and bring to the boil. Stir in the pounded chilli paste and cook for 2–3 minutes. Stir in the shrimp paste and cook for 1 minute more.

3 Add the pork and cook for 5–10 minutes, then stir in the tomatoes, fish sauce, sugar and tamarind juice. Simmer, stirring occasionally, until the sauce thickens, then stir in the chopped peanuts and spring onions. Set aside to cool.

4 Preheat the oven to the lowest setting. Grease a baking sheet. Wash the rice and put it in a pan, add the water and cover. Bring to the boil, then simmer gently for 15 minutes. Spoon the cooked rice on to the baking sheet and press it down. Leave in the oven to dry out overnight.

5 Break the rice into bitesize pieces. Heat the oil in a wok or deep-fryer. Deep-fry the cakes, in batches, for about 1 minute, until they puff up. Remove and drain. Serve with the sauce.

Spicy Potato Pancakes

Although called a pancake, these crispy spiced cakes are more like a traditional Indian bhaji. They make an ideal appetizer for a meal.

Makes 10
300g/11oz potatoes
25ml/1½ tsp garam masala or
  curry powder

4 spring onions (scallions),
  finely chopped
1 large (US extra large) egg
  white, lightly beaten
30ml/2 tbsp sunflower or
  olive oil
salt and ground black pepper
Indian chutney and relishes,
  to serve

1 Peel and grate the potatoes into a large bowl. Using your hands, squeeze the excess liquid from the grated potatoes and pat dry with kitchen paper.

2 Place the dry, grated potatoes in a separate bowl and add the spices, spring onions, egg white and seasoning. Stir to combine the ingredients.

3 Heat a large, non-stick frying pan over medium heat and add the vegetable oil.

4 Drop tablespoonfuls of the potato on to the pan and flatten out with the back of a spoon (you will need to cook the pancakes in two batches).

5 Cook the first batch for a few minutes and then flip over the pancakes. Cook for a further 3 minutes. Remove them from the pan and keep them warm in a preheated low oven while you cook the remaining batch.

6 Drain the pancakes well on kitchen paper and serve immediately with chutney and relishes.

> **Cook's Tip**
> Don't grate the potatoes too soon before you intend to use them as the flesh will quickly turn brown.

Rice Cakes Energy 361kcal/1508kJ; Protein 11.7g; Carbohydrate 42g, of which sugars 8.8g; Fat 16g, of which saturates 2.9g; Cholesterol 19mg; Calcium 38mg; Fibre 0.8g; Sodium 359mg.
Potato Pancakes Energy 50kcal/210kJ; Protein 1.3g; Carbohydrate 5.8g, of which sugars 0.5g; Fat 2.6g, of which saturates 0.3g; Cholesterol 0mg; Calcium 8mg; Fibre 0.4g; Sodium 11mg.

Curry-spiced Pakoras

These delicious batter balls make a wonderful snack with this fragrant chutney.

Makes 25

15ml/1 tbsp sunflower oil
20ml/4 tsp cumin seeds
5ml/1 tsp black mustard seeds
1 small onion, finely chopped
10ml/2 tsp grated fresh
   root ginger
2 green chillies, seeded and
   chopped
600g/1lb 5oz potatoes, cooked
200g/7oz fresh peas
juice of 1 lemon
90ml/6 tbsp chopped fresh
   coriander (cilantro) leaves
115g/4oz/1 cup gram flour

25g/1oz/¼ cup self-raising
   (self-rising) flour
40g/1½oz/⅓ cup rice flour
large pinch of turmeric
10ml/2 tsp crushed
   coriander seeds
350ml/12fl oz/1½ cups water
vegetable oil, for frying
salt and ground black pepper

For the chutney

105ml/7 tbsp coconut cream
200ml/7fl oz/scant 1 cup natural
   (plain) yogurt
50g/2oz mint leaves,
   finely chopped
5ml/1 tsp golden caster
   (superfine) sugar
juice of 1 lime

1 Heat a wok over medium heat and add the sunflower oil. When hot, fry the cumin and mustard seeds for 1–2 minutes. Add the onion, ginger and chillies to the wok and cook for 3–4 minutes. Add the cooked potatoes and peas and stir-fry for a further 5–6 minutes. Season, then stir in the lemon juice and coriander leaves. Leave the mixture to cool slightly, then divide into 25 portions. Shape each portion into a ball with your hands and chill in the refrigerator.

2 To make the chutney, place all the ingredients in a blender and process until smooth. Season, then chill. To make the batter, put the gram flour, self-raising flour and rice flour in a bowl. Season and add the turmeric and coriander seeds. Gradually whisk in the water to make a smooth batter.

3 Fill a wok one-third full of oil and heat to 180°C/350°F. Working in batches, dip the chilled balls in the batter, then drop into the oil and deep-fry for 1–2 minutes, or until golden. Drain on kitchen paper, and serve immediately with the chutney.

Onion Pakora

These delicious Indian onion fritters are made with chickpea flour, otherwise known as gram flour or besan. Serve with chutney or a yogurt dip.

Serves 4–5

675g/1½lb onions
5ml/1 tsp salt
5ml/1 tsp ground coriander
5ml/1 tsp ground cumin
2.5ml/½ tsp ground turmeric

1–2 green chillies, seeded and
   finely chopped
45ml/3 tbsp chopped fresh
   coriander (cilantro)
90g/3½oz/¾ cup gram flour
2.5ml/½ tsp baking powder
vegetable oil, for deep-frying

To serve

lemon wedges (optional)
fresh coriander (cilantro) sprigs
chutney or a yogurt and
   cucumber dip

1 Halve and thinly slice the onions in a colander, add the salt and toss. Place on a plate and leave to stand for 45 minutes, tossing once or twice. Rinse the onions, then squeeze out any excess moisture.

2 Place the onions in a bowl. Add the ground coriander, cumin, turmeric, chillies and fresh coriander. Mix well.

3 Add the gram flour and baking powder, then use your hands to mix the ingredients thoroughly. Shape the mixture by hand into 12–15 pakoras, about the size of golf balls.

4 Heat the oil for deep-frying to 180°C/350°F or until a cube of day-old bread browns in 30 seconds. Fry the pakoras, a few at a time, until they are deep golden brown all over. Drain each batch on kitchen paper and keep warm in a low oven until all the pakoras are cooked. Serve with lemon wedges, coriander sprigs and chutney or a yogurt and cucumber dip.

> **Cook's Tip**
> For a cucumber dip, stir half a diced cucumber and 1 seeded and chopped fresh green chilli into 250ml/8fl oz/1 cup natural (plain) yogurt. Season with salt and cumin.

Curry-spiced Pakoras Energy 126kcal/525kJ; Protein 4.1g; Carbohydrate 8.3g, of which sugars 2.6g; Fat 8.8g, of which saturates 5.2g; Cholesterol 0mg; Calcium 35mg; Fibre 1.3g; Sodium 16mg.
Onion Pakora Energy 207kcal/861kJ; Protein 5.4g; Carbohydrate 19.8g, of which sugars 8.2g; Fat 12.3g, of which saturates 1.4g; Cholesterol 0mg; Calcium 84mg; Fibre 4.3g; Sodium 14mg.

Onion Bhajias

A favourite snack in India, bhajias consist of a savoury vegetable mixture in a crisp and spicy batter. They can be served as an appetizer or as a side dish with curries.

Makes 20–25
2 large onions
225g/8oz/2 cups gram flour
2.5ml/½ tsp chilli powder
5ml/1 tsp ground turmeric
5ml/1 tsp baking powder
1.5ml/¼ tsp asafoetida
2.5ml/½ tsp each nigella, fennel, cumin and onion seeds, coarsely crushed
2 fresh green chillies, finely chopped
50g/2oz/2 cups fresh coriander (cilantro), chopped
vegetable oil, for deep-frying
salt

1 Using a sharp knife, slice the onions into thin rounds. Separate the slices and set them aside on a plate.

2 In a bowl mix together the flour, chilli powder, ground turmeric, baking powder and asafoetida. Add salt to taste. Sift the mixture into a large mixing bowl.

3 Add the coarsely crushed seeds, onion slices, green chillies and fresh coriander to the bowl. Mix well until all the ingredients are combined.

4 Add enough cold water to make a paste, then stir in more water to make a thick batter that coats the onions and spices.

5 Heat enough oil in a wok for deep-frying to 180°C/350°F or until a cube of day-old bread browns in 30 seconds. Drop spoonfuls of the mixture into the hot oil, and fry the bhajias until they are golden brown. Turn the bhajias over during cooking. Drain well on kitchen paper and serve hot.

> **Variation**
> This versatile bhajia batter can be used with many other vegetables, including okra, cauliflower and broccoli. Cubes of potato also work well for a more filling snack.

Goan Fish Cakes

Goan fish and shellfish are skilfully prepared with spices to make cakes of all shapes and sizes, while the rest of India makes fish kebabs.

Makes 20
450g/1lb skinned haddock or cod
2 potatoes, peeled, boiled and coarsely mashed
4 spring onions (scallions), finely chopped
4 fresh green chillies, finely chopped
5cm/2in piece fresh root ginger, crushed
a few coriander (cilantro) and mint sprigs, chopped
2 eggs
breadcrumbs, for coating
vegetable oil, for shallow-frying
salt and ground black pepper
lemon wedges and chilli sauce, to serve

1 Place the skinned fish in a lightly greased steamer and steam gently until cooked (test with a fork – the flesh should flake easily). Remove the steamer from the stove but leave the fish on the steaming tray until cool.

2 When the fish is cool, crumble it coarsely into a large bowl, using a fork. Mix in the mashed potatoes, spring onions, chillies, crushed ginger, chopped coriander and mint, and one of the eggs. Season to taste with salt and pepper.

3 Shape the mixture into about 20 cakes. Beat the remaining egg and place on a plate. Place the breadcrumbs on a separate plate. Dip the cakes in the egg, then into the breadcrumbs. Heat the oil in a frying pan and fry the cakes until brown on all sides. Serve immediately as an appetizer or as a side dish, with the lemon wedges and chilli sauce.

> **Variations**
> • To make a quicker version of these fish cakes, used canned tuna in brine and omit step 1. Make sure the tuna is thoroughly drained before use.
> • Although haddock or cod are used in this recipe, you can substitute them with other less expensive firm white fish, such as coley or whiting.

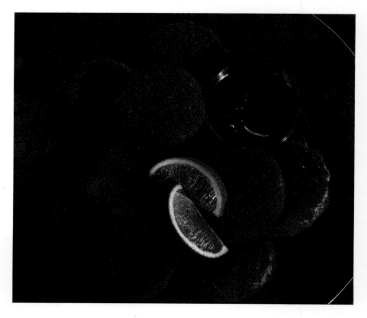

Onion Bhajias Energy 72kcal/301kJ; Protein 1.2g; Carbohydrate 8.8g, of which sugars 1.3g; Fat 3.8g, of which saturates 0.4g; Cholesterol 0mg; Calcium 23mg; Fibre 0.7g; Sodium 2mg.
Goan Fish Cakes Energy 80kcal/336kJ; Protein 5.5g; Carbohydrate 4.4g, of which sugars 0.3g; Fat 4.6g, of which saturates 0.6g; Cholesterol 27mg; Calcium 11mg; Fibre 0.2g; Sodium 43mg.

Cumin-scented Chicken

Cumin is a wonderful spice that is full of pungency, but without any harshness. Its rather warm and assertive nature gives this dish a distinctive flavour and aroma. Cumin is also known to have curative properties.

Serves 4

45ml/3 tbsp cumin seeds
45ml/3 tbsp vegetable oil
2.5ml/½ tsp black peppercorns
4 green cardamom pods
2 fresh green chillies, finely chopped
2 garlic cloves, crushed
2.5cm/1in piece fresh root ginger, grated
5ml/1 tsp ground coriander
10ml/2 tsp ground cumin
2.5ml/½ tsp salt
8 chicken pieces, such as thighs and drumsticks, skinned
5ml/1 tsp garam masala
Cucumber Raita, garnished with fresh coriander (cilantro) and chilli powder, to serve (optional)

1 Preheat a wok or deep, heavy frying pan over medium heat and dry-roast 15ml/1 tbsp of the cumin seeds for 1–2 minutes until they release their aroma. Set aside.

2 Heat the oil in a wok or large pan and fry the remaining cumin seeds, black peppercorns and cardamoms for about 2 minutes, stirring constantly.

3 Add the green chillies, garlic and grated fresh root ginger to the spices in the pan and fry for 2 minutes.

4 Add the ground coriander and cumin to the pan with the salt, and cook over medium heat. Stir the mixture constantly, for a further 1–2 minutes, until the coriander and cumin release their aromatic fragrances.

5 Add the chicken pieces to the pan, stir and mix thoroughly with the spices. Cover the pan with a lid and cook over low heat for 20–25 minutes.

6 Add the garam masala and reserved dry-roasted cumin seeds to the pan, and cook for a further 5 minutes. Place the spice-coated chicken pieces on a serving plate and serve immediately with cucumber raita, if you like.

Chicken Naan Pockets

This quick-and-easy dish is ideal for a simple lunch or supper and excellent as picnic fare. For extra flavour, you could use spicy or garlic naans, or try the ready-to-bake ones and serve warm.

Serves 4

4 naans or pitta breads
45ml/3 tbsp natural (plain) low-fat yogurt
7.5ml/1½ tsp garam masala
5ml/1 tsp chilli powder
5ml/1 tsp salt
45ml/3 tbsp lemon juice
15ml/1 tbsp chopped fresh
coriander (cilantro)
1 fresh green chilli, chopped
450g/1lb/3¼ cups chicken, skinned, boned and cubed
15ml/1 tbsp vegetable oil (optional)
8 onion rings
2 tomatoes, quartered
½ white cabbage, shredded

For the garnish
lemon wedges
2 small tomatoes, halved
mixed salad leaves
fresh coriander (cilantro)

1 Using a sharp knife, carefully cut into the middle of each naan or pitta bread to make a pocket, then set them aside while you prepare the filling.

2 In a large bowl, mix together the yogurt, garam masala, chilli powder, salt, lemon juice, fresh coriander and chopped green chilli. Pour the marinade over the chicken pieces and leave to marinate for about 1 hour.

3 When the chicken has marinated, preheat the grill (broiler) to very hot, then lower the heat to medium.

4 Place the chicken in a flameproof dish and grill (broil) for 15–20 minutes until tender and cooked through, turning the chicken pieces at least twice. If you like, baste the chicken pieces with the oil while cooking.

5 Remove from the heat and fill each naan or pitta bread with the chicken and then with the onion rings, tomatoes and cabbage. Serve immediately with the lemon wedges, tomatoes, salad leaves and fresh coriander.

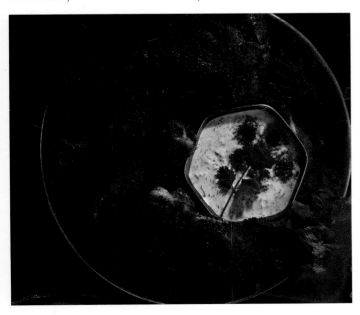

Cumin-scented Chicken Energy 269kcal/1126kJ; Protein 20.3g; Carbohydrate 22.9g, of which sugars 9.5g; Fat 11.6g, of which saturates 1.5g; Cholesterol 40mg; Calcium 136mg; Fibre 2.4g; Sodium 82mg.
Chicken Naan Pockets Energy 410kcal/1733kJ; Protein 35.8g; Carbohydrate 51.3g, of which sugars 8.5g; Fat 8.2g, of which saturates 1.3g; Cholesterol 83mg; Calcium 227mg; Fibre 3.6g; Sodium 629mg.

Quick-fried Spicy Prawns

These delicious prawns are stir-fried in a matter of moments to make a wonderfully tasty appetizer. This is fabulous food to eat with the fingers, so be sure to provide your guests with finger bowls.

Serves 4
450g/1lb large raw
    prawns (shrimp)
2.5cm/1in fresh root
    ginger, grated
2 garlic cloves, crushed
5ml/1 tsp hot chilli powder
5ml/1 tsp ground turmeric
10ml/2 tsp black mustard seeds
seeds from 4 green cardamom
    pods, crushed
50g/2oz/¼ cup ghee or butter
120ml/4fl oz/½ cup
    coconut milk
salt and ground black pepper
30–45ml/2–3 tbsp chopped fresh
    coriander (cilantro), to garnish
naan bread, to serve

1 Peel the prawns carefully, ensuring that the tails are left attached to the main body.

2 Using a small, sharp knife, make a slit along the back of each prawn and remove the dark vein. Rinse well under cold running water, drain and pat dry with kitchen paper.

3 Put the ginger, garlic, chilli powder, turmeric, mustard seeds and cardamom seeds in a bowl. Add the prawns and toss to coat completely in the spice mixture.

4 Heat a karahi, wok or large, heavy frying pan until hot. Add the ghee or butter and swirl it around until it begins to foam, taking care to not let it burn.

5 Add the spiced prawns to the pan and stir-fry for about 1–1½ minutes until they are just turning pink.

6 Stir in the coconut milk and simmer for 3–4 minutes until the prawns are just cooked through. Season to taste with salt and ground black pepper.

7 Sprinkle with the chopped fresh coriander and serve immediately, with naan bread.

Steamed Mussels in Coconut Milk

Mussels steamed in coconut milk and fresh aromatic herbs are quick and easy to prepare and great for a relaxed dinner with friends.

Serves 4
1.6kg/3½lb mussels
15ml/1 tbsp sunflower oil
6 garlic cloves, roughly chopped
15ml/1 tbsp finely chopped fresh
    root ginger
2 large red chillies, seeded and
    finely sliced
6 spring onions (scallions),
    finely chopped
2 limes
400ml/14fl oz/1⅔ cups
    coconut milk
45ml/3 tbsp light soy sauce
5ml/1 tsp caster (superfine) sugar
a large handful of chopped
    coriander (cilantro)
salt and ground black pepper

1 Scrub the mussels in cold water. Scrape off any barnacles with a knife, then pull out and discard the fibrous beard visible between the hinge on any of the shells. Discard any mussels that are not tightly closed, or that fail to close when tapped.

2 Heat a wok over high heat and then add the oil. Stir in the garlic, ginger, chillies and spring onions and stir-fry over medium to high heat for 30 seconds.

3 Grate the rind of the limes into the ginger mixture, then squeeze both fruit and add the juice to the wok with the coconut milk, soy sauce and sugar. Stir to mix.

4 Bring the mixture to the boil, then add the mussels. Return to the boil, cover and cook briskly for 5–6 minutes, or until all the mussels have opened. Discard any unopened mussels.

5 Remove the wok from the heat and stir in the chopped coriander. Season the mussels well with salt and pepper. Ladle into warmed bowls and serve immediately.

> **Cook's Tip**
> For a supper with friends, take the wok straight to the table. There's something irresistible about eating straight from the pan.

Quick-fried Prawns Energy 382kcal/1590kJ; Protein 40.8g; Carbohydrate 1g, of which sugars 0.9g; Fat 23.8g, of which saturates 3.4g; Cholesterol 439mg; Calcium 254mg; Fibre 1.9g; Sodium 440mg.
Steamed Mussels Energy 160kcal/679kJ; Protein 21.5g; Carbohydrate 6.7g, of which sugars 6.7g; Fat 5.5g, of which saturates 1g; Cholesterol 48mg; Calcium 272mg; Fibre 0.2g; Sodium 630mg.

Hot Spiced Clams

This delicious recipe uses spices to make a hot dip or sauce. Serve these clams with plenty of fresh bread to mop up the delicious juices that remain.

Serves 3–4
500g/1¼lb small clams
1 small onion, finely chopped
1 celery stick, sliced
2 garlic cloves, finely chopped
2.5cm/1in piece fresh root
   ginger, grated
30ml/2 tbsp olive oil
1.5ml/¼ tsp chilli powder
5ml/1 tsp ground turmeric
30ml/2 tbsp chopped
   fresh parsley
30ml/2 tbsp dry white wine
salt and ground black pepper
celery leaves, to garnish
fresh bread, to serve

1 Scrub the clams under cold running water, discarding any shells that are broken or open.

2 Place the onion, celery, garlic and ginger in a large pan, pour in the olive oil, and add the spices and chopped parsley and stir-fry gently for about 5 minutes. Add the clams to the pan and cook for 2 minutes.

3 Add the dry white wine to the pan, then cover and cook gently for 2–3 minutes, shaking the pan occasionally, until all the shells have opened.

4 Season with salt and ground black pepper. Discard any clams whose shells remain closed, then serve immediately with fresh bread, garnished with the celery leaves.

Cook's Tips
• One of the best and most succulent varieties of clam is the carpet shell, which is perfect used in this dish. They have grooved brown shells with a yellow lattice pattern, from which they get their common name.
• Before cooking the clams, ensure all the shells are closed and discard any that are not, or that fail to close when tapped. Any clams that do not open after cooking should also be discarded.

Spicy Shrimp and Scallop Satay

This dish is succulent, spicy and very moreish. Serve with rice and a salad or pickled vegetables and lime.

Serves 4
250g/9oz shelled shrimp or
   prawns (shrimp), deveined
   and chopped
250g/9oz shelled scallops, chopped
30ml/2 tbsp potato, tapioca or
   rice flour
5ml/1 tsp baking powder
12–16 wooden, metal, lemon
   grass or sugar cane skewers
1 lime, quartered, to serve

For the spice paste
2 shallots, chopped
2 garlic cloves, chopped
2–3 red chillies, seeded
   and chopped
25g/1oz galangal or fresh root
   ginger, chopped
15g/½oz fresh turmeric, chopped
   or 2.5ml/½ tsp ground turmeric
2–3 lemon grass stalks,
   finely chopped
15–30ml/1–2 tbsp palm or
   groundnut (peanut) oil
5ml/1 tsp shrimp paste
15ml/1 tbsp tamarind paste
5ml/1 tsp palm sugar (jaggery)

1 First make the spice paste. Using a mortar and pestle, pound the shallots, garlic, chillies, galangal or ginger, turmeric and lemon grass together to form a coarse paste.

2 Heat the oil in a wok or large, heavy frying pan, stir in the paste and fry until it becomes fragrant and begins to colour. Add the shrimp paste, tamarind and sugar and continue to cook, stirring, until the mixture darkens. Put aside and leave to cool.

3 In a bowl, pound the shrimps or prawns and scallops together to form a paste, or blend them together in an electric blender or food processor. Beat in the spice paste, followed by the flour and baking powder, and beat until combined. Put the mixture in the refrigerator for about 1 hour. If using wooden skewers, soak them in water for about 30 minutes.

4 Meanwhile, prepare the barbecue, or, if you are using the grill (broiler), preheat 5 minutes before you start cooking. Using your fingers, scoop up lumps of the shellfish paste and wrap it around the skewers. Place each skewer on the barbecue or under the grill and cook for 3 minutes on each side, until golden brown. Serve with the lime wedges.

Spiced Clams Energy 126kcal/526kJ; Protein 12.5g; Carbohydrate 4.5g, of which sugars 2.2g; Fat 6g, of which saturates 0.9g; Cholesterol 50mg; Calcium 69mg; Fibre 0.6g; Sodium 906mg.
Spicy Shrimp Energy 220kcal/922kJ; Protein 27.1g; Carbohydrate 11.5g, of which sugars 1g; Fat 7.3g, of which saturates 1g; Cholesterol 151mg; Calcium 99mg; Fibre 1.5g; Sodium 249mg.

Pan-fried Baby Squid with Moroccan Spices

Baby squid needs very little cooking and tastes wonderful with this spicy sweet and sour sauce, which teams turmeric and ginger with honey and lemon juice.

Serves 4

8 baby squid, prepared,
 with tentacles
5ml/1 tsp ground turmeric

15ml/1 tbsp smen (see Cook's
 Tip) or olive oil
2 garlic cloves, finely chopped
15g/½oz fresh root ginger,
 peeled and finely chopped
5–10ml/1–2 tsp clear honey
juice of 1 lemon
10ml/2 tsp harissa
salt
small bunch of fresh coriander
 (cilantro), chopped, to garnish

1 Gently pat dry the squid bodies with kitchen paper, inside and out, and dry the tentacles. Sprinkle the squid bodies and tentacles with the ground turmeric.

2 Heat the smen or olive oil in a large, heavy frying pan and stir in the garlic and ginger.

3 Just as the ginger and garlic begin to colour, add the squid and tentacles and fry quickly on both sides over a high heat. (Take care to not overcook the squid, otherwise it will become rubbery and unpleasant.)

4 Add the honey, lemon juice and harissa to the pan and stir to form a thick, spicy, caramelized sauce.

5 Season the mixture with salt, sprinkle with the chopped coriander and serve immediately.

Cook's Tip
Smen is a pungent, aged butter used widely in Moroccan cooking. It can also served with chunks of warm, fresh bread and is used to enhance other dishes including couscous and some tagines and stews.

Ginger and Chilli Steamed Fish Custards

These pretty little custards make an unusual and exotic appetizer for a dinner party. The pandanus leaves impart a distinctive flavour – but don't be tempted to eat them once the custards are cooked: they are inedible.

Serves 4
2 eggs
200ml/7fl oz/scant 1 cup
 coconut cream
60ml/4 tbsp chopped fresh
 coriander (cilantro)
1 red chilli, seeded and sliced
15ml/1 tbsp finely chopped
 lemon grass

2 kaffir lime leaves,
 finely shredded
30ml/2 tbsp red Thai
 curry paste
1 garlic clove, crushed
5ml/1 tsp finely grated fresh
 root ginger
2 spring onions (scallions),
 finely sliced
300g/11oz mixed firm white
 fish fillets (cod, halibut or
 haddock), skinned
200g/7oz raw tiger prawns
 (shrimp), peeled and deveined
4–6 pandanus (screwpine) leaves
salt and ground black pepper
shredded cucumber, steamed rice
 and soy sauce, to serve

1 Beat the eggs in a bowl, then stir in the coconut cream, coriander, chilli, lemon grass, lime leaves, curry paste, garlic, ginger and spring onions. Finely chop the fish and roughly chop the prawns and add to the egg mixture. Stir well and season.

2 Grease four ramekins and line them with the pandanus leaves. Divide the fish mixture between the lined ramekins, then arrange in a bamboo steamer.

3 Pour 5cm/2in water into a wok and bring to the boil. Suspend the steamer over the water, cover, reduce the heat to low and steam for 25–30 minutes, or until cooked through. Serve with shredded cucumber, steamed rice and soy sauce.

Cook's Tip
Pandanus leaves are available from Asian markets.

Baby Squid Energy 154kcal/647kJ; Protein 19.8g; Carbohydrate 5.8g, of which sugars 4.3g; Fat 5.9g, of which saturates 1g; Cholesterol 281mg; Calcium 54mg; Fibre 1g; Sodium 144mg.
Fish Custards Energy 150kcal/632kJ; Protein 26.2g; Carbohydrate 2.8g, of which sugars 2.7g; Fat 3.9g, of which saturates 1g; Cholesterol 227mg; Calcium 100mg; Fibre 0.6g; Sodium 234mg.

Turkey Sosaties with a Curried Sweet-and-Sour Sauce

These South African kebabs are simply delicious.

Serves 4
15ml/1 tbsp sunflower oil
1 onion, finely chopped
1 garlic clove, crushed
2 bay leaves
juice of 1 lemon
30ml/2 tbsp curry powder
60ml/4 tbsp apricot jam
60ml/4 tbsp apple juice
salt
675g/1½lb turkey fillet
60ml/4 tbsp crème fraîche

1 Heat the oil in a pan. Add the onion, garlic and bay leaves and cook over a low heat for 10 minutes until the onions are softened but not browned.

2 Add the lemon juice, curry powder, apricot jam and apple juice to the pan. Season with salt to taste. Cook gently for about 5 minutes. Leave to cool.

3 Cut the turkey into 2cm/¾in cubes and add to the marinade. Mix well until the turkey is well coated. Cover the bowl with clear film (plastic wrap) and leave in a cool place to marinate for at least 2 hours or overnight in the refrigerator.

4 Thread the marinated turkey pieces on to skewers, allowing the excess marinade to run back into the bowl. Grill (broil) or cook the sosaties on a barbecue for 6–8 minutes, turning several times, until cooked.

5 Meanwhile, transfer the marinade to a pan and simmer over low heat for 2 minutes to warm through. Stir in the crème fraîche and serve with the sosaties.

> **Cook's Tip**
> *Soaking bamboo skewers for about 30 minutes in a large bowl of warm water before use ensures that they won't scorch when placed under the grill.*

Chicken Satay with a Spicy Peanut Sauce

One of the classic spicy foods of the East.

Serves 4
4 skinless chicken breast fillets
10ml/2 tsp soft light brown sugar

For the marinade
5ml/1 tsp cumin seeds
5ml/1 tsp fennel seeds
7.5ml/1½ tsp coriander seeds
6 shallots, chopped
1 garlic clove, crushed
1 lemon grass stalk, root trimmed
3 macadamia nuts
2.5ml/½ tsp ground turmeric

For the peanut sauce
4 shallots, sliced
2 garlic cloves, crushed
1cm/½in cube shrimp paste
6 cashew nuts or almonds
2 lemon grass stalks, trimmed, and the lower 5cm/2in portion finely sliced
45ml/3 tbsp sunflower oil
5–10ml/1–2 tsp chilli powder
400ml/14fl oz can coconut milk
60–75ml/4–5 tbsp tamarind water
15ml/1 tbsp soft light brown sugar
175g/6oz/½ cup crunchy peanut butter

1 Cut the chicken breast fillets into thin strips, about the size of a finger. Sprinkle with the sugar and set aside.

2 Make the marinade. Dry-fry the spices, then grind to a powder. Put the shallots in a food processor and add the garlic. Add the lower 5cm/2in of the lemon grass to the processor with the nuts, ground spices and turmeric. Process to a paste and place in a bowl with the chicken. Stir well, cover and leave for 4 hours.

3 Process the shallots for the sauce with the garlic and shrimp paste. Add the nuts and the lemon grass. Process to a purée and fry in hot oil for 2–3 minutes. Add the chilli powder and cook for 2 minutes more.

4 Stir in the coconut milk and bring to the boil. Reduce the heat and stir in the tamarind water and sugar. Add the peanut butter and simmer until thick. Preheat the grill (broiler).

5 Thread the chicken on to 16 skewers. Grill (broil) for 5 minutes until golden and tender. Serve with the peanut sauce.

Turkey Sosaties Energy 325kcal/1381kJ; Protein 59.4g; Carbohydrate 12.2g, of which sugars 12.1g; Fat 4.8g, of which saturates 1.9g; Cholesterol 125mg; Calcium 18mg; Fibre 0g; Sodium 162mg.
Chicken Satay Energy 48kcal/200kJ; Protein 4.8g; Carbohydrate 2.2g, of which sugars 2.1g; Fat 2.2g, of which saturates 0.4g; Cholesterol 13mg; Calcium 3mg; Fibre 0.1g; Sodium 105mg.

Pineapple Chicken Kebabs

This chicken dish has a delicate tang and the meat is very tender. The pineapple not only tenderizes the chicken but also gives it a slight sweetness.

Serves 6

225g/8oz can pineapple chunks
5ml/1 tsp ground cumin
5ml/1 tsp ground coriander
5ml/1 tsp chilli powder
2.5ml/½ tsp crushed garlic
5ml/1 tsp salt
30ml/2 tbsp natural (plain) low-fat yogurt
15ml/1 tbsp chopped fresh coriander (cilantro)
few drops of orange food colouring (optional)
275g/10oz boneless chicken, skinned and cubed
½ red (bell) pepper, seeded
½ yellow or green (bell) pepper, seeded
1 large onion
6 cherry tomatoes
15ml/1 tbsp vegetable oil
salad leaves, to serve

1 Drain the pineapple juice into a bowl. Reserve eight large chunks of pineapple and squeeze the juice from the remaining chunks into the bowl and set aside. You should have about 120ml/4fl oz/½ cup pineapple juice.

2 In a large bowl, mix together the spices, garlic, salt, yogurt, fresh coriander and food colouring, if using. Pour in the reserved pineapple juice and mix well to combine.

3 Add the chicken to the yogurt and spice mixture, cover and leave to marinate in a cool place for about 1–1½ hours. Cut the peppers and onion into bitesize chunks.

4 Preheat the grill (broiler) to medium. Arrange the chicken pieces, vegetables and reserved pineapple chunks alternately on six metal or wooden skewers (wooden skewers should be soaked in water for 30 minutes before use to prevent them from burning under the grill).

5 Brush the kebabs lightly with the oil, then place the skewers on a flameproof dish or in a grill pan, turning the chicken pieces and basting with the marinade regularly, for about 15 minutes until cooked through. Serve with salad leaves.

Chicken Tikka

This extremely popular Indian first course is quick and easy to cook and tastes absolutely delectable. This dish can also be served as part of a spicy buffet.

Serves 6

450g/1lb boneless chicken, skinned and cubed
5ml/1 tsp crushed fresh root ginger
5ml/1 tsp crushed garlic
5ml/1 tsp chilli powder
1.5ml/¼ tsp ground turmeric
5ml/1 tsp salt
150ml/¼ pint/⅔ cup natural (plain) low-fat yogurt
60ml/4 tbsp lemon juice
15ml/1 tbsp chopped fresh coriander (cilantro)
15ml/1 tbsp vegetable oil

For the garnish
mixed salad leaves
1 small onion, cut into rings
lime wedges
fresh coriander (cilantro)

1 In a medium bowl, mix together the chicken pieces, ginger, garlic, chilli powder, turmeric and salt.

2 Stir in the yogurt, lemon juice and fresh coriander and leave to marinate for at least 2 hours.

3 Place in a grill (broiler) pan or in a flameproof dish lined with foil and baste with the oil.

4 Preheat the grill to medium. Grill (broil) the chicken for 15–20 minutes until cooked, turning and basting several times. Serve on a bed of mixed salad leaves, garnished with onion rings, lime wedges and coriander.

Cook's Tips
• To make the turning and basting of the meat easier, thread the chicken pieces on to skewers before placing under the grill (broiler) or on top of a barbecue. If you are using wooden skewers, soak them in cold water for 30 minutes prior to using to prevent them from burning under the grill.
• This dish also makes a great main course for four people. Serve with a little more salad and some pickles.

Chicken Kebabs Energy 135kcal/565kJ; Protein 13.2g; Carbohydrate 13.6g, of which sugars 10.3g; Fat 3.5g, of which saturates 0.6g; Cholesterol 32mg; Calcium 31mg; Fibre 1.7g; Sodium 35mg.
Chicken Tikka Energy 415kcal/1730kJ; Protein 46g; Carbohydrate 2g, of which sugars 0.2g; Fat 24.8g, of which saturates 8.5g; Cholesterol 203mg; Calcium 21mg; Fibre 0.5g; Sodium 172mg.

Chicken Kofta Balti with Paneer

This rather unusual appetizer looks most elegant when served in small individual karahis.

Serves 6

For the koftas
450g/1lb boneless chicken, skinned and cubed
5ml/1 tsp crushed garlic
5ml/1 tsp shredded fresh root ginger
7.5ml/1½ tsp ground coriander
7.5ml/1½ tsp chilli powder
7.5ml/1½ tsp ground fenugreek
1.5ml/¼ tsp ground turmeric

5ml/1 tsp salt
30ml/2 tbsp chopped fresh coriander (cilantro)
2 fresh green chillies, chopped
600ml/1 pint/2½ cups water
corn oil, for frying
fresh mint sprigs

For the paneer mixture
1 medium onion, sliced
1 red (bell) pepper, seeded and cut into strips
1 green (bell) pepper, seeded and cut into strips
175g/6oz paneer, cubed
175g/6oz/1½ cups corn

1 Put all the kofta ingredients, apart from the oil, into a medium pan. Bring to the boil slowly over medium heat, and cook, stirring, until all the liquid has evaporated. Remove from the heat and leave to cool slightly. Put the mixture into a food processor or blender and process for 2 minutes.

2 Transfer the mixture to a large mixing bowl. Taking a little of the mixture at a time, shape it into small balls, using your hands. You should be able to make about 12 koftas. Heat the corn oil in a karahi, wok or deep pan over high heat. Reduce the heat slightly and drop the koftas carefully into the oil. Move them around gently to ensure that they cook evenly.

3 When the koftas are lightly browned, remove them from the oil with a slotted spoon and drain well on kitchen paper. Set aside and keep warm in a low oven.

4 Heat the oil still remaining in the karahi, and flash-fry all the ingredients for the paneer mixture. This should take about 3 minutes over a high heat. Divide the paneer mixture evenly between six individual karahis. Add two koftas to each serving, and garnish with mint sprigs.

Lamb Kebabs

First introduced by the Muslims, kebabs have now become a favourite Indian dish and are often sold at open stalls; the wonderful aroma of the spicy meat wafting down the street is guaranteed to stop passers-by in their tracks to buy one.

Serves 8

For the kebabs
900g/2lb lean minced (ground) lamb
1 large onion, roughly chopped
5cm/2in piece fresh root ginger, chopped
2 garlic cloves, crushed
1 fresh green chilli, finely chopped

5ml/1 tsp chilli powder
30ml/2 tbsp chopped fresh coriander (cilantro)
5ml/1 tsp garam masala
10ml/2 tsp ground coriander
5ml/1 tsp ground cumin
5ml/1 tsp salt
1 egg
15ml/1 tbsp natural (plain) low-fat yogurt
15ml/1 tbsp vegetable oil
mixed salad, to serve

For the raita
250ml/8fl oz/1 cup natural (plain) low-fat yogurt
½ cucumber, finely chopped
30ml/2 tbsp chopped fresh mint
1.5ml/¼ tsp salt

1 Put all the ingredients for the kebabs, except the yogurt and oil, into a food processor or blender and process until the mixture binds together. Spoon into a large bowl, cover and leave to marinate for 1 hour.

2 To make the raita, mix together all the ingredients and chill for at least 15 minutes in a refrigerator.

3 Preheat the grill (broiler). Divide the lamb mixture into eight equal portions with lightly floured hands and mould into long sausage shapes. Thread the meat on to metal skewers and chill in the refrigerator for at least 1 hour.

4 Brush the kebabs lightly with the yogurt and oil and cook under a hot grill for 8–10 minutes, turning occasionally, until brown all over. Serve the kebabs on a bed of mixed salad, accompanied by the raita.

Chicken Kofta Energy 253kcal/1056kJ; Protein 24.7g; Carbohydrate 10.8g, of which sugars 6.7g; Fat 12.6g, of which saturates 2.2g; Cholesterol 57mg; Calcium 71mg; Fibre 1.8g; Sodium 471mg.
Lamb Kebabs Energy 339kcal/1409kJ; Protein 22.6g; Carbohydrate 2.7g, of which sugars 2.4g; Fat 26.5g, of which saturates 7.9g; Cholesterol 86mg; Calcium 16mg; Fibre 0.7g; Sodium 102mg.

Chargrilled Lamb with Cumin

Small pieces of tender, spicy lamb are wrapped in flat breads with red onion, parsley and lemon juice.

Serves 4–6
2 onions, grated
7.5ml/1½ tsp salt
2 garlic cloves, crushed
10ml/2 tsp cumin seeds, crushed
900g/2lb boneless shoulder of
    lamb, trimmed and cut into
    bitesize pieces

For the flat breads
225g/8oz/2 cups strong white
    bread flour
50g/2oz/¼ cup wholemeal
    (whole-wheat) flour
5ml/1 tsp salt

To serve
1 large red onion, cut in half
    lengthways and sliced
1 large bunch of fresh flat leaf
    parsley, roughly chopped
2–3 lemons, cut into wedges

1 Sprinkle the onions with the salt and leave for 15 minutes. Place a sieve (strainer) over a bowl, put in the onions and press down to extract the juice. Discard the onions left in the sieve, then mix the garlic and cumin seeds into the onion juice and toss in the lamb. Cover and leave to marinate for 3–4 hours.

2 Meanwhile, prepare the dough for the breads. Sift the flours and salt into a bowl. Make a well in the middle and gradually add 200ml/7fl oz/scant 1 cup lukewarm water, drawing in the flour from the sides. Knead the dough until firm and springy.

3 Divide the dough into 24 pieces and knead each one into a ball. Place on a floured surface and cover with a damp cloth. Leave to rest for 45 minutes while you get the barbecue ready.

4 Just before cooking, roll each ball of dough into a wide, thin circle. Dust them with flour, and keep them covered.

5 Thread the meat on to metal skewers and cook on the barbecue for 2–3 minutes on each side. At the same time, cook the flat breads on a hot griddle or other flat pan, flipping them over as they begin to go brown and buckle. Pile up on a plate.

6 Slide the meat off the skewers on to the flat breads. Sprinkle onion and parsley over and squeeze lemon juice over the top.

Curried Lamb and Potato Cakes

An unusual variation on burgers or rissoles, these little spicy lamb triangles are easy to make. They are really good served hot as part of a buffet, but they can also be eaten cold as a snack or taken on picnics.

Makes 12–15
450g/1lb new or small,
    firm potatoes
3 eggs

1 onion, grated
30ml/2 tbsp chopped
    fresh parsley
450g/1lb finely minced (ground)
    lean lamb
115g/4oz/2 cups fresh
    breadcrumbs
vegetable oil, for frying
salt and ground black pepper
sprigs of fresh mint,
    to garnish
pitta bread and herby green
    salad, to serve

1 Cook the potatoes in a large pan of boiling salted water for 20 minutes or until tender, then drain and leave to cool.

2 Beat the eggs in a large bowl. Add the onion, parsley and seasoning and beat together.

3 When the potatoes are cold, grate them coarsely and stir evenly into the egg mixture, together with the minced lamb. Knead the mixture well for 3–4 minutes until all the ingredients are thoroughly blended together.

4 Take a handful of the lamb mixture and roll it into a ball. Repeat this process until all the meat is used.

5 Roll the balls in the breadcrumbs and then mould them into fairly flat triangular shapes, about 13cm/5in long. Coat them in the breadcrumbs again.

6 Heat a 1cm/½in layer of oil in a large frying pan over medium heat. When the oil is hot, fry the potato cakes for 8–12 minutes until golden brown on both sides, turning occasionally. Drain on kitchen paper.

7 Serve the cakes immediately, garnished with mint and accompanied by pitta bread and salad.

Chargrilled Lamb Energy 433kcal/1821kJ; Protein 34.3g; Carbohydrate 37.1g, of which sugars 4.4g; Fat 17.5g, of which saturates 7.9g; Cholesterol 114mg; Calcium 83mg; Fibre 2.5g; Sodium 460mg.
Lamb Cakes Energy 181kcal/760kJ; Protein 10.8g; Carbohydrate 13.9g, of which sugars 1.1g; Fat 9.6g, of which saturates 2.8g; Cholesterol 76mg; Calcium 31mg; Fibre 0.8g; Sodium 128mg.

Shammi Kebabs

These Indian treats are
derived from the kebabs of
the Middle East. They can be
served either as appetizers
or side dishes with a
raita or chutney.

Serves 5–6

2 onions, finely chopped
250g/9oz lean lamb, boned
  and cubed
50g/2oz/¼ cup chana dhal (yellow
  lentils) or yellow split peas
5ml/1 tsp cumin seeds

5ml/1 tsp garam masala
4–6 fresh green chillies
5cm/2in piece fresh root
  ginger, grated
175ml/6fl oz/¾ cup water
a few fresh coriander (cilantro)
  and mint leaves, chopped, plus
  extra coriander sprigs
  to garnish
juice of 1 lemon
15ml/1 tbsp gram flour
2 eggs, beaten
vegetable oil, for shallow-frying
salt

1 Put the first seven ingredients and the measured water into a large pan with a pinch of salt, and bring to the boil. Simmer, covered, until the meat and dhal are cooked. Remove the lid and continue to cook for a few more minutes, to reduce the excess liquid. Set aside to cool.

2 Transfer the cooled meat mixture to a food processor or blender and process well until the mixture turns into a rough, gritty paste. You can use a mortar and pestle, if you prefer.

3 Put the paste into a large mixing bowl and add the chopped coriander and mint leaves, lemon juice and gram flour. Knead well with your fingers for a good couple of minutes, to ensure that all ingredients are evenly distributed through the mixture, and any excess liquid has been thoroughly absorbed. When the colour appears even throughout, and the mixture has taken on a semi-solid, sticky rather than powdery consistency, the kebabs are ready for shaping into portions.

4 Divide the kebab mixture into 10–12 equal portions and use your hands to roll each into a ball, then flatten slightly. Chill in the refrigerator for 1 hour. Dip the kebabs in the beaten egg and shallow-fry each side until golden brown. Pat dry on kitchen paper and serve immediately.

Sumac-spiced Burgers with Relish

The sharp-sweet red onion
relish works perfectly with
these tasty burgers, which
are based on Middle-Eastern
style lamb. Serve the
burgers and relish with pitta
bread and tabbouleh or a
green salad.

Serves 4

25g/1oz/3 tbsp bulgur wheat
500g/1¼lb minced
  (ground) lamb
1 small red onion, finely chopped
2 garlic cloves, finely chopped
1 green chilli, seeded and
  finely chopped
5ml/1 tsp ground cumin seeds
2.5ml/½ tsp ground sumac
15g/½oz chopped fresh parsley

30ml/2 tbsp chopped fresh mint
olive oil, for frying
salt and ground black pepper

For the relish

2 red (bell) peppers, halved
2 red onions, cut into 5mm/¼in
  thick slices
75–90ml/5–6 tbsp virgin olive oil
350g/12oz cherry
  tomatoes, chopped
½–1 fresh red or green chilli,
  seeded and finely chopped
30ml/2 tbsp chopped mint
30ml/2 tbsp chopped parsley
15ml/1 tbsp chopped oregano
2.5–5ml/½–1 tsp each ground
  toasted cumin and sumac
juice of ½ lemon
caster (superfine) sugar, to taste

1 Pour 150ml/¼ pint/⅔ cup hot water over the bulgur wheat and leave to stand for 15 minutes, then drain.

2 Place the bulgur wheat in a bowl and add the minced lamb, onion, garlic, chilli, cumin, sumac, parsley and mint. Mix together thoroughly, then season with 5ml/1 tsp salt and plenty of black pepper. Form the mixture into eight burgers and set aside while you make the red onion relish.

3 Grill (broil) the peppers, until the skin chars and blisters. Peel off the skin, dice and place in a bowl. Brush the onions with oil and grill until browned. Chop. Add the onions, tomatoes, chilli, mint, parsley, oregano and 2.5ml/½ tsp each of the cumin and sumac to the peppers. Stir in 60ml/4 tbsp oil and 15ml/1 tbsp of the lemon juice and salt, pepper and sugar to taste. Set aside.

4 Heat a frying pan over a high heat and grease with oil. Cook the burgers for 5–6 minutes on each side. Serve immediately.

Shammi Kebabs Energy 207kcal/861kJ; Protein 12.8g; Carbohydrate 7.7g, of which sugars 1g; Fat 14.1g, of which saturates 3.6g; Cholesterol 95mg; Calcium 40mg; Fibre 1.1g; Sodium 65mg.
Sumac Burgers Energy 537kcal/2228kJ; Protein 27.2g; Carbohydrate 19g, of which sugars 13.4g; Fat 39.6g, of which saturates 11.1g; Cholesterol 96mg; Calcium 83mg; Fibre 4.2g; Sodium 105mg.

Prawn and Spinach Pancakes

Serve these delicious filled pancakes hot. Try to use red onions, although they are not essential.

Makes 4–6
175g/6oz/1½ cups plain (all-purpose) flour
2.5ml/½ tsp salt
3 eggs
350ml/12fl oz/1½ cups semi-skimmed (low-fat) milk
15g/½oz/1 tbsp low-fat margarine

For the filling
30ml/2 tbsp vegetable oil
2 medium red onions, sliced

2.5ml/½ tsp garlic pulp
2.5cm/1in piece fresh root ginger, shredded
5ml/1 tsp chilli powder
5ml/1 tsp garam masala
5ml/1 tsp salt
2 tomatoes, sliced
225g/8oz frozen leaf spinach, thawed and drained
115g/4oz cooked prawns (shrimp)
30ml/2 tbsp chopped fresh coriander (cilantro)

For the garnish
1 tomato, quartered
fresh coriander (cilantro) sprigs
lemon wedges

1 To make the pancakes, sift the flour and salt together. Beat the eggs and add to the flour, beating constantly. Gradually stir in the milk. Leave to stand for 1 hour.

2 Heat the oil in a large frying pan and fry the onions over a medium heat until golden. Add the garlic, ginger, chilli powder, garam masala and salt, followed by the tomatoes and spinach. Add the prawns and fresh coriander. Cook for 5–7 minutes or until any excess water has been absorbed. Keep warm.

3 Heat about 2.5ml/½ tsp of the low-fat margarine in a 25cm/10in non-stick frying pan. Pour in about one-quarter of the pancake batter, tilting the pan so the batter spreads well, coats the bottom of the pan and is evenly distributed.

4 When bubbles appear on top, flip it over using a spatula and cook for a further minute or so. Transfer to a plate and keep warm. Cook the remaining pancakes in the same way.

5 Fill the pancakes with the spinach and prawns, and garnish with the tomato and coriander. Serve warm with lemon wedges.

Grilled King Prawns with Stir-fried Spices

In India, king prawns are marinated and then grilled in the tandoor to produce tandoori king prawns. Similar results are achieved here by cooking the prawns under a very hot grill.

Serves 4
45ml/3 tbsp natural (plain) yogurt
5ml/1 tsp paprika
5ml/1 tsp grated fresh root ginger
16–20 peeled, cooked king prawns (jumbo shrimp), thawed if frozen

15ml/1 tbsp vegetable oil
3 onions, sliced
2.5ml/½ tsp fennel seeds, finely crushed
2.5cm/1in piece cinnamon stick
5ml/1 tsp crushed garlic
5ml/1 tsp chilli powder
1 yellow (bell) pepper, seeded and roughly chopped
1 red (bell) pepper, seeded and roughly chopped
salt
15ml/1 tbsp fresh coriander (cilantro) leaves, left whole, to garnish

1 Blend together the yogurt, paprika, ginger and salt to taste. Add to the prawns and leave to marinate for 45 minutes.

2 Meanwhile, heat the oil in a wok, karahi or large pan and fry the sliced onions with the fennel seeds and the cinnamon stick over medium heat, stirring occasionally, until the onions have softened and turned golden.

3 Lower the heat and stir in the crushed garlic and chilli powder. Add the chopped yellow and red peppers to the pan and stir-fry gently for 3–5 minutes.

4 Remove the pan from the heat and transfer the onion and spice mixture to a warm serving dish, discarding the cinnamon stick. Set the dish aside.

5 Preheat the grill (broiler) to high. Put the marinated prawns in a grill (broiler) pan or flameproof dish and place under the grill to darken their tops and achieve a chargrilled effect. Add the prawns to the onion and spice mixture, and garnish with fresh coriander leaves. Serve immediately.

Prawn Pancakes Energy 268kcal/1127kJ; Protein 14g; Carbohydrate 33g, of which sugars 8.1g; Fat 10g, of which saturates 2.4g; Cholesterol 136mg; Calcium 229mg; Fibre 2.9g; Sodium 174mg.
Grilled King Prawns Energy 118kcal/495kJ; Protein 17.9g; Carbohydrate 3g, of which sugars 3g; Fat 3.9g, of which saturates 0.5g; Cholesterol 195mg; Calcium 83mg; Fibre 0.4g; Sodium 234mg.

Ginger Prawn and Mangetout Stir-fry

Nothing beats a stir-fry for a quick and tasty midweek meal, especially when it's spiced up with ginger, garlic and Tabasco. If you keep some prawns in the freezer most of this dish can be made with store-cupboard ingredients.

Serves 4
15ml/1 tbsp oil
2 medium onions, diced
15ml/1 tbsp tomato
   purée (paste)
5ml/1 tsp Tabasco sauce
5ml/1 tsp lemon juice
5ml/1 tsp grated fresh
   root ginger
5ml/1 tsp crushed garlic
5ml/1 tsp chilli powder
5ml/1 tsp salt
15ml/1 tbsp chopped fresh
   coriander (cilantro)
175g/6oz/1½ cups frozen
   cooked peeled prawns
   (shrimp), thawed
12 mangetouts (snow peas),
   cut in half

1 Heat the oil in a karahi, wok or heavy pan and fry the onions for 6–8 minutes until golden brown.

2 Mix the tomato purée with 30ml/2 tbsp water in a bowl. Add the Tabasco sauce, lemon juice, ginger and garlic, chilli powder and salt. Stir well until combined.

3 Lower the heat, pour the sauce over the onions and stir-fry for a few seconds until well mixed in.

4 Add the coriander, prawns and mangetouts to the pan and stir-fry for about 5–7 minutes, or until the sauce has reduced and thickened. Serve immediately.

> **Cook's Tip**
> *Mangetouts (snow peas), being small and almost flat, are perfect for stir-frying and are a popular ingredient in Indian cooking. They are particularly good stir-fried with prawns (shrimp) which need only minutes to heat through.*

Stir-fried Chilli-garlic Prawns

These spice-coated prawns make a mouthwatering appetizer or light lunch, when served with a salad, or they can be transformed into a main meal with the addition of naan bread.

Serves 4
15ml/1 tbsp vegetable oil
3 garlic cloves, roughly halved
3 tomatoes, chopped
2.5ml/½ tsp salt
5ml/1 tsp crushed dried
   red chillies
5ml/1 tsp lemon juice
mango chutney, to taste
1 fresh green chilli, chopped
16–20 peeled, cooked king
   prawns (jumbo shrimp)
fresh coriander (cilantro) sprigs
   and chopped spring onions
   (scallions), to garnish

1 In a wok, karahi or large heavy pan, heat the vegetable oil over a low heat and fry the garlic halves gently for 5–6 minutes until they are tinged with golden brown.

2 Add the chopped tomatoes, salt, crushed red chillies, lemon juice, mango chutney and the chopped fresh chilli to the pan. Stir well until all the ingredients are well combined.

3 Add the prawns to the pan, then raise the heat and stir-fry briskly, mixing the prawns with the other ingredients until they are thoroughly heated through.

4 Transfer the prawns in the sauce to a warm serving dish and garnish with fresh coriander sprigs and chopped spring onions. Serve the prawns immediately.

> **Variation**
> *This dish can be also be made with other seafood. Substitute the same quantity of mussels or scallops for the prawns (shrimp).*

> **Cook's Tip**
> *Take care not to let the garlic burn during the frying in step 1, otherwise it will impart a bitter taste to the rest of the dish.*

Ginger Prawn Stir-fry Energy 125kcal/524kJ; Protein 17.6g; Carbohydrate 5.2g, of which sugars 3.6g; Fat 3.4g, of which saturates 0.4g; Cholesterol 171mg; Calcium 96mg; Fibre 1.3g; Sodium 436mg.
Stir-fried Prawns Energy 118kcal/495kJ; Protein 17.9g; Carbohydrate 3g, of which sugars 3g; Fat 3.9g, of which saturates 0.5g; Cholesterol 195mg; Calcium 83mg; Fibre 0.4g; Sodium 234mg.

Prawn and Cauliflower Curry

This is a basic fisherman's curry. Simple to make, it would usually be eaten from a communal bowl.

Serves 4
450g/1lb raw tiger prawns (jumbo shrimp), peeled, deveined and cleaned
juice of 1 lime
15ml/1 tbsp vegetable oil
1 red onion, roughly chopped
2 garlic cloves, roughly chopped
2 Thai chillies, seeded and finely chopped
1 cauliflower, broken into florets
5ml/1 tsp sugar
2 star anise, dry-fried and ground
10ml/2 tsp fenugreek, dry-fried and ground
450ml/¾ pint/2 cups coconut milk
1 bunch fresh coriander (cilantro), chopped, to garnish
salt and ground black pepper

1 In a bowl, toss the prawns in the lime juice and set aside. Heat a wok or heavy pan and add the oil. Stir in the onion, garlic and chillies. As they brown, add the cauliflower to the pan. Stir-fry for 2–3 minutes.

2 Stir the sugar and spices into the pan. Add the coconut milk, stirring to make sure it is thoroughly combined. Reduce the heat and simmer for 10–15 minutes, or until the liquid has reduced and thickened a little.

3 Add the prawns and lime juice and cook for 1–2 minutes, or until the prawns turn pink. Season to taste, and sprinkle with coriander. Serve immediately.

Cook's Tip
To devein prawns, make a shallow cut down the back of the prawn, lift out the thin, black vein and discard, then rinse the prawns thoroughly under cold running water.

Variation
Other popular combinations include prawns (shrimp) with butternut squash or pumpkin.

Yellow Prawn Curry

This South-east Asian speciality lives up to its name with an intense turmeric yellow colour that matches the strong flavours.

Serves 4
30ml/2 tbsp coconut or palm oil
2 shallots, finely chopped
2 garlic cloves, finely chopped
2 red chillies, seeded and finely chopped
25g/1oz fresh turmeric, finely chopped, or 10ml/2 tsp ground turmeric
25g/1oz fresh root ginger, finely chopped
2 lemon grass stalks, finely sliced
10ml/2 tsp coriander seeds
10ml/2 tsp shrimp paste
1 red (bell) pepper, seeded and finely sliced
4 kaffir lime leaves
about 500g/1¼lb fresh prawns (shrimp), shelled and deveined
400g/14oz can coconut milk
salt and ground black pepper
1 green chilli, seeded and sliced, to garnish

To serve
cooked rice
4 fried shallots or fresh chillies, seeded and sliced lengthways

1 Heat the oil in a wok or heavy frying pan. Stir in the shallots, garlic, chillies, turmeric, ginger, lemon grass and coriander seeds and fry until the fragrant aromas are released.

2 Stir in the shrimp paste and cook for 2–3 minutes. Add the red pepper and lime leaves and stir-fry for a further 1 minute.

3 Add the prawns to the pan. Pour in the coconut milk, stirring to combine, and bring to the boil. Cook for 5–6 minutes until the prawns are cooked. Season with salt and pepper to taste.

4 Spoon the prawns on to a warmed serving dish and sprinkle with the sliced green chilli to garnish. Serve with rice and fried shallots or the fresh chillies on the side.

Variation
Big, juicy prawns are delectable in this dish, but you can easily substitute them with scallops, squid or mussels, or a combination of all three, depending on what is available.

Prawn Curry Energy 157kcal/664kJ; Protein 24.7g; Carbohydrate 10.4g, of which sugars 9.4g; Fat 2.2g, of which saturates 0.6g; Cholesterol 219mg; Calcium 169mg; Fibre 2.7g; Sodium 351mg.
Yellow Curry Energy 230kcal/965kJ; Protein 26.4g; Carbohydrate 16g, of which sugars 13.5g; Fat 7.2g, of which saturates 1g; Cholesterol 263mg; Calcium 226mg; Fibre 2.7g; Sodium 519mg.

Goan Prawn Curry

Goan dishes use generous amounts of chilli, mellowed by coconut milk and palm vinegar. In this delicious coconut-enriched prawn curry, cider vinegar makes an equally good alternative to palm vinegar.

Serves 4
500g/1¼lb peeled king or tiger prawns (jumbo shrimp)
2.5ml/½ tsp salt, plus extra to taste
30ml/2 tbsp palm or cider vinegar
60ml/4 tbsp sunflower or olive oil
1 large onion, finely chopped
10ml/2 tsp crushed fresh root ginger
10ml/2 tsp crushed garlic
2.5ml/½ tsp ground cumin
5ml/1 tsp ground coriander
2.5ml/½ tsp ground turmeric
2.5ml/½ tsp chilli powder
2.5ml/½ tsp ground black pepper
75g/3oz/1 cup creamed coconut, chopped, or 250ml/8floz/1 cup coconut cream
4 green chillies
30ml/2 tbsp chopped fresh coriander (cilantro) leaves
plain boiled rice, to serve

1 Put the prawns in a non-metallic bowl and add the measured salt and vinegar. Mix and set aside for 10–15 minutes.

2 Heat the sunflower or olive oil in a medium pan and add the onion. Fry over medium heat until the onion is translucent.

3 Add the ginger and garlic and continue to fry for about 2 minutes over a low heat, until lightly browned.

4 Mix the cumin, coriander, turmeric, chilli powder and pepper in a bowl and add 30ml/2 tbsp water to make a pouring consistency. Add to the onion and cook, stirring, for 4–5 minutes until the mixture is dry and the oil separates from the spice mix.

5 Next, pour in 200ml/7fl oz/¾ cup warm water, the creamed coconut and salt to taste. Stir until the coconut has dissolved.

6 Add the prawns along with all the juices in the bowl, bring the pan to the boil, reduce the heat and cook for another 5–7 minutes. When the prawns curl up, they are cooked.

7 Add the whole chillies and simmer for 2–3 minutes. Stir in the chopped coriander. Serve with plain boiled rice.

Curried Prawns in Coconut Milk

This is a mildly spiced dish where the prawns are cooked in a tangy coconut gravy along with cherry tomatoes. It is a simple but flavoursome dish that is quick to prepare.

Serves 4–6
600ml/1 pint/2½ cups coconut milk
30ml/2 tbsp yellow curry paste
2.5ml/½ tsp salt
5ml/1 tsp sugar
450g/1lb king prawns (jumbo shrimp), peeled, tails left intact, deveined
225g/8oz cherry tomatoes
fresh red chilli strips and coriander (cilantro) leaves, to garnish
juice of ½ lime, to serve

1 Pour half the coconut milk into a large heavy pan or wok and bring slowly to the boil.

2 Add the curry paste to the coconut milk in the pan, stir until it disperses, then simmer for about 10 minutes.

3 Add the salt, sugar and remaining coconut milk to the pan. Simmer for another 5 minutes.

4 Add the prawns and cherry tomatoes to the pan. Simmer very gently over a low heat for about 5 minutes until the prawns are pink and tender.

5 Serve the prawns garnished with chilli strips and fresh coriander and have the lime juice on hand for sprinkling over.

Cook's Tip
Curry paste is a useful standby, but if you prefer a more authentic flavour you can make your own curry powder and mix 30ml/2 tbsp of it with a little water to form a paste. Dry roast 75g/3oz/1 cup coriander seeds, 15ml/1 tbsp cumin seeds, 8 dried red chillies, 12 cardamom pods and 12 cloves gently for 10 minutes. Cool and add 5ml/1 tsp turmeric and 15ml/1 tbsp ground cinnamon. Grind to a fine powder then store in an airtight jar for up to 6 months.

Curried Prawns Energy 118kcal/500kJ; Protein 14.1g; Carbohydrate 11g, of which sugars 11g; Fat 2.3g, of which saturates 0.6g; Cholesterol 146mg; Calcium 116mg; Fibre 0.4g; Sodium 466mg.
Goan Prawn Curry Energy 171kcal/723kJ; Protein 21.9g; Carbohydrate 10g, of which sugars 7.4g; Fat 5.3g, of which saturates 2.5g; Cholesterol 227mg; Calcium 136mg; Fibre 1g; Sodium 344mg.

Parsi Prawn Curry

This curry comes from the west coast of India, where fresh fish and shellfish are plentiful and eaten in abundance. The larger fresh king prawns or tiger prawns are ideal to use in this simple but tasty curry.

Serves 4–6
60ml/4 tbsp vegetable oil
1 medium onion, finely sliced
6 garlic cloves, finely crushed
5ml/1 tsp chilli powder
7.5ml/1½ tsp turmeric
15ml/1 tbsp tamarind
2 medium onions or 1 large onion, finely chopped
5ml/1 tsp mint sauce
15ml/1 tbsp demerara (raw) sugar
450g/1lb fresh king prawns (jumbo shrimp), peeled and deveined
75g/3oz/3 cups fresh coriander (cilantro), chopped
salt

1 Heat the oil in a frying pan and fry the sliced onion until it becomes soft and translucent, stirring frequently. In a bowl, mix the garlic, chilli powder and turmeric with a little water to form a paste. Add to the onion and simmer for 3 minutes.

2 To make the tamarind juice, mix the tamarind pulp with 45ml/3 tbsp water in a small bowl. Discard any seeds or pulp.

3 Add the chopped onions to the frying pan and cook until they are translucent. Add the tamarind juice with the mint sauce, sugar and salt, and gently simmer for a further 3 minutes.

4 Pat the prawns dry with kitchen paper. Add to the onion and spice mixture with a small amount of water and stir-fry until the prawns turn a bright orange-pink colour.

5 When the prawns are cooked, add the fresh coriander and stir-fry over high heat for a few minutes to thicken the sauce. Serve immediately, while piping hot.

> **Cook's Tip**
> Tamarind is usually sold in blocks of mashed pods or pulp or as a concentrated juice. It is used to sour the flavour of food.

Prawn Korma

This delectable prawn curry features almonds and yogurt, along with poppy and sesame seeds, which contrast perfectly with the chilli, garlic and ginger to add a cooling dimension.

Serves 4
50g/2oz/½ cup blanched almonds
500g/1¼lb raw peeled king prawns (jumbo shrimp)
30ml/2 tbsp lemon juice
2.5ml/½ tsp ground turmeric
15ml/1 tbsp white poppy seeds
15ml/1 tbsp sesame seeds
150g/5oz/⅔ cup natural (plain) yogurt
7.5ml/1½ tsp gram flour
60ml/4 tbsp sunflower or olive oil
1 large onion, finely chopped
10ml/2 tsp ginger purée (paste)
10ml/2 tsp garlic purée (paste)
1 chilli, seeded and finely chopped
1.5–2.5ml/¼–½ tsp chilli powder
5ml/1 tsp salt, or to taste
15ml/1 tbsp toasted flaked (sliced) almonds, to garnish

1 Soak the almonds in 150ml/¼ pint/⅔ cup boiling water for 20 minutes. Meanwhile, in a large mixing bowl, mix the prawns, lemon juice and turmeric together. Set aside.

2 Grind the poppy and sesame seeds in a coffee grinder or blender until they are finely ground, about the consistency of salt. Whisk the yogurt and gram flour together and set aside.

3 In a heavy pan, heat the oil over medium heat and add the onion. Fry gently until the onion is soft and translucent, which will take around 5–6 minutes.

4 Add the ginger and garlic, the ground poppy and sesame seeds, and the chilli powder. Cook for 2–3 minutes, stirring constantly, then add the prawns, salt and the whisked yogurt. Reduce the heat to low, cover the pan with a lid and cook for another 3–4 minutes.

5 Meanwhile, purée the almonds with the water in which they were soaked in a food processor or blender, and then add this to the prawns. Stir to mix well and cook for a further 5–6 minutes or until the prawns have curled up at the ends. Transfer the korma to a serving dish and garnish with the toasted almonds before serving.

Coconut Prawn Curry

This delicious dish features chayote, also known as christophene, alligator pear or custard marrow, which belongs to the squash family. Widely used in South-east Asia and some parts of India, it is pear-shaped, and generally pale yellow or yellow-green in colour.

Serves 4

1–2 chayotes or 2–3
   courgettes (zucchini)
2 fresh red chillies, seeded
1 onion, quartered
5mm/¼in piece fresh galangal
   or 1cm/½in piece fresh root
   ginger, sliced
1 lemon grass stalk, lower
   5cm/2in sliced, top bruised
2.5cm/1in piece fresh turmeric or
   5ml/1tsp ground turmeric
200ml/7fl oz/scant 1 cup water
lemon juice, to taste
400g/14oz can coconut milk
450g/1lb cooked, peeled
   prawns (shrimp)
salt
fresh red chilli shreds, to garnish
plain boiled rice or noodles,
   to serve

1 Peel the chayotes, remove the seeds and cut into strips. If using courgettes, cut into 5cm/2in strips.

2 Grind the fresh red chillies, onion, sliced galangal or root ginger, sliced lemon grass and the turmeric to a paste in a food processor or with a pestle and mortar. Add the water to the paste mixture, with a squeeze of lemon juice and salt to taste.

3 Pour into a pan. Add the top of the lemon grass stalk. Bring to the boil and cook for 1–2 minutes. Add the chayote or courgette pieces and then cook for 2 minutes. Stir in the coconut milk. Taste and adjust the seasoning.

4 Add the prawns and cook gently for 2–3 minutes. Remove the lemon grass stalk. Garnish with the chilli shreds. Serve with plain boiled rice or noodles.

> **Variation**
> *Larger supermarkets or Asian stores usually sell chayote, but you can use courgettes (zucchini) instead.*

Paneer Balti with Prawns

Paneer is a protein-rich food and makes an excellent substitute for red meat. Here it is combined with king prawns to make a delicious dish with a truly unforgettable flavour.

Serves 4

12 cooked king prawns
   (jumbo shrimp)
175g/6oz paneer
30ml/2 tbsp tomato
   purée (paste)
60ml/4 tbsp Greek (US strained
   plain) yogurt
7.5ml/1½ tsp garam masala
5ml/1 tsp chilli powder
5ml/1 tsp crushed garlic
5ml/1 tsp salt
10ml/2 tsp mango powder
   (amchur)
5ml/1 tsp ground coriander
115g/4oz/½ cup butter
15ml/1 tbsp vegetable oil or
   sunflower oil
3 fresh green chillies, seeded
   and chopped
45ml/3 tbsp chopped fresh
   coriander (cilantro)
150ml/¼ pint/⅔ cup single
   (light) cream

1 Peel the king prawns. Using a sharp knife, remove the black intestinal vein from down the back of each prawn and discard. Cut the paneer into small cubes.

2 Put the tomato purée, yogurt, garam masala, chilli powder, garlic, salt, mango powder and ground coriander in a mixing bowl. Mix to a paste and set aside.

3 Melt the butter with the oil in a karahi, wok or deep pan. Lower the heat slightly and quickly fry the paneer and prawns for about 2 minutes. Remove the paneer and prawns with a slotted spoon and drain on kitchen paper.

4 Pour the spice paste into the fat left in the pan and cook for about 1 minute, stirring constantly.

5 Add the paneer and prawns, and cook for 7–10 minutes, stirring occasionally, until the prawns are heated through.

6 Add the fresh chillies and most of the coriander, and pour in the cream. Heat through for about 2 minutes, garnish with the remaining coriander and serve.

Coconut Prawn Curry Energy 255kcal/1066kJ; Protein 38.9g; Carbohydrate 2.4g, of which sugars 2.3g; Fat 9.9g, of which saturates 1.5g; Cholesterol 163mg; Calcium 78mg; Fibre 0.4g; Sodium 235mg.
Paneer Balti Energy 414kcal/1712kJ; Protein 15.2g; Carbohydrate 4g, of which sugars 3g; Fat 37.6g, of which saturates 21.7g; Cholesterol 162mg; Calcium 195mg; Fibre 1.5g; Sodium 419mg.

Bengali Prawn Curry

The Bay of Bengal provides enormous quantities of fish and shellfish. This fragrant curry features delectable tiger prawns.

Serves 4

675g/1½lb raw tiger prawns (jumbo shrimp)
4 dried red chillies
50g/2oz/1 cup desiccated (dry unsweetened shredded) coconut
5ml/1 tsp black mustard seeds
1 large onion, chopped
45ml/3 tbsp vegetable oil
4 bay leaves
2.5cm/1in piece fresh root ginger, chopped
2 garlic cloves, crushed
15ml/1 tbsp ground coriander
5ml/1 tsp chilli powder
5ml/1 tsp salt
4 tomatoes, finely chopped
plain boiled rice, to serve

1 Peel the prawns. Run a sharp knife along the back of each prawn to make a shallow cut and carefully remove the thin black intestinal vein and discard. You might like to leave a few of the prawns unpeeled, setting them aside to use later as a garnish for the finished dish.

2 Put the dried red chillies, coconut, mustard seeds and onion in a wok, karahi or large pan and dry-fry over medium heat for 5–6 minutes, or until the mixture begins to brown. Stir to ensure even browning and to avoid burning the coconut. Transfer to a food processor or blender and process to a coarse paste.

3 Heat the vegetable oil in the pan and fry the bay leaves for about 1 minute. Add the chopped ginger and the garlic, and fry for 2–3 minutes, stirring frequently.

4 Add the ground coriander, chilli powder, salt and the paste and fry for about 5 minutes.

5 Stir in the tomatoes and about 175ml/6fl oz/¾ cup water and simmer for 5–6 minutes or until thickened.

6 Add the prawns and cook for about 4–5 minutes, or until they turn pink. Grill (broil) the reserved whole prawns, if using, until pink. Serve the curry in a ring of plain boiled rice and garnish with the whole prawns, if using.

Prawns with Okra

This spicy prawn curry has a lovely sweet taste with a strong chilli flavour. The dish should be cooked fast to prevent the okra pods from breaking up in the pan and releasing their distinctive, sticky juice. Serve with plain rice or Indian breads.

Serves 4–6

60–90ml/4–6 tbsp vegetable oil
225g/8oz okra, washed, dried and left whole
4 cloves garlic, crushed
5cm/2in piece fresh root ginger, crushed
4–6 fresh green chillies, cut diagonally
2.5ml/½ tsp turmeric
4–6 curry leaves
5ml/1 tsp cumin seeds
450g/1lb fresh king prawns (jumbo shrimp), peeled and deveined
10ml/2 tsp soft light brown sugar
juice of 2 lemons
salt

1 Heat the oil in a frying pan and fry the okra pods over a fairly high heat until they are slightly crisp and browned on all sides. Remove the okra pods from the oil and put to one side on a piece of kitchen paper to absorb a little of the oil.

2 In the same oil, gently fry the garlic, ginger, chillies, turmeric, curry leaves and cumin seeds for 2–3 minutes. Add the prawns and mix well. Cook until the prawns are tender.

3 Add the sugar, lemon juice and fried okra, and salt to taste. Increase the heat and quickly fry for a further 5 minutes, stirring gently to prevent the okra from breaking. Adjust the seasoning, if necessary. Serve immediately.

Cook's Tip
Okra, sometimes known as 'lady's fingers', is a small, long seed pod that exudes a sticky liquid when the pod is cut. This liquid is useful for dishes that require a thick sauce, but for other dishes, such as this one, the pod must be left whole to keep in the liquid. Remove the stalk using a sharp knife but do not cut into the pod itself.

Bengali Prawn Curry Energy 237kcal/996kJ; Protein 34.9g; Carbohydrate 10g, of which sugars 6.3g; Fat 6.8g, of which saturates 3.8g; Cholesterol 338mg; Calcium 166mg; Fibre 2.6g; Sodium 344mg.
Prawns with Okra Energy 143kcal/597kJ; Protein 14.5g; Carbohydrate 3.1g, of which sugars 2.4g; Fat 8.2g, of which saturates 1.1g; Cholesterol 146mg; Calcium 121mg; Fibre 1.6g; Sodium 146mg.

Karahi Prawns and Fenugreek

The black-eyed beans, prawns and paneer in this recipe ensure that it is rich in protein. The combination of both ground and fresh fenugreek makes this a very fragrant and delicious dish.

Serves 4–6
60ml/4 tbsp corn oil
2 medium onions, sliced
2 medium tomatoes, sliced
7.5ml/1½ tsp crushed garlic
5ml/1 tsp chilli powder
5ml/1 tsp grated fresh
   root ginger
5ml/1 tsp ground cumin
5ml/1 tsp ground coriander
5ml/1 tsp salt
150g/5oz paneer, cubed
5ml/1 tsp ground fenugreek
1 bunch fresh fenugreek leaves
115g/4oz cooked
   prawns (shrimp)
2 fresh red chillies, sliced
30ml/2 tbsp chopped fresh
   coriander (cilantro)
50g/2oz/⅓ cup canned
   black-eyed beans
   (peas), drained
15ml/1 tbsp lemon juice

1 Heat the oil in a karahi, wok or deep pan. Lower the heat slightly and add the onions and tomatoes. Fry for about 3–5 minutes until the onions begin to soften.

2 Add the garlic, chilli powder, ginger, ground cumin, ground coriander, salt, paneer and the ground and fresh fenugreek. Lower the heat and stir-fry for about 2 minutes.

3 Add the prawns, red chillies, fresh coriander and black-eyed beans, and mix well. Toss over the heat for a further 3–5 minutes, or until the prawns are heated through. Sprinkle with the lemon juice and serve.

> **Cook's Tips**
> • *Paneer is a type of cheese made with the curds from boiling milk which has been acidified with lemon juice. If you cannot locate paneer, tofu or halloumi makes a good substitute.*
> • *When preparing fresh fenugreek, use the leaves whole, but remove and discard the stalks because they will impart a bitter flavour to the dish.*

Sizzling Balti Prawns in Hot Sauce

This sizzling prawn dish is cooked in a fiery hot and spicy sauce. This sauce not only contains chilli powder, but is further enhanced by the addition of ground fresh green chillies mixed with other spices.

Serves 4
2 medium onions or 1 large
   onion, roughly chopped
30ml/2 tbsp tomato
   purée (paste)
5ml/1 tsp ground coriander
1.5ml/¼ tsp ground turmeric
5ml/1 tsp chilli powder
2 fresh green chillies
45ml/3 tbsp chopped fresh
   coriander (cilantro)
30ml/2 tbsp lemon juice
5ml/1 tsp salt
45ml/3 tbsp corn oil
16 cooked king prawns
   (jumbo shrimp)
sliced green chillies,
   to garnish (optional)

1 Put the onions, tomato purée, ground coriander, turmeric, chilli powder, 2 whole green chillies, 30ml/2 tbsp of the fresh coriander, the lemon juice and salt into the bowl of a food processor. Process for about 1 minute. If the mixture seems too thick, add a little water to loosen it.

2 Heat the oil in a karahi, wok or deep pan. Lower the heat slightly and add the spice mixture. Fry the mixture for about 3–5 minutes or until the sauce has thickened slightly.

3 Add the cooked prawns to the pan and stir-fry briefly over a medium heat until heated through.

4 As soon as the prawns are heated through, transfer them to a serving dish. Garnish with the rest of the fresh coriander and the sliced green chillies, if using. Serve immediately.

> **Cook's Tips**
> • *Take care not to overcook the prawns when heating them through or they will become tough.*
> • *If the heat of this dish seems extreme, offer a cooling raita to moderate the piquant flavour.*

Karahi Prawns Energy 151kcal/629kJ; Protein 8.5g; Carbohydrate 10.1g, of which sugars 6.6g; Fat 8.7g, of which saturates 1.7g; Cholesterol 41mg; Calcium 72mg; Fibre 1.8g; Sodium 445mg.
Sizzling Balti Prawns Energy 161kcal/668kJ; Protein 13.6g; Carbohydrate 0.8g, of which sugars 0.1g; Fat 11.5g, of which saturates 1.7g; Cholesterol 146mg; Calcium 60mg; Fibre 0.2g; Sodium 143mg.

Prawn and Vegetable Balti

This fresh-tasting balti makes a delicious light lunch or supper, and is quick and simple to make.

Serves 4
175g/6oz frozen cooked
  peeled prawns (shrimp)
30ml/2 tbsp vegetable oil
1.5ml/¼ tsp onion seeds
4–6 curry leaves
115g/4oz/1 cup frozen peas
115g/4oz/⅔ cup frozen corn

1 large courgette (zucchini),
  thickly sliced
1 medium red (bell) pepper,
  seeded and roughly diced
5ml/1 tsp finely crushed
  coriander seeds
5ml/1 tsp crushed dried
  red chillies
1.5ml/½ tsp salt
15ml/1 tbsp lemon juice
15ml/1 tbsp fresh coriander
  (cilantro) leaves, to garnish
basmati rice, to serve

1 Thaw the frozen prawns and place in a sieve (strainer) to drain them of any excess liquid.

2 Heat the oil with the onion seeds and curry leaves in a karahi, wok or heavy frying pan.

3 Add the prawns to the spicy mixture in the wok and cook, stirring constantly, until the liquid has evaporated.

4 Next, add the peas, corn, courgette and red pepper. Continue to stir for 3–5 minutes.

5 Finally, add the crushed coriander seeds and dried chillies to the pan, with salt to taste and the lemon juice.

6 Serve the curry immediately, sprinkled with a few fresh coriander leaves to garnish. Accompany the balti with plain boiled basmati rice.

> **Cook's Tip**
> *Freshly crushed spices have a strong and vibrant flavour. The best way to crush whole seeds is to use an electric spice grinder or a small marble pestle and mortar.*

Karahi-style Prawns and Vegetables

Here, tender prawns, crunchy vegetables and a thick curry sauce combine to produce a dish rich in flavour and texture.

Serves 4
45ml/3 tbsp corn oil
5ml/1 tsp mixed fenugreek,
  mustard and onion seeds
2 curry leaves
½ medium cauliflower, cut into
  small florets (flowerets)
8 baby carrots, halved lengthways
6 new potatoes, thickly sliced
50g/2oz/½ cup frozen peas

2 medium onions, sliced
30ml/2 tbsp tomato purée (paste)
7.5ml/1½ tsp chilli powder
5ml/1 tsp ground coriander
5ml/1 tsp crushed fresh
  root ginger
5ml/1 tsp crushed garlic
5ml/1 tsp salt
30ml/2 tbsp lemon juice
450g/1lb cooked prawns (shrimp)
30ml/2 tbsp chopped fresh
  coriander (cilantro)
1 fresh red chilli, seeded
  and sliced
120ml/4fl oz/½ cup single
  (light) cream

1 Heat the oil in a deep frying pan or a large karahi. Lower the heat slightly and add the fenugreek, mustard and onion seeds and the curry leaves.

2 Turn up the heat and add the cauliflower, carrots, potatoes and peas. Stir-fry quickly until browned, then remove from the pan with a slotted spoon and drain on kitchen paper.

3 Add the onions to the oil left in the karahi and fry over a medium heat until golden brown.

4 While the onions are cooking, mix together the tomato purée, chilli powder, ground coriander, ginger, garlic, salt and lemon juice and pour the paste on to the onions.

5 Add the prawns to the pan and stir-fry over a low heat for about 5 minutes or until they are heated through.

6 Add the fried vegetables to the pan and mix together well.

7 Add the fresh coriander and red chilli and pour over the cream. Bring to the boil and serve immediately.

Prawn and Vegetable Balti Energy 165kcal/688kJ; Protein 11.9g; Carbohydrate 14.6g, of which sugars 7g; Fat 6.9g, of which saturates 0.9g; Cholesterol 85mg; Calcium 58mg; Fibre 2.9g; Sodium 163mg.
Karahi-style Prawns Energy 151kcal/629kJ; Protein 8.5g; Carbohydrate 10.1g, of which sugars 6.6g; Fat 8.7g, of which saturates 1.7g; Cholesterol 41mg; Calcium 72mg; Fibre 1.8g; Sodium 445mg.

Curried Noodles with Prawns

Any vegetable from the same family as courgette or squash can be used in this spicy Indonesian curry. Other noodles can also be used instead of cellophane.

Serves 4–6
450g/1lb courgettes (zucchini)
1 onion, finely sliced
1 garlic clove, finely chopped
30ml/2 tbsp vegetable oil
2.5ml/½ tsp ground turmeric
2 tomatoes, chopped
45ml/3 tbsp water
115g/4oz peeled, cooked prawns (shrimp)
25g/1oz cellophane noodles
salt

1 Use a potato or vegetable peeler to pare away thin strips from the outside of each courgette.

2 Cut the courgettes into neat slices, then set aside. Fry the onion and garlic in hot oil in a pan for 5 minutes until beginning to soften but do not allow to brown.

3 Add the turmeric, courgette slices, chopped tomatoes, water and the cooked prawns to the pan.

4 Put the noodles in a large pan and pour over enough boiling water to cover. Leave the noodles to soak for a minute.

5 Drain the noodles thoroughly and then cut them into 5cm/2in lengths. Add them to the vegetables in the pan and stir well to combine the ingredients.

6 Cover the pan with a tight-fitting lid and allow everything to cook in its own steam for 2–3 minutes. Toss well together.

7 Season the noodles with salt to taste, and transfer to a warmed serving bowl. Serve immediately.

Cook's Tip
Keep a careful eye on the time when cooking the cellophane noodles as they will soften very quickly.

Seafood Balti with Vegetables

Spicy seafood and vegetables give this curry a delicious combination of flavours.

Serves 4
For the seafood
225g/8oz cod, or firm white fish
225g/8oz cooked prawns (shrimp)
6 crab sticks, halved lengthways
15ml/1 tbsp lemon juice
5ml/1 tsp ground coriander
5ml/1 tsp chilli powder
5ml/1 tsp salt
5ml/1 tsp ground cumin
60ml/4 tbsp cornflour (cornstarch)
150ml/¼ pint/⅔ cup corn oil

For the vegetables
150ml/¼ pint/⅔ cup corn oil
2 medium onions, chopped
5ml/1 tsp onion seeds
½ cauliflower, cut into florets
115g/4oz green beans, cut into 2.5cm/1in lengths
175g/6oz/1 cup corn
5ml/1 tsp chopped fresh root ginger
5ml/1 tsp chilli powder
5ml/1 tsp salt
4 fresh green chillies, sliced
30ml/2 tbsp chopped fresh coriander (cilantro)
lime slices

1 Remove the skin from the cod or other white fish and discard. Cut the flesh into small cubes. Place into a medium mixing bowl with the prawns and crab sticks, and set aside.

2 In a separate bowl, mix together the lemon juice, ground coriander, chilli powder, salt and ground cumin. Pour this over the seafood and mix together thoroughly using your hands. Sprinkle on the cornflour and mix again. Chill for 1 hour.

3 For the vegetables, heat the oil in a deep frying pan or a karahi. Stir-fry the onions and the onion seeds until browned. Add the cauliflower, green beans, corn, ginger, chilli powder, salt, green chillies and fresh coriander. Stir-fry for 7–10 minutes over a medium heat, making sure that the florets retain their shape.

4 Spoon the fried vegetables around the edge of a shallow dish, leaving a space in the middle for the seafood, and keep warm.

5 Wash and dry the pan, then heat the oil. Fry the seafood in 2–3 batches, until they turn a golden brown, then drain. Arrange in the middle of the vegetables and keep warm while you fry the remaining seafood. Garnish with lime slices and serve.

Curried Noodles Energy 330kcal/1386kJ; Protein 13.4g; Carbohydrate 44.6g, of which sugars 4.5g; Fat 12.1g, of which saturates 2.2g; Cholesterol 73mg; Calcium 71mg; Fibre 3.3g; Sodium 337mg.
Seafood Balti Energy 454kcal/1894kJ; Protein 24.5g; Carbohydrate 31g, of which sugars 9.1g; Fat 26.7g, of which saturates 3.2g; Cholesterol 141mg; Calcium 84mg; Fibre 2.3g; Sodium 373mg.

Mussels Stuffed with Cinnamon-spiced Pilaff

These spicy stuffed mussels are filled with a fragrant pilaff containing fruits, nuts and cinnamon. They will make an ideal light lunch or a delectable supper.

Serves 4

16 large fresh mussels, cleaned
45–60ml/3–4 tbsp olive oil
2–3 shallots, finely chopped
30ml/2 tbsp pine nuts
30ml/2 tbsp currants, soaked in
    warm water for 5–10 minutes
    and drained
10ml/2 tsp ground cinnamon
5ml/1 tsp ground allspice
5–10ml/1–2 tsp sugar
5–10ml/1–2 tsp tomato
    purée (paste)
115g/4oz/generous ½ cup short
    grain or pudding rice, well
    rinsed and drained
1 small bunch each of fresh flat
    leaf parsley, mint and dill,
    finely chopped
salt and ground black pepper
lemon wedges and fresh flat leaf
    parsley sprigs, to serve

1 Keep the mussels in a bowl of cold water while you prepare the stuffing. Heat the oil in a heavy pan, stir in the shallots and cook until they soften. Add the pine nuts and currants, stir for 1–2 minutes until the pine nuts turn golden and the currants plump up, then stir in the cinnamon, allspice, sugar and tomato purée. Now add the rice, and stir until it is well coated.

2 Pour in enough water to just cover the rice. Season with salt and pepper and bring to the boil. Lower the heat, partially cover the pan and simmer for 10–12 minutes, until all the water has been absorbed. Transfer the rice on to a plate, leave to cool, then toss in the herbs.

3 Prise open each mussel, stuff a spoonful of rice into each shell, then close the shells and pack tightly into a steamer filled with water. Cover with a sheet of baking parchment, put a plate on top and weigh it down to prevent the mussels from opening. Place the lid on the steamer and bring the water to the boil. Lower the heat and steam the mussels for 15–20 minutes. Serve the stuffed mussels immediately on a bed of fresh parsley, with lemon wedges.

Curried Seafood with Coconut Milk

The pale green colour of this curry is the result of the use of green chillies and fresh herbs. You can reduce the amount of chillies if you prefer a milder curry.

Serves 4

225g/8oz raw tiger prawns
    (jumbo shrimp)
400ml/14fl oz/1⅔ cups
    coconut milk
2 kaffir lime leaves, finely shredded
30ml/2 tbsp Thai fish sauce
225g/8oz small, prepared squid,
    cut into rings, tentacles halved
450g/1lb firm white fish, skinned,
    boned and cut into chunks
2 fresh green chillies, seeded and
    finely chopped
30ml/2 tbsp torn fresh basil or
    coriander (cilantro) leaves
squeeze of fresh lime juice
cooked jasmine rice, to serve

For the curry paste

6 spring onions (scallions),
    coarsely chopped
4 fresh coriander (cilantro) stems,
    chopped, plus 45ml/3 tbsp
    chopped fresh coriander (cilantro)
4 kaffir lime leaves, shredded
8 fresh green chillies, seeded and
    coarsely chopped
1 lemon grass stalk, chopped
2.5cm/1in piece fresh root ginger,
    peeled and coarsely chopped
45ml/3 tbsp chopped fresh basil
15ml/1 tbsp vegetable oil or
    sunflower oil

1 Make the curry paste. Put all the ingredients, except the oil, in a food processor and process to a paste. Alternatively, pound together in a mortar with a pestle. Stir in the oil.

2 Heat a wok until hot, add the prawns and stir-fry, without oil, for 4 minutes, until they turn pink. Remove from the wok.

3 Leave the prawns to cool slightly, then peel the shells, saving a few with shells on for the garnish. Remove the black vein.

4 In the wok, bring the coconut milk to the boil over a medium heat. Add 30ml/2 tbsp of curry paste, the lime leaves and fish sauce. Reduce the heat and simmer gently for 10 minutes.

5 Add the squid, prawns and fish and cook for 2 minutes, until the seafood is tender. Stir in the chillies and basil or coriander. Taste and adjust the flavour with lime juice. Garnish with prawns in their shells, and serve with jasmine rice.

Mussels with Pilaff Energy 319kcal/1328kJ; Protein 13.3g; Carbohydrate 32.7g, of which sugars 7.5g; Fat 15g, of which saturates 1.9g; Cholesterol 33mg; Calcium 49mg; Fibre 0.5g; Sodium 237mg.
Curried Seafood Energy 238kcal/1005kJ; Protein 40.6g; Carbohydrate 7g, of which sugars 6.2g; Fat 5.5g, of which saturates 0.9g; Cholesterol 288mg; Calcium 145mg; Fibre 1.4g; Sodium 622mg.

Spicy Seafood Stew

This spicy soup is not a dish you can throw together in 20 minutes, but it is marvellous party food.

Serves 6
675g/1½lb small clams
2 × 400ml/14fl oz cans
  coconut milk
50g/2oz ikan bilis (dried anchovies)
900ml/1½ pints/3¾ cups water
115g/4oz shallots, finely chopped
4 garlic cloves, chopped
6 macadamia nuts or blanched
  almonds, chopped
3 lemon grass stalks, root trimmed
90ml/6 tbsp sunflower oil
1cm/½in cube shrimp paste

25g/1oz/¼ cup mild curry powder
a few curry leaves
2–3 aubergines (eggplants), total
  weight about 675g/1¼lb
675g/1½lb raw peeled
  prawns (shrimp)
10ml/2 tsp sugar
1 head Chinese leaves (Chinese
  cabbage), thinly sliced
115g/4oz/2 cups beansprouts
2 spring onions (scallions),
  finely chopped
50g/2oz crispy fried onions
115g/4oz fried tofu
675g/1½lb mixed noodles or
  one type only
prawn crackers, to serve

1 Scrub the clams and put in a large pan with 1cm/½in water. Bring to the boil, cover and steam for 3–4 minutes until the clams have opened. Drain.

2 Make up the coconut milk to 1.2 litres/2 pints/5 cups with water. To make the ikan bilis stock, put the ikan bilis in a pan and add the water. Bring to the boil and simmer for 20 minutes.

3 Meanwhile, put the shallots, garlic and nuts into a mortar. Cut off the lower 5cm/2in of two of the lemon grass stalks, chop finely and add to the mortar. Pound the mixture to a paste.

4 Heat the oil in a large heavy pan, add the shallot paste and fry for 2–3 minutes. Bruise the remaining lemon grass stalk and add to the pan. Toss over the heat for a minute. Mix the shrimp paste and curry powder to a paste with a little coconut milk, add to the pan and cook over the heat for 1 minute. Stir in the remaining coconut milk. Add the curry leaves and leave the mixture to simmer while you prepare the accompaniments.

5 Strain the ikan bilis stock into a pan. Discard the ikan bilis, bring to the boil, then add the aubergines; cook for about 10 minutes or until tender and the skins can be peeled off easily. Lift out of the stock, peel and cut into thick strips.

6 Arrange the aubergines on a serving platter. Sprinkle the prawns with sugar, add to the ikan bilis stock and cook for 2–4 minutes until pink. Add the prawns, clams, Chinese leaves, beansprouts, spring onions and crispy fried onions to the platter.

7 Gradually stir the remaining ikan bilis stock into the pan of stew and bring to the boil. Rinse the fried tofu in boiling water, cool slightly and squeeze to remove excess oil. Cut each piece in half and add to the soup. Lower the heat to a gentle simmer.

8 Cook the noodles according to the instructions, drain and pile in a dish. Remove the curry leaves and lemon grass from the stew. Place the noodles, soup and the platter of seafood and vegetables on the table, along with a bowl of prawn crackers.

Mussels and Clams with Lemon Grass and Coconut Cream

Lemon grass has an incomparable flavour and is widely used in spicy food, especially with seafood. If you cannot find clams, use a few extra mussels instead.

Serves 6
1.75kg/4–4½lb mussels
450g/1lb baby clams
120ml/4fl oz/½ cup dry white wine

1 bunch spring onions (scallions),
  finely chopped
2 lemon grass stalks, chopped
6 kaffir lime leaves, chopped
10ml/2 tsp Thai green curry paste
200ml/7fl oz/scant 1 cup
  coconut cream
30ml/2 tbsp chopped fresh
  coriander (cilantro)
salt and ground black pepper
garlic chives, to garnish

1 Clean the mussels by pulling off the beards, scrubbing the shells and removing any barnacles. Discard any mussels that are broken or do not close when tapped sharply. Wash the clams.

2 Put the dry white wine in a large pan with the spring onions, lemon grass, lime leaves and curry paste. Simmer gently until the wine has almost evaporated.

3 Add the mussels and clams to the pan, cover tightly and steam the shellfish over a high heat for 5–6 minutes, until they open.

4 Using a slotted spoon, transfer the mussels and clams to a heated serving bowl and keep hot. Discard any shellfish that remain closed. Strain the cooking liquid into a clean pan and simmer to reduce to about 250ml/8fl oz/1 cup.

5 Stir in the coconut cream and coriander, with salt and pepper to taste. Heat through. Pour the sauce over the mussels and clams and serve, garnished with garlic chives.

Cook's Tip
Buy a few extra mussels for this dish just in case there are any which have to be discarded after cooking.

Spicy Seafood Stew Energy 335kcal/1405kJ; Protein 32g; Carbohydrate 22.7g, of which sugars 5.4g; Fat 10.6g, of which saturates 1.2g; Cholesterol 325mg; Calcium 161mg; Fibre 1.7g; Sodium 385mg.
Mussels and Clams Energy 177kcal/745kJ; Protein 21.8g; Carbohydrate 1.9g, of which sugars 1.2g; Fat 7.8g, of which saturates 5.3g; Cholesterol 58mg; Calcium 212mg; Fibre 0.3g; Sodium 594mg.

Squid in Hot Yellow Sauce

Simple fishermen's dishes such as this one are cooked the length and breadth of Malaysia's coastline. To temper the heat, the dish is often served with finely shredded green mango tossed in lime juice.

Serves 4

500g/1¼lb fresh squid
juice of 2 limes
5ml/1 tsp salt
4 shallots, chopped
4 garlic cloves, chopped
25g/1oz galangal, chopped
25g/1oz fresh turmeric, chopped
6–8 red chillies, seeded and
    finely chopped
30ml/2 tbsp vegetable or
    groundnut (peanut) oil
7.5ml/1½ tsp palm
    sugar (jaggery)
2 lemon grass stalks, crushed
4 lime leaves
400ml/14fl oz/1⅔ cups
    coconut milk
salt and ground black pepper
crusty bread or steamed rice,
    to serve

1 First prepare the squid. Hold the body sac in one hand and pull off the head with the other. Sever the tentacles just above the eyes, and discard the rest of the head and innards. Clean the body sac inside and out and remove the skin. Pat the squid dry, cut it into thick slices and put them in a bowl, along with the tentacles. Mix the lime juice with the salt and rub it into the squid. Set aside for 30 minutes.

2 Meanwhile, using a mortar and pestle, food processor or blender, grind the shallots, garlic, galangal, turmeric and chillies until they form a coarse paste.

3 Heat the oil in a wok or heavy pan, and stir in the coarse paste. Cook the paste until fragrant, then stir in the palm sugar, lemon grass and lime leaves. Drain the squid of any juice and toss it around the wok, coating it in the flavourings.

4 Pour the coconut milk into the pan and bring it to the boil. Reduce the heat to low and simmer for 5–10 minutes, until the squid is tender. Take care not to overcook the squid or it will become rubbery. Season to taste with salt and ground black pepper and serve the curry immediately with chunks of fresh, crusty bread or plain steamed rice.

Indonesian Squid in Clove Sauce

This recipe combines cloves and nutmeg with tomato and soy sauce. It is an Indonesian favourite and quite delicious. Simple to prepare, it will make an ideal midweek supper for family or friends.

Serves 3–4

675g/1½lb squid
45ml/3 tbsp groundnut
    (peanut) oil
1 onion, finely chopped
2 garlic cloves, crushed
1 beefsteak tomato, skinned
    and chopped
15ml/1 tbsp dark soy sauce
2.5ml/½ tsp freshly grated nutmeg
6 whole cloves
150ml/¼ pint/⅔ cup water
juice of ½ lemon or lime
salt and ground black pepper
plain boiled rice, to serve
shredded spring onions (scallions)
    and fresh coriander (cilantro)
    sprigs, to garnish

1 Wash and clean the squid and pat dry on kitchen paper. Use a sharp kitchen knife to cut the squid into long, thin ribbons. Carefully remove the 'bone' from each tentacle, and discard.

2 Heat a wok, toss in the squid and stir constantly for 2–3 minutes, when the squid will have curled into attractive shapes or into firm rings. Lift out and set aside in a warm place.

3 Heat the oil in a clean pan and fry the onion and garlic, until soft and beginning to brown. Add the tomato, soy sauce, nutmeg, cloves, water and lemon or lime juice. Bring to the boil and then reduce the heat and add the squid, with seasoning to taste.

4 Cook the squid in the sauce for 3–5 minutes, uncovered, over a gentle heat, stirring from time to time. Take care not to overcook the squid. Serve hot or warm, with plain rice. Garnish with shredded spring onions and fresh coriander.

Variation
Instead of squid try using 450g/1lb cooked and peeled tiger prawns (shrimp) in this recipe. Add the prawns to the pan for the final 1–2 minutes until cooked through.

Squid in Yellow Sauce Energy 185kcal/780kJ; Protein 19.8g; Carbohydrate 9.4g, of which sugars 7.6g; Fat 8g, of which saturates 1.4g; Cholesterol 281mg; Calcium 50mg; Fibre 0.2g; Sodium 739mg.
Indonesian Squid Energy 154kcal/647kJ; Protein 19.8g; Carbohydrate 5.8g, of which sugars 4.3g; Fat 5.9g, of which saturates 1g; Cholesterol 281mg; Calcium 54mg; Fibre 1g; Sodium 144mg.

Fiery Octopus

Here octopus is stir-fried to give it a rich meaty texture, then smothered in a fiery chilli sauce. The dish combines the charred octopus flavour with Korean spiciness and the zing of chillies. Serve with steamed rice and a bowl of soup.

Serves 2

2 small octopuses, cleaned
  and gutted
15ml/1 tbsp vegetable oil
½ onion, sliced 5mm/¼in thick
¼ carrot, thinly sliced
½ leek, thinly sliced
75g/3oz jalapeño chillies, trimmed
2 garlic cloves, crushed
10ml/2 tsp Korean chilli powder
5ml/1 tsp dark soy sauce
45ml/3 tbsp gochujang chilli paste
30ml/2 tbsp mirin or rice wine
15ml/1 tbsp maple syrup
sesame oil and sesame seeds,
  to garnish

1 First blanch the octopuses in boiling water to soften slightly. Drain well, and cut into pieces approximately 5cm/2in long.

2 Heat the oil in a frying pan over a medium-high heat and add the onion, carrot, leek and chillies. Stir-fry for 3 minutes.

3 Add the octopus and garlic, and sprinkle over the chilli powder. Stir-fry for 3–4 minutes, or until the octopus is tender. Add the soy sauce, gochujang paste, mirin or rice wine, and maple syrup. Mix well and stir-fry for 1 minute more.

4 Transfer to a serving platter, and garnish with a drizzle of sesame oil and a sprinkling of sesame seeds.

Variation
If the taste is too fiery, mix some softened vermicelli noodles in with the stir-fry to dilute the chilli paste.

Cook's Tip
To make the octopus more tender, knead it with a handful of plain (all-purpose) flour and rinse in salted water.

Fish Head Curry

There are numerous versions of this unusual yet delectable curry throughout India and South-east Asia. Fish heads are highly prized for the succulent meat in the cheeks. Various fish can be used but this version uses red snapper.

Serves 2

30ml/2 tbsp ghee or
  vegetable oil
10ml/2 tsp brown mustard seeds
5ml/1 tsp fenugreek seeds
5ml/1 tsp cumin seeds
a handful of curry leaves
15ml/1 tbsp palm sugar (jaggery)
30ml/2 tbsp tamarind pulp,
  soaked in 150ml/¼ pint/⅔ cup
  water and strained for juice
600ml/1 pint/2½ cups coconut milk
1 large fresh fish head,
  such as red snapper (about
  900g/2lb), cleaned
5 okra, halved diagonally
2 large tomatoes, skinned, seeded
  and quartered
salt and ground black pepper
steamed plain rice and pickles,
  to serve

For the spice paste
8 shallots, chopped
6 garlic cloves, chopped
4 red chillies, seeded and
  roughly chopped
50g/2oz fresh root ginger, peeled
  and chopped
25g/1oz fresh turmeric, chopped
1 lemon grass stalk, trimmed
  and chopped
30ml/2 tbsp fish curry powder

1 To make the spice paste, grind all the ingredients together using a mortar and pestle or food processor.

2 Heat the ghee or oil in a wok or heavy pan. Stir in the mustard seeds, fenugreek and cumin seeds along with the curry leaves. Fry until the mustard seeds begin to pop.

3 Add the spice paste to the pan. Fry until fragrant, about 2–3 minutes, then stir in the palm sugar, followed by the tamarind juice and coconut milk.

4 Bring the mixture to the boil, reduce the heat and add the fish head. Simmer gently for 10 minutes, then add the okra and tomatoes. Simmer for another 10 minutes or until the fish head is cooked and tender. Season the sauce with salt and pepper and serve with steamed rice and pickles.

Fiery Octopus Energy 235kcal/988kJ; Protein 28.6g; Carbohydrate 13.2g, of which sugars 11.9g; Fat 8g, of which saturates 1.2g; Cholesterol 72mg; Calcium 76mg; Fibre 2.4g; Sodium 204mg.
Fish Head Curry Energy 417kcal/1760kJ; Protein 42.2g; Carbohydrate 30.4g, of which sugars 29.1g; Fat 15.2g, of which saturates 2.7g; Cholesterol 74mg; Calcium 231mg; Fibre 2.7g; Sodium 497mg.

Sea Bass Steamed in Coconut Milk

This is a delicious recipe for any whole white fish, such as sea bass or cod, or for large chunks of trout or salmon.

Serves 4

200ml/7fl oz coconut milk
10ml/2 tsp raw cane or
   muscovado (molasses) sugar
about 15ml/1 tbsp sesame or
   vegetable oil
2 garlic cloves, finely chopped
1 red Thai chilli, seeded and
   finely chopped
4cm/1½in fresh root ginger, peeled
   and grated
750g/1lb 10oz sea bass, gutted
   and skinned on one side
1 star anise, ground
1 bunch of fresh basil,
   stalks removed
30ml/2 tbsp cashew nuts
salt and ground black pepper

1 Heat the coconut milk with the sugar in a small pan, stirring until the sugar dissolves, then remove from the heat. Add the oil to a small frying pan and stir in the garlic, chilli and ginger. Cook until they begin to brown, then add the mixture to the coconut milk and mix well to combine.

2 Place the fish, skin side down, on a wide piece of foil and tuck up the sides to form a boat-shaped container. Using a sharp knife, cut several diagonal slashes into the flesh on the top and rub with the ground star anise. Season with salt and pepper and spoon the coconut milk over the top.

3 Sprinkle about half the basil leaves over the top of the fish and pull the sides of the foil over the top, so that it is almost enclosed (like a canoe). Gently lay the foil packet in a steamer. Cover the steamer, bring the water to the boil, then reduce the heat and simmer for 20–25 minutes, or until just cooked.

4 Meanwhile, roast the cashew nuts in the small frying pan, adding a little extra oil if necessary. Drain the nuts on kitchen paper, then grind them to crumbs.

5 When the fish is cooked, lift it out of the foil and transfer it to a serving dish. Spoon the cooking juices over, sprinkle with the cashew nut crumbs and garnish with the remaining fresh basil leaves. Serve immediately.

John Dory with Light Curry Sauce

This excellent combination of flavours also works well with other flat fish like turbot, halibut and brill. The curry taste of this dish should be subtle otherwise it will mask the delicate flavours, so use a very mild curry powder.

Serves 4

4 John Dory fillets, each about
   175g/6oz, skinned
15ml/1 tbsp sunflower oil
25g/1oz/2 tbsp butter
salt and ground black pepper
15ml/1 tbsp fresh coriander
   (cilantro) leaves and 1 mango,
   peeled and diced, to garnish

For the curry sauce
30ml/2 tbsp sunflower oil
1 carrot, chopped
1 onion, chopped
1 celery stick, chopped
white of 1 leek, chopped
2 garlic cloves, crushed
50g/2oz creamed coconut,
   crumbled or 120ml/4fl oz/½ cup
   coconut cream
2 tomatoes, peeled, seeded
   and diced
2.5cm/1in piece fresh root
   ginger, grated
15ml/1 tbsp tomato purée (paste)
5–10ml/1–2 tsp mild curry powder
500ml/17fl oz/generous 2 cups
   chicken or fish stock

1 Make the sauce. Heat the oil in a pan; add the vegetables and garlic. Cook gently until soft but not brown.

2 Add the coconut, tomatoes and ginger. Cook for 1–2 minutes, stir in the tomato purée and curry powder to taste. Add the stock, stir and season. Bring to the boil, then lower the heat, cover the pan and simmer over the lowest heat for 50 minutes.

3 Allow the sauce to cool, then pour into a food processor or blender and process until smooth. Return to a clean pan and reheat very gently, adding a little water if too thick.

4 Season the fish fillets. Heat the oil in a large frying pan, add the butter and heat until sizzling. Put in the fish and cook for about 2–3 minutes on each side, until pale golden and cooked through. Drain on kitchen paper.

5 Arrange the fillets on plates, pour the sauce around the fish and sprinkle on the mango and coriander leaves and serve.

Sea Bass Energy 235kcal/983kJ; Protein 26g; Carbohydrate 8g, of which sugars 6g; Fat 11g, of which saturates 2g; Cholesterol 100mg; Calcium 217mg; Fibre 0.3g; Sodium 0.3g.
John Dory Energy 333kcal/1391kJ; Protein 34.9g; Carbohydrate 12.5g, of which sugars 11.5g; Fat 16.3g, of which saturates 4.9g; Cholesterol 13mg; Calcium 102mg; Fibre 2.6g; Sodium 291mg.

Spiced Halibut and Tomato Curry

The chunky cubes of white fish contrast beautifully with the rich red spicy tomato sauce and taste just as good as they look. You can use any type of firm white fish for this recipe.

Serves 4

60ml/4 tbsp lemon juice
60ml/4 tbsp rice wine vinegar
30ml/2 tbsp cumin seeds
5ml/1 tsp turmeric
5ml/1 tsp chilli powder
5ml/1 tsp salt
750g/1lb 11oz thick halibut
   fillets, skinned and cubed

60ml/4 tbsp sunflower oil
1 onion, finely chopped
3 garlic cloves, finely chopped
30ml/2 tbsp finely grated
   fresh root ginger
10ml/2 tsp black
   mustard seeds
2 x 400g/14oz cans
   chopped tomatoes
5ml/1 tsp sugar
chopped coriander (cilantro)
   leaves and sliced green chilli,
   to garnish
basmati rice, pickles and
   poppadums, to serve
natural (plain) yogurt,
   to drizzle (optional)

1 Mix together the lemon juice, vinegar, cumin, turmeric, chilli powder and salt in a shallow non-metallic bowl. Add the cubed fish and turn to coat evenly. Cover and put in the refrigerator to marinate for 25–30 minutes.

2 Meanwhile, heat a wok or large frying pan over high heat and add the oil. When hot, add the onion, garlic, ginger and mustard seeds. Reduce the heat to low and cook very gently for about 10 minutes, stirring occasionally.

3 Add the tomatoes and sugar to the pan, bring to the boil, reduce the heat, cover the pan and cook gently for about 15–20 minutes, stirring occasionally.

4 Add the fish and its marinade to the pan, stir gently to mix, then cover and simmer gently for 15–20 minutes, or until the fish is cooked through and the flesh flakes easily with a fork.

5 Serve the curry ladled into shallow bowls with basmati rice, pickles and poppadums. Garnish with fresh coriander and green chillies, and drizzle over some natural yogurt, if you like.

Jamaican Fish Curry

This recipe uses some of the most common spices used in Caribbean cuisine. The taste in that region is for strong, pungent flavours rather than fiery heat.

Serves 4

2 halibut steaks, total weight
   about 500–675g/1¼–1½lb
30ml/2 tbsp groundnut
   (peanut) oil
2 cardamom pods
1 cinnamon stick
6 allspice berries
4 cloves
1 large onion, chopped
3 garlic cloves, crushed

10–15ml/2–3 tsp grated fresh
   root ginger
10ml/2 tsp ground cumin
5ml/1 tsp ground coriander
2.5ml/½ tsp cayenne pepper
4 tomatoes, peeled, seeded
   and chopped
1 sweet potato, about 225g/8oz,
   cut into 2cm/¾in cubes
475ml/16fl oz/2 cups fish stock
   or water
115g/4oz piece of creamed
   coconut or 120ml/4fl oz/½ cup
   coconut cream
1 bay leaf
225g/8oz/generous 1 cup white
   long grain rice
salt

1 Rub the halibut steaks well with salt and set aside.

2 Heat the oil in a heavy pan and stir-fry the cardamom pods, cinnamon stick, allspice berries and cloves for about 3 minutes.

3 Add the onion, garlic and ginger. Continue cooking for about 4–5 minutes over low heat until the onion is soft.

4 Add the cumin, coriander and cayenne pepper and cook briefly, stirring all the time. Stir in the tomatoes, sweet potato, fish stock or water, coconut and bay leaf. Season with salt. Bring to the boil, then lower the heat, cover and cook for 15 minutes.

5 Cook the rice according to your preferred method. Meanwhile, add the halibut to the pan of sauce and spoon the sauce over to cover them. Cover the pan and simmer gently for 10 minutes until the fish is tender and flakes easily.

6 Spoon the rice into a warmed serving dish, spoon over the curry sauce and arrange the halibut steaks on top and serve.

Halibut Curry Energy 335kcal/1409kJ; Protein 41.9g; Carbohydrate 8.4g, of which sugars 8.1g; Fat 15.2g, of which saturates 2.1g; Cholesterol 66mg; Calcium 73mg; Fibre 2.2g; Sodium 622mg.
Jamaican Curry Energy 639kcal/2669kJ; Protein 34.2g; Carbohydrate 62g, of which sugars 8.3g; Fat 28.4g, of which saturates 18.7g; Cholesterol 44mg; Calcium 74mg; Fibre 2.4g; Sodium 115mg.

Curried Halibut Steaks with Lemon, Red Chilli and Coriander

Succulent fish steaks are first marinated in herbs and spices then cooked in a tasty stock with chillies and coriander, and served with a red onion topping.

Serves 4

4 halibut or cod steaks, about 175g/6oz each
juice of 1 lemon
5ml/1 tsp garlic granules
5ml/1 tsp paprika
5ml/1 tsp ground cumin
5ml/1 tsp dried tarragon
about 60ml/4 tbsp olive oil
flour, for dusting
300ml/½ pint/1¼ cups fish stock
2 red chillies, seeded and finely chopped
30ml/2 tbsp chopped fresh coriander (cilantro)
1 red onion, cut into rings
salt and ground black pepper

1 Place the fish in a shallow bowl. Mix together the lemon juice, garlic, paprika, cumin, tarragon and a little salt and pepper.

2 Spoon the lemon mixture over the fish, cover loosely with clear film (plastic wrap) and set aside to marinate for a few hours or overnight in the refrigerator.

3 Gently heat 45ml/3 tbsp olive oil in a large non-stick frying pan, dust the fish with flour and then fry the fish for a few minutes each side, until golden brown all over.

4 Pour the fish stock around the fish, and then simmer gently, covered, for about 5 minutes, stirring occasionally until the fish is thoroughly cooked through.

5 Add the chopped red chillies and 15ml/1 tbsp of the coriander to the pan. Simmer for 5 minutes.

6 Carefully transfer the fish steaks to a serving plate. Spoon the sauce over the fish and keep warm.

7 Wipe the pan, heat 15ml/1 tbsp olive oil and stir-fry the onion rings for 1–2 minutes. Sprinkle over the fish with the remaining chopped coriander and serve immediately.

Monkfish and Okra Curry

An interesting combination of flavours and textures is used to make this delicious fish dish.

Serves 4

450g/1lb monkfish
5ml/1 tsp ground turmeric
2.5ml/½ tsp chilli powder
2.5ml/½ tsp salt
5ml/1 tsp cumin seeds
2.5ml/½ tsp fennel seeds
2 dried red chillies
45ml/3 tbsp vegetable oil
1 onion, finely chopped
2 garlic cloves, crushed
4 firm tomatoes, skinned and finely chopped
150ml/¼ pint/⅔ cup water
225g/8oz okra, trimmed and cut into 2.5cm/1in lengths
5ml/1 tsp garam masala
tomato rice or plain boiled rice, to serve

1 Remove the membrane and bones from the monkfish, cut into 2.5cm/1in cubes and place in a dish. Mix together the turmeric, chilli powder and 1.5ml/¼ tsp of the salt and rub the mixture all over the fish. Marinate for 15 minutes.

2 Put the cumin seeds, fennel seeds and chillies in a wok or a large frying pan and dry-roast for about 3–4 minutes until a fragrant aroma is released. Put the spices into a blender, or use a mortar and pestle, and grind to a coarse powder.

3 Heat 30ml/2 tbsp of the oil in the frying pan and and fry the fish for about 4–5 minutes, turning occasionally. Remove with a slotted spoon and drain on kitchen paper.

4 Add the remaining oil to the pan and gently fry the onion and garlic for about 5 minutes, until the onion is soft and translucent. Add the spice powder and the remaining salt to the pan and fry for a further 2–3 minutes.

5 Stir the chopped tomatoes and the water into the pan. Simmer the mixture gently for 5 minutes, stirring occasionally.

6 Add the prepared okra and cook for about 5–7 minutes. Return the fish to the pan with the garam masala. Cover and simmer for 5–6 minutes or until the fish is tender. Serve immediately with tomato rice or plain boiled rice.

Halibut Steaks Energy 265kcal/1106kJ; Protein 33g; Carbohydrate 5.4g, of which sugars 1.2g; Fat 12.5g, of which saturates 1.8g; Cholesterol 81mg; Calcium 47mg; Fibre 0.9g; Sodium 109mg.
Monkfish Curry Energy 203kcal/851kJ; Protein 20.9g; Carbohydrate 7.7g, of which sugars 5.4g; Fat 10.2g, of which saturates 1.5g; Cholesterol 16mg; Calcium 119mg; Fibre 3.5g; Sodium 36mg.

Tilapia in Mango and Tomato Sauce

The flesh of tilapia is white and moist, with a sweet flavour that is accentuated when it is cooked with fruit and spices, as here.

Serves 4
4 tilapia
juice of ½ lemon
2 garlic cloves, crushed
2.5ml/½ tsp dried thyme
30ml/2 tbsp chopped spring
  onion (scallion)
vegetable oil, for shallow-frying
plain (all-purpose) flour, for dusting
30ml/2 tbsp groundnut (peanut) oil
15g/½oz/1 tbsp butter
  or margarine
1 onion, finely chopped
3 tomatoes, skinned and
  finely chopped
5ml/1 tsp ground turmeric
60ml/4 tbsp white wine
1 fresh green chilli, seeded and
  finely chopped
600ml/1 pint/2½ cups
  well-flavoured fish stock
5ml/1 tsp sugar
1 under-ripe medium mango,
  peeled, stoned (pitted) and diced
15ml/1 tbsp chopped fresh parsley
salt and ground black pepper

1 Place the fish in a shallow bowl, drizzle the lemon juice all over and rub in the garlic, thyme and some salt and pepper.

2 Place some of the spring onion in the cavity of each fish, cover loosely with clear film (plastic wrap) and leave to marinate for a few hours or overnight in the refrigerator.

3 Heat a little oil in a large frying pan, coat the fish with some flour, and then fry the fish on both sides for a few minutes, until golden brown. Remove the fish to a plate and set aside.

4 Heat the groundnut oil and butter or margarine in a pan and fry the onion for 4–5 minutes, until soft. Stir in the tomatoes and cook briskly for a few minutes.

5 Add the turmeric, white wine, chilli, fish stock and sugar and stir well. Bring to the boil, then simmer gently, covered, for 10 minutes. Add the fish and cook for about 15–20 minutes.

6 Add the mango, and cook briefly for 1–2 minutes to heat through. Arrange the fish on a warmed plate with the sauce poured over. Garnish with chopped parsley and serve.

Fillet of Fish Basted with Spices and Lemon Juice

The great thing about fish is that it can be grilled without sacrificing any flavour. For this recipe, there is only a minimum amount of oil used to baste the fish.

Serves 4
4 medium flatfish fillets, such as
  plaice, sole or flounder, about
  115g/4oz each
5ml/1 tsp crushed garlic
5ml/1 tsp garam masala
5ml/1 tsp chilli powder
1.5ml/¼ tsp turmeric
2.5ml/½ tsp salt
15ml/1 tbsp finely chopped fresh
  coriander (cilantro)
15ml/1 tbsp vegetable oil or
  sunflower oil
30ml/2 tbsp lemon juice

1 Line a flameproof dish or grill (broiler) tray with foil. Rinse and pat dry the flatfish fillets and place them, slightly spaced, on the foil-lined dish or tray.

2 In a small bowl, mix together the crushed garlic, garam masala, chilli powder, turmeric, salt, chopped fresh coriander, vegetable oil and lemon juice.

3 Using a pastry brush, baste the fish fillets evenly all over with the spice and lemon juice mixture.

4 Preheat the grill to very hot, then lower the heat to medium. Grill (broil) the fillets for about 10 minutes, basting occasionally, until they are cooked right through.

5 Serve immediately with an attractive garnish, such as grated carrot, tomato quarters and lime slices, if you wish.

Variation
This recipe can also be used to cook other firm white fish fillets such as cod and haddock. Check that the fish is cooked by testing with a fork – the flesh should flake easily when it is cooked through - and be careful not to overcook.

Tilapia in Sauce Energy 238kcal/998kJ; Protein 23.4g; Carbohydrate 10.1g, of which sugars 9.6g; Fat 10.8g, of which saturates 3.1g; Cholesterol 8mg; Calcium 168mg; Fibre 2g; Sodium 97mg.
Fillet of Fish Energy 218kcal/917kJ; Protein 22.8g; Carbohydrate 11.4g, of which sugars 4.3g; Fat 9.5g, of which saturates 1.2g; Cholesterol 41mg; Calcium 36mg; Fibre 0.2g; Sodium 344mg.

Spicy Fish Curry with Tamarind

The addition of tamarind to this curry gives a slightly sour note to the spicy coconut sauce.

Serves 4
7.5ml/1½ tsp ground turmeric
5ml/1 tsp salt
450g/1lb monkfish fillet, cut into eight pieces
15ml/1 tbsp lemon juice
5ml/1 tsp cumin seeds
5ml/1 tsp coriander seeds
5ml/1 tsp black peppercorns
1 garlic clove, chopped
5cm/2in piece fresh root ginger, finely chopped
25g/1oz tamarind paste
150ml/¼ pint/⅔ cup hot water
30ml/2 tbsp vegetable oil
2 onions, halved and sliced lengthways
400ml/14fl oz/1⅔ cups coconut milk
4 mild green chillies, seeded and cut into thin strips
16 large prawns (shrimp), peeled
30ml/2 tbsp chopped fresh coriander (cilantro) leaves, to garnish

1 Mix together the ground turmeric and salt in a bowl. Place the fish in a shallow dish and sprinkle over the lemon juice, then rub the turmeric mixture over the fish. Cover and chill.

2 Put the cumin and coriander seeds and peppercorns in a blender or food processor and blend to a powder. Add the garlic and ginger and process for a few seconds more.

3 Preheat the oven to 200°C/400°F/Gas 6. Mix the tamarind paste and hot water and set aside. Heat the oil in a frying pan, add the onions and cook for 5–6 minutes, until softened and golden. Transfer the onions to a shallow ovenproof dish. Add the fish to the pan, and fry over a high heat, turning to seal on all sides. Remove from the pan and place on top of the onions.

4 Fry the ground spice mixture in the pan, stirring constantly, for 1–2 minutes. Stir in the tamarind liquid, coconut milk and chilli strips then bring to the boil. Pour over the fish.

5 Cover the dish and cook in the oven for 10 minutes. Add the prawns, and cook for a further 5 minutes, or until the prawns are pink. Do not overcook them or they will toughen. Check the seasoning, sprinkle with coriander leaves and serve.

Fish Moolie

This is a very popular South-east Asian fish curry in a coconut sauce, which is truly delicious. Choose a firm-textured fish so that the pieces stay intact during the brief cooking process. Monkfish, halibut or cod work well in this dish.

Serves 4
500g/1¼lb monkfish or other firm-textured fish fillets, skinned and cut into 2.5cm/1in cubes
2.5ml/½ tsp salt
50g/2oz/⅔ cup desiccated (dry unsweetened shredded) coconut
6 shallots, chopped
6 blanched almonds
2–3 garlic cloves, roughly chopped
2.5cm/1in piece fresh root ginger, peeled and sliced
2 lemon grass stalks, trimmed
10ml/2 tsp ground turmeric
45ml/3 tbsp vegetable oil
2 × 400ml/14fl oz cans coconut milk
1–3 fresh red chillies, seeded and sliced into rings
salt and ground black pepper
fresh chives, to garnish
plain boiled or steamed basmati rice, to serve

1 Put the fish cubes in a shallow dish and sprinkle with the salt. Dry fry the coconut in a wok, turning all the time until it is crisp and golden, then transfer into a food processor and process to an oily paste. Scrape into a bowl and reserve.

2 Add the shallots, almonds, garlic and ginger to the food processor. Chop the bulbous part of each lemon grass stalk and add to the processor with the turmeric. Process the mixture to a paste. Bruise the remaining lemon grass stalks.

3 Heat the oil in a wok. Cook the shallot and spice mixture for about 2–3 minutes. Stir in the coconut milk and bring to the boil, stirring. Add the fish, most of the chilli and the lemon grass stalks. Cook for 3–4 minutes.

4 Stir in the coconut paste and cook for a further 2–3 minutes only. Adjust the seasoning.

5 Remove the lemon grass. Transfer the moolie to a hot serving dish and sprinkle with the remaining slices of chilli. Garnish with chopped and whole chives and serve with rice.

Spicy Fish Curry Energy 220kcal/926kJ; Protein 28g; Carbohydrate 12.8g, of which sugars 10.5g; Fat 6.8g, of which saturates 1g; Cholesterol 113mg; Calcium 103mg; Fibre 1.4g; Sodium 720mg.
Fish Moolie Energy 319kcal/1335kJ; Protein 22.4g; Carbohydrate 16.7g, of which sugars 14.9g; Fat 18.6g, of which saturates 8.3g; Cholesterol 18mg; Calcium 96mg; Fibre 3g; Sodium 249mg.

Monkfish with Tomatoes and Spices

This spicy fish stew makes a really delicious lunch or light supper dish.

Serves 4
8 tomatoes
675g/1½lb monkfish
30ml/2 tbsp plain
    (all-purpose) flour
5ml/1 tsp ground coriander
2.5ml/½ tsp ground turmeric

25g/1oz/2 tbsp butter
2 garlic cloves, finely chopped
15–30ml/1–2 tbsp olive oil
40g/1½oz/4 tbsp pine
    nuts, toasted
1 preserved lemon, cut into pieces
12 black olives, pitted
salt and ground black pepper
whole slices of preserved lemon
    and chopped fresh parsley,
    to garnish

1 Peel the tomatoes by placing them briefly in boiling water, then cold water. Quarter the tomatoes, remove the cores and seeds and discard. Chop the tomato flesh roughly.

2 Cut the fish into bitesize chunks. Blend together the flour, coriander and turmeric, and season with salt and pepper to taste. Dust the fish with the seasoned flour and set aside.

3 Melt the butter in a non-stick frying pan and fry the tomatoes and garlic over low heat for 6–8 minutes, until the tomato mixture is very thick and most of the liquid has evaporated.

4 Push the tomatoes to the edge of the frying pan, moisten the pan with a little olive oil and fry the monkfish pieces in a single layer over medium heat for 3–5 minutes, turning frequently. You may have to do this in batches, so as the first batch cooks, place them on top of the tomatoes and fry the remaining fish, adding a little more oil to the pan, if necessary.

5 When all the fish is cooked, add the pine nuts and stir, scraping the bottom of the pan to remove the glazed tomatoes. The sauce should be thick and slightly charred in places.

6 Rinse the preserved lemon in cold water, discard the pulp and cut the peel into strips. Stir into the sauce with the olives, adjust the seasoning and serve garnished with whole slices of preserved lemon and parsley.

Tagine of Monkfish

The fish is marinated in chermoula, a lemony garlic and coriander paste. Monkfish is robust enough to handle the spices and the result is a very tasty dish.

Serves 4
900g/2lb monkfish, cut into chunks
15–20 small new potatoes
45–60ml/3–4 tbsp olive oil
4–5 garlic cloves, thinly sliced
15–20 cherry tomatoes
2 green (bell) peppers, grilled
    (broiled) until black, skinned,
    seeded and cut into strips

large handful of fleshy black
    olives, pits in
100ml/3½fl oz/scant ½ cup water
salt and ground black pepper
fresh bread, to serve

For the chermoula
2 garlic cloves
5ml/1 tsp coarse salt
10ml/2 tsp ground cumin
5ml/1 tsp paprika
small bunch of fresh coriander
    (cilantro), roughly chopped
juice of 1 lemon
15ml/1 tbsp olive oil

1 For the chermoula: pound the garlic and salt to a paste in a mortar and pestle. Add the cumin, paprika, coriander and lemon juice, and mix in the oil, reserving a little oil for cooking. Rub the chermoula over the monkfish. Cover and set aside for 1 hour.

2 Par-boil the potatoes for 10 minutes. Drain, then cut them in half lengthways. Heat the oil in a heavy pan and cook the garlic for 2–3 minutes. Add the tomatoes and cook until just softened.

3 Add the peppers to the tomatoes and garlic, together with the remaining chermoula, and season to taste.

4 Spread the potatoes over the base of a tagine or a deep frying pan. Spoon three-quarters of the tomato mixture over and place the marinated fish chunks on top, with the chermoula.

5 Spoon the rest of the tomato mixture on top of the fish and add the olives. Drizzle a little oil over the dish and add the water.

6 Heat until simmering, cover and cook over a medium heat for about 15 minutes, until the fish is cooked through. Serve with fresh, warm crusty bread to mop up the delicious juices.

Monkfish with Tomatoes Energy 306kcal/1283kJ; Protein 29g; Carbohydrate 5.1g, of which sugars 5.1g; Fat 19.1g, of which saturates 5g; Cholesterol 38mg; Calcium 29mg; Fibre 1.8g; Sodium 203mg.
Tagine of Monkfish Energy 406kcal/1710kJ; Protein 39.6g; Carbohydrate 25.2g, of which sugars 6.5g; Fat 17.1g, of which saturates 2.7g; Cholesterol 32mg; Calcium 98mg; Fibre 5.4g; Sodium 915mg.

Masala-stuffed Fish

Every community in India prepares stuffed fish, but this version must rank top of the list. The most popular fish in India is the pomfret. These are available from Indian and Chinese grocers or large supermarkets.

Serves 4
2 large pomfrets, or Dover or
   lemon sole
10ml/2 tsp salt
juice of 1 lemon

For the masala
115g/4oz/1⅓ cups desiccated
   (dry unsweetened
   shredded) coconut
115g/4oz/4 cups fresh coriander
   (cilantro), including the
   tender stalks
8 fresh green chillies, or
   to taste
5ml/1 tsp cumin seeds
6 garlic cloves
10ml/2 tsp sugar
10ml/2 tsp lemon juice

1 Scale the fish and cut off the fins. Gut the fish and remove the heads, if you wish. Using a sharp knife, make two diagonal gashes on each side, then pat dry with kitchen paper.

2 Rub the fish inside and out with salt and lemon juice. Cover and leave to stand in a cool place for about 1 hour. Pat dry.

3 For the masala, grind all the ingredients together using a pestle and mortar or food processor.

4 Stuff the fish with most of the masala mixture. Rub the rest into the gashes and all over the fish on both sides.

5 Place each fish on a separate piece of greased foil. Tightly wrap the foil over each fish. Place in a steamer and steam for 20 minutes, or bake in a preheated oven for 30 minutes at 200°C/400°F/Gas 6 or until cooked. Remove the fish from the foil and serve immediately.

> **Cook's Tip**
> *Try this fish steamed in banana leaves, as it is served in India.*

Cod in a Spicy Mushroom Sauce

Grilling the cod fillets before adding them to the spicy sauce in this recipe helps to prevent the fish from breaking up during the cooking process.

Serves 4
4 cod fillets
15ml/1 tbsp lemon juice
15ml/1 tbsp vegetable oil
1 medium onion, chopped
1 bay leaf
4 black peppercorns, crushed
115g/4oz/1 cup mushrooms
175ml/6fl oz/¾ cup natural
   (plain) low-fat yogurt
5ml/1 tsp grated fresh
   root ginger
5ml/1 tsp crushed garlic
2.5ml/½ tsp garam masala
2.5ml/½ tsp chilli powder
5ml/1 tsp salt
15ml/1 tbsp fresh coriander
   (cilantro) leaves, to garnish
lightly cooked green beans,
   to serve

1 Preheat the grill (broiler). Remove the skin and any bones from the cod fillets. Sprinkle with lemon juice, then par-cook under the grill for 5 minutes on each side. Remove the fillets from the heat and set aside.

2 Heat the oil in a karahi or wok and fry the onion with the bay leaf and peppercorns for 2–3 minutes. Lower the heat, add the whole mushrooms and stir-fry for a further 4–5 minutes.

3 In a bowl mix together the natural yogurt, grated ginger and crushed garlic, garam masala, chilli powder and salt. Pour this over the onion and mushrooms and stir-fry for 3 minutes.

4 Add the cod fillets to the sauce and cook for a further 2 minutes. Serve garnished with the fresh coriander and accompanied by lightly cooked green beans.

> **Cook's Tip**
> *If you can find tiny button (white) mushrooms they look very attractive in this dish. Alternatively, choose from the many other pretty coloured varieties, such as ceps and oyster mushrooms.*

Masala-stuffed Fish Energy 305kcal/1267kJ; Protein 25.1g; Carbohydrate 5.2g, of which sugars 5.1g; Fat 20.5g, of which saturates 15.4g; Cholesterol 63mg; Calcium 102mg; Fibre 5.4g; Sodium 143mg.
Cod in Mushroom Sauce Energy 202kcal/847kJ; Protein 31.7g; Carbohydrate 6.9g, of which sugars 3.4g; Fat 5.7g, of which saturates 0.9g; Cholesterol 70mg; Calcium 116mg; Fibre 0.3g; Sodium 131mg.

Curried Cod in a Tomato Sauce

Dusting the cod with spices before cooking gives it a delectable coating.

Serves 4

30ml/2 tbsp cornflour
    (cornstarch)
5ml/1 tsp salt
5ml/1 tsp garlic powder
5ml/1 tsp chilli powder
5ml/1 tsp ground ginger
5ml/1 tsp ground fennel seeds
5ml/1 tsp ground coriander
2 medium cod fillets, each cut
    into 2 pieces
15ml/1 tbsp vegetable oil
mashed potatoes, to serve

For the sauce

30ml/2 tbsp tomato purée (paste)
5ml/1 tsp garam masala
5ml/1 tsp chilli powder
5ml/1 tsp crushed garlic
5ml/1 tsp grated fresh
    root ginger
2.5ml/½ tsp salt
175ml/6fl oz/¾ cup water
15ml/1 tbsp vegetable oil
1 bay leaf
3 or 4 black peppercorns
1cm/½in piece cinnamon stick
15ml/1 tbsp chopped fresh
    coriander (cilantro)
15ml/1 tbsp chopped fresh
    mint leaves

1 Mix together the cornflour, salt, garlic powder, chilli powder, ground ginger, ground fennel seeds and ground coriander. Use to coat the four cod pieces.

2 Preheat the grill (broiler) to very hot, then reduce the heat slightly and place the cod under the heat. After about 5 minutes spoon the oil over the cod. Turn the cod over and repeat the process. Cook for a further 5 minutes, check that the fish is cooked through and set aside.

3 Make the sauce by mixing together the tomato purée, garam masala, chilli powder, garlic, ginger, salt and water. Set aside.

4 Heat the oil in a karahi or wok and add the bay leaf, peppercorns and cinnamon. Pour the sauce into the pan and reduce the heat to low. Bring slowly to the boil, stirring occasionally, then simmer for about 5 minutes.

5 Gently slide the pieces of fish into this mixture and cook for a further 2 minutes. Add the chopped fresh coriander and mint and serve the dish with mashed potatoes.

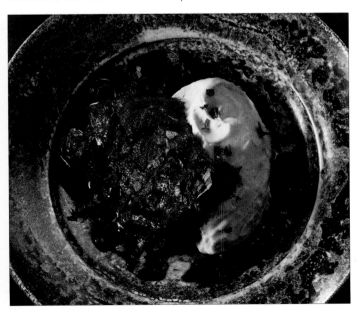

Balti Fried Fish

Pieces of succulent white fish are coated in a spicy marinade before being pan-fried. This dish is delicious served with pungent chutneys and Indian breads.

Serves 4–6

675g/1½lb cod, or any other firm,
    white fish
1 medium onion, sliced

15ml/1 tbsp lemon juice
5ml/1 tsp salt
5ml/1 tsp garlic pulp
5ml/1 tsp crushed dried red chillies
7.5ml/1½ tsp garam masala
30ml/2 tbsp chopped fresh
    coriander (cilantro)
2 medium tomatoes
30ml/2 tbsp cornflour
    (cornstarch)
150ml/¼ pint/⅔ cup corn oil

1 Skin the fish and cut the flesh into small cubes. Put the fish pieces into the refrigerator to chill.

2 Put the onion into a bowl and add the lemon juice, salt, garlic, crushed red chillies, garam masala and fresh coriander. Mix together well and set to one side.

3 Skin the tomatoes by dropping them into boiling water for a few seconds. Remove with a slotted spoon and gently peel off the skins. Chop the tomatoes roughly and add to the onion mixture in the bowl. Place the contents of the bowl into a food processor or blender and process for about 30 seconds.

4 Remove the fish from the refrigerator. Pour the contents of the food processor or blender over the fish and mix together well to coat the fish evenly. Add the cornflour and mix again until the fish pieces are well coated.

5 Heat the oil in a karahi or deep frying pan. Lower the heat slightly and add the fish pieces, a few at a time. Turn them gently with a slotted spoon as they will break easily. Cook for about 5 minutes until the fish is lightly browned.

6 Remove the fish pieces from the pan and drain on kitchen paper to absorb any excess oil. Keep warm and continue frying the remaining fish. Serve the fish immediately with a selection of Indian chutneys and breads.

Curried Cod Energy 294kcal/1229kJ; Protein 41.8g; Carbohydrate 2.7g, of which sugars 2.7g; Fat 12.8g, of which saturates 1.9g; Cholesterol 104mg; Calcium 26mg; Fibre 0.9g; Sodium 143mg.
Balti Fried Fish 369kcal/1539kJ; Protein 36.2g; Carbohydrate 6.7g, of which sugars 3.2g; Fat 22.2g, of which saturates 3.7g; Cholesterol 94mg; Calcium 46mg; Fibre 1.4g; Sodium 370mg.

Red-hot Fish Curry

The island of Bali has wonderful fish, surrounded as it is by sparkling blue sea. This simple fish curry is packed with many of the characteristic flavours associated with Indonesia.

Serves 4–6
675g/1½lb cod or haddock fillet
1cm/½in cube shrimp paste
2 red or white onions
2.5cm/1in fresh root ginger,
   peeled and sliced
1cm/½in fresh galangal, peeled
   and sliced
2 garlic cloves
1–2 fresh red chillies, seeded,
   or 10ml/2 tsp chilli sambal, or
   5–10ml/1–2 tsp chilli powder
90ml/6 tbsp sunflower oil
15ml/1 tbsp dark soy sauce
5ml/1 tsp tamarind pulp, soaked
   in 30ml/2 tbsp warm water
250ml/8fl oz/1 cup water
celery leaves or chopped fresh
   chilli, to garnish
boiled rice, to serve

1 Skin the fish fillets, remove any bones and then cut the flesh into bitesize pieces. Pat the fish dry with kitchen paper and set aside in a cool place until needed.

2 Grind the shrimp paste, onions, ginger, fresh galangal, garlic and fresh chillies, if using, to a paste in a food processor or blender or with a mortar and pestle. Stir in the chilli sambal or the chilli powder, if using.

3 Heat 30ml/2 tbsp of the oil and fry the spice mixture, stirring, until it gives off a rich aroma.

4 Add the soy sauce to the pan. Strain the soaked tamarind pulp, discarding the seeds and pulp, and add the juice and water to the pan, mixing well. Cook gently for 2–3 minutes.

5 In a separate pan, fry the fish fillets in the remaining oil for 2–3 minutes. Turn the fish once only so that the pieces stay whole and don't break apart. Lift out with a slotted spoon and place them in the pan with the sauce.

6 Simmer the fish in the sauce for a further 3 minutes and serve with boiled rice. Garnish with feathery celery leaves or a little chopped fresh chilli, if you like.

Chunky Fish Balti with Peppers

Try to find peppers in different colours to make this wonderful dish as colourful as possible.

Serves 2–4
450g/1lb cod, or any other firm
   white fish, such as haddock
7.5ml/1½ tsp ground cumin
10ml/2 tsp mango powder
   (amchur)
5ml/1 tsp ground coriander
2.5ml/½ tsp chilli powder
5ml/1 tsp salt
5ml/1 tsp grated fresh
   root ginger
45ml/3 tbsp cornflour
   (cornstarch)
150ml/¼ pint/⅔ cup corn oil
1 each green, orange and red
   (bell) peppers, seeded
   and chopped
8–10 cherry tomatoes

1 Skin the fish and cut it into small cubes. Put the cubes in a large mixing bowl and add the ground cumin, mango powder, ground coriander, chilli powder, salt, grated ginger and cornflour. Mix together thoroughly until the fish is well coated with the spice mix.

2 Heat the oil in a karahi, wok or large, deep pan. Lower the heat slightly and add the fish pieces, three or four at a time. Fry for about 3 minutes, turning constantly.

3 Drain the cooked fish pieces on kitchen paper and transfer to a serving dish. Keep the cooked fish warm in a low oven while you fry the remaining fish pieces.

4 Fry the chopped peppers in the oil remaining in the pan for about 4–5 minutes. The pieces of pepper should still be slightly crisp. Drain well on kitchen paper.

5 Add the cooked peppers to the fish and garnish with the cherry tomatoes. Serve immediately.

> **Cook's Tip**
> Amchur is an Indian seasoning made by grinding dried unripe mangoes into a powder and is used to add sourness.

Red-hot Fish Curry Energy 322kcal/1342kJ; Protein 33g; Carbohydrate 8g, of which sugars 5g; Fat 18g, of which saturates 2g; Cholesterol 84mg; Calcium 53mg; Fibre 1.1g; Sodium 200mg.
Chunky Fish Balti Energy 296kcal/1236kJ; Protein 22.9g; Carbohydrate 22.9g, of which sugars 11.1g; Fat 13g, of which saturates 1.6g; Cholesterol 52mg; Calcium 51mg; Fibre 3.8g; Sodium 98mg.

Fish Fillets with a Chilli Sauce

For this recipe, the fish fillets are first marinated with finely chopped fresh coriander and lemon juice, then cooked quickly before being served with a chilli sauce. It makes a delicious and quick light lunch or supper dish that will be enjoyed by all the family.

Serves 4

4 flat-fish fillets, such as plaice,
   sole or flounder, about
   115g/4oz each
30ml/2 tbsp lemon juice
15ml/1 tbsp finely chopped fresh
   coriander (cilantro)
15ml/1 tbsp oil
lime wedges and a fresh
   coriander sprig, to garnish
yellow basmati rice, flavoured
   with turmeric or saffron,
   to serve

For the sauce

5ml/1 tsp grated fresh
   root ginger
30ml/2 tbsp tomato
   purée (paste)
5ml/1 tsp sugar
5ml/1 tsp salt
15ml/1 tbsp chilli sauce
15ml/1 tbsp malt vinegar
300ml/½ pint/1¼ cups water

1 Rinse and pat dry the fish fillets and place in a medium bowl. Add the lemon juice, coriander and oil and rub into the fish. Leave to marinate for at least 1 hour.

2 Make the sauce. Mix the grated ginger, tomato purée, sugar, salt and chilli sauce in a bowl. Stir in the vinegar and water.

3 Pour into a small pan and simmer gently over a low heat for about 6 minutes, stirring occasionally.

4 Meanwhile, preheat the grill (broiler) to medium. Lift the fish fillets out of the marinade and place them in a grill pan. Grill (broil) for about 5–7 minutes.

5 When the fish is cooked, arrange it on a warmed serving dish.

6 The chilli sauce should now be fairly thick – about the consistency of a thick chicken soup. Spoon the sauce over the fish fillets, garnish with the lime wedges and coriander sprig and serve immediately with yellow basmati rice.

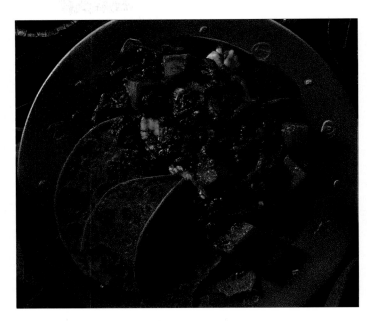

Indian Fish Stew

Cooking fish with vegetables is very much a tradition in eastern regions. This hearty dish with potatoes, peppers and tomatoes is perfect served with breads such as chapatis or parathas.

Serves 4

30ml/2 tbsp vegetable oil
5ml/1 tsp cumin seeds
1 onion, chopped
1 red (bell) pepper,
   thinly sliced
1 garlic clove, crushed
2 fresh red chillies, seeded and
   finely chopped
2 bay leaves
2.5ml/½ tsp salt
5ml/1 tsp ground cumin
5ml/1 tsp ground coriander
5ml/1 tsp chilli powder
400g/14oz can chopped
   tomatoes
2 large potatoes, cut into
   2.5cm/1in chunks
300ml/½ pint/1¼ cups fish
   stock
4 cod fillets
chapatis or parathas, to serve

1 Heat the oil in a wok, karahi or large pan over a medium heat and fry the cumin seeds for 30–40 seconds until they begin to splutter. Add the onion, red pepper, garlic, chillies and bay leaves and fry for 5–7 minutes more until the onions have browned.

2 Add the salt, ground cumin, ground coriander and chilli powder and cook for 1–2 minutes.

3 Stir the tomatoes, potatoes and fish stock into the pan. Bring the mixture to the boil and simmer for a further 10 minutes, or until the potatoes are almost tender.

4 Add the fish fillets, then cover the pan and allow to simmer for 5–6 minutes until the fish is just cooked. Serve immediately with warm chapatis or parathas.

Cook's Tip
Avoid reheating this dish. Serve it as soon as it is cooked because cod flesh flakes very easily. If preparing in advance, follow the recipe up to the end of step 3, then cover the sauce and store in the refrigerator. Complete step 4 before serving.

Fish Fillets Energy 162kcal/684kJ; Protein 26.8g; Carbohydrate 3.8g, of which sugars 3.7g; Fat 4.5g, of which saturates 1g; Cholesterol 75mg; Calcium 37mg; Fibre 0.8g; Sodium 708mg.
Indian Fish Stew Energy 332kcal/1396kJ; Protein 36.9g; Carbohydrate 27.6g, of which sugars 7.9g; Fat 9.2g, of which saturates 1.3g; Cholesterol 81mg; Calcium 59mg; Fibre 2.9g; Sodium 132mg.

Vietnamese Fried Fish with Dill

In this classic dish from Vietnam, the dill is just as important as the fish, and they complement each other beautifully. A simple accompaniment of plain rice or noodles is all that is needed to make an impressive meal.

Serves 4

75g/3oz/⅔ cup rice flour
7.5ml/1½ tsp ground turmeric
500g/1¼lb white fish fillets, such as cod, skinned and cut into bitesize chunks
vegetable oil, for deep-frying
1 large bunch fresh dill
15ml/1 tbsp groundnut (peanut) oil
30ml/2 tbsp roasted peanuts
4 spring onions (scallions), cut into bitesize pieces
1 small bunch of fresh basil, stalks removed, leaves finely chopped
1 small bunch of fresh coriander (cilantro), stalks removed
1 lime, cut into quarters, and nuoc cham (Vietnamese fish sauce), to serve

1 Mix the flour with the turmeric and toss the fish chunks in it until well coated. Heat the oil in a wok or heavy pan and cook the fish in batches until crisp and golden. Drain the cooked fish well on kitchen paper.

2 Sprinkle some of the dill fronds on a serving dish, arrange the fish on top and keep warm. Chop some of the remaining dill fronds and set aside for the garnish.

3 Heat the groundnut oil in a small pan or wok. Stir in the peanuts and cook for 1 minute, then add the spring onions, the remaining dill fronds, basil and coriander. Stir-fry for no more than 30 seconds, then spoon the herbs and peanuts over the fish. Garnish with the chopped dill and serve with lime wedges and nuoc cham to drizzle over the top.

> **Cook's Tip**
> Nuoc cham is a popular Vietnamese condiment and dipping sauce made from dried red chillies, garlic and sugar, mixed with water, fish sauce and lime juice.

Spicy Fish Tagine

This aromatic one-pot dish proves how good fish can be. Serve with couscous, which can be steamed over the cooking pot.

Serves 8

1.3kg/3lb firm fish fillets, skinned and cut into 5cm/2in chunks
60ml/4 tbsp olive oil
1 large aubergine (eggplant), cut into 1cm/½in cubes
2 courgettes (zucchini), cut into 1cm/½in cubes
4 onions, chopped
400g/14oz can chopped tomatoes
400ml/14fl oz/1⅔ cups passata (bottled strained tomatoes)
200ml/7fl oz/scant 1 cup fish stock
1 preserved lemon, chopped
90g/3½oz/scant 1 cup olives
60ml/4 tbsp chopped fresh coriander (cilantro), plus extra whole leaves to garnish
salt and ground black pepper

For the harissa

3 large fresh red chillies, seeded and chopped
3 garlic cloves, peeled
15ml/1 tbsp ground coriander
30ml/2 tbsp ground cumin
5ml/1 tsp ground cinnamon
grated rind of 1 lemon
30ml/2 tbsp sunflower oil or vegetable oil

1 Make the harissa. Blend everything in a food processor to a smooth paste. Put the fish in a wide bowl and add 30ml/2 tbsp of the harissa. Toss to coat, cover and chill for at least 1 hour.

2 Heat half the oil in a heavy pan. Add the aubergine cubes and fry for 10 minutes, or until they are golden brown. Add the courgettes and fry for 2 minutes. Remove the vegetables from the pan using a slotted spoon and set aside.

3 Add the remaining oil to the pan, add the onions and cook gently for about 10 minutes until golden brown. Stir in the remaining harissa and cook for 5 minutes, stirring occasionally.

4 Add the vegetables to the pan, then stir in the tomatoes, the passata and stock. Bring to the boil, then simmer for 20 minutes.

5 Stir the fish chunks and preserved lemon into the pan. Add the olives. Cover and simmer over low heat for 15–20 minutes. Season to taste with salt and pepper. Stir in the coriander. Serve with couscous, if you like, and garnish with coriander leaves.

Vietnamese Fried Fish Energy 350kcal/1458kJ; Protein 27g; Carbohydrate 17g, of which sugars 1g; Fat 19g, of which saturates 3g; Cholesterol 85mg; Calcium 112mg; Fibre 1.2g; Sodium 0.2g.
Spicy Fish Tagine Energy 263kcal/1099kJ; Protein 32.3g; Carbohydrate 8.3g, of which sugars 7g; Fat 11.3g, of which saturates 1.7g; Cholesterol 75mg; Calcium 57mg; Fibre 3.2g; Sodium 360mg.

Burmese Fish Stew

This tasty seafood curry originated in Burma but has also proved enticingly popular farther afield.

Serves 8
675g/1½lb huss, cod or mackerel, cleaned but left on the bone
3 lemon grass stalks
2.5cm/1in piece fresh root ginger
30ml/2 tbsp fish sauce
3 onions, roughly chopped
4 garlic cloves, roughly chopped
2–3 fresh red chillies, seeded and chopped
5ml/1 tsp ground turmeric
75ml/5 tbsp groundnut (peanut) oil, for frying
400g/14oz can coconut milk
25g/1oz/¼ cup rice flour
25g/1oz/¼ cup gram flour
540g/1lb 5oz canned bamboo shoots, rinsed, drained and sliced
salt and ground black pepper
wedges of hard-boiled egg, thinly sliced red onions, chopped spring onions (scallions), deep-fried prawns (shrimp) and fried chillies, to garnish
rice noodles, to serve

1 Place the fish in a large pan and pour in cold water to cover. Bruise two lemon grass stalks and half the ginger and add to the pan. Bring to the boil, add the fish sauce and cook for 10 minutes. Lift out the fish with a slotted spoon, and allow to cool. Meanwhile, strain the stock into a bowl. Discard any skin and bones from the fish and break the flesh into small pieces.

2 Cut off the lower 5cm/2in of the remaining lemon grass stalk and discard; roughly chop the remaining lemon grass. Place in a food processor or blender, along with the remaining ginger, the onions, garlic, chillies and turmeric. Process to a paste. Heat the oil in a wok or large pan, and fry the paste for 2 minutes. Remove the pan from the heat and add the fish pieces.

3 Stir the coconut milk into the reserved stock and pour into a large pan. Add water to make up to 2.5 litres/4 pints/10 cups. In a jug (pitcher), mix the rice flour and gram flour to a thin cream with some stock. Stir into the mixture. Bring to the boil, stirring.

4 Add the bamboo shoots to the pan and cook for 10 minutes. Stir in the fish mixture, season to taste, and cook until heated through. Guests pour the soup over the noodles, and add the egg, onions, spring onions, prawns and chillies as a garnish.

Green Fish Curry

A delicious paste of fresh coriander, tamarind, root ginger, shallots and chilli is used to marinate the fish in this recipe, creating a refreshing taste.

Serves 4
675g/1½lb fillet of cod, haddock or other white fish
2 shallots, roughly chopped
25g/1oz/2 tbsp fresh root ginger, roughly chopped
2–4 fresh green chillies, roughly chopped and seeded
15g/½oz/¼ cup coriander (cilantro) leaves and stalks, roughly chopped
5ml/1 tsp tamarind mixed with 10ml/2 tsp water and strained or 30ml/2 tbsp lemon juice
5ml/1 tsp salt, or to taste
75g/3oz/⅔ cup gram flour, sifted
vegetable oil or sunflower oil, for deep-frying
plain boiled rice, to serve

1 Wash the fish gently under running water and pat dry with absorbent kitchen paper. Cut into 5cm/2in pieces. Place the fish pieces in a large mixing bowl.

2 Process the shallots, ginger, chillies, coriander, tamarind or lemon juice and salt in a food processor or blender. Add the blended ingredients to the fish, and using a metal spoon, mix gently, but thoroughly. Set aside for about 30 minutes.

3 Add the sifted gram flour and 30–45ml/2–3 tbsp water, if necessary, and mix thoroughly until the fish is coated with the paste. You can add a little more water if the paste is not wet enough, to ensure the fish is coated thoroughly.

4 Heat the oil in a wok or other suitable pan for deep-frying over medium to high heat, then fry the fish in batches for about 2½ minutes on each side until it is a golden brown colour. Drain the fried fish on absorbent kitchen paper and serve with any vegetable or lentil dish, accompanied by plain boiled rice.

Variation
Serve these spicy fish pieces with chunky chips (French fries) for a meal of 'fish and chips', Indian style.

Green Fish Curry Energy 357kcal/1490kJ; Protein 35g; Carbohydrate 13.6g, of which sugars 1.6g; Fat 18.3g, of which saturates 2.2g; Cholesterol 81mg; Calcium 55.8mg; Fibre 2.6g; Sodium 116mg.
Burmese Fish Stew Energy 344kcal/1436kJ; Protein 23.3g; Carbohydrate 18.5g, of which sugars 4g; Fat 18.3g, of which saturates 10.8g; Cholesterol 135mg; Calcium 87mg; Fibre 2.5g; Sodium 146mg.

Chicken and Coconut Milk Curry

This is a mild coconut curry flavoured with turmeric, coriander and cumin seeds. Serve with noodles or rice.

Serves 4
60ml/4 tbsp vegetable oil
I large garlic clove, crushed
I chicken, weighing about 1.5kg/
   3–3½lb, chopped into
   12 large pieces
400ml/14fl oz/1⅔ cups
   coconut cream
250ml/8fl oz/1 cup
   chicken stock
30ml/2 tbsp fish sauce
30ml/2 tbsp sugar
juice of 2 limes

To garnish
2 small fresh red chillies, seeded
   and finely chopped
I bunch spring onions (scallions),
   thinly sliced

For the curry paste
5ml/1 tsp dried chilli flakes or
   chopped fresh red chilli
2.5ml/½ tsp salt
5cm/2in piece fresh turmeric
   or 5ml/1 tsp ground
   turmeric
2.5ml/½ tsp coriander seeds
2.5ml/½ tsp cumin seeds
5ml/1 tsp dried shrimp paste

1 First make the curry paste. Blend all the ingredients into a smooth paste using a pestle and mortar, food processor or spice grinder.

2 Heat the oil in a wok or large frying pan and cook the garlic until golden. Add the chicken pieces and brown on all sides. Remove the chicken and set aside.

3 Reheat the oil in the pan and add the curry paste and then half the coconut cream. Cook for a few minutes, stirring occasionally, until fragrant.

4 Return the chicken to the wok or pan, add the stock, mixing well, then add the remaining coconut cream, the fish sauce, sugar and lime juice. Stir well and bring to the boil, then lower the heat and simmer for 15 minutes.

5 Spoon the curry into four warm serving bowls, garnish with the chopped fresh chillies and spring onions. Serve immediately accompanied by noodles or rice, if you like.

Coronation Chicken

Devised for Elizabeth II's coronation in 1953, this salad has been popular ever since.

Serves 8
½ lemon
2.25kg/5lb chicken
I onion, quartered
I carrot, quartered
I large bouquet garni
8 black peppercorns, crushed
salt
watercress sprigs, to garnish

For the sauce
I small onion, chopped
15g/½oz/1 tbsp butter
15ml/1 tbsp curry paste
15ml/1 tbsp tomato purée (paste)
125ml/4fl oz/½ cup red wine
I bay leaf
juice of ½ lemon, or to taste
10–15ml/2–3 tsp apricot jam
300ml/½ pint/1¼ cups mayonnaise
125ml/4fl oz/½ cup
   whipping cream
salt and ground black pepper

1 Put the lemon half in the chicken cavity, then place it in a close-fitting pan. Add the vegetables, bouquet garni, peppercorns and a little salt to the pan.

2 Add water to come two-thirds of the way up the chicken, bring just to the boil, cover and cook very gently for 1½ hours, until the chicken juices run clear. Leave to cool.

3 When the chicken is cool enough to handle, remove all the skin and bones, and chop the flesh into bitesize pieces.

4 To make the sauce, cook the onion in the butter until soft. Add the curry paste, tomato purée, wine, bay leaf and lemon juice, then cook gently for 10 minutes. Stir in the jam, press through a sieve (strainer) and cool.

5 Beat the sauce into the mayonnaise. Whip the cream and fold it in. Add seasoning and lemon juice, then stir in the chicken. Garnish and serve immediately.

> **Cook's Tip**
> A few walnut pieces or slices of celery would add some extra crunch and texture to the dish.

Coronation Chicken Energy 587kcal/2429kJ; Protein 10.1g; Carbohydrate 17.1g, of which sugars 4.7g; Fat 51.6g, of which saturates 8.8g; Cholesterol 228mg; Calcium 97mg; Fibre 1.1g; Sodium 401mg.
Chicken Curry Energy 706kcal/2935kJ; Protein 48.1g; Carbohydrate 15.8g, of which sugars 15.6g; Fat 50.4g, of which saturates 12.8g; Cholesterol 240mg; Calcium 91mg; Fibre 1.5g; Sodium 305mg.

Fragrant Chicken Curry

This dish is perfect for a party as the chicken and sauce can be prepared in advance and combined and heated at the last minute.

Serves 4
45ml/3 tbsp vegetable oil
1 onion, coarsely chopped
2 garlic cloves, crushed
15ml/1 tbsp Thai red curry paste
115g/4oz creamed coconut
   dissolved in 900ml/1½
   pints/3¾ cups boiling water,
   or 1 litre/1¾ pints/4 cups
   coconut milk

2 lemon grass stalks,
   coarsely chopped
6 kaffir lime leaves, chopped
150ml/¼ pint/⅔ cup Greek
   (US strained plain) yogurt
30ml/2 tbsp apricot jam
1 cooked chicken, about
   1.5kg/3–3½lb
30ml/2 tbsp chopped fresh
   coriander (cilantro)
salt and ground black pepper
kaffir lime leaves, shredded,
   toasted shredded coconut and
   fresh coriander (cilantro),
   to garnish
plain boiled rice, to serve

1 Heat the oil in a large pan. Add the onion and garlic and cook over low heat for 5–10 minutes until soft.

2 Stir in the red curry paste. Cook, stirring constantly, for 2–3 minutes. Stir in the diluted creamed coconut or coconut milk, then add the lemon grass, lime leaves, yogurt and apricot jam. Stir well. Cover and simmer for 30 minutes.

3 Remove from the heat and cool slightly. Transfer the sauce to a food processor or blender and process to a purée, then strain it back into the rinsed-out pan, pressing as much of the puréed mixture as possible through the sieve (strainer) with the back of a wooden spoon. Set aside while you prepare the chicken.

4 Remove the skin from the chicken and discard, slice the meat off the bones and cut it into bitesize pieces. Add to the sauce.

5 Bring the curry sauce back to simmering point. Stir in the chopped fresh coriander and season with salt and black pepper. Garnish with extra lime leaves, toasted shredded coconut and coriander. Serve immediately with rice, sprinkled with coriander leaves and black pepper.

Thai Chicken Curry

This is a flavourful and fragrant Thai curry with a lovely creamy taste thanks to the coconut milk. It is quite easy to make so will be ideal for a quick midweek meal for the whole family.

Serves 6
400ml/14oz can coconut milk
6 skinless chicken breast fillets,
   finely sliced
225g/8oz can bamboo shoots,
   drained and sliced
30ml/2 tbsp Thai fish sauce
15ml/1 tbsp soft light
   brown sugar
cooked jasmine rice, to serve

For the green curry paste
4 fresh green chillies, seeded
1 lemon grass stalk, sliced
1 small onion, sliced
3 garlic cloves
1cm/½in piece galangal or
   fresh root ginger, peeled
grated rind of ½ lime
5ml/1 tsp coriander seeds
5ml/1 tsp cumin seeds
2.5ml/½ tsp Thai fish sauce

To garnish
1 fresh red chilli, seeded and
   cut into fine strips
finely pared rind of ½ lime,
   finely shredded
fresh Thai purple basil or
   coriander (cilantro), chopped

1 First make the green curry paste: put all the ingredients in a food processor or blender and process to a thick paste. Set aside while you prepare the rest of the dish.

2 Bring half the coconut milk to the boil in a wok or large frying pan, then reduce the heat and simmer gently for about 5 minutes, or until reduced by half. Stir in the green curry paste and simmer for a further 5 minutes.

3 Add the finely sliced chicken breast fillets to the pan with the remaining coconut milk, bamboo shoots, fish sauce and sugar. Stir well to combine all the ingredients and bring the curry back to simmering point, then simmer gently for about 10 minutes, or until the chicken slices are cooked through. The mixture will look grainy or curdled during cooking but this is quite normal and is nothing to worry about.

4 Spoon the curry and rice into warmed bowls, garnish with the chilli, lime rind, and basil or coriander, and serve.

Fragrant Chicken Energy 837kcal/3472kJ; Protein 50.2g; Carbohydrate 14.2g, of which sugars 13.7g; Fat 64.6g, of which saturates 29.2g; Cholesterol 253mg; Calcium 85mg; Fibre 0.3g; Sodium 240mg.
Thai Chicken Energy 236kcal/991kJ; Protein 33.8g; Carbohydrate 7.2g, of which sugars 5.9g; Fat 8.3g, of which saturates 1.6g; Cholesterol 165mg; Calcium 149mg; Fibre 3.1g; Sodium 253mg.

Curried Apricot and Chicken Casserole

A mildly spiced and fruity chicken dish, slowly baked in the oven and served with almond rice.

Serves 4
15ml/1 tbsp vegetable oil
8 large chicken thighs, skinned and boned
1 onion, finely chopped
5ml/1 tsp medium curry powder
30ml/2 tbsp plain (all-purpose) flour
450ml/¾ pint/scant 2 cups hot chicken stock
juice of 1 large orange
8 ready-to-eat dried apricots, halved
15ml/1 tbsp sultanas (golden raisins)
salt and ground black pepper

For the almond rice
225g/8oz/1 cup cooked rice
15g/½oz/1 tbsp butter
50g/2oz/½ cup toasted almonds

1 Preheat the oven to 190°C/375°F/Gas 5. Heat the oil in a large frying pan. Cut the chicken into cubes and brown quickly all over in the oil. Add the onion to the pan and cook gently until soft and lightly browned.

2 Transfer to a large, flameproof casserole, sprinkle in the curry powder and cook again for a few minutes. Add the flour, and blend in the stock and orange juice. Bring to the boil and season with salt and black pepper.

3 Add the apricots and sultanas to the pan, cover with a tight-fitting lid and cook in the oven for 1 hour, or until tender. Adjust the seasoning to taste.

4 To make the almond rice, reheat the pre-cooked rice thoroughly with the butter and season to taste. Stir in the toasted almonds. Serve immediately alongside the chicken.

Variation
This recipe is also works well with chicken breast fillets or with diced turkey breast fillets or other boneless turkey meat. Replace the chicken thigh meat with the same amount of an alternative meat of your choice, if you like.

Chicken Coconut Stew

In this recipe, chicken on the bone is cooked in a sumptuous, rich coconut broth. In south-west India, it is served with 'appam', a plain rice flour pancake, but it is also good with plain boiled basmati rice, which soaks up the tangy, green chilli-infused sauce.

Serves 4
675g/1½lb chicken leg or breast joints on the bone
60ml/4 tbsp sunflower oil or olive oil
2.5cm/1in piece of cinnamon stick
6 cardamom pods, bruised
4 cloves
12–15 curry leaves
1 large onion, finely chopped
10ml/2 tsp ginger purée
10ml/2 tsp garlic purée
2 green chillies, sliced at an angle
2.5ml/½ tsp ground turmeric
400g/14fl oz/1½ cups canned coconut milk
5ml/1 tsp salt, or to taste
500g/1¼lb medium potatoes
175g/6oz/1½ cups frozen garden peas
plain boiled basmati rice, to serve

1 Skin the chicken joints, and cut each one into two pieces, then set them aside.

2 Heat the oil in a large pan over a low heat and add the cinnamon, cardamom pods, cloves and curry leaves. Sauté these for 25–30 seconds and add the onion. Increase the heat to medium and fry until the onion is soft, about 5–6 minutes, then add the ginger, garlic and chillies and cook for 2–3 minutes longer to allow the flavours to blend.

3 Add the turmeric, stir well, then add the chicken. Increase the heat from medium to high and stir until the chicken browns. Pour in the coconut milk and add the salt, stir and mix well. Reduce the heat to low, cover and simmer for 15–20 minutes.

4 Halve the potatoes, add to the stew and pour in 250ml/8fl oz/1 cup warm water. Bring to the boil, reduce the heat to low, then cover and cook for an additional 20 minutes, or until the chicken is cooked and the potatoes are tender.

5 Add the peas, cook for 5 minutes longer and remove from the heat. Serve with plain boiled basmati rice.

Chicken Casserole Energy 500kcal/2105kJ; Protein 54.1g; Carbohydrate 37g, of which sugars 13.2g; Fat 16g, of which saturates 3.6g; Cholesterol 148mg; Calcium 86mg; Fibre 3.1g; Sodium 150mg.
Chicken Coconut Stew Energy 552kcal/2309kJ; Protein 40g; Carbohydrate 43.6g, of which sugars 16g; Fat 25.5g, of which saturates 6.9g; Cholesterol 192.5mg; Calcium 104.5mg; Fibre 5.4g; Sodium 271mg.

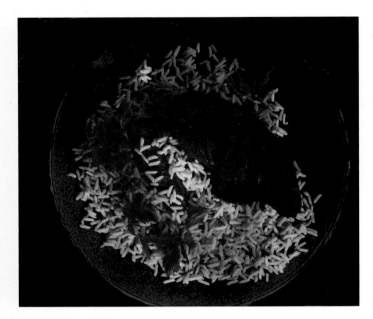

Chicken in a Spicy Marinade

The flavour of this dish will be more intense if the chicken is marinated overnight. Poussin portions will need less cooking time than chicken quarters.

Serves 4

1.5kg/3–3½lb chicken or 2 poussins
4 garlic cloves, crushed
2 lemon grass stems, lower
  5cm/2in sliced
1cm/½in fresh lengkuas or fresh
  root ginger, peeled and sliced
5ml/1 tsp ground turmeric
475ml/16fl oz/2 cups water
3–4 bay leaves
45ml/3 tbsp each dark and light
  soy sauce
50g/2oz butter or margarine
salt
celery leaves, to garnish
plain boiled rice or noodles,
  to serve

1 Cut the chicken into four or eight portions. Halve the poussins or quarter them, if you are serving this as part of a buffet. Slash the fleshy part of each portion twice and set aside.

2 Grind the garlic, sliced lemon grass, lengkuas or root ginger, turmeric and salt together into a paste in a food processor or with a mortar and pestle. Rub the paste into the chicken pieces and leave for at least 30 minutes. Wear rubber gloves for this, if you like, as the turmeric will stain your hands heavily; or wash your hands immediately after mixing, if you prefer.

3 Transfer the chicken or poussin pieces to a wok and pour in the water. Add the bay leaves and bring to the boil. Cover and cook gently for 30 minutes, adding a little more water if necessary. Stir from time to time.

4 Add the two soy sauces to the pan together with the butter or margarine. Stir well to combine the ingredients.

5 Cook until the chicken or poussin is well-coated and the sauce has almost been absorbed. Transfer the chicken or poussin pieces to a preheated grill (broiler) or barbecue, or an oven preheated to 200°C/400°F/Gas 6, to finish cooking. Cook for a further 10–15 minutes, turning the pieces often so they become golden brown all over. Baste with the remaining sauce while cooking. Garnish with celery leaves. Serve with rice.

Chicken with Aromatic Spices

With the inclusion of nutmeg and cloves, this dish combines both taste and aroma. It is best cooked a day or two in advance to allow the flavours to mellow and permeate the flesh of the chicken.

Serves 4

1.3–1.6kg/3–3½lb chicken,
  cut into quarters, or
  4 chicken quarters
5ml/1 tsp sugar
30ml/2 tbsp coriander seeds
10ml/2 tsp cumin seeds
6 whole cloves
2.5ml/½ tsp grated nutmeg
2.5ml/½ tsp ground turmeric
1 small onion
2.5cm/1in piece fresh root ginger,
  thinly sliced
300ml/½ pint/1¼ cups chicken
  stock or water
salt and ground black pepper
deep-fried onions, to garnish
plain boiled basmati rice,
  to serve

1 Cut each chicken quarter in half to make eight pieces. Place the pieces in a flameproof casserole, sprinkle with the sugar and season to taste with salt and pepper. Toss the chicken pieces and seasoning together. Use the chicken backbone and any remaining carcass, if using, to make a fresh chicken stock for use later in the recipe, if you like.

2 In a preheated wok or large pan, dry-fry the coriander and cumin seeds and the whole cloves until the spices give off a good aroma. Add the nutmeg and turmeric and heat briefly. Remove and cool. Grind in a spice grinder or food processor or with a mortar and pestle.

3 In a food processor, process the onion and ginger until finely chopped. Otherwise, finely chop the onion and ginger and pound to a paste with a mortar and pestle. Add the spices and stock or water and mix well.

4 Pour the spice mixture over the chicken in the flameproof casserole, and stir well. Cover the casserole and cook over a low heat for 45–50 minutes until the chicken pieces are tender.

5 Serve the chicken with the sauce on plain boiled basmati rice, sprinkled with crisp deep-fried onions.

Chicken in a Marinade Energy 634kcal/2642kJ; Protein 65g; Carbohydrate 8.3g, of which sugars 3.6g; Fat 38.3g, of which saturates 5.8g; Cholesterol 302mg; Calcium 210mg; Fibre 4.4g; Sodium 320mg.
Chicken with Spices Energy 604kcal/2514kJ; Protein 55.7g; Carbohydrate 4.1g, of which sugars 2.2g; Fat 40.6g, of which saturates 10.8g; Cholesterol 330mg; Calcium 66mg; Fibre 1.7g; Sodium 269mg.

Ethiopian Curried Chicken

The long-simmered stews eaten in Ethiopia are known as wats. This delectable curry is made in a slow cooker to replicate the traditional techniques used in making wats.

Serves 4
30ml/2 tbsp vegetable oil
2 large onions, chopped
3 garlic cloves, chopped
2.5cm/1in piece peeled and finely chopped fresh root ginger
175ml/6fl oz/¾ cup chicken or vegetable stock
250ml/8fl oz/1 cup passata (bottled strained tomatoes)
or 400g/14oz can chopped tomatoes
seeds from 5 cardamom pods
2.5ml/½ tsp ground turmeric
large pinch of ground cinnamon
large pinch of ground cloves
large pinch of grated nutmeg
1.3kg/3lb chicken, cut into 8–12 portions
4 hard-boiled eggs
cayenne pepper or hot paprika, to taste
salt and ground black pepper
roughly chopped fresh coriander (cilantro) and onion rings, to garnish
flatbread or rice, to serve

1 Heat the oil in a large pan, add the onions and cook for 10 minutes until softened. Add the garlic and ginger to the pan and cook for about 1–2 minutes.

2 Add the stock and the passata or chopped tomatoes to the pan. Bring to the boil and cook, stirring frequently, for about 10 minutes, or until the mixture has thickened, then season.

3 Transfer the mixture to the ceramic cooking pot and stir in the cardamom, turmeric, cinnamon, cloves and nutmeg. Add the chicken in a single layer, pushing the pieces well down so that they are covered by the sauce. Cover the slow cooker with the lid and cook on high for 3 hours.

4 Remove the shells from the eggs, then prick the eggs a few times with a fork or very fine skewer. Add to the sauce and cook for 30–45 minutes, or until the chicken is cooked through and tender. Season to taste with cayenne pepper or hot paprika. Garnish with the fresh coriander and onion rings and serve immediately with flatbread or rice.

Spicy Chicken in Cashew Nut Sauce

This mildly spiced, slow-cooker dish has a rich yet delicately flavoured sauce.

Serves 4
1 large onion, roughly chopped
1 garlic clove, crushed
15ml/1 tbsp tomato purée (paste)
50g/2oz/½ cup cashew nuts
7.5ml/1½ tsp garam masala
5ml/1 tsp chilli powder
1.5ml/¼ tsp ground turmeric
5ml/1 tsp salt
15ml/1 tbsp lemon juice
15ml/1 tbsp natural (plain) yogurt
30ml/2 tbsp vegetable oil
450g/1lb chicken breast fillets, skinned and cubed
175g/6oz/2¼ cups button (white) mushrooms
15ml/1 tbsp sultanas (golden raisins)
300ml/½ pint/1¼ cups chicken or vegetable stock
30ml/2 tbsp chopped fresh coriander (cilantro), plus extra to garnish
rice and fruit chutney, to serve

1 Put the onion, garlic, tomato purée, cashew nuts, garam masala, chilli powder, turmeric, salt, lemon juice and yogurt in a food processor and process to a paste.

2 Heat the oil in a large frying pan or wok and fry the cubes of chicken for a few minutes, or until just beginning to brown. Using a slotted spoon, transfer the chicken to the ceramic cooking pot, leaving the oil in the pan.

3 Add the spice paste and mushrooms to the pan, lower the heat and fry gently, stirring frequently, for 3–4 minutes. Transfer the mixture to the ceramic pot.

4 Add the sultanas to the pot and stir in the chicken or vegetable stock. Cover with the lid and switch the slow cooker to high. Cook for 3–4 hours, stirring halfway through the cooking time. The chicken should be cooked through and very tender, and the sauce fairly thick.

5 Stir the chopped coriander into the sauce, then taste and add a little more salt and pepper, if necessary. Serve the curry from the ceramic cooking pot or transfer to a warmed serving dish and garnish with a sprinkling of chopped fresh coriander. Serve with rice and a fruit chutney, such as mango.

Ethiopian Chicken Energy 388kcal/1629kJ; Protein 54.6g; Carbohydrate 13g, of which sugars 9.6g; Fat 13.4g, of which saturates 2.8g; Cholesterol 13mg; Calcium 81mg; Fibre 2.5g; Sodium 311mg.
Chicken in Cashew Sauce Energy 239kcal/1006kJ; Protein 31.6g; Carbohydrate 10.7g, of which sugars 7.6g; Fat 8.1g, of which saturates 1.7g; Cholesterol 78.9mg; Calcium 39mg; Fibre 1.9g; Sodium 696mg.

Curried Chicken with Shallots

This richly spiced dish makes a delectable main course for a light summer dinner.

Serves 4

675g/1½lb skinned chicken thigh or breast fillets, cut into 5cm/2in cubes
juice of ½ lemon
5ml/1 tsp salt or to taste
60ml/4 tbsp sunflower oil
2 medium onions, finely chopped
15ml/1 tbsp ginger purée
15ml/1 tbsp garlic purée
7.5ml/1½ tsp ground coriander
5ml/1 tsp ground cumin
5ml/1 tsp ground turmeric
2.5–5ml/½–1 tsp chilli powder
225g/8oz canned chopped tomatoes, with their juice
15ml/1 tbsp ghee
8–10 small whole shallots
2.5–5ml/½–1 tsp garam masala
15ml/1 tbsp chopped fresh mint or 5ml/1 tsp dried mint
4–5 whole green chillies
10ml/2 tbsp chopped fresh coriander (cilantro) leaves
naan bread and a vegetable side dish, to serve

1 Put the chicken in a bowl and add the lemon juice and salt. Mix thoroughly, cover and set aside in a cool place for 30 minutes.

2 In a medium-sized pan, preferably non-stick, heat the oil and sauté the onions, ginger and garlic over a medium heat for 7–8 minutes. Add the coriander, cumin, turmeric and chilli powder and cook gently for about one minute, then add the tomatoes. Cook, stirring regularly, until the tomatoes reach a paste-like consistency and the oil separates from the paste.

3 Increase the heat to high and add the chicken. Cook, stirring constantly, for 4–5 minutes. Pour in 250ml/8fl oz/1 cup warm water, bring it to the boil and reduce the heat to low. Cover and cook for 15–20 minutes, stirring occasionally for even flavour.

4 In a separate pan, heat the ghee over a medium heat. Add the shallots and stir-fry until lightly browned, then stir in the garam masala. Add this mixture to the chicken and stir over a medium heat until the sauce has thickened.

5 Add the mint, chillies and chopped coriander. Stir them in and cook for 1–2 minutes longer. Serve with naan bread and a vegetable side dish.

Spiced Cambodian Chicken Curry

Many recipes for Cambodian chicken or seafood curries exist, but they all use Indian curry powder and coconut milk in their sauces.

Serves 4

45ml/3 tbsp Indian curry powder or garam masala
15ml/1 tbsp ground turmeric
500g/1¼lb skinless chicken thighs or chicken portions
25ml/1½ tbsp raw cane sugar
30ml/2 tbsp sesame oil
2 shallots, chopped
2 garlic cloves, chopped
4cm/1½in galangal, peeled and chopped
2 lemon grass stalks, chopped
10ml/2 tsp chilli paste or dried chilli flakes
2 medium sweet potatoes, peeled and cubed
45ml/3 tbsp nuoc cham (Vietnamese fish sauce)
600ml/1 pint/2½ cups coconut milk
1 small bunch each fresh basil and coriander (cilantro), stalks removed
salt and ground black pepper

1 In a small bowl, mix together the curry powder or garam masala and the turmeric. Put the chicken in a bowl and coat with half of the spice. Set aside.

2 To make the caramel sauce, heat the sugar in a small pan with 7.5ml/1½ tsp water, until the sugar dissolves and the syrup turns golden. Remove from the heat and set aside.

3 Heat a wok or heavy pan and add the oil. Stir-fry the shallots, garlic, galangal and lemon grass.

4 Stir in the rest of the turmeric and curry powder or garam masala with the chilli paste or flakes, followed by the chicken, and cook for 2–3 minutes, stirring frequently.

5 Add the sweet potatoes, then the nuoc mam, caramel sauce, coconut milk and 150ml/¼ pint/⅔ cup water, mixing thoroughly to combine the flavours. Bring to the boil, reduce the heat and cook for about 15 minutes until the chicken is cooked through.

6 Season and stir in half the basil and coriander. Garnish with the remaining herbs and serve immediately.

Curried Chicken Energy 401kcal/1678kJ; Protein 42.6g; Carbohydrate 18.2g, of which sugars 10.6g; Fat 18.3g, of which saturates 3.3g; Cholesterol 75mg; Calcium 99mg; Fibre 3.7g; Sodium 143mg.
Cambodian Curry Energy 387kcal/1632kJ; Protein 31g; Carbohydrate 38g, of which sugars 19g; Fat 14g, of which saturates 3g; Cholesterol 131mg; Calcium 1.8mg; Fibre 1g; Sodium 1000mg.

Malay Clay-pot Chicken

This dish is cooked in a low oven where the gentle heat is evenly distributed and retained by a clay pot, resulting in very tender meat.

Serves 4–6
1 × 1.3–1.6kg/3–3½lb chicken, oven-ready
45ml/3 tbsp grated fresh coconut
30ml/2 tbsp vegetable oil
2 shallots or 1 small onion, finely chopped
2 garlic cloves, crushed
5cm/2in piece lemon grass
2.5cm/1in piece fresh galangal or fresh root ginger, thinly sliced
2 fresh green chillies, seeded and chopped
12mm/½in cube shrimp paste
400g/14oz can coconut milk
300ml/½ pint/1¼ cups hot chicken stock
2 kaffir lime leaves (optional)
15ml/1 tbsp sugar
15ml/1 tbsp rice or wine vinegar
2 ripe tomatoes
30ml/2 tbsp chopped fresh coriander (cilantro) leaves, to garnish

1 To joint the chicken, remove the legs and wings with a sharp knife. Skin the pieces, divide the drumsticks from the thighs and, using kitchen scissors, remove the lower part of the chicken, leaving only the breast piece. Remove as many of the bones as you can. Cut the breast into four or six pieces and set aside.

2 Dry-fry the coconut in a large wok until evenly browned. Add the oil, shallots or onion, garlic, lemon grass, galangal or ginger, chillies and shrimp paste. Fry for 2–4 minutes to release the flavours. Preheat the oven to 180°C/350°F/Gas 4. Add the chicken to the wok and brown with the spices for 2–3 minutes.

3 Strain the coconut milk, and add the thin part with the chicken stock, lime leaves, if using, sugar and vinegar. Transfer to a glazed clay pot, cover and bake in the centre of the oven for 50 minutes, or until the chicken is tender. Stir in the thick part of the coconut milk and return to the oven for 5–10 minutes.

4 Place the tomatoes in a bowl and cover with boiling water to loosen and remove the skins. Halve the tomatoes, then remove the seeds and chop into large dice. Add the tomatoes to the finished dish, sprinkle with the chopped coriander and serve. Plain rice would make a good accompaniment.

Chicken with Spices and Soy Sauce

This simple but delicious curry is an example of Nonya cuisine – the food of the Chinese Malaysians.

Serves 4
1.3–1.6kg/3–3½lb chicken, jointed and cut into 16 pieces
3 onions, sliced
about 1 litre/1¾ pints/4 cups water
3 garlic cloves, crushed
3–4 fresh chillies, seeded and sliced, or 15ml/1 tbsp chilli powder
45ml/3 tbsp vegetable oil
2.5ml/½ tsp grated nutmeg
6 cloves
5ml/1 tsp tamarind pulp, soaked in 45ml/3 tbsp warm water
30–45ml/2–3 tbsp dark or light soy sauce
salt
fresh green and red chillies, shredded, to garnish
plain boiled or steamed basmati rice, to serve

1 Place the chicken pieces in a large pan with one of the sliced onions. Pour over enough water to just cover. Bring to the boil and then reduce the heat and simmer gently for 20 minutes.

2 Grind the remaining onions, with the garlic and chillies or chilli powder, to a fine paste in a food processor or with a mortar and pestle. Heat a little of the oil in a wok or frying pan and cook the paste to bring out the flavour. Stir frequently so that the paste does not brown.

3 When the chicken has cooked for 20 minutes, lift it out of the stock and into the spicy mixture. Toss everything together over a fairly high heat so that the spices permeate the chicken pieces. Reserve 300ml/½ pint/1¼ cups of the chicken stock to add to the pan later.

4 Stir in the nutmeg and cloves. Strain the tamarind, discarding the pulp, and add the tamarind juice and soy sauce to the chicken. Cook for a further 2–3 minutes, then add the reserved stock.

5 Taste and adjust the seasoning and cook, uncovered, for a further 25–35 minutes, or until the chicken pieces are tender.

6 Transfer the chicken to a bowl, top with shredded green and red chillies, and serve with rice.

Malay Clay-pot Chicken Energy 372kcal/1560kJ; Protein 36.2g; Carbohydrate 46.8g, of which sugars 1g; Fat 4g, of which saturates 1.2g; Cholesterol 93mg; Calcium 54mg; Fibre 0.7g; Sodium 721mg.
Chicken with Spices Energy 630kcal/2615kJ; Protein 48.8g; Carbohydrate 13.8g, of which sugars 10.7g; Fat 42.5g, of which saturates 10.6g; Cholesterol 248mg; Calcium 52mg; Fibre 2.6g; Sodium 798mg.

Indian Stuffed Chicken

At one time this dish was cooked only in royal palaces and the ingredients varied according to individual chefs. The saffron and the rich stuffing make it a truly royal dish.

Serves 4–6
1 sachet saffron powder
2.5ml/½ tsp grated nutmeg
15ml/1 tbsp warm milk
1.3kg/3lb whole chicken
75g/3oz/6 tbsp ghee
75ml/5 tbsp hot water

For the stuffing
3 medium onions, finely chopped
2 fresh green chillies, chopped
50g/2oz/⅓ cup sultanas
  (golden raisins)
50g/2oz/½ cup ground almonds
50g/2oz ready-to-eat dried
  apricots, soaked until soft
3 hard-boiled eggs, peeled and
  coarsely chopped
salt

For the masala
4 spring onions (scallions),
  finely chopped
2 garlic cloves, crushed
5ml/1 tsp Chinese
  five-spice powder
4–6 green cardamom pods
2.5ml/½ tsp turmeric
5ml/1 tsp ground black pepper
30ml/2 tbsp natural
  (plain) yogurt
50g/2oz/1 cup desiccated (dry
  unsweetened shredded)
  coconut, toasted

1 Mix together the saffron, nutmeg and milk. Use to brush the inside of the chicken and over the skin. Heat 50g/2oz/4 tbsp of the ghee in a large frying pan and fry the chicken on all sides to seal it. Remove and keep warm.

2 To make the stuffing, in the same ghee, fry the onions, chillies and sultanas for 2–3 minutes. Allow to cool and add the ground almonds, apricots, chopped eggs and salt. Use to stuff the chicken.

3 Heat the remaining ghee in a large, heavy pan and gently fry all the masala ingredients except the coconut for 2–3 minutes. Add the water. Place the chicken on the bed of masala, cover the pan and cook until the chicken is tender.

4 Remove the chicken from the pan. Cook the liquid to reduce excess fluids in the masala. When the mixture thickens, pour over the chicken. Sprinkle with toasted coconut and serve hot.

Chicken and Sweet Potato Curry

Lemon grass, garlic and sweet potatoes give this South-east Asian curry a wonderful aromatic flavour.

Serves 4
1 chicken, about 1.3–1.6kg/
  3–3½lb
225g/8oz sweet potatoes
60ml/4 tbsp vegetable oil
1 onion, finely sliced
3 garlic cloves, crushed
30–45ml/2–3 tbsp Thai
  curry powder
5ml/1 tsp sugar
10ml/2 tsp Thai fish sauce
600ml/1 pint/2½ cups
  coconut milk
1 lemon grass stalk, cut in half
350g/12oz rice vermicelli, soaked
  in hot water until soft
salt
1 lemon, cut into wedges,
  to serve

For the garnish
115g/4oz beansprouts
2 spring onions (scallions), finely
  sliced diagonally
2 red chillies, seeded and
  finely sliced
8–10 mint leaves

1 Skin the chicken. Cut the flesh into small pieces and set aside. Peel the sweet potatoes and cut them into large chunks, about the same size as the chicken pieces.

2 Heat half the oil in a large heavy pan. Add the onion and garlic and fry until the onion softens.

3 Add the chicken pieces to the pan and stir-fry until they change colour. Stir in the curry powder. Season with salt and sugar and mix thoroughly, then stir in the fish sauce. Pour in the coconut milk and add the lemon grass. Stir well and cook over low heat for about 15 minutes.

4 Meanwhile, heat the remaining oil in a large frying pan. Fry the sweet potatoes until lightly golden. Using a slotted spoon, add them to the chicken. Cook for 10–15 minutes more, or until both the chicken and sweet potatoes are tender.

5 Drain the rice vermicelli and cook it in a pan of boiling water for 3–5 minutes. Drain well. Place in shallow bowls, with the chicken curry. Garnish with beansprouts, spring onions, chillies and mint leaves and serve with lemon wedges.

Indian Stuffed Chicken Energy 658kcal/2727kJ; Protein 34.1g; Carbohydrate 17.9g, of which sugars 14.9g; Fat 50.5g, of which saturates 19.2g; Cholesterol 234mg; Calcium 95mg; Fibre 3.7g; Sodium 158mg.
Chicken Curry Energy 763kcal/3199kJ; Protein 51.6g; Carbohydrate 92g, of which sugars 11.6g; Fat 21.3g, of which saturates 4.1g; Cholesterol 109mg; Calcium 170mg; Fibre 4g; Sodium 545mg.

Savoury Chicken Korma

There are many types of korma, and contrary to popular belief, a korma is not an actual dish, but a technique that is used in Indian cooking.

Serves 4

675g/1½lb boned chicken thighs or breast fillets, skinned and cut into 5cm/2in pieces
75g/3oz/⅓ cup whole milk natural (plain) yogurt
10ml/2 tsp gram flour
5ml/1 tsp salt
10ml/2 tsp crushed fresh root ginger
10ml/2 tsp crushed garlic
60ml/4 tbsp ghee or unsalted butter
2.5cm/1in piece of cinnamon stick
1 large onion, finely sliced
2.5ml/½ tsp ground turmeric
15ml/1 tbsp ground coriander
2.5ml/½ tsp chilli powder, or to taste
50g/2oz/½ cup raw unsalted cashew nuts, soaked in boiling water for about 15 minutes
150ml/¼ pint/⅔ cup double (heavy) cream
2.5ml/½ tsp ground cardamom
2.5ml/½ tsp ground mace

1 Put the chicken in a large mixing bowl. Beat the yogurt and the gram flour together and add to the chicken. Add the salt, ginger and garlic, and mix thoroughly. Cover and leave in the dish to marinate for about an hour or so.

2 Heat the ghee or butter in a heavy pan over medium heat and add the cinnamon, followed by the onion. Stir-fry for 5–6 minutes until the onion is soft and translucent.

3 Add the turmeric, coriander and chilli powder, stir-fry for 1 minute, then place the marinated chicken into the pan.

4 Increase the heat slightly and stir-fry the ingredients for about 3–4 minutes until the chicken changes colour. Pour in 300ml/ ½ pint/1¼ cups warm water, bring it to the boil, reduce the heat to low, cover and simmer for 15 minutes.

5 Drain the cashew nuts and purée them in a food processor or blender with the cream. Add to the chicken and simmer for 2–3 minutes. Stir in the ground cardamom and mace, remove from the heat and serve.

Chicken in Golden Saffron Sauce

Saffron is said to be worth its weight in gold, and its characteristic bouquet adds a unique aroma and flavour to this succulent dish.

Serves 4

50g/2oz blanched almonds
675g/1½lb skinless, boneless chicken thighs or breast fillets, cut into 5cm/2in cubes
10ml/2 tsp crushed garlic
10ml/2 tsp crushed fresh root ginger
5ml/1 tsp ground cumin
7.5ml/1½ tsp ground coriander
2.5–5ml/½–1 tsp crushed dried chillies
1 large onion, finely chopped
75g/3oz/⅓ cup natural (plain) yogurt
10ml/2 tsp gram flour
4 cloves
4 green cardamom pods, split at the top of each pod
2.5cm/1in piece of cinnamon stick
25g/1oz ghee or unsalted butter
300ml/½ pint/1¼ cups full cream (whole) milk
2.5ml/½ tsp saffron strands, pounded and soaked in 15ml/ 1 tbsp hot milk
2.5ml/½ tsp garam masala
1–2 fresh green chillies, seeded and cut into julienne strips, to garnish
naan bread, to serve

1 Soak the almonds in 150ml/¼ pint/⅔ cup boiling water for 20 minutes. Put the chicken, garlic, ginger, cumin, coriander, crushed chillies and onion in a heavy pan. Beat the yogurt and gram flour together and add to the pan. Add the cloves, cardamom pods and cinnamon, and place the pan over medium heat. Stir until the contents sizzle. Reduce the heat to low, cover the pan with a lid and cook for 20–25 minutes.

2 Remove the lid and increase the heat to high. Cook until the liquid is reduced to a thick batter-like consistency, stirring frequently. Add the ghee or butter and stir-fry the chicken for another 3–4 minutes until the fat rises to the surface.

3 Purée the almonds with the soaking water and add to the pan. Stir in the milk, the saffron and the soaking milk. Bring it to the boil. Reduce the heat and simmer for 5–6 minutes.

4 Stir in the garam masala. Transfer to a serving dish and garnish with the green chilli. Serve immediately with naan bread.

Savoury Korma Energy 343kcal/1450kJ; Protein 54g; Carbohydrate 18g, of which sugars 10.7g; Fat 6.8g, of which saturates 2.6g; Cholesterol 151mg; Calcium 66mg; Fibre 1.8g; Sodium 197mg.
Chicken in Saffron Energy 554kcal/2321kJ; Protein 75.6g; Carbohydrate 5.1g, of which sugars 4.7g; Fat 25.9g, of which saturates 12.2g; Cholesterol 255mg; Calcium 146mg; Fibre 0.8g; Sodium 792mg.

Creamy Chicken Korma

This chicken korma recipe calls for creamy coconut milk and chilli. Subtle flavours are added with a little nutmeg and mace.

Serves 4
50g/2oz/½ cup raw cashew nuts
200g/7oz/¾ cup thick set natural (plain) yogurt
10ml/2 tsp gram flour
10ml/2 tsp crushed fresh root ginger
10ml/2 tsp crushed garlic
2.5ml/½ tsp ground turmeric
2.5–5ml/½–1 tsp chilli powder
5ml/1 tsp salt, or to taste

675g/1½lb skinless chicken breast fillets, cut into 5cm/2in cubes
75g/3oz/6 tbsp ghee or unsalted butter
2.5cm/1in piece of cinnamon stick
6 green cardamom pods, bruised
6 cloves
2 bay leaves
1 large onion, finely chopped
15ml/1 tbsp sesame seeds, finely ground
200ml/7fl oz/¾ cup canned coconut milk
1.5ml/¼ tsp freshly grated nutmeg
1.5ml/¼ tsp ground mace
Indian bread or boiled basmati rice, to serve

1 Soak the cashew nuts in 150ml/¼ pint/⅔ cup boiling water for 20 minutes. Whisk the yogurt and gram flour together until smooth. Add the ginger, garlic, turmeric, chilli powder and salt. Mix well and stir into the chicken. Set aside for 30–35 minutes.

2 Reserve 5ml/1 tsp of ghee or butter and melt the remainder in a medium pan over a low heat. Add the cinnamon, cardamom, cloves and bay leaves. Stir-fry for 3–4 minutes.

3 Increase the heat and fry the onion until translucent. Stir in the ground sesame seeds and the chicken. Cook for 5 minutes. Add the coconut milk and 150ml/¼ pint/⅔ cup warm water. Bring to the boil, reduce the heat, cover and simmer for 20 minutes.

4 Meanwhile, purée the cashews with the water in which they were soaked and add to the chicken. Simmer, uncovered, for 5–6 minutes until the sauce thickens.

5 Melt the reserved ghee or butter in a pan over low heat. Add the nutmeg and mace, then cook gently for 30 seconds. Stir the spiced butter into the chicken. Serve with rice or bread.

Classic Chicken Curry

This recipe uses plenty of curry powder to give it a real bite. It is best served with plain boiled rice to moderate the spicy flavours.

Serves 4
675g/1½lb chicken leg or breast joint pieces on the bone
2.5ml/½ tsp ground turmeric
15ml/1 tbsp plain (all-purpose) flour
5ml/1 tsp salt, or to taste
1 large onion, roughly chopped

2.5cm/1in piece of fresh root ginger, roughly chopped
4–5 garlic cloves, roughly chopped
60ml/4 tbsp sunflower oil or olive oil
25ml/1½ tbsp curry powder
2.5ml/½ tsp chilli powder (optional)
175g/6oz fresh tomatoes, peeled and chopped
30ml/2 tbsp chopped fresh coriander (cilantro)
plain boiled or steamed basmati rice, to serve

1 Skin the chicken and separate the legs from the thighs. If you are using breast meat, cut each one into three pieces. Mix the turmeric, flour and salt together and rub this mixture into the chicken. Set aside the chicken in a cool place to marinate while you prepare the other flavourings.

2 Put the onion, ginger and garlic in a food processor to make a purée; alternatively, you can pound them together into a paste using a mortar and pestle.

3 Heat the sunflower or olive oil in a medium pan and add the puréed ingredients. Cook over medium heat for about 8–10 minutes, stirring regularly so that the paste does not burn.

4 Add the curry powder and chilli powder, if using, and cook for 2–3 minutes. Add about 30ml/2 tbsp water and continue to cook for a further 2–3 minutes.

5 Add the chicken, increase the heat to medium-high and stir until the chicken begins to brown. Add 425ml/15fl oz/1¾ cups warm water, bring it to the boil, cover and reduce the heat to low. Cook for another 35–40 minutes and add the tomatoes. Cook for 2–3 minutes longer, stir in the chopped coriander and remove from the heat. Serve with rice.

Creamy Korma Energy 398kcal/1671kJ; Protein 46.4g; Carbohydrate 19.1g, of which sugars 12.5g; Fat 16g, of which saturates 3.8g; Cholesterol 76mg; Calcium 195mg; Fibre 2.1g; Sodium 265mg.
Classic Curry Energy 392kcal/1632kJ; Protein 24.3g; Carbohydrate 12.5g, of which sugars 7.3g; Fat 27.6g, of which saturates 5.8g; Cholesterol 135mg; Calcium 67mg; Fibre 2.6g; Sodium 108mg.

82

Goan Chicken Curry

Coconut in all its forms is widely used to enrich Goan cuisine.

Serves 4
75g/3oz/1 cup desiccated
   (dry unsweetened shredded)
   coconut
30ml/2 tbsp vegetable oil
2.5ml/½ tsp cumin seeds
4 black peppercorns
15ml/1 tbsp fennel seeds
15ml/1 tbsp coriander seeds
2 onions, finely chopped
2.5ml/½ tsp salt
8 small chicken pieces,
   such as thighs and
   drumsticks, skinned
fresh coriander (cilantro) sprigs
   and lemon wedges, to garnish

1 Put the desiccated coconut in a bowl with 45ml/3 tbsp water. Leave to soak for 15 minutes.

2 Heat 15ml/1 tbsp of the oil in a karahi, wok or large pan and fry the cumin seeds, peppercorns, fennel and coriander seeds over a low heat for 3–4 minutes until they begin to splutter and release their fragrant aromas.

3 Add the finely chopped onions and fry for about 5 minutes without browning, stirring occasionally, until the onion has softened and turned translucent.

4 Stir in the coconut, along with the soaking water and salt, and continue to fry for a further 5 minutes, stirring occasionally to prevent the mixture from sticking to the pan.

5 Put the coconut mixture into a food processor or blender and process to form a coarse paste. Spoon into a bowl and set aside until required.

6 Heat the remaining oil and fry the chicken for 10 minutes. Add the coconut paste and cook over low heat for 15–20 minutes, or until the coconut mixture is golden brown and the chicken is cooked through and tender.

7 Transfer the curry to a warmed serving plate, and garnish with sprigs of fresh coriander and the lemon wedges. Chutney, rice or lentils make good accompaniments.

Tandoori Chicken

The word tandoori refers to a method of cooking in a charcoal-fired clay oven called a tandoor. In northern India and Pakistan, a wide variety of foods are cooked in this type of oven, but in western countries the method is most popular for chicken.

Serves 4
30ml/2 tbsp vegetable oil
2 small onions, cut into wedges
2 garlic cloves, sliced
4 skinless chicken breast fillets,
   cut into cubes
100ml/3½fl oz/⅓ cup water
300g/11oz jar tandoori sauce
salt and ground black pepper
fresh coriander (cilantro) sprigs,
   to garnish

To serve
5ml/1 tsp ground turmeric
350g/12oz/1⅔ cups basmati rice

1 Heat the oil in a flameproof casserole. Add the onions and garlic, and cook for about 3 minutes, or until the onion is beginning to soften, stirring frequently.

2 Add the cubes of chicken to the casserole and cook for 6 minutes. Stir the water into the tandoori sauce and pour it over the chicken. Bring to the boil, then reduce the heat and simmer for 10 minutes, or until the chicken pieces are cooked through and the sauce is slightly reduced and thickened.

3 Meanwhile, bring a large pan of lightly salted water to the boil, add the turmeric and rice and bring back to the boil. Stir once, reduce the heat to prevent the water from boiling over and simmer the rice for 12 minutes, or according to the time suggested on the packet, until tender.

4 Drain the rice well and serve immediately alongside the tandoori chicken on warmed individual serving plates, garnished with the sprigs of fresh coriander.

> **Cook's Tip**
> You will find jars of ready-made tandoori sauce in large supermarkets and Asian stores and markets.

Tandoori Chicken Energy 592kcal/2479kJ; Protein 44g; Carbohydrate 77.5g, of which sugars 4.5g; Fat 11.4g, of which saturates 1.1g; Cholesterol 105mg; Calcium 54mg; Fibre 0.4g; Sodium 826mg.
Goan Chicken Curry Energy 353kcal/1472kJ; Protein 33.3g; Carbohydrate 7.1g, of which sugars 5.4g; Fat 21.5g, of which saturates 11.9g; Cholesterol 158mg; Calcium 34mg; Fibre 3.6g; Sodium 143mg.

Balti Chicken in Saffron Sauce

This is a beautifully aromatic chicken dish that is partly cooked in the oven.

Serves 4
50g/2oz/¼ cup butter
30ml/2 tbsp corn oil
1.2–1.3kg/2½–3lb chicken, skinned and cut into 8 pieces
1 medium onion, chopped
5ml/1 tsp crushed garlic
2.5ml/½ tsp crushed black peppercorns
2.5ml/½ tsp crushed cardamom pods
2.5ml/¼ tsp ground cinnamon
7.5ml/1½ tsp chilli powder
150ml/¼ pint/⅔ cup natural (plain) yogurt
50g/2oz/½ cup ground almonds
15ml/1 tbsp lemon juice
5ml/1 tsp salt
5ml/1 tsp saffron strands
150ml/¼ pint/⅔ cup water
150ml/¼ pint/⅔ cup single (light) cream
30ml/2 tbsp chopped fresh coriander (cilantro)
fruity pilau or boiled rice, to serve

1 Preheat the oven to 180°C/350°F/Gas 4. Melt the butter with the corn oil in a karahi, wok or deep frying pan. Add the chicken pieces and fry until lightly browned, about 5–7 minutes. Remove the chicken from the pan using a slotted spoon, leaving behind the fat.

2 Add the onion to the same pan, and fry over a medium heat. Meanwhile, mix together the next 10 ingredients in a bowl. When the onions are lightly browned, pour the spice mixture into the pan and stir-fry for about 1 minute.

3 Add the chicken pieces, and continue to fry for a further 2 minutes stirring constantly. Pour in the water and bring to a simmer. Transfer the contents of the pan to a flameproof casserole and cover with a lid, or, if using a karahi with heatproof handles, cover with foil. Transfer to the preheated oven and cook for about 30–35 minutes.

4 Once you are sure that the chicken is cooked right through, remove it from the oven. Transfer the mixture to a frying pan or place the karahi on the stove and stir in the cream.

5 Reheat gently for about 2 minutes. Garnish with fresh coriander and serve with a fruity pilau or boiled rice.

Balti Chicken Pasanda

Yogurt and cream give this tasty dish its characteristic richness. Serve it with garlic and coriander naan to complement the almonds.

Serves 4
60ml/4 tbsp Greek (US strained plain) yogurt
2.5ml/½ tsp black cumin seeds
4 cardamom pods
6 whole black peppercorns
10ml/2 tsp garam masala
2.5cm/1in cinnamon stick
15ml/1 tbsp ground almonds
5ml/1 tsp crushed garlic
5ml/1 tsp grated fresh root ginger
5ml/1 tsp chilli powder
5ml/1 tsp salt
675g/1½lb skinless, boneless chicken, cut into bitesize cubes
75ml/5 tbsp corn oil
2 medium onions, diced
3 fresh green chillies, seeded and finely chopped
30ml/2 tbsp chopped fresh coriander (cilantro), plus extra to garnish
120ml/4fl oz/½ cup single (light) cream

1 Mix the Greek yogurt, black cumin seeds, cardamom pods, whole black peppercorns, garam masala and cinnamon stick together in a medium mixing bowl. Add the ground almonds, crushed garlic, grated ginger, chilli powder and salt and mix together well to combine.

2 Add the chicken cubes, stir to coat, and leave in the spice mixture to marinate for about 2 hours.

3 Heat the corn oil in a large karahi, wok or deep frying pan. Add the onions and fry for 2–3 minutes.

4 Add the chicken pieces mixture to the pan and stir until they are well blended with the onions.

5 Cook for 12–15 minutes over a medium heat until the sauce thickens and the chicken is cooked through.

6 Add the chopped green chillies and fresh coriander to the chicken in the wok, and pour in the single cream. Bring to the boil, stirring constantly, and serve the dish garnished with more fresh coriander, if you like.

Balti Chicken Pasanda Energy 434kcal/1812kJ; Protein 44.9g; Carbohydrate 13.2g, of which sugars 7.4g; Fat 23g, of which saturates 6g; Cholesterol 135mg; Calcium 107mg; Fibre 1.4g; Sodium 129mg.
Balti Chicken Energy 554kcal/2321kJ; Protein 75.6g; Carbohydrate 5.1g, of which sugars 4.7g; Fat 25.9g, of which saturates 12.2g; Cholesterol 255mg; Calcium 146mg; Fibre 0.8g; Sodium 792mg.

Creamy Mughlai-style Chicken with Almonds

This recipe, with the heady and unmistakable aroma of saffron and the captivating flavour of a silky almond sauce, is perfect for a special occasion or family feast. This curry is inspired by the cuisine of the Mughal dynasty in India.

Serves 4–6

1 large onion
2 eggs
4 skinless chicken breast fillets
15–30ml/1–2 tbsp garam masala
90ml/6 tbsp ghee or vegetable oil
5cm/2in piece fresh root ginger, finely crushed
4 garlic cloves, finely crushed
4 cloves
4 green cardamom pods
5cm/2in piece cinnamon stick
2 bay leaves
15–20 saffron threads
150ml/¼ pint/⅔ cup natural (plain) yogurt, beaten with 5ml/1 tsp cornflour (cornstarch)
75ml/2½fl oz/⅓ cup double (heavy) cream
50g/2oz/½ cup ground almonds
salt and ground black pepper

1 Chop the onion finely. Break the eggs into a mixing bowl and beat with salt and black pepper. Rub the chicken breast fillets all over with the garam masala, then brush with the beaten egg.

2 In a karahi, wok, or large pan, heat the ghee or vegetable oil and fry the prepared chicken pieces until browned on both sides. Remove the chicken from the pan with a slotted spoon and keep warm.

3 In the same pan, fry the chopped onion, ginger, garlic, cloves, cardamom pods, cinnamon and bay leaves. When the onion turns golden, remove the pan from the heat, allow the contents to cool a little and add the saffron and yogurt mixture to the pan. Stir well to prevent the yogurt from curdling.

4 Return the chicken to the pan, along with any juices, and gently cook until the chicken is cooked through and tender. Adjust the seasoning. Just before serving, pour in the cream. Fold it in then repeat the process with the ground almonds. Serve immediately.

Karahi Chicken with Fresh Fenugreek

Fresh fenugreek is a flavour that many people are unfamiliar with, and this recipe is a good introduction to this delicious herb. The chicken is boiled before being quickly stir-fried, to make sure that it is cooked all the way through.

Serves 4

115g/4oz boneless chicken thigh meat, skinned and cut into strips
115g/4oz chicken breast fillet, skinned and cut into strips
2.5ml/½ tsp crushed garlic
5ml/1 tsp chilli powder
2.5ml/½ tsp salt
10ml/2 tsp tomato purée (paste)
30ml/2 tbsp vegetable oil
1 bunch fresh fenugreek leaves
15ml/1 tbsp chopped fresh coriander (cilantro)
300ml/½ pint/1¼ cups water
pilau rice and wholemeal (whole-wheat) chapatis, to serve (optional)

1 Bring a pan of water to the boil, add the chicken strips and cook for about 5–7 minutes. Drain the chicken strips well and set aside while you prepare the rest of the dish.

2 In a mixing bowl, combine the crushed garlic, chilli powder and salt with the tomato purée.

3 Heat the oil in a large, heavy pan. Lower the heat and stir in the tomato purée and spice mixture.

4 Add the chicken pieces to the spices and stir-fry for about 5–7 minutes, then lower the heat further.

5 Add the fenugreek leaves and chopped fresh coriander to the pan. Continue to cook for 5–7 minutes, stirring frequently, until all the ingredients are well mixed.

6 Pour in the water, cover the pan and bring to the boil. Reduce the heat to medium and simmer for about 5 minutes, stirring several times during the cooking.

7 Place the chicken in a serving dish and serve with pilau rice and warm wholemeal chapatis, if you like.

Mughlai-style Chicken Energy 350kcal/1453kJ; Protein 25.8g; Carbohydrate 4.3g, of which sugars 3g; Fat 25.7g, of which saturates 6.8g; Cholesterol 139mg; Calcium 94mg; Fibre 0.8g; Sodium 99mg.
Karahi Chicken Energy 127kcal/529kJ; Protein 13g; Carbohydrate 1.7g, of which sugars 0.7g; Fat 7.7g, of which saturates 1.2g; Cholesterol 60mg; Calcium 42mg; Fibre 0.9g; Sodium 64mg.

Balti Chicken with Paneer and Peas

This is rather an unusual combination, but it really works well. Serve with plain boiled rice.

Serves 4
1 small chicken, about 675g/1½lb
30ml/2 tbsp tomato
 purée (paste)
45ml/3 tbsp natural (plain)
 low-fat yogurt
7.5ml/1½ tsp garam masala
5ml/1 tsp crushed garlic
5ml/1 tsp grated fresh root ginger
pinch of ground cardamom
15ml/1 tbsp chilli powder
1.5ml/¼ tsp ground turmeric
5ml/1 tsp salt
5ml/1 tsp sugar
10ml/2 tsp vegetable oil
2.5cm/1in cinnamon stick
2 black peppercorns
300ml/½ pint/1¼ cups water
115g/4oz paneer, cubed
30ml/2 tbsp fresh coriander
 (cilantro) leaves
2 fresh green chillies, seeded
 and chopped
50g/2fl oz/¼ cup low-fat fromage
 frais or ricotta cheese
75g/3oz/¾ cup frozen
 peas, thawed

1 Skin the chicken and cut it into six to eight equal pieces.

2 Mix the tomato purée, yogurt, garam masala, garlic, ginger, cardamom, chilli powder, turmeric, salt and sugar in a bowl.

3 Heat the oil with the whole spices in a karahi, wok or heavy pan, then pour the yogurt mixture into the oil. Lower the heat and cook gently for about 3 minutes, then pour in the water and bring to a simmer.

4 Add the chicken pieces to the pan. Cook for 2 minutes, stirring frequently, then cover the pan and cook over a medium heat for about 10 minutes.

5 Add the paneer cubes to the pan, followed by half the coriander leaves and half the green chillies. Mix well and cook for a further 5–7 minutes.

6 Stir in the fromage frais or ricotta and peas, heat through and serve with the reserved coriander and chillies.

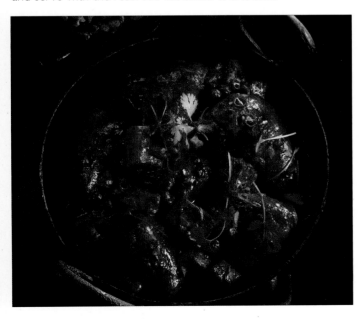

Balti Chicken with Vegetables

This is an excellent recipe to cook when you need a small amount of chicken to go a long way. The carrots and courgette add lots of extra colour as well as boosting the dish's nutritional value.

Serves 4–6
60ml/4 tbsp corn oil
2 medium onions, sliced
4 garlic cloves, thickly sliced
450g/1lb skinless chicken breast
 fillets, cut into strips
5ml/1 tsp salt
30ml/2 tbsp lime juice
3 fresh green chillies, chopped
2 medium carrots, cut into batons
2 medium potatoes, peeled and
 cut into 1cm/½in strips
1 medium courgette (zucchini),
 cut into batons

For the garnish
4 lime slices
15ml/1 tbsp chopped fresh
 coriander (cilantro)
2 fresh green chillies, seeded and
 cut into thin strips (optional)

1 Heat the oil in a large karahi, wok or deep pan. Lower the heat slightly and add the sliced onions. Fry until the onions are lightly browned and softened.

2 Add half the garlic slices and fry for a few seconds before adding the chicken strips and salt. Cook everything together, stirring frequently, until all the moisture has evaporated and the chicken is lightly browned.

3 Add the lime juice, green chillies and all the vegetables to the pan. Increase the heat and add the rest of the garlic. Stir-fry for 7–10 minutes, or until the chicken is cooked through and the vegetables are just tender.

4 Transfer the curry to a warmed serving dish and garnish with the lime slices, fresh chopped coriander and green chilli strips, if you like. Serve immediately.

Cook's Tip
Try other fresh vegetables in this dish, such as green beans, mangetouts (snow peas) and (bell) peppers.

Chicken with Paneer Energy 313kcal/1303kJ; Protein 27.7g; Carbohydrate 7.3g, of which sugars 5.6g; Fat 19.3g, of which saturates 5.9g; Cholesterol 117mg; Calcium 87mg; Fibre 1.3g; Sodium 75mg.
Chicken with Vegetables Energy 248kcal/1039kJ; Protein 21.2g; Carbohydrate 22.1g, of which sugars 10g; Fat 8.9g, of which saturates 1.2g; Cholesterol 53mg; Calcium 63mg; Fibre 3.7g; Sodium 70mg.

Chicken with Mixed Chillies

Minced chicken is seldom cooked in Indian or Pakistani homes. However, it works very well in this dish.

Serves 4
275g/10oz skinless chicken
    breast fillets
2 thick red chillies
3 thick green chillies
45ml/3 tbsp corn oil
6 curry leaves
3 medium onions, sliced
7.5ml/1½ tsp crushed garlic
7.5ml/1½ tsp ground coriander
7.5ml/1½ tsp crushed fresh
    root ginger
5ml/1 tsp chilli powder
5ml/1 tsp salt
15ml/1 tbsp lemon juice
30ml/2 tbsp chopped fresh
    coriander (cilantro) leaves
chapatis and lemon wedges,
    to serve

1 Cut the chicken breast fillets into medium pieces. Add to a pan of boiling water and boil gently for about 10–12 minutes until soft and cooked through. Drain well.

2 Place the chicken in a food processor to mince (grind), or use a meat mincer if available.

3 Cut the chillies in half lengthways and remove the seeds, if you like. If you want a more fiery dish, you can retain the seeds and add them to the pan with the rest of the chillies. Cut the chilli flesh into thin strips.

4 Heat the oil in a non-stick wok or large frying pan and fry the curry leaves and onions until the onions are a soft golden brown, stirring frequently.

5 Lower the heat and stir the crushed garlic, ground coriander, crushed ginger, chilli powder and salt into the onions.

6 Add the minced chicken to the pan and stir-fry for about 3–5 minutes until it is beginning to brown.

7 Add the lemon juice, the chilli strips and most of the fresh coriander leaves. Stir-fry for a further 3–5 minutes, then serve, garnished with the remaining coriander leaves and accompanied by chapatis and lemon wedges.

Chicken with Golden Turmeric

Fresh turmeric is a root like ginger. It has a completely different taste to dried turmeric and produces a luxurious golden colour in a dish. Dried and ground turmeric can be used instead and will produce an acceptable colour, although the flavour will be somewhat different.

Serves 4
1.3–1.6kg/3–3½lb chicken, cut
    into 8 pieces, or 4 chicken
    quarters, halved
15ml/1 tbsp soft light brown sugar
3 macadamia nuts or 6 almonds
2 garlic cloves, crushed
1 large onion, quartered
2.5cm/1in piece fresh galangal
    or 1cm/½in piece fresh root
    ginger, sliced, or 5ml/1 tsp
    galangal powder
1–2 lemon grass stalks, lower
    5cm/2in sliced, top bruised
1cm/½in cube shrimp paste
4cm/1½in piece fresh turmeric,
    sliced, or 10ml/2 tsp
    ground turmeric
15ml/1 tbsp tamarind pulp,
    soaked in 150ml/¼ pint/⅔ cup
    warm water
60–90ml/4–6 tbsp vegetable oil
400g/14oz can coconut milk
salt and ground black pepper
deep-fried onions,
    to garnish (optional)

1 Rub each of the chicken joints all over with a little of the light brown sugar and set them aside.

2 Grind the nuts and garlic in a food processor with the onion, galangal or ginger, sliced lemon grass, shrimp paste and turmeric. Alternatively, pound the ingredients to a paste with a mortar and pestle. Strain the tamarind pulp and reserve the juice.

3 Heat the oil in a wok or large pan, and cook the paste, without browning, until it gives off a spicy aroma. Add the pieces of chicken and toss well in the spices. Add the strained tamarind juice. Spoon the coconut cream off the top of the milk and set it to one side.

4 Add the coconut milk to the pan. Cover and cook for 45 minutes, or until the chicken is tender.

5 Before serving, stir in the coconut cream. Season to taste and serve, garnished with deep-fried onions, if using.

Chicken with Chillies Energy 196kcal/819kJ; Protein 18.4g; Carbohydrate 10.2g, of which sugars 7.3g; Fat 9.4g, of which saturates 1.2g; Cholesterol 48mg; Calcium 60mg; Fibre 2.4g; Sodium 49mg.
Chicken with Turmeric Energy 706kcal/2935kJ; Protein 48.1g; Carbohydrate 15.8g, of which sugars 15.6g; Fat 50.4g, of which saturates 12.8g; Cholesterol 240mg; Calcium 91mg; Fibre 1.5g; Sodium 305mg.

Chicken Tikka Masala

This classic Indian curry features tender pieces of chicken cooked in a creamy tomato sauce with ginger and chillies, and served on naan bread.

Serves 4

675g/1½lb skinless chicken breast fillets
90ml/6 tbsp tikka paste
60ml/4 tbsp natural (plain) yogurt
30ml/2 tbsp vegetable oil
1 onion, chopped
1 garlic clove, crushed
1 green chilli, seeded and chopped
2.5cm/1in piece fresh root ginger, grated
15ml/1 tbsp tomato purée (paste)
15ml/1 tbsp ground almonds
250ml/8fl oz/1 cup water
45ml/3 tbsp butter, melted
50ml/2fl oz/¼ cup double (heavy) cream
15ml/1 tbsp lemon juice
fresh coriander (cilantro) sprigs, natural (plain) yogurt and toasted cumin seeds, to garnish
naan bread, to serve

1 Cut the chicken into 2.5cm/1in pieces. Put 45ml/3 tbsp of the tikka paste and all of the yogurt into a bowl. Add the chicken, coat thoroughly and leave to marinate for 20 minutes. Soak some wooden skewers in water for 30 minutes.

2 For the tikka sauce, heat the oil and fry the onion, garlic, chilli and ginger for 5 minutes. Add the remaining tikka paste and fry for 2 minutes. Stir in the tomato purée, almonds and water. Simmer gently for about 15 minutes.

3 Thread the chicken on to the soaked wooden skewers. Preheat the grill (broiler) to medium. Brush the chicken with the butter and grill (broil) under a medium heat for 15 minutes, turning occasionally.

4 Pour the tikka sauce into a food processor or blender and process until smooth. Return the sauce to the pan.

5 Add the cream and lemon juice, remove the chicken from the skewers, add to the pan and simmer for 5 minutes. Garnish with coriander, yogurt and toasted cumin seeds and serve with naan bread.

Hot Chilli Chicken

Not for the faint-hearted, this delicious fiery, hot curry is made with a spicy chilli masala paste.

Serves 4

30ml/2 tbsp tomato purée (paste)
2 garlic cloves, roughly chopped
2 green chillies, roughly chopped
5 dried red chillies
2.5ml/½ tsp salt
1.5ml/¼ tsp sugar
5ml/1 tsp chilli powder
2.5ml/½ tsp paprika
15ml/1 tbsp curry paste
30ml/2 tbsp vegetable oil
2.5ml/½ tsp cumin seeds
1 onion, finely chopped
2 bay leaves
5ml/1 tsp ground coriander
5ml/1 tsp ground cumin
1.5ml/¼ tsp ground turmeric
400g/14oz can chopped tomatoes
150ml/¼ pint/⅔ cup water
8 chicken thighs, skinned
5ml/1 tsp garam masala
fresh green chillies, seeded and sliced, to garnish
chapatis and natural (plain) yogurt, to serve

1 Put the tomato purée, garlic, green and dried red chillies, salt, sugar, chilli powder, paprika and curry paste into a food processor or blender and process to a smooth paste. Alternatively, grind all the ingredients together to a paste using a mortar and pestle.

2 Heat the oil in a large heavy pan or wok and fry the cumin seeds for about 2 minutes. Add the onion and bay leaves to the pan and fry for a further 5 minutes.

3 Add the spice paste to the pan and fry for 2–3 minutes until it releases a fragrant aroma. Add the remaining ground spices and cook, stirring constantly, for 2 minutes.

4 Add the chopped tomatoes and the measured water to the pan. Bring the mixture to the boil, reduce the heat and simmer for 5 minutes until the sauce thickens.

5 Add the chicken and garam masala to the sauce. Cover the pan with a lid and simmer for about 25–30 minutes until the chicken is tender. Serve with chapatis and natural yogurt, garnished with sliced green chillies.

Chicken Tikka Energy 416kcal/1730kJ; Protein 46g; Carbohydrate 2.1g, of which sugars 0.2g; Fat 24.8g, of which saturates 8.5g; Cholesterol 203mg; Calcium 21mg; Fibre 0.5g; Sodium 172mg.
Hot Chilli Chicken Energy 269kcal/1128kJ; Protein 27g; Carbohydrate 9g, of which sugars 7g; Fat 15g,0 of which saturates 3g; Cholesterol 120mg; Calcium 68mg; Fibre 1.5g; Sodium 400g.

Balti Chilli Chicken with Whole Green Chillies

Hot and spicy is the best way to describe this mouthwatering balti dish. The smell of the fresh chillies while they are cooking is simply irresistible.

Serves 4–6

75ml/5 tbsp corn oil
8 large fresh green chillies, slit
2.5ml/½ tsp mixed onion seeds and cumin seeds
4 curry leaves
5ml/1 tsp grated fresh root ginger

5ml/1 tsp chilli powder
5ml/1 tsp ground coriander
5ml/1 tsp crushed garlic
5ml/1 tsp salt
2 medium onions, chopped
675g/1½lb skinless chicken fillets, cubed
15ml/1 tbsp lemon juice
15ml/1 tbsp roughly chopped fresh mint
15ml/1 tbsp roughly chopped fresh coriander (cilantro)
8–10 cherry tomatoes

1 Heat the oil in a karahi, wok or deep frying pan. Lower the heat slightly and add the slit green chillies. Cook, stirring frequently, until the skin starts to change colour.

2 Add the onion seeds and cumin seeds, curry leaves, ginger, chilli powder, ground coriander, garlic, salt and onions, and fry for a minute, stirring constantly.

3 Add the chicken pieces to the pan. Stir-fry over a medium heat for about 7–10 minutes, or until the chicken is cooked right through. Take care not to overcook the chicken or it will become dry in texture.

4 Sprinkle on the lemon juice and add the roughly chopped fresh mint and coriander. Dot with the cherry tomatoes and serve immediately from the pan.

Cook's Tip
Frying the chillies and the whole and ground spices helps to release their lovely fragrant aromas.

Kashmiri Chicken Curry

Surrounded by the snow-capped Himalayas, Kashmir is popularly known as the 'Switzerland of the East'. The state is also renowned for its rich culinary heritage, and this aromatic dish is one of the simplest among the region's repertoire.

Serves 4–6

20ml/4 tsp Kashmiri masala paste
60ml/4 tbsp tomato ketchup

5ml/1 tsp Worcestershire sauce
5ml/1 tsp Chinese five-spice powder
5ml/1 tsp sugar
8 chicken joints, skinned
5cm/2in piece fresh root ginger
45ml/3 tbsp vegetable oil
4 garlic cloves, crushed
juice of 1 lemon
15ml/1 tbsp coriander (cilantro) leaves, finely chopped
salt
plain boiled rice, to serve (optional)

1 To make the marinade, mix the masala paste, tomato ketchup, Worcestershire sauce and five-spice powder with the sugar and a little salt. Leave the mixture to rest in a warm place until the sugar has dissolved.

2 Rub the chicken pieces all over with the marinade and set aside in a cool place for at least 2 hours, or preferably in the refrigerator overnight. Bring the chicken back to room temperature before cooking.

3 Thinly peel the ginger, using a sharp knife or vegetable peeler. Grate the peeled root finely.

4 Heat the oil in a karahi, wok or large pan and fry half the ginger and all the garlic until golden.

5 Add the chicken to the pan and fry until both sides are sealed. Cover and cook until the chicken is tender, and the oil has separated from the sauce.

6 Sprinkle the chicken with the lemon juice, remaining grated ginger and chopped coriander leaves, and mix in well. Serve the chicken piping hot. Plain boiled rice would make a good accompaniment to this curry.

Balti Chilli Chicken Energy 244kcal/1016kJ; Protein 21g; Carbohydrate 1.6g, of which sugars 0.5g; Fat 17.2g, of which saturates 2.2g; Cholesterol 56mg; Calcium 47mg; Fibre 0.7g; Sodium 56mg.
Kashmiri Chicken Energy 256kcal/1066kJ; Protein 16.9g; Carbohydrate 12.3g, of which sugars 10.2g; Fat 15.8g, of which saturates 3.5g; Cholesterol 75mg; Calcium 93mg; Fibre 2.4g; Sodium 411mg.

Baby Chicken in a Chilli Tamarind Sauce

The tamarind in this recipe gives the dish a tasty sweet-and-sour flavour.

Serves 4–6

60ml/4 tbsp tomato ketchup
15ml/1 tbsp tamarind paste
60ml/4 tbsp water
7.5ml/1½ tsp chilli powder
7.5ml/1½ tsp salt
15ml/1 tbsp sugar
7.5ml/1½ tsp crushed fresh root ginger
7.5ml/1½ tsp crushed garlic
30ml/2 tbsp desiccated (dry unsweetened shredded) coconut
30ml/2 tbsp sesame seeds
5ml/1 tsp poppy seeds
5ml/1 tsp ground cumin
7.5ml/1½ tsp ground coriander
2 X 450g/1lb baby chickens, skinned and cut into 6–8 pieces each
75ml/5 tbsp corn oil
about 20 curry leaves
2.5ml/½ tsp onion seeds
3 large dried red chillies
2.5ml/½ tsp fenugreek seeds
10–12 cherry tomatoes
45ml/3 tbsp chopped fresh coriander (cilantro)
2 fresh green chillies, chopped

1 Put the tomato ketchup, tamarind paste and water into a large mixing bowl and use a fork to blend everything together.

2 Add the chilli powder, salt, sugar, ginger, garlic, coconut, sesame and poppy seeds, ground cumin and ground coriander to the mixture. Stir well until combined.

3 Add the chicken pieces and stir until they are well coated with the spice mixture. Set to one side.

4 Heat the oil in a deep frying pan or a large karahi. Add the curry leaves, onion seeds, dried red chillies and fenugreek seeds and fry for about 1 minute.

5 Add the chicken pieces to the pan, along with their spice paste, mixing as you go. Simmer gently for about 12–15 minutes, or until the chicken is thoroughly cooked.

6 Stir in the tomatoes, fresh coriander and green chillies for a minute to heat through, and serve immediately.

Balti Chicken

This recipe has a beautifully delicate flavour, and is another very popular balti dish. Choose a young chicken as the result will be more flavoursome.

Serves 4–6

1–1.3kg/2¼–3lb chicken, skinned and cut into 8 pieces
45ml/3 tbsp corn oil
3 medium onions, sliced
3 medium tomatoes, halved and sliced
2.5cm/1in cinnamon stick
2 large black cardamom pods
4 black peppercorns
2.5ml/½ tsp black cumin seeds
5ml/1 tsp crushed fresh root ginger
5ml/1 tsp crushed garlic
5ml/1 tsp garam masala
5ml/1 tsp chilli powder
5ml/1 tsp salt
30ml/2 tbsp natural (plain) yogurt
60ml/4 tbsp lemon juice
30ml/2 tbsp chopped fresh coriander (cilantro)
2 fresh green chillies, chopped

1 Wash and trim the chicken pieces, and set to one side. Heat the oil in a large wok or deep frying pan. Add the onions and fry until they are golden brown. Add the tomatoes and stir well.

2 Add the cinnamon stick, cardamoms, peppercorns, black cumin seeds, ginger, garlic, garam masala, chilli powder and salt. Lower the heat and stir-fry for 3–5 minutes.

3 Add the chicken pieces two at a time, and stir-fry for at least 7 minutes until the spice mixture has penetrated the chicken. Add the yogurt to the pan and mix well.

4 Lower the heat and cover the pan with a piece of foil. Cook gently for about 15 minutes, checking to make sure the sauce is not sticking. Finally, stir in the lemon juice, fresh coriander and green chillies, and serve immediately.

> **Variation**
> Although chicken is most tender and flavoursome when cooked on the bone, you can substitute 675g/1½lb boned and cubed chicken breast fillets, if you wish.

Baby Chicken Energy 268kcal/1120kJ; Protein 26g; Carbohydrate 4.1g, of which sugars 4g; Fat 16.6g, of which saturates 4.5g; Cholesterol 70mg; Calcium 60mg; Fibre 2.2g; Sodium 152mg.
Balti Chicken Energy 231kcal/971kJ; Protein 29.6g; Carbohydrate 11.1g, of which sugars 6.2g; Fat 8.1g, of which saturates 1.3g; Cholesterol 79mg; Calcium 45mg; Fibre 1.7g; Sodium 77mg.

Balti Butter Chicken

Butter chicken is one of the most popular balti chicken dishes. Cooked in butter, with a subtle blend of aromatic spices, cream and almonds, this mild dish will be enjoyed by everyone.

Serves 4–6
150ml/¼ pint/⅔ cup natural (plain) yogurt
50g/2oz/½ cup ground almonds
7.5ml/1½ tsp chilli powder
1.5ml/¼ tsp crushed bay leaves
1.5ml/¼ tsp ground cloves
1.5ml/¼ tsp ground cinnamon
5ml/1 tsp garam masala
4 green cardamom pods
2.5cm/1in piece fresh root ginger, grated
1 garlic clove, crushed
400g/14oz/2 cups canned chopped tomatoes
6.5ml/1¼ tsp salt
1kg/2¼lb/6½ cups skinless chicken breast fillets, cubed
75g/3oz/6 tbsp butter
15ml/1 tbsp corn oil
2 medium onions, sliced
30ml/2 tbsp chopped fresh coriander (cilantro)
60ml/4 tbsp single (light) cream
coriander (cilantro) sprigs, to garnish

1 Put the yogurt, ground almonds, all the dry spices, ginger, garlic, tomatoes and salt into a mixing bowl and blend together thoroughly. Put the chicken into a large mixing bowl and pour over the yogurt mixture. Set aside.

2 Melt the butter and oil together in a medium wok or deep frying pan. When the oil is hot, add the onions and fry for about 3 minutes, stirring frequently.

3 Add the chicken mixture and stir-fry for 7–10 minutes. Stir in about half of the coriander and mix well.

4 Pour the cream over the chicken mixture and stir in well. Bring to the boil. Serve immediately garnished with the remaining chopped coriander and a few extra coriander sprigs.

> **Variation**
> Replace the natural (plain) yogurt with Greek (US strained plain) yogurt for an even richer and creamier flavour.

Chicken and Tomato Balti

If you like tomatoes, you will love this tangy chicken curry. It makes a delicious semi-dry balti and is also excellent served with a spicy lentil dish and plain boiled rice.

Serves 4
60ml/4 tbsp corn oil
6 curry leaves
2.5ml/½ tsp mixed onion and mustard seeds
8 medium tomatoes, sliced
5ml/1 tsp ground coriander
5ml/1 tsp chilli powder
5ml/1 tsp salt
5ml/1 tsp ground cumin
5ml/1 tsp crushed garlic
675g/1½lb skinless, boneless chicken, cubed
150ml/¼ pint/⅔ cup water
15ml/1 tbsp sesame seeds, roasted
15ml/1 tbsp chopped fresh coriander (cilantro)

1 Heat the oil in a karahi, wok or deep frying pan. Add the curry leaves and mixed onion and mustard seeds.

2 Toss the seeds over the heat for 1–2 minutes so that they become fragrant. Do not let the seeds burn.

3 Lower the heat slightly and add the tomatoes.

4 While the tomatoes are gently cooking, mix together the ground coriander, chilli powder, salt, ground cumin and crushed garlic in a mixing bowl.

5 Add the spices to the tomatoes in the wok or pan and stir well to combine the ingredients thoroughly.

6 Add the chicken pieces to the pan and stir well. Cook for about 5 minutes more, stirring frequently.

7 Pour the water into the pan and continue cooking, stirring occasionally, until the sauce reduces and thickens and the chicken is fully cooked and tender.

8 Sprinkle the roasted sesame seeds and chopped fresh coriander over the chicken and tomato balti. Serve immediately, from the pan with plain boiled rice, if you like.

Butter Chicken Energy 606kcal/2540kJ; Protein 84g; Carbohydrate 6.8g, of which sugars 3.4g; Fat 27.3g, of which saturates 3.8g; Cholesterol 239mg; Calcium 57mg; Fibre 1.3g; Sodium 214mg.
Chicken and Tomato Energy 347kcal/1457kJ; Protein 43.4g; Carbohydrate 7.3g, of which sugars 4.7g; Fat 16.5g, of which saturates 2.4g; Cholesterol 118mg; Calcium 58mg; Fibre 1.8g; Sodium 118mg.

Chicken Murgh

This is a marvellous way to re-heat tandoori chicken.

Serves 4

For the chicken tikka
juice of ½ lemon
5ml/1 tsp salt or to taste
675g/1½lb skinless chicken breast
   fillets, cut into 5cm/2in cubes
120ml/4floz/½ cup Greek
   (US strained plain) yogurt
15ml/1 tbsp crushed garlic
15ml/1 tbsp crushed fresh ginger
2.5ml/½ tsp ground turmeric
5ml/1 tsp garam masala
2.5ml/½ tsp chilli powder
10ml/2 tsp cornflour (cornstarch)
5ml/1 tsp sugar
45ml/3 tbsp sunflower oil
50g/2oz/4 tbsp butter, melted

For the sauce
150g/5oz/10 tbsp
   unsalted butter
5cm/2in cinnamon stick, broken up
3 cardamom pods, bruised
4 cloves
2 green chillies, roughly chopped
15ml/1 tbsp crushed fresh ginger
15ml/1 tbsp crushed garlic
5–10ml/1–2 tsp chilli powder
400g/14oz canned
   chopped tomatoes
30ml/2 tbsp tomato purée
   (paste)
10ml/2 tsp sugar
10ml/2 tsp salt
200ml/7fl oz/¾ cup warm water
10ml/2 tsp dried fenugreek leaves
150ml/¼ pint/½ cup double
   (heavy) cream

1 Rub the lemon juice and salt into the chicken. Whisk the yogurt and stir in the remaining tikka ingredients, except the melted butter. Stir into the chicken, cover and chill overnight.

2 Pre-heat the grill (broiler) to high and brush the skewers with oil. Thread the chicken on to skewers and place on the grill pan. Cook for 5 minutes. Mix the marinade with melted butter. Brush over the chicken and cook for 3–4 minutes. Turn over and baste. Cook for 2–3 minutes. Remove from the heat.

3 For the sauce, melt half the butter. Add the spices, chillies, ginger, garlic and chilli powder. Cook for 2–3 minutes. Add the remaining ingredients except the cream. Simmer for 20 minutes. Cool. Purée until smooth with a hand blender or sieve (strainer).

4 Return the pan to the heat, and add the remaining butter and cream. Let the mixture come to a simmer, then add the chicken. Simmer for 5–6 minutes, and serve with boiled rice.

Chicken with Orange and Pepper

Use virtually fat-free fromage frais to give this curry a rich, creamy flavour. Low-fat cream cheese can be used as a substitute if fromage frais is not available.

Serves 4
225g/8oz fromage frais or low-fat
   cream cheese
50ml/2fl oz/¼ cup natural (plain)
   low-fat yogurt
120ml/4fl oz/½ cup orange juice

7.5ml/1½ tsp crushed fresh
   root ginger
5ml/1 tsp crushed garlic
5ml/1 tsp ground black pepper
5ml/1 tsp salt
5ml/1 tsp ground coriander
1 baby chicken, about 675g/1½lb,
   skinned and cut into 8 pieces
15ml/1 tbsp corn oil
1 bay leaf
1 large onion, chopped
15ml/1 tbsp fresh mint leaves
1 green chilli, seeded and chopped

1 In a large mixing bowl, whisk together the fromage frais or low-fat cream cheese, natural yogurt, orange juice, ginger, garlic, pepper, salt and coriander.

2 Add the chicken pieces to the bowl, ensuring it is well coated, and set aside for 3–4 hours to marinate.

3 Heat the oil with the bay leaf in a wok or large frying pan and fry the onion until soft and translucent.

4 Pour the chicken mixture into the pan and cook for about 3–5 minutes over medium heat. Lower the heat, cover the pan with a lid and cook for a further 10–12 minutes, adding a little water if the sauce is too thick.

5 When the chicken is cooked through, add the fresh mint and chilli and cook for 1–2 minutes. Serve immediately.

> **Cook's Tip**
> If you prefer the taste of curry leaves, you can use them instead of the bay leaf, but you need to double the quantity. Try to find fresh leaves in Asian food stores and markets – dried leaves lose much of their spicy aroma.

Chicken Murgh Energy 793kcal/3293kJ; Protein 45.8g; Carbohydrate 14.2g, of which sugars 9g; Fat 64.4g, of which saturates 37.1g; Cholesterol 227mg; Calcium 102mg; Fibre 1.2g; Sodium 1491mg.
Chicken with Orange Energy 268kcal/1129kJ; Protein 34.9g; Carbohydrate 14.8g, of which sugars 11.9g; Fat 8.3g, of which saturates 2.8g; Cholesterol 99mg; Calcium 96mg; Fibre 0.3g; Sodium 111mg.

Balti Chicken in Hara Masala Sauce

This creamy chicken curry, made with yogurt and fromage frais or ricotta cheese, can be served as an accompaniment to any of the rice dishes in this book.

Serves 4

1 crisp green eating apple, peeled, cored and cut into small cubes
60ml/4 tbsp fresh coriander (cilantro) leaves
30ml/2 tbsp fresh mint leaves
120ml/4fl oz/½ cup natural (plain) low-fat yogurt
45ml/3 tbsp low-fat fromage frais or ricotta cheese
2 fresh green chillies, seeded and chopped
1 bunch spring onions (scallions), chopped
5ml/1 tsp salt
5ml/1 tsp sugar
5ml/1 tsp crushed garlic
5ml/1 tsp grated fresh root ginger
15ml/1 tbsp vegetable oil
225g/8oz skinless chicken breast fillets, cubed
25g/1oz/2 tbsp sultanas (golden raisins)

1 Place the apple, 45ml/3 tbsp of the coriander, the mint, yogurt, fromage frais or ricotta, chillies, spring onions, salt, sugar, garlic and ginger in a food processor and pulse for 1 minute.

2 Heat the oil in a karahi, wok or heavy frying pan. Pour in the yogurt mixture and cook over low heat for about 2 minutes, stirring frequently.

3 Next, add the chicken pieces and blend everything together. Cook over medium to low heat for 12–15 minutes or until the chicken is fully cooked and tender.

4 Stir in the sultanas and the remaining 15ml/1 tbsp fresh coriander leaves and serve immediately.

> **Cook's Tip**
> This dish makes an attractive centrepiece for a dinner party served with rice and a selection of Indian breads.

Chicken with Green Mango

Green or unripe mango is meant only for cooking purposes. These fruits are smaller than eating mangoes, and they have a sharper taste. They can be bought from Indian stores but if not available, cooking apples make an easy alternative.

Serves 4

1 green (unripe) mango or cooking apple
450g/1lb chicken breast fillets, skinned and cubed
1.5ml/¼ tsp onion seeds
5ml/1 tsp grated fresh root ginger
2.5ml/½ tsp crushed garlic
5ml/1 tsp chilli powder
1.5ml/¼ tsp ground turmeric
5ml/1 tsp salt
5ml/1 tsp ground coriander
30ml/2 tbsp vegetable oil
2 onions, sliced
4 curry leaves
300ml/½ pint/1¼ cups water
2 tomatoes, quartered
2 fresh green chillies, chopped
30ml/2 tbsp chopped fresh coriander (cilantro)

1 To prepare the mango, peel the skin and slice the flesh thickly. Discard the stone (pit) from the middle. Place the mango slices in a bowl, cover and set aside. If using apple, coat the slices with lemon juice to prevent discoloration.

2 Put the cubed chicken into a large mixing bowl and add the onion seeds, ginger, garlic, chilli powder, turmeric, salt and ground coriander. Mix the spices with the chicken, then stir in half the mango or apple slices.

3 Heat the oil in a wok, karahi or large pan over medium heat, and fry the sliced onions until golden brown. Add the curry leaves to the pan, and stir very gently to release their flavour.

4 Gradually add the chicken to the pan, stirring all the time. Stir-fry briskly over medium heat until the chicken is opaque.

5 Add the water, lower the heat and simmer for about 12–15 minutes, stirring, until the chicken is cooked and the water has completely evaporated.

6 Add the remaining mango or apple slices, the tomatoes, green chillies and fresh coriander. Serve immediately.

Balti Chicken Energy 299kcal/1254kJ; Protein 41.5g; Carbohydrate 3.4g, of which sugars 1.7g; Fat 13.5g, of which saturates 1.9g; Cholesterol 118mg; Calcium 28mg; Fibre 0.6g; Sodium 106mg.
Chicken with Mango Energy 264kcal/1107kJ; Protein 26.6g; Carbohydrate 18.1g, of which sugars 13.1g; Fat 10.1g, of which saturates 1.8g; Cholesterol 118mg; Calcium 56mg; Fibre 3.1g; Sodium 114mg.

Baby Chicken Curry with Spiced Apples

This mild yet aromatic dish is pleasantly flavoured with a warming combination of spices and chilli. Yogurt and almonds make a creamy sauce, which is given an additional lift by the use of sliced apples.

Serves 4
10ml/2 tsp vegetable oil
2 medium onions, diced
1 bay leaf
2 cloves
2.5cm/1in piece cinnamon stick
4 black peppercorns
1 baby chicken, about 675g/1½lb,
   skinned and cut into 8 pieces
5ml/1 tsp garam masala
5ml/1 tsp grated fresh root ginger
5ml/1 tsp crushed garlic
5ml/1 tsp salt
5ml/1 tsp chilli powder
15ml/1 tbsp ground almonds
150ml/¼ pint/⅔ cup natural
   (plain) low-fat yogurt
2 green eating apples, peeled,
   cored and roughly sliced
15ml/1 tbsp chopped fresh
   coriander (cilantro)
15g/½oz flaked (sliced) almonds,
   lightly toasted, and fresh
   coriander leaves, to garnish

1 Heat the oil in a karahi, wok or heavy pan and fry the onions with the bay leaf, cloves, cinnamon and peppercorns for about 3–5 minutes until the onions are beginning to soften and turn translucent but have not yet begun to brown.

2 Add the chicken pieces to the onions in the pan and continue to stir-fry for at least another 3 minutes.

3 Lower the heat and add the garam masala, ginger, garlic, salt, chilli powder and ground almonds to the pan and cook, stirring constantly, for about 2–3 minutes.

4 Pour the yogurt into the pan and stir for a couple more minutes. Add the apples and chopped coriander, cover and cook for about 10–15 minutes.

5 Check that the chicken is cooked through and serve the curry immediately, garnished with the flaked almonds and the whole coriander leaves.

Sweet-and-sour Balti Chicken

This dish combines a tangy sweet-and-sour flavour with a deliciously creamy texture. It is excellent served with pilau or plain basmati rice or Indian breads, such as naan or paratha.

Serves 4
45ml/3 tbsp tomato
   purée (paste)
30ml/2 tbsp Greek (US strained
   plain) yogurt
7.5ml/1½ tsp garam masala
5ml/1 tsp chilli powder
5ml/1 tsp crushed garlic
30ml/2 tbsp mango chutney
5ml/1 tsp salt
2.5ml/½ tsp sugar
60ml/4 tbsp corn oil
675g/1½lb skinless, boneless
   chicken, cubed
150ml/¼ pint/⅔ cup water
2 fresh green chillies, seeded
   and chopped
30ml/2 tbsp chopped fresh
   coriander (cilantro)
30ml/2 tbsp single (light) cream

1 Mix the tomato purée, Greek yogurt, garam masala, chilli powder, crushed garlic, mango chutney, salt and sugar in a medium mixing bowl. Stir well.

2 Heat the oil in a karahi, wok or deep pan. Lower the heat slightly and pour in the spice mixture. Bring to the boil and cook for about 2 minutes, stirring occasionally.

3 Add the chicken pieces and stir until they are well coated.

4 Stir the water into the pan to thin the sauce slightly. Continue cooking for about 5–7 minutes, or until the chicken is fully cooked and tender.

5 Finally, add the fresh chillies, coriander and cream, cook for a further 2 minutes over low heat, then serve.

> **Variation**
> If you like, you could lightly fry 1 sliced green (bell) pepper and 115g/4oz/1½ cups whole small button (white) mushrooms in 15ml/1 tbsp oil and add them to the spice mixture along with the chicken pieces in step 3.

Chicken Curry Energy 349kcal/1450kJ; Protein 25g; Carbohydrate 14.2g, of which sugars 11.8g; Fat 21.8g, of which saturates 5.6g; Cholesterol 108mg; Calcium 140mg; Fibre 2.8g; Sodium 124mg.
Sweet-and-sour Chicken Energy 355kcal/1486kJ; Protein 43.8g; Carbohydrate 10.1g, of which sugars 6.5g; Fat 15.9g, of which saturates 3g; Cholesterol 122mg; Calcium 85mg; Fibre 1.1g; Sodium 160mg.

Khara Masala Balti Chicken

Whole spices, called khara in India, are used in this balti curry, giving it a wonderfully rich and deep flavour. This is a dry dish so it is best served with a side dish that has plenty of sauce, such as a dhal and a creamy raita.

Serves 4
3 curry leaves
1.5ml/¼ tsp mustard seeds
1.5ml/¼ tsp fennel seeds
1.5ml/¼ tsp onion seeds
2.5ml/½ tsp crushed dried
   red chillies
2.5ml/½ tsp white cumin seeds
1.5ml/¼ tsp fenugreek seeds
2.5ml/½ tsp crushed pomegranate
   seeds
5ml/1 tsp salt
5ml/1 tsp grated fresh
   root ginger
3 garlic cloves, sliced
60ml/4 tbsp corn oil
4 fresh green chillies, slit
1 large onion, sliced
1 medium tomato, sliced
675g/1½lb skinless, boneless
   chicken, cubed
15ml/1 tbsp chopped fresh
   coriander (cilantro)

1 In a large mixing bowl, combine the curry leaves, mustard seeds, fennel seeds, onion seeds, crushed red chillies, cumin seeds, fenugreek seeds, crushed pomegranate seeds and salt. Mix well to combine all the ingredients.

2 Add the grated ginger and garlic cloves to the spice mixture in the bowl and stir well to combine.

3 Heat the oil in a medium karahi, wok or deep pan. Add the spice mixture, then the green chillies.

4 Spoon the sliced onion into the pan and fry over medium heat for about 5–7 minutes, stirring constantly to coat and flavour the onion with the spices.

5 Finally add the tomato and chicken pieces, and cook over medium heat for about 10–12 minutes, stirring frequently to prevent the sauce sticking to the pan. The chicken should be cooked through and the sauce reduced.

6 Serve immediately from the pan, garnished with chopped fresh coriander.

Red Hot Chicken Curry

This curry has a satisfyingly thick sauce, and uses sweet red and green bell peppers to give the dish a vibrant colour and flavour. You can use whatever chicken meat you prefer for this dish.

Serves 4
2 medium onions
½ red (bell) pepper
½ green (bell) pepper
30ml/2 tbsp vegetable oil
1.5ml/¼ tsp fenugreek seeds
1.5ml/¼ tsp onion seeds
2.5ml/½ tsp crushed garlic
2.5ml/½ tsp grated fresh
   root ginger
5ml/1 tsp ground coriander
5ml/1 tsp chilli powder
5ml/1 tsp salt
400g/14oz can tomatoes
30ml/2 tbsp lemon juice
350g/12oz chicken, skinned
   and cubed
30ml/2 tbsp chopped fresh
   coriander (cilantro)
3 fresh green chillies, chopped
fresh coriander (cilantro),
   to garnish

1 Using a sharp knife, dice the onions. Seed the peppers and cut the flesh into even chunks.

2 In a medium, heavy pan, heat the oil and stir-fry the fenugreek and onion seeds until they turn a shade darker. Add the chopped onions, crushed garlic and fresh ginger. Fry for about 5 minutes until the onions turn soft and golden brown. Reduce the heat to very low.

3 In a bowl, mix together the ground coriander, chilli powder, salt, canned tomatoes and lemon juice. Stir well.

4 Pour this mixture into the pan and increase the heat to medium. Stir-fry for about 3 minutes.

5 Add the chicken cubes and stir-fry for 5–7 minutes.

6 Add the chopped fresh coriander and green chillies and the red and green pepper chunks to the pan and stir well.

7 Lower the heat, cover the pan and allow to simmer for about 10 minutes, until the chicken cubes are cooked. Serve the curry hot, garnished with fresh coriander.

Khara Masala Energy 299kcal/1254kJ; Protein 41.5g; Carbohydrate 3.4g, of which sugars 1.7g; Fat 13.5g, of which saturates 1.9g; Cholesterol 118mg; Calcium 28mg; Fibre 0.6g; Sodium 106mg.
Red Hot Chicken Energy 177kcal/747kJ; Protein 24.2g; Carbohydrate 15.8g, of which sugars 11.2g; Fat 2.5g, of which saturates 0.5g; Cholesterol 61mg; Calcium 51mg; Fibre 3.1g; Sodium 560mg.

Spicy Chicken Jalfrezi

A jalfrezi curry is a stir-fried dish cooked with onions, ginger and garlic in a rich pepper sauce.

Serves 4

675g/1½lb skinless chicken
   breast fillets
30ml/2 tbsp vegetable oil
5ml/1 tsp cumin seeds
1 onion, finely chopped
1 green (bell) pepper,
   finely chopped
1 red (bell) pepper, finely chopped

1 garlic clove, crushed
2cm/¾in piece fresh root ginger,
   finely chopped
15ml/1 tbsp curry paste
1.5ml/¼ tsp chilli powder
5ml/1 tsp ground coriander
5ml/1 tsp ground cumin
2.5ml/½ tsp salt
400g/14oz can chopped
   tomatoes
30ml/2 tbsp chopped fresh
   coriander (cilantro), plus leaves,
   to garnish
plain boiled rice, to serve

1 Remove any visible fat from the chicken with a sharp knife and discard. Cut the chicken meat into 2.5cm/1in pieces.

2 Heat the oil in a wok or large frying pan and fry the cumin seeds for 2–3 minutes until they begin to splutter.

3 Add the onion, green and red peppers, garlic and ginger to the pan and fry for 6–8 minutes.

4 Add the curry paste to the pan and fry for about 2 minutes, stirring constantly, until it releases its fragrant aromas.

5 Stir the chilli powder, ground coriander, cumin and salt into the pan and stir in about 15ml/1 tbsp cold water. Cook, stirring constantly, for a further 2–4 minutes.

6 Add the chicken to the pan and cook for about 5 minutes, stirring occasionally. Add the chopped tomatoes and the fresh coriander to the pan and stir well.

7 Cover the pan with a lid and simmer over low heat for about 15–20 minutes, or until the chicken is cooked through and tender. Garnish with the coriander and serve immediately with plain boiled rice, if you like.

Balti Chicken Madras

This is a fairly hot chicken curry, which is excellent served with either plain boiled rice, pilau rice or naan bread. Reduce the number of chillies if you prefer a milder curry.

Serves 4

275g/10oz skinless chicken
   breast fillets
45ml/3 tbsp tomato purée (paste)
large pinch of ground fenugreek
1.5ml/¼ tsp ground fennel seeds
5ml/1 tsp grated fresh root ginger

7.5ml/1½ tsp ground coriander
5ml/1 tsp crushed garlic
5ml/1 tsp chilli powder
1.5ml/¼ tsp ground turmeric
30ml/2 tbsp lemon juice
5ml/1 tsp salt
300ml/½ pint/1¼ cups water
15ml/1 tbsp vegetable oil
2 medium onions, diced
2–4 curry leaves
2 fresh green chillies, seeded
   and chopped
15ml/1 tbsp fresh coriander
   (cilantro) leaves
naan bread or boiled rice, to serve

1 Remove any visible fat from the chicken breast fillets and cut the meat into bitesize pieces.

2 Place the tomato purée in a bowl and mix in the fenugreek, fennel seeds, ginger, coriander, garlic, chilli powder, turmeric, lemon juice, salt and measured water.

3 Heat the oil in a karahi, wok or heavy pan and fry the diced onions together with the curry leaves until the onions are golden brown and softened.

4 Add the chicken pieces to the onions and stir over the heat for about 1 minute to seal the meat.

5 Next, pour in the prepared spice mixture and continue to stir the chicken for about 2 minutes.

6 Lower the heat and cook for about 8–10 minutes, stirring frequently to prevent any of the mixture from catching and burning on the bottom of the pan.

7 Seed and chop the chillies. Add the chillies and coriander leaves and serve immediately with naan bread or rice.

Spicy Jalfrezi Energy 338kcal/1422kJ; Protein 44.8g; Carbohydrate 20.1g, of which sugars 14g; Fat 9.5g, of which saturates 1.5g; Cholesterol 118mg; Calcium 66mg; Fibre 3.8g; Sodium 120mg.
Chicken Madras Energy 159kcal/667kJ; Protein 19.3g; Carbohydrate 11.5g, of which sugars 7.8g; Fat 4.4g, of which saturates 0.6g; Cholesterol 48mg; Calcium 65mg; Fibre 2.4g; Sodium 573mg.

Chicken Dopiaza

Dopiaza translates literally as 'two onions' and describes this chicken curry in which two types of onion – medium and small – are used at different stages.

Serves 4
30ml/2 tbsp vegetable oil
8 small onions, halved
2 bay leaves
8 green cardamom pods
4 cloves
3 dried red chillies
8 black peppercorns
2 medium onions, finely chopped
2 garlic cloves, crushed
2.5cm/1in piece fresh root ginger, finely chopped
5ml/1 tsp ground coriander
5ml/1 tsp ground cumin
2.5ml/½ tsp ground turmeric
5ml/1 tsp chilli powder
2.5ml/½ tsp salt
4 tomatoes, peeled and finely chopped
120ml/4fl oz/½ cup water
8 chicken pieces, such as thighs and drumsticks, skinned
plain boiled rice, to serve

1 Heat half the oil in a wok or large heavy pan and fry the small onions over medium heat for about 8–10 minutes, or until golden brown. Remove and set aside.

2 Add the remaining oil and fry the bay leaves, cardamoms, cloves, chillies and peppercorns for 2 minutes.

3 Add the medium onions, garlic and ginger and fry for 5 minutes. Add the ground spices and salt and cook for 2 minutes.

4 Add the tomatoes and water and simmer for 5 minutes until the sauce thickens. Add the chicken and cook for 15 minutes.

5 Add the reserved small onions, then cover and cook for a further 10 minutes, or until the chicken is cooked through. Spoon the mixture on to a serving dish or individual plates. Serve immediately with plain boiled rice.

Cook's Tip
Soak the small onions in boiling water for about 2–3 minutes to make them easier to peel.

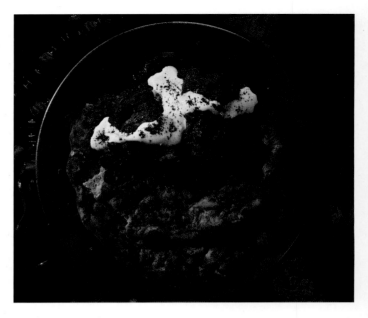

Chicken Saag

This mildly spiced curry uses a popular Indian combination of spinach and chicken. This dish is best made using fresh spinach.

Serves 4
225g/8oz fresh spinach leaves, washed but not dried
2.5cm/1in piece fresh root ginger, grated
2 garlic cloves, crushed
1 fresh green chilli, seeded and roughly chopped
200ml/7fl oz/scant 1 cup water
15ml/1 tbsp vegetable oil
2 bay leaves
1.5ml/¼ tsp black peppercorns
1 onion, finely chopped
4 tomatoes, peeled and finely chopped
10ml/2 tsp curry powder
5ml/1 tsp salt
5ml/1 tsp chilli powder
45ml/3 tbsp natural (plain) low-fat yogurt
8 chicken thighs, skinned
naan bread, to serve
natural low-fat yogurt and chilli powder, to garnish

1 Cook the spinach leaves, without extra water, in a tightly covered pan for 5 minutes. Put the cooked spinach, ginger, garlic and chilli with 50ml/2fl oz/¼ cup of the measured water into a food processor or blender and process to a thick purée. Set aside while you prepare the other ingredients.

2 Heat the oil in a large, heavy pan, add the bay leaves and black peppercorns and fry for 2 minutes. Stir in the onion and fry for a further 6–8 minutes until the onion has browned.

3 Add the tomatoes to the pan, lower the heat and simmer gently for about 5–8 minutes.

4 Stir in the curry powder, salt and chilli powder. Cook for 2 minutes over medium heat, stirring once or twice. Stir in the spinach purée and the remaining measured water, then simmer for 5 minutes. Add the yogurt, 15ml/1 tbsp at a time, and simmer for 5 minutes.

5 Add the chicken thighs and stir to coat them in the sauce. Cover and cook for 25–30 minutes until the chicken is tender. Serve on naan bread, drizzle over some natural yogurt and dust with chilli powder.

Chicken Dopiaza Energy 331kcal/1391kJ; Protein 44.7g; Carbohydrate 9.8g, of which sugars 4.8g; Fat 13.1g, of which saturates 2.6g; Cholesterol 210mg; Calcium 51mg; Fibre 1.4g; Sodium 194mg.
Chicken Saag Energy 238kcal/998kJ; Protein 34.7g; Carbohydrate 6.8g, of which sugars 5.6g; Fat 8.2g, of which saturates 1.7g; Cholesterol 158mg; Calcium 155mg; Fibre 3g; Sodium 735mg.

Balti Chicken in a Lentil Sauce

Traditionally, this curry is made with lamb, but it is just as delicious when made with chicken breast meat.

Serves 4
30ml/2 tbsp chana dhal (yellow lentils)
50g/2oz/¼ cup masoor dhal or red split peas
15ml/1 tbsp vegetable oil
2 medium onions, chopped
5ml/1 tsp crushed garlic
5ml/1 tsp grated fresh root ginger
2.5ml/½ tsp ground turmeric
7.5ml/1½ tsp chilli powder
5ml/1 tsp garam masala
2.5ml/½ tsp ground coriander

7.5ml/1½ tsp salt
175g/6oz skinless chicken breast fillets, cubed
45ml/3 tbsp fresh coriander (cilantro) leaves
1 or 2 fresh green chillies, seeded and chopped
30–45ml/2–3 tbsp lemon juice
300ml/½ pint/1¼ cups water
2 tomatoes, peeled and halved

For the tarka
5ml/1 tsp vegetable oil
2.5ml/½ tsp cumin seeds
2 garlic cloves
2 dried red chillies
4 curry leaves

1 Put the dhal or peas in a pan with water and bring to the boil. Cook for 30–45 minutes until soft and mushy. Drain and set aside. Heat the oil in a karahi, wok or heavy frying pan and fry the onions until soft and golden brown. Add the garlic, ginger, turmeric, chilli powder, garam masala, ground coriander and salt to the pan and stir well.

2 Next, add the chicken pieces to the pan and fry for about 5–7 minutes, stirring constantly over a medium heat to seal in the juices and lightly brown the meat.

3 Add half the fresh coriander, the green chillies, lemon juice and water and cook for 3–5 minutes. Stir in the cooked lentils, then add the tomatoes. Sprinkle over the remaining coriander leaves. Take the pan off the heat and set aside.

4 To make the tarka, heat the oil and add the cumin seeds, whole garlic cloves, dried red chillies and curry leaves. Heat for about 30 seconds then spread over the top of the chicken and lentils. Serve the dish immediately.

Chicken Dhansak with Chillies

Dhansak curries originate from the Parsee community and are traditionally made with lentils and meat.

Serves 4
75g/3oz/½ cup green lentils
475ml/16fl oz/2 cups chicken stock
45ml/3 tbsp vegetable oil
5ml/1 tsp cumin seeds
2 curry leaves
1 onion, finely chopped
2.5cm/1in piece fresh root ginger, chopped

1 green chilli, seeded and finely chopped
5ml/1 tsp ground cumin
5ml/1 tsp ground coriander
1.5ml/¼ tsp salt
1.5ml/¼ tsp chilli powder
400g/14oz can chopped tomatoes
8 chicken pieces, skinned
60ml/4 tbsp chopped fresh coriander (cilantro)
5ml/1 tsp garam masala
fresh coriander (cilantro) sprigs, to garnish
plain and yellow rice, to serve

1 Rinse the lentils under cold running water, and carefully pick through to remove any stones. Put the lentils into a large heavy pan with the chicken stock. Bring to the boil, cover the pan and simmer for about 15–20 minutes. Remove the pan from the heat and set aside.

2 Heat the oil in a karahi or large heavy pan. Fry the cumin seeds and curry leaves for 2 minutes until the fragrant aromas are released and the cumin seeds begin to splutter.

3 Add the onion, ginger and chilli to the pan. Cook for about 5 minutes, until the onion begins to soften and turn translucent. Stir in the ground cumin, ground coriander, salt and chilli powder with 30ml/2 tbsp water.

4 Add the chopped tomatoes and the chicken pieces. Cover the pan and simmer for 10–15 minutes.

5 Add the lentils with the chicken stock, chopped fresh coriander and garam masala and cook for 10 minutes, or until the chicken is cooked through and tender when pierced with a knife. Transfer the chicken to a bowl. Garnish with coriander sprigs and serve with plain and yellow rice.

Balti Chicken Energy 196kcal/823kJ; Protein 20.3g; Carbohydrate 9.8g, of which sugars 2.6g; Fat 8.7g, of which saturates 1.2g; Cholesterol 47mg; Calcium 41mg; Fibre 2.5g; Sodium 51mg.
Chicken Dhansak Energy 392kcal/1653kJ; Protein 54.9g; Carbohydrate 16.7g, of which sugars 4g; Fat 12.4g, of which saturates 1.9g; Cholesterol 140mg; Calcium 52mg; Fibre 2.9g; Sodium 135mg.

Balti Chicken with Chillied Lentils

This is rather an unusual combination of flavours, but highly recommended. The mango powder gives a delicious tangy flavour to this spicy dish.

Serves 4–6

75g/3oz/½ cup chana dhal (yellow lentils)
60ml/4 tbsp corn oil
2 medium leeks, chopped
6 large dried red chillies
4 curry leaves
5ml/1 tsp mustard seeds
10ml/2 tsp mango powder
2 medium tomatoes, chopped
2.5ml/½ tsp chilli powder
5ml/1 tsp ground coriander
5ml/1 tsp salt
450g/1lb chicken, skinned, boned and cubed
15ml/1 tbsp chopped fresh coriander (cilantro)

1 Wash the yellow lentils and and carefully pick through to remove any stones or bits of grit.

2 Put the lentils into a pan with enough water to cover, and boil for about 10 minutes until they are soft but not mushy. Drain and set aside in a bowl.

3 Heat the oil in a medium karahi or large frying pan. Lower the heat slightly and add the leeks, dried red chillies, curry leaves and mustard seeds to the pan. Stir-fry gently for a few minutes until the leeks soften and the spices are fragrant.

4 Add the mango powder, tomatoes, chilli powder, ground coriander, salt and chicken, and stir-fry for 8–10 minutes.

5 Mix in the cooked lentils and fry for a further 2 minutes, or until you are sure that the chicken is cooked right through. Garnish with the fresh coriander and serve immediately accompanied by naan or paratha bread.

Cook's Tip
Chana dhal, a yellow split lentil, is available from Asian stores and larger supermarkets. However, yellow split peas are a good substitute if you cannot find them.

Chicken and Pasta Balti

This is not a traditional balti dish, as pasta is not eaten widely in India or Pakistan, however, it is a delicious fusion curry. Pomegranate seeds give this curry an unusual and delicious tangy flavour. Use vari-coloured pasta shells for a most attractive appearance.

Serves 4–6

75g/3oz/¾ cup small pasta shells
75ml/5 tbsp corn oil
4 curry leaves
4 whole dried red chillies
1 large onion, sliced
5ml/1 tsp crushed garlic
5ml/1 tsp chilli powder
5ml/1 tsp grated fresh root ginger
5ml/1 tsp crushed pomegranate seeds
5ml/1 tsp salt
2 medium tomatoes, chopped
175g/6oz/1⅓ cups chicken, skinned, boned and cubed
225g/8oz/1½ cups canned chickpeas, drained
115g/4oz/⅔ cup corn
50g/2oz mangetouts (snow peas), diagonally sliced
15ml/1 tbsp chopped fresh coriander (cilantro) (optional)
chutneys and pickles, to serve

1 Cook the pasta in boiling water, following the directions on the packet. Add 15ml/1 tbsp of the oil to the water to stop the pasta from sticking together. When it is cooked, drain well and set to one side while you prepare the other ingredients.

2 Heat the remaining oil in a deep, heavy frying pan or a large karahi, and add the curry leaves, whole dried chillies and the onion. Fry for about 5 minutes.

3 Add the garlic, chilli powder, ginger, pomegranate seeds, salt and tomatoes. Stir-fry for about 3 minutes.

4 Next add the chicken, chickpeas, corn and mangetouts to the onion mixture in the pan. Cook over a medium heat for about 5–7 minutes, stirring frequently.

5 Add in the pasta and stir well. Cook for a further 7–10 minutes until the chicken is cooked through.

6 Serve this curry garnished with the fresh coriander, if you like, and accompanied by Indian chutneys and pickles.

Balti Chicken Energy 196kcal/822kJ; Protein 20.3g; Carbohydrate 9.8g, of which sugars 2.6g; Fat 8.7g, of which saturates 1.2g; Cholesterol 47mg; Calcium 41mg; Fibre 2.5g; Sodium 51mg.
Chicken Balti Energy 350kcal/1468kJ; Protein 20.6g; Carbohydrate 29.4g, of which sugars 5.9g; Fat 17.6g, of which saturates 2.7g; Cholesterol 36mg; Calcium 51mg; Fibre 4.2g; Sodium 157mg.

Balti Chicken with Spicy Potatoes

The baby potatoes in this dish are first tossed in spices and then baked separately in the oven before being added to the balti chicken, making an unusual yet delectable curry.

Serves 4

150ml/¼ pint/⅔ cup natural
    (plain) low-fat yogurt
25g/1oz/¼ cup ground almonds
7.5ml/1½ tsp ground coriander
2.5ml/½ tsp chilli powder
5ml/1 tsp garam masala
15ml/1 tbsp coconut milk
5ml/1 tsp crushed garlic
5ml/1 tsp grated fresh root ginger

30ml/2 tbsp chopped fresh
    coriander (cilantro)
1 fresh red chilli, seeded
    and chopped
225g/8oz skinless chicken
    breast fillets, cubed
15ml/1 tbsp vegetable oil
2 medium onions, sliced
3 green cardamom pods
2.5cm/1in cinnamon stick
2 cloves

For the potatoes

15ml/1 tbsp vegetable oil
8 baby potatoes, thickly sliced
1.5ml/¼ tsp cumin seeds
15ml/1 tbsp finely chopped
    fresh coriander (cilantro)

1 In a large bowl, mix together the first eight ingredients with half the fresh coriander and half the red chilli. Place the chicken pieces in the mixture, mix well, then cover and leave to marinate for about 2 hours.

2 Meanwhile, start to prepare the spicy potatoes. Heat the oil in a karahi, wok or heavy pan. Add the sliced potatoes, cumin seeds and fresh coriander and quickly stir-fry for 2–3 minutes.

3 Preheat the oven to 180°C/350°F/Gas 4. Spoon the potatoes into a baking dish, cover and bake in the oven for about 30 minutes or until they are cooked through.

4 Halfway through the potatoes' cooking time, heat the oil and fry the onions, cardamoms, cinnamon and cloves for 2 minutes.

5 Add the chicken mixture to the fried onions and stir-fry for 5–7 minutes. Lower the heat, cover and cook for 5–7 minutes until cooked through. Top the balti with the potatoes and garnish with the fresh coriander and red chilli before serving.

Balinese Spiced Duck

This delicious duck dish is popular in Bali and across the neighbouring islands.

Serves 4

8 skinless duck breast fillets,
    fat trimmed
50g/2oz desiccated (dry
    unsweetened shredded) coconut
175ml/6fl oz/¾ cup coconut milk
salt and ground black pepper
deep-fried onions, to garnish
salad leaves or herb sprigs, to serve

For the spice paste

1 small onion or 4–6 shallots,
    finely sliced
2 garlic cloves, sliced
2.5cm/½ in fresh root ginger,
    peeled and sliced
1cm/½in fresh lengkuas, peeled
    and sliced
2.5cm/1in fresh turmeric or
    2.5ml/½ tsp ground turmeric
1–2 red chillies, seeded and sliced
4 macadamia nuts or 8 almonds
5ml/1 tsp coriander seeds, dry-fried

1 Place the duck fat trimmings in a heated frying pan, without oil, and allow the fat to render. Reserve the fat.

2 Dry-fry the desiccated coconut in a preheated pan until crisp and brown in colour.

3 To make the spice paste, blend the onion or shallots, garlic, ginger, lengkuas, fresh or ground turmeric, chillies, nuts and coriander seeds to a paste in a food processor.

4 Spread the spice paste over the duck portions and leave to marinate in a cool place for 3–4 hours. Preheat the oven to 160°C/325°F/Gas 3. Shake off the spice paste and transfer the duck fillets to an oiled roasting pan. Cover with a double layer of foil and cook the duck in the oven for 2 hours.

5 Turn the oven temperature up to 190°C/375°F/Gas 5. Heat the reserved fat in a pan, add the paste and fry for 2 minutes. Stir in the coconut milk and simmer for 2 minutes. Discard the duck juices then cover the duck with the spice mix and sprinkle with the toasted coconut. Cook in the oven for 20–30 minutes.

6 Arrange the duck on a warm serving platter and sprinkle with the deep-fried onions. Season to taste and serve with the salad leaves or fresh herb sprigs of your choice.

Balti Chicken Energy 169kcal/711kJ; Protein 16.8g; Carbohydrate 16.2g, of which sugars 5.9g; Fat 4.6g, of which saturates 0.6g; Cholesterol 39mg; Calcium 128mg; Fibre 4.4g; Sodium 75mg.
Balinese Spiced Duck Energy 305kcal/1270kJ; Protein 18.7g; Carbohydrate 9.2g, of which sugars 4.2g; Fat 22g, of which saturates 9.3g; Cholesterol 63mg; Calcium 79mg; Fibre 2.8g; Sodium 108mg.

Indian Lamb and Chickpea Burgers

Serve this spicy Indian burger in a bun with a dollop of chilli sauce and a salad made with tomatoes, onion and lettuce, or serve it unaccompanied as a delicious appetizer.

Serves 4–6

50g/2oz/⅓ cup chickpeas, soaked overnight in a pan of water
2 onions, finely chopped
250g/9oz lean lamb, cut into small cubes
5ml/1 tsp cumin seeds
5ml/1 tsp garam masala
4–6 fresh green chillies, roughly chopped
5cm/2in piece fresh root ginger, crushed
175ml/6fl oz/¾ cup water
a few fresh coriander (cilantro) and mint leaves, chopped
juice of 1 lemon
15ml/1 tbsp gram flour
2 eggs, beaten
vegetable oil, for shallow-frying
salt
½ lime, to garnish

1 Drain the chickpeas and cook them in a pan of boiling water for 1 hour. Drain again, return to the pan and add the onions, lamb, cumin seeds, garam masala, chillies, ginger and water, and salt to taste. Bring to the boil. Simmer, covered, for about 2 hours until the meat and chickpeas are cooked.

2 Remove the lid and continue to cook uncovered to reduce the excess liquid. Leave to cool, and then grind to a paste in a food processor, blender or with a mortar and pestle.

3 Scrape the mixture into a mixing bowl and add the fresh coriander and mint, lemon juice and flour. Knead well. Divide the mixture into 10–12 portions and roll each into a ball, then flatten slightly. Chill in the refrigerator for 1 hour.

4 Dip the burgers in the beaten egg and shallow-fry each side until golden brown. Serve immediately, with the lime.

Variation
Chicken breast meat or lean pork would also work well in these burgers instead of the lamb.

Spicy Spring Roast Lamb

Coating a leg of lamb with a spicy, fruity rub gives it a wonderful flavour.

Serves 6

1.6kg/3½lb lean leg of spring lamb
5ml/1 tsp chilli powder
5ml/1 tsp crushed garlic
5ml/1 tsp ground coriander
5ml/1 tsp ground cumin
5ml/1 tsp salt
15ml/1 tbsp dried breadcrumbs
45ml/3 tbsp natural (plain) low-fat yogurt
30ml/2 tbsp lemon juice
30ml/2 tbsp sultanas (golden raisins)
15ml/1 tbsp vegetable oil

For the garnish
mixed salad leaves
fresh coriander (cilantro)
2 tomatoes, quartered
1 large carrot, shredded
lemon wedges

1 Preheat the oven to 180°C/350°F/Gas 4. Trim any excess fat from the lamb. Rinse the joint, pat it dry and set aside on a sheet of foil large enough to enclose it completely.

2 In a medium bowl, mix together the chilli powder, garlic, ground coriander, ground cumin and salt.

3 Mix together the breadcrumbs, yogurt, lemon juice and sultanas in a food processor or blender.

4 Add the contents of the food processor to the spice mixture together with the oil and mix together well. Pour this on to the leg of lamb and rub all over the meat.

5 Enclose the meat in the foil and place in an ovenproof dish. Cook in the oven for about 1½ hours.

6 Remove the lamb from the oven, open up the foil wrapping and, using the back of a spoon, spread the mixture evenly over the top of the meat. Return the lamb, uncovered this time, to the oven for another 45–50 minutes or until the meat is cooked right through and tender.

7 Slice the meat and serve with the mixed salad leaves, fresh coriander, tomatoes, carrot and lemon wedges.

Indian Lamb Burgers Energy 245kcal/1019kJ; Protein 14g; Carbohydrate 14.4g, of which sugars 4.9g; Fat 15.1g, of which saturates 3.7g; Cholesterol 95mg; Calcium 60mg; Fibre 2.1g; Sodium 67mg.
Spring Roast Lamb Energy 478kcal/1987kJ; Protein 39.1g; Carbohydrate 3.5g, of which sugars 0.6g; Fat 34.4g, of which saturates 10.1g; Cholesterol 145mg; Calcium 37mg; Fibre 0g; Sodium 119mg.

Creamy Lamb Korma

This is a delicious creamy and aromatic curry. It is perfect for those who prefer a spicy curry that is not too hot.

Serves 4–6

15ml/1 tbsp white sesame seeds
15ml/1 tbsp white poppy seeds
50g/2oz almonds, blanched
2 green chillies, seeded
5cm/2in piece fresh root
   ginger, sliced
6 garlic cloves, sliced
1 onion, finely chopped
45ml/3 tbsp ghee or vegetable oil
6 green cardamoms
5cm/2in piece cinnamon stick
4 cloves
900g/2lb lean lamb, cubed
5ml/1 tsp ground cumin
5ml/1 tsp ground coriander
salt
300ml/½ pint/1¼ cups double
   (heavy) cream mixed with
   2.5ml/½ tsp cornflour
   (cornstarch)
roasted sesame seeds, to garnish

1 Heat a heavy frying pan without any liquid or oil and dry-roast the sesame and poppy seeds, almonds, chillies, ginger, garlic and onion for about 3–5 minutes until the aromatic fragrances of the spices are released.

2 Leave the mixture to cool slightly and grind to a fine paste using a mortar and pestle or a food processor. Heat the ghee or oil in a wok or frying pan.

3 Add the cardamoms, cinnamon and cloves to the pan. Stir-fry the spices until the cloves begin to swell.

4 Add the lamb, ground cumin and coriander, and the prepared paste to the pan. Season with salt, to taste.

5 Cover the pan and cook over a low heat until the lamb is almost done, about 30–40 minutes.

6 Remove the pan from the heat, leave it to cool a little and then gradually fold in the double cream, reserving about 15ml/1 tsp to use as a garnish.

7 To serve, gently reheat the lamb uncovered and serve hot, garnished with the sesame seeds and the remaining cream.

Lamb Korma with Mint

This is a superb curry of lamb cooked in a creamy sauce flavoured with mint, coconut, chillies and a subtle blend of spices. It is quick and easy to cook because the lamb is sliced into thin strips, making it ideal for a simple midweek meal for family or friends.

Serves 4

2 fresh green chillies
120ml/4fl oz/½ cup natural
   (plain) low-fat yogurt
50ml/2fl oz/¼ cup coconut milk
15ml/1 tbsp ground almonds
5ml/1 tsp salt
5ml/1 tsp crushed garlic
5ml/1 tsp grated fresh
   root ginger
5ml/1 tsp garam masala
1.5ml/¼ tsp ground cardamom
large pinch of ground cinnamon
15ml/1 tbsp chopped fresh mint
15ml/1 tbsp vegetable oil
2 medium onions, diced
1 bay leaf
4 black peppercorns
225g/8oz lean lamb, cut
   into strips
150ml/¼ pint/⅔ cup water
fresh mint leaves, roughly torn,
   to garnish

1 Finely chop the chillies. Whisk the yogurt with the chillies, coconut milk, ground almonds, salt, garlic, ginger, garam masala, cardamom, cinnamon and mint.

2 Heat the oil in a karahi, wok or heavy pan and fry the onions with the bay leaf and peppercorns for about 5 minutes.

3 When the onions are soft and golden brown, add the lamb and stir-fry for about 2 minutes.

4 Pour in the yogurt and coconut mixture and the water, lower the heat, cover and cook for about 15 minutes or until the lamb is cooked through, stirring occasionally. Uncover and stir the mixture over the heat for a further 2 minutes to reduce the sauce. Serve garnished with fresh mint leaves.

> **Cook's Tip**
> Basmati rice with peas and curry leaves goes very well with this curry.

Creamy Lamb Korma Energy 220kcal/916kJ; Protein 14.2g; Carbohydrate 14.5g, of which sugars 11.1g; Fat 12.2g, of which saturates 3.8g; Cholesterol 42mg; Calcium 101mg; Fibre 2.1g; Sodium 90mg.
Lamb Korma with Mint Energy 197kcal/823kJ; Protein 14.5g; Carbohydrate 13.6g, of which sugars 9.9g; Fat 10g, of which saturates 3.5g; Cholesterol 43mg; Calcium 101mg; Fibre 1.8g; Sodium 583mg.

Malay Lamb Korma with Coconut Milk

Adapted from the traditional Indian korma, the creamy Malay version is flavoured with coconut milk. This tasty curry is often accompanied by a fragrant rice or flatbread and a salad or sambal.

Serves 4–6

25g/1oz fresh root ginger, peeled and chopped
4 garlic cloves, chopped
2 red chillies, seeded and chopped
10ml/2 tsp garam masala
10ml/2 tsp ground coriander
5ml/1 tsp ground cumin
5ml/1 tsp ground turmeric

675g/1½lb lamb shoulder, cut into bitesize cubes
45ml/3 tbsp ghee, or 30ml/2 tbsp vegetable oil and 15g/½ oz/ 1 tbsp butter
2 onions, halved lengthways and sliced along the grain
2.5ml/½ tsp sugar
4–6 cardamom pods, bruised
1 cinnamon stick
400ml/14fl oz/1⅔ cups coconut milk
salt and ground black pepper
30ml/2 tbsp roasted peanuts, crushed, and fresh coriander (cilantro) and mint leaves, coarsely chopped, to garnish

1 Using a mortar and pestle or food processor, grind the ginger, garlic and chillies to a paste. Stir in the garam masala, ground coriander, cumin and turmeric. Put the lamb into a shallow dish and rub the paste into it. Cover and leave to marinate for 1 hour.

2 Heat the ghee or oil and butter in a heavy pan or flameproof pot. Add the onions and sugar, and cook until brown and almost caramelized. Stir in the cardamom pods and cinnamon stick and add the lamb with all the marinade. Mix well and cook until the meat is browned all over.

3 Pour in the coconut milk, stir well and bring to the boil. Reduce the heat, cover the pan and cook the meat gently for 30–40 minutes until tender. Make sure the meat doesn't become dry and stir in a little extra coconut milk, or water, if necessary.

4 Season to taste with salt and pepper. Sprinkle the peanuts over and garnish with the coriander and mint. Serve immediately.

Fragrant Lamb Curry

Essentially a Muslim dish known as rezala, this curry comes from Bengal.

Serves 4

1 large onion, roughly chopped
10ml/2 tsp grated fresh root ginger
10ml/2 tsp crushed garlic
4–5 cloves
2.5ml/½ tsp black peppercorns
6 green cardamom pods
5cm/2in cinnamon stick, halved
8 lamb rib chops
60ml/4 tbsp vegetable oil
1 large onion, finely sliced

175ml/6fl oz/¾ cup natural (plain) yogurt
50g/2oz/¼ cup butter
5ml/1 tsp salt
2.5ml/½ tsp ground cumin
2.5ml/½ tsp hot chilli powder
2.5ml/½ tsp freshly grated nutmeg
2.5ml/½ tsp sugar
15ml/1 tbsp lime juice
pinch of saffron, steeped in 15ml/1 tbsp hot water for 10–15 minutes
15ml/1 tbsp rose water
rose petals or other flower petals, to garnish

1 Process the onion in a blender or food processor. Add a little water if necessary to form a purée. Put the purée in a glass bowl and add the grated ginger, crushed garlic, cloves, peppercorns, cardamom pods, and cinnamon. Mix well.

2 Put the lamb in a glass dish and add the spice mixture. Mix thoroughly, cover and leave to marinate for 3–4 hours.

3 In a wok, karahi or large pan, heat the oil over a medium-high heat and fry the sliced onion for 6–7 minutes, until golden brown. Remove the onion slices, squeezing out as much oil as possible back into the pan. Drain the onion on kitchen paper. In the remaining oil, fry the lamb chops for 5 minutes, stirring frequently. Reduce the heat, cover and simmer for 5–7 minutes.

4 Meanwhile, mix the yogurt and butter together in a pan and cook over a low heat for 5 minutes, then stir into the lamb chops along with the salt. Add the cumin and chilli powder and cover the pan. Cook for 45–50 minutes until the chops are tender.

5 Add the nutmeg and sugar, cook for 1–2 minutes and add the lime juice, saffron and rose water. Stir well and simmer for 2 minutes. Serve garnished with the fried onion and rose petals.

Malay Lamb Korma Energy 267kcal/1117kJ; Protein 24.3g; Carbohydrate 8.5g, of which sugars 6.8g; Fat 15.4g, of which saturates 6.4g; Cholesterol 86mg; Calcium 46mg; Fibre 1.2g; Sodium 211mg.
Fragrant Lamb Curry Energy 399kcal/1664kJ; Protein 22.6g; Carbohydrate 35.1g, of which sugars 7.5g; Fat 18.8g, of which saturates 7.8g; Cholesterol 74mg; Calcium 70mg; Fibre 1.4g; Sodium 131mg.

Curried Moroccan Lamb with Honey and Prunes

This sweet and spicy dish is eaten by Moroccan Jews at Rosh Hashanah, the Jewish New Year. Ras al hanout is a mixture of spices that may include cardamom, clove, cinnamon, paprika, cumin, nutmeg and turmeric.

Serves 6
130g/4½oz/generous ½ cup pitted prunes
350ml/12fl oz/1½ cups hot tea
1kg/2¼lb stewing or braising lamb, cut into chunky portions
1 onion, chopped
75–90ml/5–6 tbsp chopped fresh parsley
2.5ml/½ tsp ground ginger
2.5ml/½ tsp curry powder or ras al hanout
pinch of freshly grated nutmeg
10ml/2 tsp ground cinnamon
1.5ml/¼ tsp saffron threads
30ml/2 tbsp hot water
75–120ml/5–9 tbsp honey, to taste
250ml/8fl oz/1 cup beef or lamb stock
115g/4oz/1 cup blanched almonds, toasted
30ml/2 tbsp chopped fresh coriander (cilantro) leaves
3 hard-boiled eggs, cut into wedges
salt and ground black pepper

1 Preheat the oven to 180°C/350°F/Gas 4. Put the prunes in a bowl, pour over the tea and cover. Leave to soak and plump up.

2 Meanwhile, put the lamb, chopped onion, parsley, ginger, curry powder or ras al hanout, nutmeg, cinnamon, salt and pepper in a roasting pan. Mix together well. Cover and cook in the oven for about 2 hours, or until the meat is tender.

3 Drain the pitted prunes; add their liquid to the lamb. Combine the saffron and hot water in a small bowl and add to the pan with the honey and stock.

4 Place in the preheated oven and bake, uncovered, for about 30 minutes, turning the lamb occasionally.

5 Add the prunes to the pan and stir gently to mix. Serve the dish sprinkled with the toasted almonds and chopped coriander, and topped with the wedges of hard-boiled egg.

Lamb Dhansak

This piquant curry features lamb with a medley of spices.

Serves 4
45ml/3 tbsp sunflower oil
1 large onion, finely chopped
10ml/2 tsp ginger purée
10ml/2 tsp garlic purée
5ml/1 tsp coriander seeds
2.5ml/½ tsp cumin seeds
4 green cardamom pods
2.5cm/1in cinnamon stick, broken
10–12 black peppercorns
2 bay leaves
5–6 fenugreek seeds
2.5ml/½ tsp black mustard seeds
5ml/1 tsp chilli powder or to taste

675g/1½lb boned leg of lamb, cut into 5cm/2in cubes
150g/5oz canned tomatoes
5ml/1 tsp salt, or to taste

For the lentils and vegetables
75g/3oz/⅓ cup each yellow split peas and red split lentils
30ml/2 tbsp sunflower oil
1 medium onion, finely chopped
2 green chillies, chopped
5ml/1 tsp ground turmeric
1 small aubergine (eggplant), cubed
5ml/1 tsp salt or to taste
30ml/2 tbsp lime juice
15ml/1 tbsp chopped coriander (cilantro), plus extra to garnish

1 In a heavy pan, heat the oil and fry the onion until soft, then add the ginger and garlic and fry until brown. Grind the coriander, cumin, cardamom, cinnamon, peppercorns, bay leaves, fenugreek and mustard seeds finely in a food processor. Add the chilli and ground spices to the onion and cook for 2 minutes.

2 Add the meat and fry over a high heat until brown. Add the tomatoes and salt, and pour in 120ml/4fl oz/½ cup warm water. Bring the pan to the boil, cover and simmer for 35–40 minutes.

3 Wash the split peas and lentils and drain. Heat the oil in a medium pan and fry the onion and chillies until browned, about 8–9 minutes. Stir in the turmeric, lentils and aubergine.

4 Pour in 600ml/1 pint/2½ cups warm water, and simmer for 20–25 minutes, stirring. Add salt, then push the lentils through a sieve (strainer). Discard any coarse mixture left in the sieve.

5 Add the lime juice to the lentils. Pour over the lamb and simmer for 20 minutes, stirring occasionally. Stir in the coriander and remove from the heat. Serve garnished with coriander.

Moroccan Lamb Energy 618kcal/2564kJ; Protein 42.7g; Carbohydrate 0.8g, of which sugars 0.1g; Fat 49.3g, of which saturates 21.2g; Cholesterol 183mg; Calcium 16mg; Fibre 0.2g; Sodium 150mg.
Lamb Dhansak Energy 470kcal/1970kJ; Protein 32.7g; Carbohydrate 36.5g, of which sugars 9g; Fat 22.7g, of which saturates 7.1g; Cholesterol 85.5mg; Calcium 106mg; Fibre 4.8g; Sodium 133mg.

Spiced Lamb in a Yogurt Sauce

The lamb is first marinated and then cooked slowly in a hot yogurt sauce. It is served with dried apricots that have been lightly sautéed with spices.

Serves 4

15ml/1 tbsp tomato purée (paste)
175ml/6fl oz/⅔ cup natural (plain) low-fat yogurt
5ml/1 tsp garam masala
1.5ml/¼ tsp cumin seeds
5ml/1 tsp salt
5ml/1 tsp crushed garlic
5ml/1 tsp crushed fresh root ginger
5ml/1 tsp chilli powder
225g/8oz lean spring lamb, cut into strips
15ml/3 tsp corn oil
2 medium onions, finely sliced
25g/1oz low-fat spread
2.5cm/1in cinnamon stick
2 green cardamom pods
5 ready-to-eat dried apricots, quartered
15ml/1 tbsp fresh coriander (cilantro) leaves

1 In a bowl, blend together the tomato purée, yogurt, garam masala, cumin seeds, salt, garlic, ginger and chilli powder. Place the lamb in the sauce and leave to marinate for about 1 hour.

2 Heat 10ml/2 tsp of the oil in a non-stick wok or frying pan and fry the onions until crisp and golden brown.

3 Remove the onions using a slotted spoon, allow to cool and then grind down by processing briefly in a food processor or with a pestle in a mortar. Reheat the oil remaining in the wok and return the onions to the wok or frying pan.

4 Add the lamb and stir-fry for about 2 minutes. Cover, lower the heat and cook for 15 minutes, or until the meat is cooked through. If required, add about 150ml/¼ pint/⅔ cup water during the cooking. Remove from the heat and set aside.

5 Heat the low-fat spread with the remaining oil in a pan and drop in the cinnamon stick and cardamoms.

6 Add the dried apricots to the pan and stir over low heat for about 2 minutes to heat through. Pour this over the lamb. Serve immediately garnished with the coriander.

Kashmiri-style Lamb with Chilli

This deliciously creamy curry originated in Kashmir in north-west India.

Serves 4–6

60ml/4 tbsp vegetable oil
1.5ml/¼ tsp asafoetida
900g/2lb lean lamb, cubed
5cm/2in piece fresh root ginger, crushed
2 garlic cloves, crushed
60ml/4 tbsp rogan josh masala paste
5ml/1 tsp chilli powder
8–10 strands saffron (optional)
salt
150ml/¼ pint/⅔ cup natural (plain) low-fat yogurt, beaten, plus extra to serve
flaked (sliced) almonds, to garnish

1 Heat the oil in a frying pan and fry the asafoetida and lamb, stirring well to seal the meat. Reduce the heat, cover, then cook for about 10 minutes.

2 Add the remaining ingredients except the yogurt and almonds and mix well. If the meat is too dry, add a very small quantity of boiling water. Cover and cook on a low heat for a further 10 minutes.

3 Remove the pan from the heat and leave to cool a little. Add the yogurt, 15ml/1 tbsp at a time, stirring constantly to avoid curdling. Cook uncovered over a low heat until the gravy becomes thick. Spoon the curry on to a large serving dish. Garnish with the flaked almonds and serve immediately while still hot with a spoonful of yogurt.

Cook's Tips

• *Ready-made spice pastes are the perfect way to speed up the time you spend in the kitchen. There are many varieties and they are widely available in large supermarkets and Asian stores so you are sure to find one that suits your dish without too much trouble.*

• *Saffron strands are the dried stigmas of a crocus flower, which impart a fabulous yellow-orange colour to this dish. Harvesting and processing saffron is very labour-intensive, therefore it is by far the most expensive spice in the world.*

Spiced Lamb Energy 302kcal/1259kJ; Protein 16.4g; Carbohydrate 19.6g, of which sugars 15.4g; Fat 18.3g, of which saturates 4.9g; Cholesterol 44mg; Calcium 139mg; Fibre 2.7g; Sodium 141mg.
Kashmiri-style Lamb Energy 410kcal/1709kJ; Protein 32.2g; Carbohydrate 5.4g, of which sugars 1.9g; Fat 29.3g, of which saturates 9.4g; Cholesterol 114mg; Calcium 78mg; Fibre 0g; Sodium 153mg.

Spicy Lamb Stew with Cassava

Spicy stews are very much part of the Peruvian kitchen, and cooks will appreciate this clever combination of ingredients. This kind of stew is called seco (dry) to distinguish it from the soupy aguadito. It contains potatoes, cassava, coriander, hot chilli sauce and spices. It is served with rice and often with beans too, and with chilli sauce for those who like extra heat in their stew.

Serves 4
500g/1¼lb boneless lamb
   leg steaks
90ml/6 tbsp vegetable oil
1 medium onion, finely chopped
5ml/1 tsp ground cumin
15ml/1 tbsp chilli sauce
1 bunch coriander (cilantro)
1 litre/1¾ pints/4 cups water
500g/1¼lb white potatoes, peeled
   and halved
500g/1¼lb cassava, peeled and
   cut into 7.5cm/3in chunks
250g/9oz/2 cups shelled fresh
   green peas
salt
plain boiled rice and chilli sauce,
   to serve

1 Cut the meat into 5cm/2in pieces. Heat the oil in a large pan and fry the meat over a medium to high heat until browned on all sides. Reduce the heat, add the onion and fry until it is golden, then add the cumin and chilli sauce and stir well.

2 Purée the coriander in a blender or processor with 250ml/8fl oz/1 cup of the water. Add the coriander paste to the pan with the remaining water and bring to the boil, then add the potatoes, cassava and peas. Season.

3 Cover the pan and leave to simmer for 30 minutes, or until the meat and vegetables are tender. Serve immediately with white rice and chilli sauce.

Cook's Tip
Cassava is a starchy root vegetable, native to South America. If you cannot obtain cassava, then substitute potatoes, turnips or swede (rutabaga) for equally delicious results.

Balti Lamb with Yogurt and Spices

This is a traditional tikka recipe, in which the lamb is marinated in a mixture of yogurt and spices. The lamb is usually cut into bitesize cubes, but the cooking time for the curry can be halved by cutting it into thinner strips instead, as is done with this recipe.

Serves 4
450g/1lb lamb, cut into strips
175ml/6fl oz/¾ cup natural
   (plain) yogurt
5ml/1 tsp ground cumin
5ml/1 tsp ground coriander
5ml/1 tsp chilli powder
5ml/1 tsp crushed garlic
5ml/1 tsp salt
5ml/1 tsp garam masala
30ml/2 tbsp chopped fresh
   coriander (cilantro)
30ml/2 tbsp lemon juice
30ml/2 tbsp corn oil
15ml/1 tbsp tomato
   purée (paste)
1 large green (bell) pepper,
   seeded and sliced
3 large fresh red chillies

1 Put the lamb strips, yogurt, ground cumin, ground coriander, chilli powder, garlic, salt, garam masala, fresh coriander and lemon juice into a large mixing bowl and stir thoroughly. Set aside for at least 1 hour to marinate.

2 Heat the corn oil in a deep, heavy frying pan or a medium karahi or wok. Lower the heat slightly and add the tomato purée to the pan.

3 Add the lamb strips to the pan, a few at a time, leaving any excess marinade behind in the bowl.

4 Cook the lamb, stirring frequently, for about 7–10 minutes or until it is well browned all over.

5 Finally, add the green pepper slices and the whole red chillies. Heat through, checking that the lamb is cooked, and serve.

Cook's Tip
Use tender cuts of lamb for this curry, such as leg or loin meat, so that it cooks quickly in the pan.

Spicy Lamb Energy 662kcal/2771kJ; Protein 34.2g; Carbohydrate 62.1g, of which sugars 16.1g; Fat 32.6g, of which saturates 8.7g; Cholesterol 95mg; Calcium 113mg; Fibre 9.2g; Sodium 180mg.
Balti Lamb Energy 221kcal/923kJ; Protein 15.2g; Carbohydrate 13.1g, of which sugars 9.5g; Fat 12.6g, of which saturates 6.5g; Cholesterol 57mg; Calcium 122mg; Fibre 1.5g; Sodium 136mg.

Balti Lamb Tikka

One of the best ways of tenderizing meat is to marinate it in papaya, which must be unripe or it will lend its sweetness to what should be a savoury dish.

Serves 4

675g/1½lb lean lamb, cubed
1 unripe papaya
45ml/3 tbsp natural (plain) yogurt
5ml/1 tsp crushed fresh root ginger
5ml/1 tsp chilli powder
5ml/1 tsp crushed garlic
1.5ml/¼ tsp turmeric
10ml/2 tsp ground coriander
5ml/1 tsp ground cumin
5ml/1 tsp salt
30ml/2 tbsp lemon juice
15ml/1 tbsp chopped fresh coriander (cilantro), plus extra to garnish
1.5ml/¼ tsp red food colouring
300ml/½ pint/1¼ cups corn oil
lemon wedges and onion rings, to garnish

1 Place the lamb in a bowl. Peel and halve the papaya, and scoop out the seeds. Cut the flesh into cubes and blend in a food processor or blender, adding a little water if necessary.

2 Pour 30ml/2 tbsp of the papaya over the lamb and rub it in well with your fingers. Set aside for at least 3 hours.

3 Mix together the yogurt, ginger, chilli powder, garlic, turmeric, ground coriander, cumin, salt, lemon juice, fresh coriander, food colouring and 30ml/2 tbsp of oil. Pour over the lamb and mix.

4 Heat the remaining oil in a deep frying pan or a karahi. Lower the heat slightly and add the lamb cubes, a few at a time. Deep-fry each batch for 5–7 minutes or until the lamb is cooked. Keep warm while the remainder is fried.

5 Transfer to a serving dish and garnish with lemon wedges, onion rings and fresh coriander. Serve with raita and naan.

Cook's Tip
A meat tenderizer, available from supermarkets, can be used in place of the papaya. However, the meat will need a longer marinating time and should be left to tenderize overnight.

Spicy Lamb with Mint Peas

A simple curry for a family meal, this is easy to prepare and very versatile. It is equally delicious whether served with plain boiled rice or bread. Another excellent use for the lamb mixture is for filling samosas.

Serves 4
15ml/1 tbsp vegetable oil
1 medium onion, chopped
2.5ml/½ tsp crushed garlic
2.5ml/½ tsp grated fresh root ginger
2.5ml/½ tsp chilli powder
1.5ml/¼ tsp ground turmeric
5ml/1 tsp ground coriander
5ml/1 tsp salt
2 medium tomatoes, sliced
275g/10oz lean leg of lamb, minced (ground)
1 large carrot, sliced or cut into batons
75g/3oz/½ cup petits pois (baby peas)
15ml/1 tbsp chopped fresh mint
15ml/1 tbsp chopped fresh coriander (cilantro)
1 fresh green chilli, chopped
fresh coriander (cilantro) sprigs, to garnish

1 In a deep, heavy frying pan, heat the oil and fry the chopped onion over a medium heat for 5 minutes until golden.

2 Meanwhile, in a small mixing bowl, mix the garlic, ginger, chilli powder, turmeric, ground coriander and salt. Stir well.

3 Add the sliced tomatoes and the spice mixture to the cooked onion in the frying pan and fry for about 2–3 minutes, stirring constantly.

4 Add the minced lamb to the mixture and cook for about 7–10 minutes, stirring frequently, to seal.

5 Break up any lumps of meat which may form in the pan, using a potato masher, if necessary.

6 Finally add the carrot, petits pois, chopped fresh mint and coriander and the chopped green chilli and mix well.

7 Cook, stirring for 2–3 minutes until the carrot slices or batons and the petits pois are cooked, then serve immediately, garnished with fresh coriander sprigs.

Balti Lamb Tikka Energy 438kcal/1827kJ; Protein 34.4g; Carbohydrate 7.8g, of which sugars 7.7g; Fat 30.3g, of which saturates 10.4g; Cholesterol 128mg; Calcium 74mg; Fibre 2.3g; Sodium 162mg.
Spicy Lamb with Peas Energy 192kcal/802kJ; Protein 15.8g; Carbohydrate 7.6g, of which sugars 5.7g; Fat 11.2g, of which saturates 4.1g; Cholesterol 52mg; Calcium 49mg; Fibre 2.9g; Sodium 77mg.

Keema Lamb with Curry Leaves

This delicious dry curry is made by cooking minced lamb in its own juices with a few spices and herbs. Serve with a saucy side dish or a yogurt raita.

Serves 4
10ml/2 tsp corn oil
2 medium onions, chopped
10 curry leaves
6 green chillies
350g/12oz lean minced
  (ground) lamb
5ml/1 tsp crushed garlic
5ml/1 tsp crushed fresh
  root ginger
5ml/1 tsp chilli powder
1.5ml/¼ tsp ground turmeric
5ml/1 tsp salt
2 tomatoes, skinned
  and quartered
15ml/1 tbsp chopped fresh
  coriander (cilantro)

1 Heat the oil in a non-stick wok or frying pan. Stir-fry the onions together with the curry leaves and three of the whole green chillies for 3–4 minutes, until the onions begin to soften and turn translucent but not browned.

2 Put the lamb into a large mixing bowl and add the garlic and crushed ginger, chilli powder, turmeric and salt. Mix well to blend everything together thoroughly.

3 Add the lamb mixture to the pan with the onions and cook for about 7–10 minutes, stirring frequently and lowering the heat to medium if necessary.

4 Add the tomatoes and coriander to the pan. Stir in the remaining whole green chillies. Continue to stir-fry for a further 2 minutes before serving.

Cook's Tips
• *This curry also makes a terrific brunch or light lunch. Serve it with a fried egg per diner, and light Indian breads such as pooris or chapatis.*
• *This curry would make an ideal filling for samosas, the spicy Indian snacks. Cook as above but ensure that all the ingredients are finely chopped before using.*

Koftas in Spicy Sauce

Little meatballs are called koftas in Indian cooking and are usually served in a spicy curry sauce. This curry is popular in most Indian homes.

Serves 4
225g/8oz/1 cup lean minced
  (ground) lamb
10ml/2 tsp poppy seeds
1 medium onion, chopped
5ml/1 tsp grated fresh
  root ginger
5ml/1 tsp crushed garlic
5ml/1 tsp salt
5ml/1 tsp chilli powder
7.5ml/1½ tsp ground coriander
30ml/2 tbsp fresh coriander
  (cilantro) leaves
1 small egg, (US medium) beaten

For the sauce
75ml/2½fl oz/⅓ cup natural
  (plain) low-fat yogurt
30ml/2 tbsp tomato
  purée (paste)
5ml/1 tsp chilli powder
5ml/1 tsp salt
5ml/1 tsp crushed garlic
5ml/1 tsp crushed fresh
  root ginger
5ml/1 tsp garam masala
10ml/2 tsp vegetable oil
1 cinnamon stick
400ml/14fl oz/1⅔ cups water

1 Place the lamb in a food processor and mince it further for about 1 minute. Scrape the meat into a bowl, sprinkle the poppy seeds on top and set aside.

2 Place the onion in the food processor with the next five ingredients and half the fresh coriander. Blend for about 30 seconds, then add it to the lamb. Add the egg and mix well. Leave to stand for about 1 hour.

3 To make the sauce, whisk together the yogurt, tomato purée, chilli powder, salt, crushed garlic, ginger and garam masala. Heat the oil with the cinnamon stick in a pan for about 1 minute, then pour in the sauce. Lower the heat and cook for 1 minute. Remove from the heat and set aside.

4 Roll small balls of the meat mixture using your hands. Return the sauce to the heat and stir in the water. Drop in the koftas one by one. Add the remaining coriander to the pan, cover with a lid and cook for about 7–10 minutes, stirring occasionally. Serve immediately.

Keema Lamb Energy 239kcal/998kJ; Protein 19.7g; Carbohydrate 13.5g, of which sugars 9.3g; Fat 12.3g, of which saturates 4.9g; Cholesterol 67mg; Calcium 50mg; Fibre 2.5g; Sodium 578mg.
Koftas in Spicy Sauce Energy 208kcal/868kJ; Protein 14.7g; Carbohydrate 11.8g, of which sugars 1.2g; Fat 11.6g, of which saturates 4.7g; Cholesterol 57mg; Calcium 24mg; Fibre 1g; Sodium 63mg.

Balti Mini Lamb Kebabs

In this unusual balti dish the meat patties are cooked on skewers before being added to the karahi along with the other vegetables. This makes a great meal on its own or serve with Indian breads.

Serves 6

450g/1lb lean minced (ground) lamb

1 medium onion, finely chopped

5ml/1 tsp garam masala

5ml/1 tsp crushed garlic

2 medium fresh green chillies, finely chopped

30ml/2 tbsp chopped fresh coriander (cilantro), plus extra to garnish

5ml/1 tsp salt

15ml/1 tbsp plain (all-purpose) flour

60ml/4 tbsp corn oil

12 baby (pearl) onions

4 fresh green chillies, sliced

12 cherry tomatoes

1 Mix the lamb, onion, garam masala, garlic, green chillies, fresh coriander, salt and flour in a medium bowl, using your hands. Transfer the mixture to a food processor or blender and process for about 1–2 minutes, until the mixture has turned even finer in texture.

2 Put the mixture back into the bowl. Break off small pieces and wrap them around skewers to form small sausage shapes. Put about two of these shapes on each skewer.

3 Continue making up the sausage shapes until you have used up all the mixture. Preheat the grill (broiler) to its maximum setting. Baste the meat with 15ml/1 tbsp of the oil and grill (broil) the kebabs for 12–15 minutes, turning and basting occasionally, until the meat is evenly browned.

4 Heat the remaining 45ml/3 tbsp of the oil in a karahi, wok or deep pan. Lower the heat slightly and add the whole baby onions. As soon as the onions start to darken, add the fresh chillies and tomatoes to the pan.

5 Slide the lamb patties off their skewers and add them to the onion and tomato mixture. Stir gently for about 3 minutes until they are heated through. Transfer to a warmed serving dish and garnish with fresh coriander.

Balti Lamb Koftas with Vegetables

These koftas look attractive served on their bed of vegetables, especially if you make them quite small.

Serves 4

For the koftas

450g/1lb lean minced (ground) lamb

5ml/1 tsp garam masala

5ml/1 tsp ground cumin

5ml/1 tsp ground coriander

5ml/1 tsp crushed garlic

5ml/1 tsp chilli powder

5ml/1 tsp salt

15ml/1 tbsp chopped fresh coriander (cilantro)

1 small onion, finely diced

150ml/¼ pint/⅔ cup corn oil

For the vegetables

45ml/3 tbsp corn oil

1 bunch spring onions (scallions), roughly chopped

½ large red (bell) pepper, seeded and chopped

½ large green (bell) pepper, seeded and chopped

175g/6oz/1 cup corn

225g/8oz/1½ cups canned butter (lima) beans, drained

½ cauliflower, cut into florets

4 fresh green chillies, chopped

5ml/1 tsp chopped fresh mint

15ml/1 tbsp chopped fresh coriander (cilantro)

15ml/1 tbsp grated fresh root ginger

lime slices

15ml/1 tbsp lemon juice

1 Put the lamb into a food processor or blender and process for 1 minute. Transfer the lamb into a bowl. Add the garam masala, ground cumin, ground coriander, garlic, chilli powder, salt, fresh coriander and onion, and mix everything thoroughly. Cover the bowl and set aside in the refrigerator.

2 Heat the oil for the vegetables in a deep frying pan or a medium karahi. Add the spring onions and stir-fry for 2 minutes. Add the peppers, corn, butter beans, cauliflower and chillies, and stir-fry over a high heat for about 2 minutes. Set to one side.

3 Roll small pieces of the kofta mixture into walnut-sized portions. Heat the oil for the koftas in a frying pan. Cook the koftas in batches, turning until they are evenly browned.

4 Put the vegetables back over a medium heat, and add the koftas. Stir gently for about 5 minutes, or until everything is heated through. Garnish with the mint, coriander, ginger and lime slices. Just before serving, sprinkle over the lemon juice.

Balti Mini Lamb Kebabs Energy 253kcal/1053kJ; Protein 15.8g; Carbohydrate 8.1g, of which sugars 3.9g; Fat 17.8g, of which saturates 5.8g; Cholesterol 58mg; Calcium 37mg; Fibre 1.1g; Sodium 56mg.
Balti Lamb Koftas Energy 634kcal/2639kJ; Protein 31.2g; Carbohydrate 28.3g, of which sugars 10.1g; Fat 45g, of which saturates 10.7g; Cholesterol 87mg; Calcium 76mg; Fibre 5.6g; Sodium 446mg.

Chilli Lamb Chops

It is best to marinate the chops overnight, as this makes them very tender and also helps them to absorb the maximum amount of spicy flavour.

Serves 4

8 small lean spring lamb chops
1 large red chilli, seeded
30ml/2 tbsp chopped fresh
   coriander (cilantro)
15ml/1 tbsp chopped fresh mint
5ml/1 tsp salt
5ml/1 tsp soft light brown sugar
5ml/1 tsp garam masala
5ml/1 tsp crushed garlic
5ml/1 tsp crushed fresh root ginger
175ml/6fl oz/¾ cup natural
   (plain) low-fat yogurt
10ml/2 tsp corn oil

1 Trim the lamb chops with a sharp knife to remove any excess fat. Place them in a large bowl.

2 Finely chop the chilli, then mix with the coriander, mint, salt, brown sugar, garam masala, crushed garlic and crushed ginger.

3 Pour the yogurt into the herb mixture and, using a small whisk or a fork, mix thoroughly.

4 Pour this mixture over the top of the chops and turn them with your fingers to make sure that they are completely covered. Leave to marinate overnight in the refrigerator.

5 Heat the oil in a wok or large frying pan and add the chops. Lower the heat and allow to cook over a medium heat. Turn the chops over then continue frying until they are cooked right through, about 20 minutes, turning again if needed.

6 When the lamb is cooked, place on to warmed plates and serve immediately with a crisp salad.

> **Cook's Tip**
> These chops can also be cooked under a grill (broiler), and they are great for cooking on a barbecue. Remember to baste the meat with oil before grilling (broiling).

Lamb in Mango-flavoured Sauce

This recipe has a pleasant sweet-and-sour taste combined with the heady bouquet of spices.

Serves 4

675g/1½lb boned leg of lamb
60ml/4 tbsp sunflower oil
1 large onion, finely chopped
10ml/2 tsp ginger purée
10ml/2 tsp garlic purée
5ml/1 tsp ground turmeric
10ml/2 tsp ground cumin
2.5–5ml/½–1 tsp chilli powder
50g/2oz/¼ cup thick set natural
   (plain) yogurt
10ml/2 tsp gram flour
5ml/1 tsp salt, or to taste
2 firm, ripe tomatoes, skinned
   and chopped
115g/4oz dried ready-to-eat mango
2.5ml/½ tsp garam masala
25ml/1½ tbsp red wine vinegar
30ml/2 tbsp chopped coriander
   (cilantro) leaves
naan bread, to serve

1 Remove all visible fat from the meat, then cut into 5cm/2in cubes and set aside.

2 In a heavy pan, heat the oil over a medium heat and add the onion. Fry for 3–4 minutes, stirring constantly, then add the ginger and garlic.

3 Continue to fry the ginger and garlic for a further 3–4 minutes, then add the turmeric, cumin and chilli powder. Stir-fry for 30 seconds and add 3 tbsp water. Stir-fry until the water has evaporated and repeat this process twice more.

4 Add the meat to the pan and reduce the heat to low. Whisk the yogurt and the gram flour together, and then add this mixture to the meat. Blend thoroughly, cover the pan and cook for around 40–45 minutes.

5 Add the salt, tomatoes and mango. Simmer, uncovered, for 10–12 minutes, or until the sauce has thickened to a good 'gravy-like' consistency.

6 Stir in the garam masala, vinegar and half of the chopped coriander. Serve in bowls and garnish with the remaining chopped coriander. Naan bread of any variety makes an ideal accompaniment to this dish.

Chilli Lamb Energy 183kcal/764kJ; Protein 15.5g; Carbohydrate 14.1g, of which sugars 9.1g; Fat 7.8g, of which saturates 3.2g; Cholesterol 43mg; Calcium 102mg; Fibre 1.8g; Sodium 77mg.
Lamb in Mango Energy 534kcal/2230kJ; Protein 38.8g; Carbohydrate 23.6g, of which sugars 17g; Fat 32.6g, of which saturates 10.8g; Cholesterol 133mg; Calcium 98mg; Fibre 3.8g; Sodium 176mg.

Apricot Lamb Curry

This recipe comes from the wonderful fruit-laden valley of Kashmir. The curries of Kashmir are renowned for the imaginative use of all the exotic fruits and nuts that grow abundantly in that state. Serve this curry with an apricot chutney to complement the fruit in the recipe.

Serves 4–6
900g/2lb stewing lamb

30ml/2 tbsp vegetable oil
2.5cm/1in piece cinnamon stick
4 green cardamom pods
1 onion, chopped
15ml/1 tbsp curry paste
5ml/1 tsp ground cumin
5ml/1 tsp ground coriander
1.5ml/¼ tsp salt
175g/6oz/¾ cup ready-to-eat
  dried apricots
350ml/12fl oz/1½ cups
  lamb stock
fresh coriander (cilantro),
  to garnish

1 Cut away and discard any visible fat from the lamb, then cut the meat into 2.5cm/1in cubes.

2 Heat the oil in a wok, karahi or large pan and fry the cinnamon stick and cardamoms for 2 minutes. Add the onion and fry for 6–8 minutes until soft.

3 Add the curry paste and fry for about 2 minutes. Stir in the cumin, coriander and salt and fry for 2–3 minutes.

4 Add the cubed lamb, dried apricots and the lamb stock to the pan. Cover the pan with a tight-fitting lid and cook over a medium heat for 1–1½ hours, until the lamb is tender.

5 Transfer to a serving dish and garnish with the fresh coriander. Pilau rice and apricot chutney would make good accompaniments to this dish.

Cook's Tip
Choose whichever curry paste you prefer for this dish. Look for a hot variety if you prefer your curries with plenty of kick. A milder paste will also work well.

Ethiopian Lamb Berbere

This dish from Ethiopia is a powerful blend of chillies with herbs and spices.

Serves 4
450g/1lb lamb fillet
45ml/3 tbsp olive oil
1 red onion, sliced
2.5ml/½ tsp grated fresh
  root ginger
2 garlic cloves, crushed

½ fresh green chilli, seeded and
  finely chopped (optional)
15ml/1 tbsp clarified butter or ghee
salt and ground black pepper

For the berbere
2.5ml/½ tsp each chilli powder,
  paprika, ground ginger, ground
  cinnamon, ground cardamom
  seeds and dried basil
5ml/1 tsp garlic powder

1 To make the berbere, combine all the ingredients in a small bowl and transfer into an airtight container. Berbere will keep for several months if stored in a cool, dry place. Trim the lamb of any fat and then cut the meat into 2cm/¾in cubes.

2 Heat the oil in a large frying pan or wok and fry the meat and onion for about 5–6 minutes, stirring occasionally, until the meat is browned on all sides and the onion has softened.

3 Add the ginger and garlic to the pan, together with 10ml/2 tsp of the berbere, then cook over a medium-high heat, stirring frequently, for a further 5–10 minutes.

4 Add the chilli to the pan, if using, and season well with salt and black pepper. Just before serving, add the butter or ghee and stir well. Serve immediately.

Cook's Tip
Clarified butter is traditionally used for this recipe. It can be made by gently heating unsalted butter, up to boiling point, and then scooping off and discarding the milk solids that rise to the surface. You are then left with clarified butter, which is a clear yellow liquid. Ghee is an Indian version of clarified butter which is made by simmering butter until all the moisture has evaporated and the butter caramelizes.

Apricot Lamb Curry Energy 765kcal/3192kJ; Protein 58.5g; Carbohydrate 27.5g, of which sugars 23.4g; Fat 47.5g, of which saturates 14.7g; Cholesterol 218mg; Calcium 53mg; Fibre 2.5g; Sodium 181mg.
Ethiopian Lamb Energy 336kcal/1392kJ; Protein 22g; Carbohydrate 1.2g, of which sugars 0.9g; Fat 27g, of which saturates 10.3g; Cholesterol 92mg; Calcium 9mg; Fibre 0.2g; Sodium 92mg.

Balti Bhoona Lamb

Bhooning is the term for a traditional Indian technique when stir-frying curries, which simply involves making semi-circular movements while the curry is cooking, scraping the bottom of the pan each time in the centre. Serve this dish of spring lamb with freshly made chapatis or naan breads.

Serves 4
225–275g/8–10oz boneless lean
   spring lamb
3 medium onions
15ml/1 tbsp vegetable oil
15ml/1 tbsp tomato
   purée (paste)
5ml/1 tsp crushed garlic
7.5ml/1½ tsp finely grated
   fresh root ginger, plus 15ml/
   1 tbsp shredded
5ml/1 tsp salt
1.5ml/¼ tsp ground turmeric
600ml/1 pint/2½ cups water
15ml/1 tbsp lemon juice
15ml/1 tbsp chopped fresh
   coriander (cilantro)
15ml/1 tbsp chopped
   fresh mint
1 fresh red chilli, seeded
   and chopped

1 Using a sharp knife, remove any excess fat from the lamb and cut the meat into small cubes.

2 Dice the onions finely. Heat the oil in a karahi, wok or heavy pan and fry the onions until soft.

3 Meanwhile, mix together the tomato purée, garlic and grated ginger, salt and turmeric. Pour the spice mixture on to the onions in the pan and stir-fry for a few seconds.

4 Add the lamb and continue to stir-fry for about 2–3 minutes. Stir in the water, lower the heat, cover the pan and cook for 15–20 minutes, stirring occasionally.

5 When the water has almost evaporated, start bhooning or stirring over a medium heat, making sure that the sauce does not catch on the bottom of the pan. Continue for 5–7 minutes.

6 Pour in the lemon juice, followed by the shredded ginger, chopped fresh coriander, mint and red chilli. Stir to mix, then serve straight from the pan.

Spicy Lamb with Courgettes

For this simple curry, lamb is cooked first with yogurt, and then sliced courgettes, which have already been browned, are added to the mixture.

Serves 4
15ml/1 tbsp vegetable oil
2 medium onions, chopped
225g/8oz lean lamb steaks, cut
   into strips
120ml/4fl oz/½ cup natural
   (plain) low-fat yogurt
5ml/1 tsp garam masala
5ml/1 tsp chilli powder
5ml/1 tsp crushed garlic
5ml/1 tsp grated fresh
   root ginger
2.5ml/½ tsp ground coriander
2 medium courgettes (zucchini),
   thickly sliced
15ml/1 tbsp chopped fresh
   coriander (cilantro), to garnish

1 Heat the oil in a karahi, wok or heavy pan and fry the onions until golden brown (see Cook's Tip).

2 Add the lamb strips to the pan and stir-fry with the onions for about 1 minute to seal the meat.

3 Put the yogurt, garam masala, chilli powder, garlic, ginger and ground coriander into a bowl. Whisk the mixture together.

4 Pour the yogurt mixture over the lamb and cook for about 2 minutes, stirring frequently. Cover the pan and cook over a medium to low heat for about 12–15 minutes.

5 Preheat the grill (broiler) to medium-high. Place the courgettes in a flameproof dish and brown lightly under the heat for about 3 minutes, turning once.

6 Check that the lamb is cooked through and tender and that the sauce is quite thick, then add the courgettes to the curry and serve garnished with the fresh coriander.

> **Cook's Tip**
> It is best to stir the onions only occasionally so that their moisture will be retained.

Balti Bhoona Lamb Energy 188kcal/785kJ; Protein 13.7g; Carbohydrate 12.1g, of which sugars 7.8g; Fat 10g, of which saturates 3.3g; Cholesterol 43mg; Calcium 69mg; Fibre 2.5g; Sodium 67mg.
Spicy Lamb Energy 198kcal/824kJ; Protein 15.8g; Carbohydrate 11.4g, of which sugars 8.3g; Fat 10.4g, of which saturates 3.7g; Cholesterol 43mg; Calcium 120mg; Fibre 1.7g; Sodium 84mg.

Balti Lamb with Peas and Potatoes

Fresh mint leaves are used in this curry, but if they are unobtainable or out of season, you can use ready-minted frozen peas to bring an added freshness. Serve with plain boiled rice.

Serves 4

225g/8oz boneless lean spring lamb
120ml/4fl oz/½ cup natural (plain) low-fat yogurt
1 cinnamon stick
2 green cardamom pods
3 black peppercorns
5ml/1 tsp crushed garlic
5ml/1 tsp grated fresh root ginger
5ml/1 tsp chilli powder
5ml/1 tsp garam masala
5ml/1 tsp salt
30ml/2 tbsp roughly chopped fresh mint
15ml/1 tbsp vegetable oil
2 medium onions, sliced
300ml/½ pint/1¼ cups water
1 large potato, diced
115g/4oz/1 cup frozen peas
1 firm tomato, peeled, seeded and diced

1 Using a sharp knife, trim any excess fat from the lamb and cut the meat into strips. Place it in a bowl.

2 Add the yogurt, cinnamon, cardamoms, peppercorns, garlic, ginger, chilli powder, garam masala, salt and half the mint. Stir well, cover the bowl and leave in a cool place to marinate for a minimum of 2 hours.

3 Heat the oil in a karahi, wok or heavy pan and fry the onions until golden brown. Stir in the lamb and the marinade and stir-fry for about 3 minutes.

4 Pour in the water, lower the heat and cook for 15 minutes until the meat is cooked right through and tender. Meanwhile, cook the diced potato in a pan of boiling water until just soft, but do not let it go mushy.

5 Add the peas and cooked potato to the lamb and stir gently to combine all the ingredients.

6 Finally, add the remaining mint and the tomato and cook for a further 5 minutes before serving.

Spicy Lamb and Potato Stew

Indian spices help to transform a simple lamb and potato stew into a mouthwatering curry that is fit for princes. It's a meal in itself so requires no accompaniments, although naan breads will go well if you are feeding many people.

Serves 6

675g/1½lb lean lamb fillet (tenderloin)
15ml/1 tbsp vegetable oil
1 onion, finely chopped
2 bay leaves
1 fresh green chilli, seeded and finely chopped
2 garlic cloves, finely chopped
10ml/2 tsp ground coriander
5ml/1 tsp ground cumin
2.5ml/½ tsp ground turmeric
2.5ml/½ tsp chilli powder
2.5ml/½ tsp salt
2 tomatoes, peeled and roughly chopped
600ml/1 pint/2½ cups chicken stock
2 large potatoes, cut into large chunks
chopped fresh coriander (cilantro), to garnish

1 Remove any visible fat from the lamb and cut the meat into neat 2.5cm/1in cubes.

2 Heat the oil in a large, heavy pan and fry the onion, bay leaves, chilli and garlic for 5 minutes.

3 Add the cubed meat to the pan and cook for a further 6–8 minutes until lightly browned.

4 Add the ground coriander, ground cumin, ground turmeric, chilli powder and salt and cook the spices for 3–4 minutes, stirring constantly to prevent the spices from sticking to the bottom of the pan and burning.

5 Add the tomatoes and stock and simmer for 5 minutes. Bring to the boil, cover and simmer for 1 hour.

6 Add the bitesize chunks of potato to the simmering mixture, stir in, and cook for a further 30–40 minutes, or until the meat is tender and much of the excess juices have evaporated, leaving a thick but minimal sauce. Garnish with chopped fresh coriander and serve piping hot.

Balti Lamb with Peas Energy 317kcal/1322kJ; Protein 18.1g; Carbohydrate 25.6g, of which sugars 10.7g; Fat 16.8g, of which saturates 4.4g; Cholesterol 43mg; Calcium 113mg; Fibre 3.8g; Sodium 89mg.
Spicy Lamb and Potato Stew Energy 284kcal/1192kJ; Protein 24g; Carbohydrate 14.1g, of which sugars 3.1g; Fat 15.1g, of which saturates 6.3g; Cholesterol 86mg; Calcium 23mg; Fibre 1.3g; Sodium 109mg.

Balti Lamb with Fresh Fenugreek

The combination of lamb with fresh fenugreek works very well in this dish, which is delicious accompanied by plain boiled rice and mango chutney.

Serves 4
450g/1lb lean minced
  (ground) lamb
5ml/1 tsp grated fresh root ginger
5ml/1 tsp crushed garlic
7.5ml/1½ tsp chilli powder
5ml/1 tsp salt
1.5ml/¼ tsp turmeric
45ml/3 tbsp corn oil
2 medium onions, sliced
2 medium potatoes, peeled,
  par-boiled and roughly diced
1 bunch fresh fenugreek,
  chopped
2 tomatoes, chopped
50g/2oz/½ cup frozen peas
30ml/2 tbsp chopped fresh
  coriander (cilantro)
3 fresh red chillies, seeded
  and sliced, to garnish

1 Put the minced lamb, grated ginger, garlic, chilli powder, salt and turmeric into a large bowl, and mix together thoroughly. Set aside while you prepare the other ingredients.

2 Heat the oil in a karahi, wok or deep pan. Add the onion slices and fry for about 5 minutes until golden brown.

3 Add the minced lamb to the pan and fry over a medium heat for 5–7 minutes, stirring frequently.

4 Stir the par-boiled potatoes, chopped fenugreek, tomatoes and frozen peas into the pan and cook for a further 5–7 minutes, stirring constantly.

5 Just before serving, stir in the fresh coriander. Spoon the curry into a large serving dish or on to individual plates and serve hot. Garnish with fresh red chillies.

> **Cook's Tip**
> Look for fresh fenugreek in large supermarkets and Asian stores. Only use the leaves from the plant in this curry as the stalks can taste rather bitter.

Balti Lamb Chops with Potatoes

These chops are marinated before being cooked in a delicious spicy sauce.

Serves 8
8 lamb chops
30ml/2 tbsp olive oil
150ml/¼ pint/⅔ cup lemon juice
5ml/1 tsp salt
15ml/1 tbsp chopped fresh mint
  and coriander (cilantro)
mint sprigs and lime slices,
  to garnish

For the sauce
45ml/3 tbsp corn oil
8 medium tomatoes, chopped
1 bay leaf
5ml/1 tsp garam masala
30ml/2 tbsp natural (plain) yogurt
5ml/1 tsp crushed garlic
5ml/1 tsp chilli powder
5ml/1 tsp salt
2.5ml/½ tsp black cumin seeds
3 black peppercorns
2 medium potatoes, peeled,
  roughly chopped and boiled
  until just tender

1 Put the chops into a large bowl. Mix together 15ml/1 tbsp of the olive oil, lemon juice, salt and fresh mint and coriander. Pour the oil mixture over the chops and rub it in well with your fingers. Leave to marinate for at least 3 hours.

2 To make the sauce, heat the corn oil in a deep frying pan or a karahi. Lower the heat and add the chopped tomatoes. Stir-fry for 2 minutes. Gradually add the bay leaf, garam masala, yogurt, garlic, chilli powder, salt, black cumin seeds and peppercorns, and stir-fry for a further 2–3 minutes.

3 Lower the heat again and add the cooked potatoes, mixing everything together. Remove from the heat and set aside.

4 Heat the remaining olive oil in a separate frying pan. Lower the heat slightly, add the chops and fry them on both sides until they are cooked through. This will take 10–12 minutes. Remove with a slotted spoon and drain on kitchen paper.

5 Heat the sauce in the karahi, bringing it to the boil. Add the chops and lower the heat. Simmer for 5–7 minutes.

6 Transfer the curry to a warmed serving dish and garnish with the mint sprigs and lime slices before serving.

Balti Lamb with Fenugreek 418kcal/1748kJ; Protein 27.3g; Carbohydrate 28.8g, of which sugars 9.2g; Fat 22.4g, of which saturates 7.1g; Cholesterol 86mg; Calcium 93mg; Fibre 4.5g; Sodium 123mg.
Balti Lamb Chops Energy 276kcal/1154kJ; Protein 16.5g; Carbohydrate 11.4g, of which sugars 3.5g; Fat 18.7g, of which saturates 5.2g; Cholesterol 57mg; Calcium 30mg; Fibre 1.7g; Sodium 80mg.

Beef Curry in Sweet Peanut Sauce

This curry is deliciously rich and thick. It is usually served with rice, but would also make a good filling for pitta breads.

Serves 4–6
600ml/1 pint/2½ cups
   coconut milk
45ml/3 tbsp red curry paste
45ml/3 tbsp fish sauce
30ml/2 tbsp light muscovado
   (brown) sugar

2 lemon grass stalks, bruised
450g/1lb rump (round) steak,
   cut into thin strips
75g/3oz/¾ cup roasted
   peanuts, ground
2 fresh red chillies, sliced
5 kaffir lime leaves, torn
salt and ground black pepper
2 salted eggs, cut in wedges,
   and 10–15 Thai basil
   leaves, to garnish

1 Pour half the coconut milk into a large, heavy pan or wok. Place over a medium heat and bring slowly to the boil, stirring constantly until the milk separates.

2 Stir the red curry paste into the coconut milk and cook for 2–3 minutes until the mixture is fragrant and thoroughly blended. Add the fish sauce, sugar and bruised lemon grass stalks. Mix well until combined.

3 Continue to cook until the colour deepens. Gradually add the remaining coconut milk, stirring constantly. Bring back to the boil, stirring constantly.

4 Add the beef and peanuts. Cook, stirring constantly, for 8–10 minutes, or until most of the liquid has evaporated. Add the chillies and lime leaves. Season to taste and serve, garnished with wedges of salted eggs and Thai basil leaves.

Cook's Tip
Red curry paste is a popular ingredient in Thai cuisine. It includes red chillies, shallots, garlic, galangal, lemon grass, shrimp paste and kaffir lime zest. A wide range of ready-made Thai curry paste is available in Asian stores as well as large supermarkets.

Dry Beef and Peanut Butter Curry

Although this is called a dry curry, the method of cooking helps to keep the beef succulent.

Serves 4–6
400g/14oz can coconut milk
900g/2lb stewing beef,
   finely chopped

300ml/½ pint/1¼ cups
   beef stock
30–45ml/2–3 tbsp red curry paste
30ml/2 tbsp crunchy
   peanut butter
juice of 2 limes
lime slices, shredded coriander
   (cilantro) and fresh red chilli
   slices, to garnish

1 Strain the coconut milk into a bowl, retaining the thicker coconut milk in the sieve (strainer).

2 Pour the thin coconut milk from the bowl into a large, heavy pan or wok, then scrape in half the residue from the sieve. Reserve the remaining thick coconut milk. Add the chopped beef to the pan. Pour in the beef stock and bring the mixture to the boil. Reduce the heat, cover the pan and simmer gently for about 50 minutes.

3 Strain the beef, reserving the cooking liquid, and place a cupful of this liquid in a wok. Stir in 30–45ml/2–3 tbsp of the curry paste, according to taste. Boil rapidly until all the liquid has evaporated. Stir in the reserved thick coconut milk, the peanut butter and the beef. Simmer, uncovered, for 15–20 minutes, adding a little more cooking liquid if the mixture starts to stick to the pan, but keep the curry dry.

4 Just before serving, stir in the lime juice. Serve in warmed individual bowls, garnished with the lime slices, shredded coriander and sliced red chillies.

Variation
The curry is equally delicious made with lean leg or shoulder of lamb, or with pork fillet (tenderloin).

Beef Curry Energy 227kcal/953kJ; Protein 21g; Carbohydrate 14.3g, of which sugars 11.5g; Fat 9.9g, of which saturates 2.6g; Cholesterol 44mg; Calcium 92mg; Fibre 2.5g; Sodium 723mg.
Dry Beef Curry Energy 296kcal/1238kJ; Protein 35.2g; Carbohydrate 4.9g, of which sugars 4.5g; Fat 15.2g, of which saturates 4.8g; Cholesterol 103mg; Calcium 66mg; Fibre 0.7g; Sodium 262mg.

Green Beef Curry with Thai Aubergines

This is a very quick curry so it is essential that you use good-quality meat. Sirloin is recommended here, but tender rump or even fillet steak could be used instead, if they are available.

Serves 4–6

450g/1lb beef sirloin
15ml/1 tbsp vegetable oil
45ml/3 tbsp Thai green curry paste
600ml/1 pint/2½ cups
   coconut milk
4 kaffir lime leaves, torn
15–30ml/1–2 tbsp Thai fish sauce
5ml/1 tsp palm sugar (jaggery) or
   light muscovado (brown) sugar
150g/5oz small Thai aubergines
   (eggplants), halved
a small handful of fresh Thai basil,
   roughly chopped
2 fresh green chillies, plus extra
   Thai basil sprigs, to garnish

1 Trim off any excess fat from the beef. Using a sharp knife, cut it into long, thin strips. This is easiest to do if it is well chilled, so place it into the freezer for about 10 minutes first if you have time. Set it aside while preparing the other ingredients.

2 Heat the oil in a large, heavy pan or wok. Add the curry paste and cook for 1–2 minutes, until it is fragrant.

3 Stir in half the coconut milk, a little at a time. Cook, stirring frequently, for about 5–6 minutes, until an oily sheen appears on the surface of the liquid.

4 Add the beef to the pan with the kaffir lime leaves, fish sauce, sugar and aubergine halves. Cook for 2–3 minutes, then stir in the remaining coconut milk.

5 Bring back to a simmer and cook until the meat and aubergines are tender. Stir in the Thai basil.

6 Prepare the garnish. Slit the fresh green chillies and scrape out the pith and seeds and discard. Shred the chillies finely. Spoon the curry into a heated dish or on to warmed individual plates. Sprinkle the finely shredded chillies over the top of the curry, add the sprigs of basil and serve immediately.

Citrus Beef Curry

This superbly aromatic curry is not too hot but it is nonetheless packed with flavour. For a special family meal, it goes perfectly with fried noodles.

Serves 4

450g/1lb rump (round) steak
30ml/2 tbsp sunflower oil
30ml/2 tbsp medium curry paste
2 bay leaves
400ml/14fl oz/1⅔ cups
   coconut milk
300ml/½ pint/1¼ cups
   beef stock
30ml/2 tbsp lemon juice
45ml/3 tbsp fish sauce
15ml/1 tbsp sugar
115g/4oz baby (pearl) onions,
   peeled but left whole
225g/8oz new potatoes, scrubbed
   and halved
115g/4oz/1 cup unsalted roasted
   peanuts, roughly chopped
115g/4oz fine green
   beans, halved
1 red (bell) pepper, seeded and
   thinly sliced
unsalted roasted peanuts,
   to garnish

1 Trim any fat off the beef and use a sharp knife to cut it into 5cm/2in strips. Slicing the meat is easier if it is very cold, so place it in the freezer for 10 minutes before slicing, if time.

2 Heat the oil in a large, heavy pan, add the curry paste and cook over a medium heat for 30 seconds, stirring constantly.

3 Add the beef to the pan and cook, stirring constantly, for about 2 minutes until it is beginning to brown and is thoroughly coated with the spices.

4 Stir in the bay leaves, coconut milk, stock, lemon juice, fish sauce and sugar, and bring to the boil, stirring.

5 Add the onions and potatoes, then bring back to the boil, reduce the heat and simmer, uncovered, for 5 minutes.

6 Stir in the peanuts, beans and pepper and simmer for a further 10 minutes, or until the beef and potatoes are tender. Serve in warmed shallow bowls, with a fork and spoon, to enjoy all the rich and creamy juices. Sprinkle with extra unsalted roasted peanuts, to garnish.

Green Beef Curry Energy 147kcal/619kJ; Protein 18.2g; Carbohydrate 6.4g, of which sugars 6.3g; Fat 5.6g, of which saturates 1.9g; Cholesterol 38mg; Calcium 36mg; Fibre 0.5g; Sodium 341mg.
Citrus Beef Curry Energy 476kcal/1990kJ; Protein 33.8g; Carbohydrate 27.5g, of which sugars 16.3g; Fat 26.4g, of which saturates 6.6g; Cholesterol 69mg; Calcium 77mg; Fibre 4.1g; Sodium 169mg.

Beef and Chorizo Stew

This spicy dish from the Philippines can be made with beef, chicken or pork, all of which are cooked the same way. If using pork or chicken, take care that it is cooked through.

Serves 4–6

30–45ml/2–3 tbsp groundnut (peanut) or corn oil
1 onion, chopped
2 garlic cloves, chopped
40g/1½oz fresh root ginger, chopped
2 x 175g/6oz chorizo sausages, cut diagonally into bitesize pieces
700g/1lb 9oz lean rump (round) beef, cut into bitesize pieces
4 tomatoes, skinned, seeded and quartered
900ml/1½ pints/3¾ cups beef or chicken stock
2 plantains, peeled and sliced diagonally
2 x 400g/14oz cans chickpeas, rinsed and drained
salt and ground black pepper
1 small bunch fresh coriander (cilantro) leaves, roughly chopped, to garnish

To accompany

corn oil, for deep-frying
1–2 firm bananas or 1 plantain, peeled and sliced diagonally
stir-fried greens

1 Heat the oil in a wok with a lid or a flameproof casserole, stir in the onion, garlic and ginger and fry until they begin to brown. Add the chorizo sausages and beef and fry until they begin to brown. Add the tomatoes and pour in the stock. Bring to the boil, reduce the heat, cover and simmer for 45 minutes.

2 Add the plantains and chickpeas to the stew and cook for a further 20–25 minutes, adding a little extra water if the cooking liquid reduces too much.

3 Meanwhile, heat enough oil for deep-frying in a wok or large, shallow pan. Deep-fry the bananas or plantain, in batches, for about 3 minutes, until crisp and golden brown. Remove from the pan, drain on kitchen paper and set aside.

4 Season the stew with salt and pepper to taste and sprinkle with chopped coriander leaves to garnish. Serve with the deep-fried bananas or plantain and stir-fried greens.

Beef Tagine with Sweet Potatoes

This warming dish of tender beef and succulent sweet potatoes is eaten during the winter in Morocco, where it can get surprisingly cold.

Serves 4

675–900g/1½–2lb braising or stewing beef
30ml/2 tbsp sunflower oil
a good pinch of ground turmeric
1 large onion, chopped
1 red or green chilli, seeded and chopped
7.5ml/1½ tsp paprika
a good pinch of cayenne pepper
2.5ml/½ tsp ground cumin
450g/1lb sweet potatoes
15ml/1 tbsp chopped fresh parsley
15ml/1 tbsp chopped fresh coriander (cilantro)
15g/½oz/1 tbsp butter
salt and ground black pepper

1 Cube the beef. Heat the oil in a flameproof casserole and fry the meat, with the turmeric and seasoning, for 3–4 minutes until evenly brown, stirring frequently.

2 Cover the pan with a tight-fitting lid and cook for 15 minutes over a fairly gentle heat, without lifting the lid. Preheat the oven to 180°C/350°F/Gas 4.

3 Add the onion, chilli, paprika, cayenne pepper and cumin to the casserole, with just enough water to cover the meat. Cover tightly and cook in the oven for 1–1½ hours until the meat is very tender, checking occasionally and adding a little extra water to keep the stew moist.

4 Meanwhile, peel the sweet potatoes and slice them straight into a bowl of salted water. Transfer to a pan, bring to the boil and simmer for 3 minutes until just tender. Drain.

5 Stir the herbs into the meat. Arrange the potato slices over the top of the meat and dot with the butter. Cover again and bake for a further 10 minutes.

6 Increase the oven temperature to 200°C/400°F/Gas 6 or heat the grill (broiler). Remove the lid of the casserole and cook in the oven or under the grill for a further 5–10 minutes until the potatoes are golden. Serve immediately.

Beef and Chorizo Stew Energy 583kcal/2441kJ; Protein 40.5g; Carbohydrate 35.8g, of which sugars 6.2g; Fat 31.9g, of which saturates 11.1g; Cholesterol 91mg; Calcium 104mg; Fibre 6.1g; Sodium 778mg.
Beef Tagine Energy 301kcal/1254kJ; Protein 21.9g; Carbohydrate 12g, of which sugars 3.2g; Fat 18.7g, of which saturates 4.6g; Cholesterol 61mg; Calcium 18mg; Fibre 1.4g; Sodium 67mg.

Beef Tagine with Peas and Saffron

Saffron is cultivated commercially in Morocco and is a favourite ingredient in dishes like this classic fresh pea and preserved lemon tagine.

Serves 6
1.2kg/2½lb chuck steak
   or stewing beef, trimmed
   and cubed
30ml/2 tbsp olive oil
1 onion, chopped
25g/1oz fresh root ginger, peeled
   and finely chopped
5ml/1 tsp ground ginger
pinch of cayenne pepper
pinch of saffron threads
1.2kg/2½lb shelled fresh peas
2 tomatoes, skinned
   and chopped
1 preserved lemon, chopped
a handful of brown
   kalamata olives
salt and ground black pepper
bread or couscous, to serve

1 Put the cubed beef in a tagine, flameproof casserole or large heavy pan with the olive oil, chopped onion, fresh and ground ginger, cayenne pepper and saffron and season with salt and plenty of ground black pepper.

2 Pour in enough water to cover the meat completely, stir well to combine, and then bring to the boil.

3 Reduce the heat and then cover the pan with a lid and simmer for about 1½ hours, until the meat is very tender. Cook for a little longer, if necessary.

4 Add the peas, tomatoes, preserved lemon and olives. Stir well and cook, uncovered, for about 10 minutes, or until the peas are tender and the sauce has reduced. Check the seasoning and serve with bread or plain couscous.

> **Cook's Tip**
> *Saffron is the yellow-orange stigmas from a small purple crocus. It is the world's most expensive spice because each flower has only three stigmas, which are hand-picked and then dried. About 15,000 stigmas are needed to produce 25g/1oz of saffron. Store in an airtight container in a cool, dark place for up to 6 months.*

Mussaman Beef

This dish is traditionally based on beef, but chicken, lamb or tofu can be used instead. Mussaman curry paste, available from specialist Asian stores, imparts a rich, sweet and spicy flavour.

Serves 4–6
675g/1½lb stewing steak
600ml/1 pint/2½ cups
   coconut milk
250ml/8fl oz/1 cup coconut cream
45ml/3 tbsp Mussaman curry paste
30ml/2 tbsp Thai fish sauce
15ml/1 tbsp palm sugar
   (jaggery) or light muscovado
   (brown) sugar
60ml/4 tbsp tamarind juice
   (tamarind paste mixed with
   warm water)
6 green cardamom pods
1 cinnamon stick
1 large potato, about 225g/8oz,
   cut into even chunks
1 onion, cut into wedges
50g/2oz/½ cup roasted peanuts

1 Trim off any excess fat from the stewing steak, then, using a sharp knife, cut it into 2.5cm/1in chunks. Pour the coconut milk into a large, heavy pan and bring to the boil over a medium heat. Add the chunks of beef to the coconut milk, reduce the heat to low, partially cover the pan and simmer gently for about 40–45 minutes, or until tender.

2 Pour the coconut cream into a separate pan. Cook over a medium heat, stirring constantly, for about 5 minutes, or until it separates. Stir in the Mussaman curry paste and cook rapidly for 2–3 minutes, until fragrant and thoroughly blended.

3 Add the coconut cream and curry paste mixture to the pan with the beef and stir until thoroughly blended. Simmer for a further 4–5 minutes, stirring occasionally.

4 Stir the fish sauce, sugar, tamarind juice, cardamom pods, cinnamon stick, potato chunks and onion wedges into the beef curry. Continue to simmer for a further 15–20 minutes, or until the potato is cooked and tender.

5 Add most of the roasted peanuts to the pan and stir well. Cook for 5 minutes, then transfer to warmed individual bowls, garnish with the reserved peanuts and serve immediately.

Beef Tagine Energy 492kcal/2049kJ; Protein 57.9g; Carbohydrate 25.6g, of which sugars 7g; Fat 18.2g, of which saturates 6g; Cholesterol 126mg; Calcium 61mg; Fibre 10.1g; Sodium 134mg.
Mussaman Beef Energy 626kcal/2610kJ; Protein 44.6g; Carbohydrate 24.8g, of which sugars 15.4g; Fat 39.3g, of which saturates 22.7g; Cholesterol 98mg; Calcium 74mg; Fibre 1.6g; Sodium 288mg.

Spicy Meat Loaf with a Chilli and Egg Topping

This deliciously spicy meat loaf is baked in the oven. It provides a hearty meal for the whole family on a cold winter day.

Serves 4–6
5 eggs
450g/1lb minced (ground) beef
30ml/2 tbsp grated fresh root ginger
30ml/2 tbsp crushed garlic
6 fresh green chillies, chopped
2 small onions, finely chopped
2.5ml/½ tsp ground turmeric
50g/2oz/2 cups fresh coriander (cilantro), chopped
175g/6oz potato, grated
salt
lemon twist, to garnish
salad leaves, to serve

1 Preheat the oven to 180°C/350°F/Gas 4. In a large mixing bowl, beat two eggs until they are fluffy and pour them into a greased 900g/2lb loaf tin (pan).

2 Knead together the meat, ginger and garlic, 4 green chillies, 1 chopped onion, 1 beaten egg, the ground turmeric, fresh coriander, potato and salt.

3 Pack the mixture into the loaf tin, filling the corners, and smooth the surface with a knife. Place in the preheated oven and cook for about 45–50 minutes.

4 Meanwhile, beat the remaining eggs and fold in the remaining green chillies and onion. Remove the loaf tin from the oven and pour the mixture all over the meat.

5 Return the tin to the oven and cook until the eggs have just set. Serve the loaf immediately on a bed of salad leaves, garnished with a twist of lemon.

> **Cook's Tip**
> It is always best to buy meat for mincing by the piece if possible so that you can choose lean meat with little fat and remove any remaining fat before you mince it.

Beef Kofta Curry

Koftas come in various shapes and sizes. In this variation, the more commonly used lamb is replaced by beef, which works well with the hot curry sauce.

Serves 4
For the meatballs
450g/1lb minced (ground) beef
45ml/3 tbsp finely chopped onion
15ml/1 tbsp chopped fresh coriander (cilantro)
15ml/1 tbsp natural (plain) yogurt
about 60ml/4 tbsp plain (all-purpose) flour
10ml/2 tsp ground cumin
5ml/1 tsp garam masala
5ml/1 tsp ground turmeric
5ml/1 tsp ground coriander
1 fresh green chilli, seeded and finely chopped
2 garlic cloves, crushed
1.5ml/¼ tsp black mustard seeds
1 egg (optional)
salt and ground black pepper

For the curry sauce
30ml/2 tbsp butter
1 onion, finely chopped
2 garlic cloves, crushed
45ml/3 tbsp curry powder
4 green cardamom pods
600ml/1 pint/2½ cups hot beef stock or water
15ml/1 tbsp tomato purée (paste)
30ml/2 tbsp natural (plain) yogurt
15ml/1 tbsp chopped fresh coriander (cilantro)

1 To make the meatballs, put the beef into a large bowl, add all the remaining meatball ingredients and mix well with your hands. Roll the mixture into small balls and set aside.

2 For the curry sauce, heat the butter in a pan over a medium heat. Fry the onion and garlic for 8 minutes, until the onion is soft.

3 Reduce the heat and then add the curry powder and cardamon pods and cook for a few minutes, stirring well.

4 Slowly stir in the stock or water, the tomato purée, yogurt and chopped coriander and stir well. Simmer for 10 minutes.

5 Add the koftas to the sauce a few at a time, allow to cook briefly and then add a few more, until all of the koftas are in the pan. Simmer, uncovered, for about 20 minutes, until the koftas are cooked. The sauce will thicken slightly but add a little water if it is drying out too much. Serve immediately.

Spicy Meat Loaf Energy 272kcal/1133kJ; Protein 22.1g; Carbohydrate 7.3g, of which sugars 2g; Fat 17.6g, of which saturates 6.6g; Cholesterol 204mg; Calcium 73mg; Fibre 1.5g; Sodium 129mg.
Beef Kofta Curry Energy 313kcal/1301kJ; Protein 25.8g; Carbohydrate 4.9g, of which sugars 3.7g; Fat 21.3g, of which saturates 11.3g; Cholesterol 90mg; Calcium 42mg; Fibre 1g; Sodium 192mg.

Persian Tangy Beef and Herb Koresh

In modern-day Iran, as in ancient Persia, rice is eaten at almost every meal. That the diet is never dull is thanks to the koresh. This is a delicately spiced sauce or stew that serves as a topping. This is a classic meat koresh, but there are also vegetarian versions, often with fruit and herbs.

Serves 4
45ml/3 tbsp olive oil
1 large onion, chopped

450g/1lb lean stewing beef, cut
    into bitesize cubes
15ml/1 tbsp fenugreek leaves,
    stalks discarded
10ml/2 tsp ground turmeric
2.5ml/½ tsp ground cinnamon
600ml/1 pint/2½ cups water
25g/1oz fresh parsley, chopped
25g/1oz fresh chives, chopped
400g/14oz can red kidney beans
juice of 1 lemon
salt and ground black pepper
plain boiled basmati rice,
    to serve

1 Heat 30ml/2 tbsp of the oil in a large pan or flameproof casserole and fry the onion for 4–5 minutes, until lightly golden.

2 Add the beef to the pan and fry for a further 10 minutes until browned on all sides.

3 Add the fenugreek, turmeric and cinnamon and cook for about 1 minute, then add the water and bring to the boil. Cover with a tight-fitting lid and simmer over a low heat for about 45 minutes, stirring occasionally.

4 Heat the remaining oil in a small frying pan and fry the fresh parsley and chives over a medium heat for about 2–3 minutes, stirring frequently so that they do not burn.

5 Rinse the kidney beans thoroughly and drain well. Stir them into the beef in the pan with the fried herbs and lemon juice. Season with salt and black pepper.

6 Simmer the stew for a further 30–35 minutes, until the meat is tender. Serve immediately on a bed of plain boiled rice.

Balti Beef

There's no marinating involved with this simple curry, which can be prepared and cooked in less than an hour. Use whatever lean beef is available, whether rump, fillet or sirloin.

Serves 4
1 red (bell) pepper
1 green (bell) pepper
15ml/1 tbsp vegetable oil

5ml/1 tsp cumin seeds
2.5ml/½ tsp fennel seeds
1 onion, cut into thick wedges
1 garlic clove, crushed
2.5cm/1in piece fresh root ginger,
    finely chopped
1 fresh red chilli, finely chopped
15ml/1 tbsp curry paste
2.5ml/½ tsp salt
675g/1½lb lean rump (round)
    or fillet steak (beef tenderloin),
    cut into thick strips
naan bread, to serve

1 Halve the red and green peppers, discard the seeds and cut the peppers into 2.5cm/1in chunks.

2 Heat the oil in a karahi, wok or frying pan and fry the cumin and fennel seeds for 2 minutes or until they begin to splutter. Add the onion, garlic, ginger and chilli and fry for a further 5 minutes, stirring constantly.

3 Stir the curry paste and salt into the pan and cook for a further 3–4 minutes, stirring constantly.

4 Add the peppers to the pan and toss over the heat for about 5 minutes. Stir in the beef strips and continue to fry for 10–12 minutes or until the meat is tender. Serve from the pan, with warm naan bread.

> **Variations**
> • This recipe would also work well with chicken breast fillet in place of the rump (round) or fillet steak.
> • You could add mangetouts (snow peas), trimmed and left whole, to the dish for added crunch. As the peas need only the minimum amount of cooking, add them for the last 5 minutes of cooking time only.

Persian Tangy Beef Energy 357kcal/1491kJ; Protein 32.5g; Carbohydrate 22.9g, of which sugars 7.3g; Fat 15.5g, of which saturates 4g; Cholesterol 71mg; Calcium 117mg; Fibre 7.7g; Sodium 468mg.
Balti Beef Energy 374kcal/1556kJ; Protein 39.7g; Carbohydrate 7.8g, of which sugars 6.2g; Fat 20.5g, of which saturates 7g; Cholesterol 98mg; Calcium 43mg; Fibre 2.5g; Sodium 129mg.

Spicy Beef with Green Beans

Green beans slowly cooked with beef is a variation on a traditional Indian curry which uses lamb. The sliced red pepper provides a contrast to the colour of the beans and chillies, and adds extra flavour.

Serves 4

275g/10oz fine green beans,
   cut into 2.5cm/1in pieces
15ml/1 tbsp vegetable oil
1 onion, sliced
5ml/1 tsp grated fresh root ginger
5ml/1 tsp crushed garlic
5ml/1 tsp chilli powder
6.5ml/1¼ tsp salt
1.5ml/¼ tsp ground turmeric
2 tomatoes, chopped
450g/1lb lean beef, cubed
475ml/16fl oz/2 cups water
1 red (bell) pepper, seeded
   and sliced
15ml/1 tbsp chopped fresh
   coriander (cilantro)
2 fresh green chillies, chopped
warm chapatis, to serve (optional)

1 Blanch the beans in boiling water for 3–4 minutes, then rinse under cold running water, drain and set aside.

2 Heat the oil in a large, heavy pan and gently fry the onion slices, stirring frequently, until golden brown.

3 In a bowl, mix the ginger, garlic, chilli powder, salt, turmeric and chopped tomatoes. Spoon the mixture into the pan and stir-fry with the onion for 5–7 minutes.

4 Add the cubed beef and stir-fry for a further 3 minutes. Pour in the water, bring it to the boil and lower the heat. Half-cover the pan and cook for 1–1¼ hours until most of the water has evaporated and the meat is tender. If the mixture looks like it is drying out during cooking, add a little more water.

5 Add the green beans to the pan and mix everything together well. Finally, add the red pepper, chopped fresh coriander and green chillies. Cook the mixture with the lid removed, stirring occasionally, for a further 7–10 minutes, or until the green beans and pepper are tender.

6 Spoon into a large bowl or individual plates. Serve the beef hot, with warm chapatis, if you like.

Beef and Aubergine Curry

This slow-cooked creamy curry is full of spicy flavours with an extra chilli kick from the fresh chilli garnish.

Serves 6

120ml/4fl oz/½ cup sunflower oil
2 onions, thinly sliced
2.5cm/1in fresh root ginger, sliced
   and cut into matchsticks
1 garlic clove, crushed
2 fresh red chillies, seeded and
   very finely sliced
2.5cm/1in fresh turmeric, crushed,
   or 5ml/1 tsp ground turmeric
1 lemon grass stem, lower part
   sliced finely, top bruised
675g/1½lb braising steak, cut in
   even strips
400ml/14fl oz can coconut milk
300ml/½ pint/1¼ cups water
1 aubergine (eggplant), sliced
   and patted dry
5ml/1 tsp tamarind pulp, soaked
   in 60ml/4 tbsp warm water
salt and ground black pepper
finely sliced chilli (optional) and
   deep-fried onions, to garnish
plain boiled basmati rice,
   to serve

1 Heat half the oil and fry the onions, ginger and garlic for 3–4 minutes. Add the chillies, turmeric and the sliced lower part of the lemon grass. Push to one side of the pan and then turn up the heat and add the beef, stirring until it changes colour.

2 Add the coconut milk, water, lemon grass top and seasoning. Cover and simmer gently for 1½ hours, or until the meat is tender.

3 Towards the end of the cooking time heat the remaining oil in a frying pan. Fry the aubergine slices until brown all over.

4 Add the browned aubergine slices to the beef curry and cook for a further 15 minutes. Stir gently from time to time. Strain the tamarind and stir the juice into the curry. Taste and adjust the seasoning. Place into a warm serving dish. Garnish with the sliced chilli, if using, and deep-fried onions, and serve immediately with the boiled rice.

> **Cook's Tip**
> If you want to make this curry ahead of time, follow the above method to the end of step 2 and finish later.

Beef with Green Beans Energy 309kcal/1289kJ; Protein 29.7g; Carbohydrate 15.1g, of which sugars 10g; Fat 15g, of which saturates 4.9g; Cholesterol 65mg; Calcium 70mg; Fibre 3.8g; Sodium 83mg.
Beef and Aubergine Curry Energy 394kcal/1638kJ; Protein 26g; Carbohydrate 12g, of which sugars 10g; Fat 27g, of which saturates 5g; Cholesterol 71mg; Calcium 54mg; Fibre 203g; Sodium 700mg.

Stewed Beef Curry

This deliciously aromatic curry uses stewing beef, which is succulent and tender after long, slow simmering in the spicy, fragrant sauce.

Serves 4
900g/2lb lean stewing beef
15ml/1 tbsp vegetable oil
1 large onion, finely chopped
4 cloves
4 green cardamom pods
2 green chillies, finely chopped
2.5cm/1in piece fresh root ginger, finely chopped
2 garlic cloves, crushed
2 dried red chillies
15ml/1 tbsp curry paste
10ml/2 tsp ground coriander
5ml/1 tsp ground cumin
2.5ml/½ tsp salt
150ml/¼ pint/⅔ cup beef stock
handful of fresh coriander (cilantro) sprigs, to garnish
boiled rice, to serve

1 Trim any visible fat from the beef with a sharp knife and cut the meat into 2.5cm/1in cubes.

2 Heat the oil in a large, heavy frying pan and stir-fry the onion, cloves and cardamom pods for about 5 minutes. Add the fresh green chillies, ginger, garlic and dried red chillies and fry for a further 2 minutes until the spices release their fragrances and the fresh chillies have softened a little.

3 Add the curry paste to the pan and fry for 2 minutes until fragrant. Add the cubed beef and fry for 5–8 minutes until all the meat pieces are lightly browned.

4 Add the coriander, cumin, salt and hot stock. Cover and simmer gently for 1–1½ hours or until the meat is tender. Garnish with fresh coriander sprigs and serve immediately, accompanied by boiled rice.

> **Cook's Tip**
> *When whole cardamom pods are used as a flavouring in curries, they are not meant to be eaten. In India, they are fished out while eating and left on the side of the plate, along with any bones from the meat in the dish.*

Chilli Beef and Tomato Curry

When served with boiled yam or rice, this delicious curry makes a hearty dish, certain to be popular with anybody who likes their food spicy.

Serves 4
450g/1lb stewing beef
5ml/1 tsp dried thyme
45ml/3 tbsp palm or vegetable oil
1 large onion, finely chopped
2 garlic cloves, crushed
4 canned plum tomatoes, chopped, plus 60ml/4 tbsp of the juice
15ml/1 tbsp tomato purée (paste)
2.5ml/½ tsp mixed (apple pie) spice
1 fresh red chilli, seeded and chopped
900ml/1½ pints/3¾ cups chicken stock or water
1 large aubergine (eggplant)
salt and ground black pepper

1 Cut the beef into cubes and season with 2.5ml/½ tsp of the thyme and salt and black pepper.

2 Heat 15ml/1 tbsp of the oil in a large pan and fry the meat, in batches if necessary, for 8–10 minutes, stirring constantly, until evenly browned all over. Transfer to a large bowl using a slotted spoon and set aside.

3 Heat the remaining oil in the pan and fry the onion and garlic for a few minutes until the onion begins to soften.

4 Add the tomatoes and tomato juice to the pan and simmer for a further 8–10 minutes, stirring occasionally.

5 Add the tomato purée, mixed spice, chilli and remaining thyme to the pan and stir well.

6 Add the cubed beef and the chicken stock or water to the pan. Bring to the boil, reduce the heat, cover the pan and simmer gently for 30 minutes.

7 Cut the aubergine into 1cm/½in dice. Stir into the beef mixture and cook, covered, for a further 30 minutes until the beef is completely tender. Taste the sauce, adjust the seasoning if necessary, and serve immediately.

Stewed Beef Curry Energy 442kcal/1840kJ; Protein 52.2g; Carbohydrate 2.8g, of which sugars 0.1g; Fat 24.7g, of which saturates 9g; Cholesterol 131mg; Calcium 25mg; Fibre 0g; Sodium 147mg.
Chilli Beef Curry Energy 251kcal/1050kJ; Protein 27.2g; Carbohydrate 7.2g, of which sugars 6.2g; Fat 12.8g, of which saturates 2.9g; Cholesterol 75mg; Calcium 29mg; Fibre 3g; Sodium 87mg.

Beef Rendang

This spicy dish is slowly simmered on top of the stove and is usually served with the meat quite dry. If you prefer more sauce, add a little more water.

Serves 6–8
2 onions or 5–6 shallots, chopped
4 garlic cloves, chopped
2.5cm/1in piece fresh galangal, peeled and sliced, or 15ml/1 tbsp galangal paste
2.5cm/1in piece fresh root ginger, peeled and sliced
4–6 fresh red chillies, seeded and roughly chopped
lower part only of 1 lemon grass stalk, sliced

2.5cm/1in piece fresh turmeric, peeled and sliced, or 5ml/1 tsp ground turmeric
1kg/2¼lb prime beef, in one piece
5ml/1 tsp coriander seeds, dry-fried
5ml/1 tsp cumin seeds, dry-fried
2 kaffir lime leaves, torn into small pieces
2 x 400ml/14fl oz cans coconut milk
300ml/½ pint/1¼ cups water
30ml/2 tbsp dark soy sauce
5ml/1 tsp tamarind pulp, soaked in 60ml/4 tbsp warm water
8–10 small new potatoes, scrubbed
salt and ground black pepper
deep-fried onions, sliced fresh red chillies and spring onions (scallions), to garnish

1 Put the onions or shallots in a food processor. Add the garlic, galangal, ginger, chillies, sliced lemon grass and turmeric. Process to a fine paste or grind using a pestle and mortar.

2 Cut the meat into cubes using a large, sharp knife, then place the cubes in a bowl. Grind the dry-fried coriander and cumin seeds, then add to the meat with the onion and chilli paste and kaffir lime leaves; stir well. Cover and leave in a cool place to marinate for at least 1 hour.

3 Pour the coconut milk and water into a wok or large pan, then stir in the spiced meat and the soy sauce. Strain the tamarind water and add to the wok or pan. Stir over a medium heat until the liquid boils, then simmer gently, half-covered with a lid, for about 1½ hours.

4 Add the potatoes to the pan and simmer for 20–25 minutes, or until the meat and potatoes are tender. Season and serve, garnished with deep-fried onions, chillies and spring onions.

Madras Beef Curry

Although Madras is renowned for the best vegetarian food in the country, meat-based recipes such as this beef curry are also extremely popular. This particular recipe is a contribution by the area's small Muslim community.

Serves 4–6
60ml/4 tbsp vegetable oil
1 large onion, finely sliced
3–4 cloves
4 green cardamoms

2 whole star anise
4 fresh green chillies, chopped
2 fresh or dried red chillies, chopped
45ml/3 tbsp Madras masala paste
5ml/1 tsp ground turmeric
450g/1lb lean beef, cubed
60ml/4 tbsp tamarind juice
sugar, to taste
salt
a few fresh coriander (cilantro) leaves, chopped, to garnish
pilau rice and mixed salad, to serve

1 Heat the vegetable oil in a wok, karahi or large pan over a medium heat. Add the onion slices and fry for 8–9 minutes, stirring occasionally, until they soften and turn golden brown.

2 Lower the heat, add all the spice ingredients to the pan, and fry for a further 2–3 minutes, stirring constantly, until the spices release their fragrances.

3 Add the beef to the pan and mix well. Cover and cook over a low heat until the beef is cooked through and tender. Cook uncovered on a high heat for the last few minutes to reduce any excess liquid and produce a thicker sauce.

4 Fold in the tamarind juice, sugar and salt. Reheat the dish and garnish with the chopped coriander leaves. Serve with pilau rice and a simple mixed salad.

Cook's Tip
If your beef isn't the leanest, to help tenderize it you can add about 60ml/4 tbsp white wine vinegar in step 2, along with the meat, and omit the tamarind juice.

Beef Rendang Energy 289kcal/1210kJ; Protein 30.2g; Carbohydrate 15.4g, of which sugars 8.6g; Fat 12.2g, of which saturates 5g; Cholesterol 73mg; Calcium 63mg; Fibre 1.4g; Sodium 465mg.
Madras Beef Curry Energy 524kcal/2180kJ; Protein 37.6g; Carbohydrate 13.8g, of which sugars 7.4g; Fat 36g, of which saturates 13.8g; Cholesterol 133mg; Calcium 65mg; Fibre 2.6g; Sodium 160mg.

Oxtail in Hot Tangy Sauce

Considered a delicacy in some parts of South-east Asia, oxtail and the tails of water buffalo are generally cooked for special feasts and celebrations. Served with steamed rice, or chunks of fresh, crusty bread, it makes a very tasty supper dish.

Serves 4–6

8 shallots, chopped
8 garlic cloves, chopped
4–6 fresh red chillies, seeded and chopped
25g/1oz fresh galangal, chopped
30ml/2 tbsp rice flour or plain (all-purpose) flour
15ml/1 tbsp ground turmeric
8–12 oxtail joints, cut roughly the same size and trimmed of fat
45ml/3 tbsp vegetable oil
225g/8oz tamarind pulp
400g/14oz can plum tomatoes, drained and chopped
2 lemon grass stalks, halved and bruised
a handful of fresh kaffir lime leaves
30–45ml/2–3 tbsp sugar
salt and ground black pepper
fresh coriander (cilantro) leaves, roughly chopped

1 Using a mortar and pestle or food processor, grind the shallots, garlic, chillies and galangal to a coarse paste.

2 Mix the flour with the ground turmeric and spread it on a flat surface. Roll the oxtail in the flour and set aside.

3 Heat the oil in a heavy pan or flameproof pot. Stir in the spice paste and cook until fragrant and golden. Add the oxtail joints and brown on all sides.

4 Soak the tamarind pulp in 600ml/1 pint/2½ cups water, squeeze it, strain the juice and discard the pulp and seeds. Add the tomatoes, lemon grass stalks, lime leaves and tamarind juice.

5 Pour in enough water to cover the oxtail, and bring it to the boil. Skim off any fat from the surface. Reduce the heat, cover the pan with a lid and simmer the oxtail for 2 hours.

6 Stir in the sugar, season with salt and pepper and continue to cook, uncovered, for a further 30–40 minutes, until the meat is very tender. Sprinkle with the coriander and serve the curry immediately straight from the pan.

Slow-cooked Buffalo in Coconut Milk

Cook this slowly for tender meat and a rich sauce.

Serves 6

1kg/2¼lb buffalo or beef, cubed
115g/4oz fresh coconut, grated
45ml/3 tbsp coconut oil
2 onions, sliced
3 lemon grass stalks, halved
2 cinnamon sticks
3–4 lime leaves
1.2 litres/2 pints/5 cups coconut milk
15ml/1 tbsp tamarind paste dissolved in 90ml/6 tbsp water
15ml/1 tbsp sugar
salt and ground black pepper
15ml/1 tbsp vegetable oil,
6 shallots, cooked rice and a salad, to serve

For the spice paste

8 red chillies, seeded and chopped
8 shallots, chopped
4–6 garlic cloves, chopped
50g/2oz galangal, chopped
25g/1oz fresh turmeric, chopped
15ml/1 tbsp coriander seeds
10ml/2 tsp cumin seeds
5ml/1 tsp black peppercorns

1 First make the spice paste. Grind the chillies, shallots, garlic, galangal and turmeric to a smooth paste. In a frying pan, dry-fry the coriander, cumin and peppercorns for 2–3 minutes. Grind the dry-fried spices to a powder then stir into the spice paste.

2 Put the buffalo or beef in a large bowl and mix in the spice paste. Leave to marinate for at least 2 hours.

3 Dry-fry the coconut in a heavy pan until brown. Grind the coconut in a food processor. Set aside.

4 Heat the oil in a flameproof casserole. Add the onions, lemon grass, cinnamon and lime leaves, and fry for 5 minutes. Add the beef and paste and fry until browned. Add the coconut milk and tamarind juice and bring to the boil. Reduce the heat and simmer gently for 2–4 hours for beef (4 hours for buffalo).

5 Stir in the sugar and coconut, cover and cook for 4 hours if using buffalo and 2–4 hours if using beef, stirring occasionally, until the meat is tender and the sauce is very thick. Season.

6 Fry the shallots in the oil. Spoon the meat on to a serving dish, garnish with the shallots and serve with rice and a salad.

Oxtail Energy 386kcal/1611kJ; Protein 34.5g; Carbohydrate 11.3g, of which sugars 6.6g; Fat 22.6g, of which saturates 7.7g; Cholesterol 125mg; Calcium 31mg; Fibre 1.2g; Sodium 191mg.
Slow-cooked Buffalo Energy 494kcal/2064kJ; Protein 40.6g; Carbohydrate 20.9g, of which sugars 18.8g; Fat 28.2g, of which saturates 17g; Cholesterol 97mg; Calcium 95mg; Fibre 3.9g; Sodium 335mg.

Pineapple and Coconut Curry

This sweet and spicy curry benefits from being made the day before, enabling the flavours to mingle longer. In Indonesia it is often eaten at room temperature, but it is also delicious hot.

15ml/1 tbsp palm
  sugar (jaggery)
400ml/14fl oz/1⅔ cups
  coconut milk
salt and ground black pepper
1 small bunch fresh coriander
  (cilantro) leaves, finely chopped,
  to garnish

Serves 4
1 small, firm pineapple
15–30ml/1–2 tbsp palm or
  coconut oil
4–6 shallots, finely chopped
2 garlic cloves, finely chopped
1 red chilli, seeded and
  finely chopped

For the spice paste
4 cloves
4 cardamom pods
1 small cinnamon stick
5ml/1 tsp coriander seeds
2.5ml/½ tsp cumin seeds
5–10ml/1–2 tsp water

1 First make the spice paste. Using a mortar and pestle or spice grinder, grind all the spices together to a powder. In a small bowl mix the spice powder with the water to make a smooth paste. Set aside.

2 Remove the skin from the pineapple then cut the flesh lengthways into quarters and remove the core. Cut each pineapple quarter widthways into chunky slices and set aside.

3 Heat the oil in a wok or large, heavy frying pan, stir in the shallots, garlic and chilli and stir-fry until fragrant and beginning to colour. Stir in the spice paste and stir-fry for 1 minute. Toss the pineapple slices into the wok, making sure they are well coated in the spicy mixture.

4 Stir the sugar into the coconut milk and pour into the wok. Bring to the boil, reduce the heat and simmer for 3–4 minutes to thicken the sauce, but don't allow the pineapple to become too soft. Season to taste with salt and pepper.

5 Transfer the curry into a warmed serving dish and top with the coriander to garnish. Serve hot or at room temperature.

Tamarind-laced Vegetables

The flavours in this dish make it popular in southern India.

10ml/2 tsp cumin seeds
50g/2oz/⅔ cup desiccated (dry
  unsweetened shredded) coconut
2–3 green chillies, chopped
200ml/7fl oz/¾ cup buttermilk
30ml/2 tbsp tamarind juice
30ml/2 tbsp sunflower oil
2.5ml/½ tsp black mustard seeds
2.5ml/½ tsp cumin seeds
2–3 whole dried red chillies
6–8 curry leaves
1.5ml/¼ tsp asafoetida
15ml/1 tbsp fresh coriander
  (cilantro), chopped
plain boiled basmati rice, to serve

Serves 4
125g/4½oz green beans, cut into
  2.5cm/1in lengths
200g/7oz carrots, cut into
  1cm/½in thick circles
225g/8oz potatoes, cubed
1 small aubergine (eggplant), about
  200g/7oz, quartered lengthways
  and cut into 2.5cm/1in pieces
2.5ml/½ tsp ground turmeric
5ml/1 tsp salt or to taste
200g/7oz cauliflower, divided into
  1cm/½in florets

1 Put the green beans, carrots, potatoes and aubergine into a large pan and add 350ml/12fl oz/1½ cups hot water. Add the turmeric and salt. Bring to the boil, reduce the heat to low and cover the pan. Cook for 5–6 minutes, then add the cauliflower. Cover and cook until the vegetables are tender, but still firm.

2 Meanwhile, heat a small heavy pan over a medium heat. Dry-roast the 10ml/2tsp cumin seeds for 30–40 seconds. Remove from the pan and dry-roast the coconut and green chillies until lightly browned. Allow to cool. Using a mortar and pestle or spice grinder, grind with the roasted cumin seeds until fine.

3 Add the ground roasted ingredients, buttermilk and tamarind juice to the vegetables. Cook gently for 4–5 minutes, then remove from the heat.

4 Heat the oil in a small pan over a medium heat. When hot, but not smoking, add the mustard seeds, followed by the 2.5ml/½tsp cumin seeds, red chillies, curry leaves and asafoetida. Blacken the chillies, then pour the spices over the vegetables. Stir in the chopped coriander and remove from the heat. Stand covered, for 5–6 minutes. Serve with basmati rice.

Pineapple Curry Energy 135kcal/573kJ; Protein 1.6g; Carbohydrate 25.4g, of which sugars 23.6g; Fat 3.8g, of which saturates 0.5g; Cholesterol 0mg; Calcium 87mg; Fibre 2.9g; Sodium 131mg.
Tamarind Vegetables Energy 252kcal/1050kJ; Protein 7.55g; Carbohydrate 22.5g, of which sugars 10.7g; Fat 15.5g, of which saturates 7.7g; Cholesterol 1.75mg; Calcium 119mg; Fibre 6.1g; Sodium 57mg.

Tofu and Vegetable Thai Curry

Coconut milk, chillies, galangal, lemon grass and kaffir lime leaves give this curry a wonderful flavour.

Serves 4
175g/6oz firm tofu, drained
45ml/3 tbsp dark soy sauce
15ml/1 tbsp sesame oil
5ml/1 tsp chilli sauce
2.5cm/1in piece fresh root ginger,
 finely grated
30ml/2 tbsp vegetable oil
1 onion, sliced
400ml/14fl oz/1⅔ cups coconut milk
150ml/¼ pint/⅔ cup water
1 red (bell) pepper, seeded
 and chopped
175g/6oz green beans, halved
225g/8oz cauliflower florets
225g/8oz broccoli florets
115g/4oz/1½ cups shiitake
 or button (white)
 mushrooms, halved
shredded spring onions (scallions),
 to garnish
boiled rice or noodles, to serve

For the curry paste
2 fresh green chillies, seeded
 and chopped
1 lemon grass stalk, chopped
2.5cm/1in piece fresh
 galangal, chopped
2 kaffir lime leaves
10ml/2 tsp ground coriander
a few sprigs fresh coriander
 (cilantro), including the stalks

1 Cut the drained tofu into 2.5cm/1in cubes and place in an ovenproof dish. Mix together the soy sauce, sesame oil, chilli sauce and ginger and pour over the tofu. Toss gently, then leave to marinate for 4 hours or overnight, turning occasionally.

2 For the curry paste, place the ingredients and 45ml/3 tbsp water in a food processor and blend for a few seconds.

3 Preheat the oven to 190°C/375°F/Gas 5. Heat the oil in a flameproof casserole. Fry the onion for 7–8 minutes. Add the paste and the coconut milk. Add the water and bring to the boil.

4 Stir in the red pepper, beans, cauliflower and broccoli, then cover and place in the oven.

5 Place the tofu and marinade in the oven for 30 minutes. Stir them into the curry with the mushrooms. Reduce the oven to 180°C/350°F/Gas 4 and cook for a further 15 minutes. Garnish with spring onions and serve with rice or noodles.

Malay Vegetable Curry with Coconut

Originally from southern India, this delicious curry has found its way into many Malay homes. Made with firm vegetables, roots and gourds, all cut into long bitesize pieces, it is substantial and flexible – choose your own assortment of vegetables.

Serves 4
2–3 green chillies, seeded
 and chopped
25g/1oz fresh root ginger, peeled
 and chopped
5–10ml/1–2 tsp roasted
 cumin seeds
10ml/2 tsp sugar
5–10ml/1–2 tsp ground turmeric
1 cinnamon stick
5ml/1 tsp salt
2 carrots, cut into bitesize sticks
2 sweet potatoes, cut into
 bitesize sticks
2 courgettes (zucchini), partially
 peeled in strips, seeded and
 cut into bitesize sticks
1 green plantain, peeled and cut
 into bitesize sticks
a small coil of yard-long beans
 or a few green beans, cut into
 bitesize sticks
a handful fresh curry leaves
1 fresh coconut, grated
250ml/8fl oz/1 cup Greek (US
 strained plain) yogurt
salt and ground black pepper

1 Using a mortar and pestle or food processor, grind the chillies, ginger, roasted cumin seeds and sugar to a paste.

2 In a heavy pan, bring 450ml/15fl oz/scant 2 cups water to the boil. Stir in the turmeric, cinnamon stick and salt. Add the carrots and cook for 1 minute. Add the sweet potatoes and cook for 2 minutes. Add the courgettes, plantain and beans and cook for a further 2 minutes.

3 Reduce the heat, stir in the spice paste and curry leaves, and cook gently for 4–5 minutes, or until the vegetables are tender but not soft and mushy, and the liquid has greatly reduced.

4 Gently stir in half the coconut. Take the pan off the heat and fold in the yogurt. Season to taste with salt and pepper.

5 Quickly roast the remaining coconut in a heavy pan over a high heat, until nicely browned. Sprinkle a little over the curry in the pan, and serve the rest with the curry and flatbread.

Malay Curry Energy 419kcal/1753kJ; Protein 9.9g; Carbohydrate 47.7g, of which sugars 19.4g; Fat 23g, of which saturates 16.9g; Cholesterol 0mg; Calcium 176mg; Fibre 9g; Sodium 104mg.
Tofu Thai Curry Energy 210kcal/873kJ; Protein 11g; Carbohydrate 15.1g, of which sugars 13.3g; Fat 12g, of which saturates 1.8g; Cholesterol 0mg; Calcium 328mg; Fibre 5g; Sodium 927mg.

Tofu, Green Bean and Mushroom Red Curry

This is one of those versatile recipes that should be in every curry lover's repertoire. This version uses green beans, but other types of vegetable work equally well.

Serves 4–6
600ml/1 pint/2½ cups
   coconut milk
10ml/2 tsp palm sugar (jaggery)
   or honey
15ml/1 tbsp Thai red
   curry paste
225g/8oz/3¼ cups button
   (white) mushrooms
115g/4oz green beans, trimmed
175g/6oz firm tofu, rinsed,
   drained and cut into
   2cm/¾in cubes
4 kaffir lime leaves, torn
2 fresh red chillies, seeded
   and sliced
fresh coriander (cilantro) leaves,
   to garnish

1 Pour about one-third of the coconut milk into a wok or pan. Cook until it starts to separate and an oily sheen appears on the surface of the hot liquid.

2 Add the palm sugar or honey and red curry paste to the coconut milk. Mix thoroughly, then add the mushrooms. Stir and cook for 1 minute over a medium heat.

3 Stir in the remaining coconut milk. Bring back to the boil, then add the green beans and tofu cubes. Simmer gently for 4–5 minutes more, stirring occasionally.

4 Stir in the kaffir lime leaves and sliced red chillies. Spoon the tofu and green bean curry into a serving dish, garnish with the coriander leaves and serve immediately.

> **Cook's Tip**
> Unless there are compelling health reasons, do not use low-fat coconut milk for this curry. The flavour of the full-cream product is superior. If you buy the canned product and have some left over, freeze it in ice cube trays – handy for future sauces.

Spicy Tofu with Basil and Peanuts

In Vietnam, aromatic pepper leaves are often used as the herb element in this dish but, because these are quite difficult to find outside South-east Asia, you can use basil leaves instead. Tofu can be very bland in flavour, but when marinated in lemon grass, chillies and spices, it becomes a memorable dish.

Serves 3–4
3 lemon grass stalks,
   finely chopped
45ml/3 tbsp soy sauce
2 red Serrano chillies, seeded
   and finely chopped
2 garlic cloves, crushed
5ml/1 tsp ground turmeric
10ml/2 tsp sugar
300g/11oz tofu, rinsed, drained,
   patted dry and cut into
   bitesize cubes
30ml/2 tbsp groundnut
   (peanut) oil
45ml/3 tbsp roasted
   peanuts, chopped
1 bunch fresh basil, stalks
   removed
salt

1 In a large mixing bowl, stir together the lemon grass, soy sauce, chopped chillies, garlic, turmeric and sugar, stirring briskly until the sugar has dissolved.

2 Add a little salt to the bowl to taste and add the tofu, making sure it is well coated in the marinade. Set aside to marinate for at least 1 hour.

3 Heat a wok or heavy pan. Pour in the oil, add the marinated tofu, and fry, stirring frequently, until it is golden brown on all sides. Add the peanuts and most of the basil leaves to the pan and mix well to combine the ingredients.

4 Divide the tofu among individual serving dishes, sprinkle the remaining basil leaves over the top and serve the curry either hot or at room temperature.

> **Variation**
> Lime, coriander (cilantro) or curry leaves would all work well in this simple and delicious stir-fry.

Tofu Curry Energy 59kcal/250kJ; Protein 3.8g; Carbohydrate 7.5g, of which sugars 7.1g; Fat 1.8g, of which saturates 0.4g; Cholesterol 0mg; Calcium 188mg; Fibre 0.8g; Sodium 291mg.
Spicy Tofu with Basil Energy 120kcal/500kJ; Protein 3g; Carbohydrate 5g, of which sugars 3g; Fat 10g, of which saturates 2g; Cholesterol 0mg; Calcium 36mg; Fibre 3.3g; Sodium 200mg.

Okra and Tomato Tagine with Garlic and Coriander

Although this spicy vegetable stew is a North African speciality, similar dishes exist throughout the Middle East.

Serves 4
350g/12oz okra
5–6 tomatoes

2 small onions
2 garlic cloves, crushed
1 fresh green chilli, seeded and roughly chopped
5ml/1 tsp paprika
small handful of fresh coriander (cilantro)
30ml/2 tbsp sunflower oil
juice of 1 lemon

1 Trim the okra and then cut it into 1cm/½in lengths. Skin and seed the tomatoes and roughly chop the flesh.

2 Roughly chop one of the onions and place it in a blender or food processor with the garlic, chilli, paprika, coriander and 60ml/4 tbsp water. Process to make a paste.

3 Thinly slice the second onion and fry it in the oil in a pan for 5–6 minutes, until golden brown. Transfer to a plate and set aside. Reduce the heat and pour the onion and coriander paste into the pan. Cook for 1–2 minutes, stirring frequently.

4 Add the okra, tomatoes, lemon juice and about 120ml/4fl oz/ ½ cup water. Stir well to mix, cover tightly and simmer over a low heat for about 15 minutes, until the okra is tender. Transfer to a serving dish, sprinkle with the fried onion rings and serve.

> **Variations**
> • Okra is a vegetable that is particularly popular in Egypt, where it is cultivated commercially on a grand scale. The vegetable is also known as 'ladies' fingers'. When cut before being cooked, the pods ooze a glue-like substance, which gives the dish a distinctive texture.
> • Use three or four shallots instead of onions, for a milder flavour, plus canned chopped tomatoes, if you prefer.

Israeli Vegetable Curry

This fiery tomato and aubergine stew is typical of Israeli cooking, for which aubergines and all things hot and spicy are staples.

Serves 4–6
about 60ml/4 tbsp olive oil
1 large aubergine (eggplant) cut into bitesize chunks
2 onions, thinly sliced
3–5 garlic cloves, chopped
1–2 green (bell) peppers, thinly sliced or chopped
1–2 fresh hot chillies, chopped

4 fresh or canned tomatoes, diced
30–45ml/2–3 tbsp tomato purée (paste), if using fresh tomatoes
5ml/1 tsp ground turmeric
pinch of curry powder or ras al hanout
cayenne pepper, to taste
400g/14oz can chickpeas, drained and rinsed
juice of ½–1 lemon
30–45ml/2–3 tbsp chopped fresh coriander (cilantro) leaves
salt

1 Heat half the oil in a frying pan, add the aubergine chunks and fry until brown, adding more oil if necessary. When cooked, transfer the aubergine to a strainer, standing over a large bowl, and leave to drain thoroughly on kitchen paper.

2 Heat the remaining oil in the pan, add the onions, garlic, peppers and chillies and fry until softened.

3 Add the diced tomatoes, tomato purée, if using, spices and salt, and cook, stirring, until the mixture thickens to a sauce consistency. Add a little water if necessary.

4 Add the chickpeas to the sauce and cook for about 5 minutes, then add the aubergine, stir to mix well and cook for 5–10 minutes until the flavours are well combined. Add lemon juice to taste, then add the coriander leaves. Chill before serving.

> **Variation**
> To make a Middle Eastern-style ratatouille, cut two courgettes (zucchini) and one red (bell) pepper into chunks. Add to the pan with the onions and garlic and continue as before.

Okra Tagine Energy 113kcal/471kJ; Protein 4.1g; Carbohydrate 9.2g, of which sugars 8g; Fat 7g, of which saturates 1.1g; Cholesterol 0mg; Calcium 181mg; Fibre 5.8g; Sodium 23mg.
Israeli Vegetable Curry Energy 362kcal/1536kJ; Protein 26g; Carbohydrate 60.9g, of which sugars 5.2g; Fat 3.6g, of which saturates 0.6g; Cholesterol 0mg; Calcium 117mg; Fibre 8g; Sodium 46mg.

Spicy Chickpea and Aubergine Stew

This is a Lebanese dish, but similar recipes are found all over the Mediterranean. The vegetables have a warm, smoky flavour, subtly enriched with spices. Crunchy fried onion rings provide a contrast of taste and texture. Serve the stew on a bed of rice.

Serves 4
3 large aubergines (eggplants), cut into cubes
200g/7oz/1 cup chickpeas, soaked overnight
60ml/4 tbsp olive oil
3 garlic cloves, chopped
2 large onions, chopped
2.5ml/½ tsp ground cumin
2.5ml/½ tsp ground cinnamon
2.5ml/½ tsp ground coriander
3 × 400g/14oz cans chopped tomatoes
salt and ground black pepper
cooked rice, to serve

For the garnish
30ml/2 tbsp olive oil
1 onion, sliced
1 garlic clove, sliced
sprigs of coriander (cilantro)

1 Place the aubergines in a colander and sprinkle them with salt. Sit the colander in a bowl and leave for 30 minutes, to allow the bitter juices to escape. Rinse with cold water and pat dry using a piece of kitchen paper.

2 Drain the chickpeas and put in a pan with enough water to cover. Bring to the boil, reduce the heat and simmer for about 30 minutes, or until tender. Drain.

3 Heat the oil in a large pan. Add the garlic and onions and cook gently until soft. Add the spices and cook, stirring, for a few seconds. Add the aubergine and stir to coat with the spices and onion. Cook for 5 minutes.

4 Add the tomatoes and chickpeas and season with salt and pepper. Cover and simmer for 20 minutes.

5 To make the garnish, heat the oil in a frying pan and, when very hot, add the sliced onion and garlic. Fry until golden and crisp. Serve the stew with rice, topped with the onion and garlic and garnished with coriander.

Aubergine and Sweet Potato Stew

This aubergine and sweet potato stew cooked in a coconut sauce is scented with fragrant lemon grass, ginger and lots of garlic.

Serves 6
60ml/4 tbsp sunflower oil
400g/14oz baby aubergines (eggplants), halved, or 2 standard aubergines, cut into chunks
225g/8oz red shallots or other small shallots or pickling onions
5ml/1 tsp fennel seeds, crushed
4–5 garlic cloves, thinly sliced
25ml/1½ tbsp finely chopped fresh root ginger
475ml/16fl oz/2 cups vegetable stock
2 lemon grass stalks, outer layers discarded, finely chopped
15g/½oz fresh coriander, stalks and leaves chopped separately
3 kaffir lime leaves, lightly bruised
2–3 small red chillies
45–60ml/3–4 tbsp Thai green curry paste
675g/1½lb sweet potatoes, peeled and cut into thick chunks
400ml/14fl oz/1⅔ cups coconut milk
2.5–5ml/½–1 tsp light muscovado (brown) sugar
250g/9oz mushrooms, sliced
juice of 1 lime, to taste
salt and ground black pepper
18 fresh Thai basil leaves or ordinary basil, to garnish

1 Heat half the oil in a lidded wok or deep frying pan. Cook the aubergines over a medium heat, stirring occasionally, until lightly browned on all sides. Remove and set aside.

2 Slice 4–5 of the shallots or 3–4 onions and set aside. Fry the remaining whole shallots or onions until lightly browned. Set aside. Heat the remaining oil and cook the sliced shallots, fennel seeds, garlic and ginger very gently until soft. Add the stock, lemon grass, coriander stalks and any roots, lime leaves and whole chillies. Cover with a lid and simmer gently for 5 minutes.

3 Stir in 30ml/2 tbsp of the curry paste and the sweet potatoes. Simmer for 10 minutes, then return the aubergines and browned shallots to the pan and cook for 5 minutes.

4 Stir in the coconut milk and the sugar. Season to taste, then stir in the mushrooms and simmer for 5 minutes. Stir in more curry paste and lime juice to taste, followed by the coriander leaves. Serve in warmed bowls, garnished with basil leaves.

Spicy Chickpea Stew Energy 201kcal/843kJ; Protein 7.1g; Carbohydrate 22.3g, of which sugars 10.4g; Fat 10g, of which saturates 1.4g; Cholesterol 0mg; Calcium 57mg; Fibre 5.9g; Sodium 175mg.
Aubergine Stew Energy 228kcal/960kJ; Protein 4.3g; Carbohydrate 34g, of which sugars 13.4g; Fat 9.3g, of which saturates 1.2g; Cholesterol 0mg; Calcium 130mg; Fibre 7.2g; Sodium 159mg.

Moroccan-spiced Aubergine Tagine

Spiced with coriander, cumin, cinnamon, turmeric and a dash of chilli sauce, this Moroccan-style stew makes a filling supper dish when served with couscous.

Serves 4

1 small aubergine (eggplant), cut into 1cm/½in dice
2 courgettes (zucchini), sliced
60ml/4 tbsp olive oil
1 large onion, sliced
2 garlic cloves, chopped
150g/5oz/2 cups brown cap (cremini) mushrooms, halved
15ml/1 tbsp ground coriander
10ml/2 tsp cumin seeds
15ml/1 tbsp ground cinnamon
10ml/2 tsp ground turmeric
225g/8oz new potatoes, quartered
600ml/1 pint/2⅓ cups passata (bottled strained tomatoes)
15ml/1 tbsp tomato purée (paste)
15ml/1 tbsp chilli sauce
75g/3oz/½ cup ready-to-eat unsulphured dried apricots
400g/14oz/3 cups canned chickpeas, drained and rinsed
salt and ground black pepper
15ml/1 tbsp chopped fresh coriander (cilantro), to garnish

1 Place the the aubergine and courgettes in a colander, sprinkle with salt and leave for 30 minutes. Rinse and pat dry with a dish towel. Heat the grill (broiler) to high. Arrange the courgettes and aubergine on a baking tray and toss in 30ml/2 tbsp of the olive oil. Cook for 20 minutes, turning occasionally, until tender and golden.

2 Meanwhile, heat the remaining oil in a large heavy pan and cook the onion and garlic for 5 minutes until softened, stirring occasionally. Add the mushrooms and sauté for 3 minutes until tender. Add the spices and cook for 1 minute more, stirring, to allow the flavours to mingle.

3 Add the potatoes and cook for about 3 minutes, stirring. Pour in the passata, tomato purée and 150ml/¼ pint/⅔ cup water. Cover and cook for 10 minutes to thicken the sauce.

4 Add the aubergine, courgettes, chilli sauce, apricots and chickpeas. Season and cook, partially covered, for about 15 minutes until the potatoes are tender. Add a little extra water if the tagine becomes too dry. Sprinkle with chopped fresh coriander and serve immediately.

Cambodian Aubergine Curry

Aubergine curries are popular throughout South-east Asia, the Thai version being the most famous. All are hot and aromatic, enriched with coconut milk. This spicy Cambodian recipe uses the herbal paste kroeung.

Serves 4–6

15ml/1 tbsp vegetable oil
4 garlic cloves, crushed
2 shallots, sliced
2 dried chillies
45ml/3 tbsp kroeung
15ml/1 tbsp vegetable paste or mam roi
15ml/1 tbsp palm sugar (jaggery)
600ml/1 pint/2½ cups coconut milk
250ml/8fl oz/1 cup vegetable stock
4 aubergines (eggplants), trimmed and cut into bitesize pieces
6 kaffir lime leaves
1 bunch fresh basil, stalks removed, leaves chopped
salt and ground black pepper
fragrant jasmine rice and 2 limes, cut into quarters, to serve

1 Heat the oil in a wok or heavy pan. Stir in the garlic, shallots and whole chillies and stir-fry until they begin to colour.

2 Stir in the kroeung, vegetable paste or mam roi and palm sugar and stir-fry until the mixture begins to darken.

3 Pour the coconut milk and stock into the pan, and add the aubergines and lime leaves. Stir well so that all the ingredients are well combined. Bring slowly to the boil.

4 Partially cover the pan and simmer over a low heat for about 25–30 minutes until the aubergines are tender. Stir in the chopped fresh basil and check the seasoning. Serve the curry immediately with jasmine rice and lime wedges.

Cook's Tip

Kroeung is an aromatic, medium to hot red curry paste. A typical formulation of this popular ingredient contains dried red chillies, galangal root, coriander root, shallots, chopped kaffir lime rind and leaves, lemon grass, garlic and turmeric. Look for it in large supermarkets and Asian stores.

Aubergine Tagine Energy 359kcal/1509kJ; Protein 13.9g; Carbohydrate 45g, of which sugars 19.3g; Fat 15g, of which saturates 2.1g; Cholesterol 0mg; Calcium 123mg; Fibre 9.7g; Sodium 597mg.
Aubergine Curry Energy 72kcal/305kJ; Protein 1.6g; Carbohydrate 11.2g, of which sugars 10.7g; Fat 3g, of which saturates 1g; Cholesterol 0mg; Calcium 46mg; Fibre 2.8g; Sodium 113mg.

Pumpkin and Peanut Yellow Curry

This is a hearty, soothing Thai curry that is perfect for autumn or winter evenings. Its cheerful colour alone will brighten you up – and it tastes terrific.

Serves 4

30ml/2 tbsp vegetable oil
4 garlic cloves, crushed
4 shallots, finely chopped
30ml/2 tbsp Thai yellow
   curry paste
600ml/1 pint/2½ cups
   vegetable stock
2 kaffir lime leaves, torn

15ml/1 tbsp chopped galangal
450g/1lb pumpkin, peeled, seeded
   and diced
225g/8oz sweet potatoes, diced
90g/3½oz/scant 1 cup peanuts,
   roasted and chopped
300ml/½ pint/1¼ cups
   coconut milk
90g/3½oz/1½ cups brown cap
   (cremini) mushrooms, sliced
15ml/1 tbsp soy sauce
30ml/2 tbsp Thai
   mushroom ketchup
50g/2oz/⅓ cup pumpkin seeds,
   toasted, and fresh green chilli
   flowers, to garnish

1 Heat the oil in a large pan. Add the garlic and shallots and cook over a medium heat, stirring occasionally, for 10 minutes, until softened and golden. Do not let them burn.

2 Add the yellow curry paste and stir-fry over a medium heat for 30 seconds, until the mixture is fragrant.

3 Add the stock, lime leaves, galangal, pumpkin and sweet potatoes. Bring to the boil, stirring frequently, then reduce the heat to low and simmer gently for 15 minutes.

4 Add the peanuts, coconut milk and mushrooms. Stir in the soy sauce and mushroom ketchup and simmer for 5 minutes more. Spoon into warmed individual serving bowls, garnish with the pumpkin seeds and chilli flowers and serve.

Cook's Tip
The well-drained vegetables from a curry of this kind would make a very tasty filling for a pastry or pie. This may not be a Thai tradition, but it is a good example of fusion food.

Corn and Cashew Nut Curry

This is a substantial curry, thanks largely to the potatoes and corn kernels, which makes it a great winter-warming dish. It is deliciously aromatic, but, as the spices are added in relatively small amounts, the resulting flavour and heat is fairly mild.

Serves 4

30ml/2 tbsp vegetable oil
4 shallots, chopped
90g/3½ oz/scant 1 cup
   cashew nuts
5ml/1 tsp red curry paste
400g/14oz potatoes, peeled
   and cut into chunks
1 lemon grass stalk, finely chopped

200g/7oz can chopped tomatoes
600ml/1 pint/2½ cups
   boiling water
200g/7oz/generous 1 cup
   drained canned whole
   kernel corn
4 celery sticks, sliced
2 kaffir lime leaves, central rib
   removed, rolled into cylinders
   and thinly sliced
15ml/1 tbsp tomato ketchup
15ml/1 tbsp light soy sauce
5ml/1 tsp palm sugar (jaggery)
   or light muscovado
   (brown) sugar
4 spring onions (scallions),
   thinly sliced
small bunch fresh basil,
   roughly chopped

1 Heat the oil in a wok or deep frying pan. Add the shallots and stir-fry over a medium heat for 2–3 minutes, until softened. Add the cashew nuts to the pan and stir-fry for a few minutes until they are golden but take care not to let them burn.

2 Stir the red curry paste into the pan. Cook for 1 minute, stirring constantly, then add the potatoes, lemon grass, tomatoes and boiling water and stir well.

3 Bring back to the boil, then reduce the heat to low, cover and simmer gently for 15–20 minutes, or until the potatoes are tender when tested with the tip of a knife.

4 Stir the corn, celery, lime leaves, ketchup, soy sauce and sugar into the pan. Simmer further for about 5 minutes, until heated through, then spoon the curry into warmed serving bowls. Sprinkle with the sliced spring onions and chopped fresh basil and serve immediately.

Pumpkin Curry Energy 306kcal/1279kJ; Protein 9.6g; Carbohydrate 24.5g, of which sugars 11.4g; Fat 19.6g, of which saturates 3.3g; Cholesterol 0mg; Calcium 160mg; Fibre 6.4g; Sodium 409mg.
Corn and Cashew Curry Energy 298kcal/1245kJ; Protein 8.8g; Carbohydrate 27.6g, of which sugars 8.9g; Fat 17.7g, of which saturates 3.1g; Cholesterol 0mg; Calcium 33mg; Fibre 3.5g; Sodium 981mg.

Hot and Spicy Thai Vegetable Curry

This spicy curry made with coconut milk has a creamy richness that contrasts wonderfully with the heat of the chilli. Thai yellow curry paste is available in supermarkets, but you will really taste the difference when you make it yourself.

Serves 4
30ml/2 tbsp sunflower oil
200ml/7fl oz/scant 1 cup
    coconut cream
300ml/½ pint/1¼ cups
    coconut milk
150ml/¼ pint/⅔ cup vegetable
    stock
200g/7oz green beans, cut into
    2cm/¾in lengths
200g/7oz baby corn
4 baby courgettes (zucchini),
    thickly sliced

1 small aubergine (eggplant),
    cubed or sliced
30ml/2 tbsp Thai
    mushroom ketchup
10ml/2 tsp palm sugar (jaggery)
fresh coriander (cilantro) leaves,
    to garnish
noodles or rice, to serve

For the yellow curry paste
10ml/2 tsp hot chilli powder
10ml/2 tsp ground coriander
10ml/2 tsp ground cumin
5ml/1 tsp turmeric
15ml/1 tbsp chopped fresh
    galangal
10ml/2 tsp finely grated garlic
30ml/2 tbsp finely chopped
    lemon grass
4 red Asian or brown shallots,
    finely chopped
5ml/1 tsp finely chopped
    lime rind

1 To make the curry paste, place all the ingredients in a food processor and blend with 30–45ml/2–3 tbsp of cold water to make a smooth paste. Add a little more water to the paste if the mixture seems too dry.

2 Heat a large wok over a medium heat and add the sunflower oil. When hot add 30–45ml/2–3 tbsp of the curry paste and stir-fry for 1–2 minutes. Add the coconut cream and cook gently for 8–10 minutes, or until the mixture starts to separate.

3 Add the coconut milk, stock and vegetables and cook gently for 8–10 minutes, until the vegetables are just tender.

4 Stir in the mushroom ketchup and palm sugar, garnish with coriander leaves and serve with noodles or rice.

Spicy Chickpea Tagine

This tangy Moroccan tagine features the traditional preserved lemon. The flavour of preserved lemon is wonderful. It adds a real zing to the nuttiness of the chickpeas.

Serves 4
150g/5oz/¾ cup chickpeas,
    soaked overnight, or
    2 x 400g/14oz cans chickpeas,
    rinsed and drained

30ml/2 tbsp sunflower oil
    or vegetable oil
1 large onion, chopped
1 garlic clove, crushed (optional)
400g/14oz can chopped
    tomatoes
5ml/1 tsp ground cumin
350ml/12fl oz/1½ cups
    vegetable stock
¼ preserved lemon
30ml/2 tbsp chopped fresh
    coriander (cilantro)
Moroccan bread, to serve

1 If using dried chickpeas, cook them in plenty of boiling water for 1–1½ hours until tender. Drain well.

2 Place the chickpeas in a bowl of cold water and rub them between your fingers to remove the skins.

3 Heat the oil in a pan or flameproof casserole and fry the onion and garlic, if using, for 8–10 minutes, until golden.

4 Add the chickpeas, tomatoes, cumin and vegetable stock to the pan and stir well to combine.

5 Bring to the boil and simmer for 30–40 minutes, until most of the liquid has evaporated.

6 Rinse the preserved lemon and cut away the flesh and pith. Cut the peel into slivers and stir it into the chickpeas together with the coriander. Serve immediately with Moroccan bread.

> **Cook's Tip**
> *Preserved lemon is popular in North Africa, particularly Morocco, where the distinctive yellow globes in glass jars glimmer like miniature suns in the markets.*

Hot Thai Curry Energy 279kcal/1161kJ; Protein 9.8g; Carbohydrate 17.4g, of which sugars 13.3g; Fat 19.4g, of which saturates 3.6g; Cholesterol 5mg; Calcium 99mg; Fibre 3.3g; Sodium 824mg.
Chickpea Tagine Energy 207kcal/871kJ; Protein 9.7g; Carbohydrate 26.4g, of which sugars 7.1g; Fat 7.8g, of which saturates 0.9g; Cholesterol 0mg; Calcium 87mg; Fibre 5.6g; Sodium 56mg.

Spiced Peppers with Eggs and Lentils

These oven-baked filled peppers make a tasty side dish. They are delicious with fish or pork chops, but also make an excellent light meal for vegetarians.

Serves 4
75g/3oz/½ cup Puy lentils
2.5ml/½ tsp ground turmeric
2.5ml/½ tsp ground coriander
2.5ml/½ tsp paprika
450ml/¾ pint/1¾ cups
   vegetable stock
2 large (bell) peppers, halved
   lengthways and seeded
a little vegetable oil
15ml/1 tbsp chopped fresh mint
4 eggs
salt and ground black pepper
sprigs of coriander (cilantro),
   to garnish

1 Put the lentils in a pan with the spices and stock. Bring to the boil, stirring occasionally, and simmer for 30–40 minutes. If necessary, add more water during cooking.

2 Brush the peppers with oil and place close together on a baking tray. Stir the mint into the lentils, then fill the peppers with the mixture. Preheat the oven to 190°C/375°F/Gas 5.

3 Crack the eggs, one at a time, into a small saucer and carefully pour into the middle of a pepper. Stir into the lentils and sprinkle with seasoning. Bake for 10 minutes until the egg white is just set. Garnish with coriander and serve.

> **Cook's Tip**
> Use beef tomatoes instead of peppers. Cut a lid off the tomatoes and scoop out their middles using a spoon. Fill with lentils and eggs and bake as before.

> **Variation**
> Add a little extra flavour to the lentil mixture by adding chopped onion and tomatoes sautéed in olive oil.

Red Curry Stuffed Sweet Peppers

This is an unusual recipe where the stuffed peppers are steamed rather than baked, but the result is beautifully light and tender. The filling incorporates typical Thai ingredients such as red curry paste and soy sauce. Kaffir lime leaves also add a delicate citrus flavour.

Serves 4
3 garlic cloves
2 coriander (cilantro) roots
400g/14oz/3 cups brown cap
   (cremini) or button (white)
   mushrooms, quartered
5ml/1 tsp Thai red curry paste
1 egg, lightly beaten
30ml/2 tbsp soy sauce or light
   soy sauce
2.5ml/½ tsp sugar
3 kaffir lime leaves,
   finely chopped
4 yellow (bell) peppers, halved
   lengthways and seeded

1 Finely chop the garlic cloves and coriander roots. Pound or blend the garlic with the coriander roots using a pestle and mortar or spice grinder. Scrape into a bowl.

2 Put the mushrooms in a food processor and pulse briefly until they are finely chopped.

3 Add to the garlic mixture, then stir in the Thai red curry paste, beaten egg and soy sauce. Add the sugar and kaffir lime leaves to the mixture.

4 Place the pepper halves in a single layer in a steamer basket. Spoon the mixture loosely into the pepper halves. Do not pack the mixture down tightly or the filling will dry out too much.

5 Bring the water in the steamer to the boil, then lower the heat to a simmer. Steam the peppers for 15 minutes, or until the flesh is tender. Serve hot.

> **Variations**
> Use red or orange (bell) peppers rather than yellow, if you prefer, or a combination of the two.

Spiced Peppers Energy 188kcal/788kJ; Protein 11.8g; Carbohydrate 16.3g, of which sugars 5.9g; Fat 9g, of which saturates 2.1g; Cholesterol 190mg; Calcium 58mg; Fibre 2.6g; Sodium 82mg.
Red Curry Energy 103kcal/429kJ; Protein 6.1g; Carbohydrate 14.4g, of which sugars 12g; Fat 2.7g, of which saturates 0.7g; Cholesterol 48mg; Calcium 30mg; Fibre 4.4g; Sodium 297mg.

Fiery Jungle Curry

This fiery, flavoursome vegetarian curry is almost dominated by the chilli. Its many variations make it a favourite with Buddhist monks who value the way it adds variety to their vegetarian diet. Jungle curry can be served with plain rice or noodles, or chunks of crusty bread. It can be eaten for breakfast or enjoyed as a pick-me-up at any time of day.

Serves 4

30ml/2 tbsp vegetable oil or
    extra virgin olive oil
2 onions, roughly chopped
2 lemon grass stalks, roughly
    chopped and bruised
4 fresh green chillies, seeded
    and finely sliced
4cm/1½in galangal or
    fresh root ginger, peeled
    and chopped
3 carrots, peeled, halved
    lengthways and sliced
115g/4oz yard-long beans
grated rind of 1 lime
15ml/3 tsp soy sauce
15ml/1 tbsp rice vinegar
5ml/1 tsp black
    peppercorns, crushed
15ml/1 tbsp sugar
10ml/2 tsp ground turmeric
115g/4oz canned bamboo shoots
75g/3oz spinach, steamed and
    roughly chopped
150ml/¼ pint/⅔ cup coconut milk
chopped fresh coriander (cilantro)
    and mint leaves, to garnish

1 Heat a wok or heavy frying pan and add the oil. Once hot, stir in the onions, lemon grass, chillies and galangal or ginger and stir-fry for 2–3 minutes.

2 Add the carrots and beans to the pan along with the lime rind and stir-fry for 1–2 minutes.

3 Stir in the soy sauce and rice vinegar and mix well.

4 Add the crushed peppercorns, sugar and turmeric to the pan, then stir in the bamboo shoots and the chopped spinach.

5 Stir the coconut milk into the pan and simmer over a low heat for about 10 minutes, until all the vegetables are tender.

6 Garnish with chopped fresh coriander and mint leaves and serve the curry immediately with rice, noodles or crusty bread.

Israeli Stuffed Onions, Potatoes and Courgettes

The vegetarian filling of these vegetables is tomato-red, Yemenite-spiced and accented with the tart taste of lemon. They are delicious cold and are good served as an appetizer as well as a main course.

Serves 4

4 potatoes, peeled
4 onions, skinned
4 courgettes (zucchini), cut in
    half widthways
2–4 garlic cloves, chopped
45–60ml/3–4 tbsp olive oil
45–60ml/3–4 tbsp tomato
    purée (paste)
1.5ml/¼ tsp ras al hanout
    or curry powder
large pinch of ground allspice
seeds of 2–3 cardamom pods
juice of ½ lemon
30–45ml/2–3 tbsp chopped
    fresh parsley
90–120ml/6–8 tbsp
    vegetable stock
salt and ground black pepper
salad, to serve (optional)

1 Bring a large pan of salted water to the boil. Starting with the potatoes, then the onions and finally the courgettes, add to the boiling water and cook until they become almost tender but not cooked right through. Allow about 10 minutes for the potatoes, 8 minutes for the onions and about 4–6 minutes for the courgettes. Remove the vegetables from the pan and set aside to cool slightly.

2 When the vegetables are cool enough to handle, hollow them out. Preheat the oven to 190°C/375°F/Gas 5.

3 Finely chop the cut-out vegetable flesh and put it in a bowl. Add the garlic, half the olive oil, the tomato purée, ras al hanout or curry powder, allspice, cardamom seeds, lemon juice, parsley, salt and pepper and mix well together. Use the stuffing mixture to fill the hollowed vegetables.

4 Arrange the stuffed vegetables in a baking tin (pan) and drizzle with the stock and the remaining oil. Roast for about 35–40 minutes, or until golden brown. Serve warm with a simple salad, if you like.

Fiery Jungle Curry Energy 119kcal/496kJ; Protein 3.8g; Carbohydrate 18.6g, of which sugars 15.3g; Fat 3.8g, of which saturates 0.5g; Cholesterol 0mg; Calcium 125mg; Fibre 4.3g; Sodium 60mg.
Israeli Stuffed Onions Energy 347kcal/1452kJ; Protein 10.2g; Carbohydrate 56.7g, of which sugars 22.1g; Fat 10.3g, of which saturates 1.6g; Cholesterol 0mg; Calcium 135mg; Fibre 8.2g; Sodium 62mg.

Curried Parsnip Pie

Sweet, creamy parsnips are beautifully complemented by the addition of curry spices and cheese in this delectable pie. It is sure to go down a treat with the whole family.

Serves 4
For the pastry
115g/4oz/½ cup butter
225g/8oz/1 cup plain
  (all-purpose) flour
5ml/1 tsp dried thyme or oregano
cold water, to mix
salt and ground black pepper

For the filling
8 shallots, peeled
2 large parsnips, thinly sliced
2 carrots, thinly sliced
25g/1oz/2 tbsp butter
30ml/2 tbsp wholemeal
  (whole-wheat) flour
15ml/1 tbsp mild curry paste
300ml/½ pint/1¼ cups milk
115g/4oz cheese, grated
45ml/3 tbsp fresh coriander
  (cilantro) or parsley, chopped
1 egg yolk, beaten with 10ml/
  2 tsp water
salt and ground black pepper

1 Make the pastry by rubbing the butter into the flour until it resembles fine breadcrumbs. Season and stir in the thyme or oregano, then mix with enough cold water to make a firm dough.

2 Blanch the shallots with the parsnips and carrots in water for 5 minutes. Drain, reserving 300ml/½ pint/1¼ cups of the stock.

3 In a clean pan, melt the butter, and stir in the flour and curry paste to make a roux. Whisk in the milk until smooth. Simmer for a minute or two. Stir in the cheese and seasoning, then mix into the vegetables with the coriander or parsley. Pour into a pie dish, fix a pie funnel in the centre and allow to cool.

4 Roll out the pastry, large enough to fit the pie dish. Re-roll the trimmings into long strips. Brush the edges of the dish with egg yolk wash and fit on the strips. Carefully lift the rolled pastry over the pie top, pressing it down. Cut off any excess and crimp the edges. Cut a hole for the funnel and make decorations with the trimmings. Brush with egg yolk wash.

5 Place the dish on a baking sheet and chill for 30 minutes while you preheat the oven to 200°C/400°F/Gas 6. Bake the pie for 25–30 minutes until golden brown and crisp on top.

Curried Stuffed Peppers

These fabulous peppers are served at weddings in India.

Serves 4–6
15ml/1 tbsp sesame seeds
15ml/1 tbsp white poppy seeds
5ml/1 tsp coriander seeds
60ml/4 tbsp desiccated (dry
  unsweetened shredded) coconut
½ onion, sliced
2.5cm/1in piece fresh root
  ginger, sliced
4 garlic cloves, sliced
1 bunch of fresh coriander

(cilantro), stalks removed,
  roughly chopped
6 fresh green chillies
60ml/4 tbsp vegetable oil
2 potatoes, boiled and
  coarsely mashed
2 each green, red and yellow
  (bell) peppers
30ml/2 tbsp sesame oil
5ml/1 tsp cumin seeds
15ml/1 tbsp tamarind pulp
  soaked in 45ml/3 tbsp water,
  pulp and seeds discarded
salt

1 In a frying pan, dry-fry the sesame, poppy and coriander seeds, then add the coconut and continue to roast until the coconut turns golden brown. Add the onion, ginger, garlic, coriander, and two of the chillies, and roast for a further 5 minutes. Cool, and grind to a paste using a mortar and pestle or food processor. Set aside.

2 Heat 30ml/2 tbsp of the oil in a frying pan and fry the ground paste for about 4–5 minutes. Add the potatoes and salt to the pan, and stir well until the spices have blended evenly into the mashed potatoes.

3 Trim the bases of the peppers so that they can stand upright, then slice off the tops and reserve. Remove the seeds and any white pith. Fill the peppers with equal amounts of the potato mixture and replace the tops.

4 Slit the remaining chillies and remove the seeds, if you like. Heat the sesame oil and remaining vegetable oil in a large pan and fry the cumin seeds and the slit green chillies. When the chillies turn white, add the tamarind juice and bring to the boil.

5 Place the peppers over the mixture, cover the pan and cook until the peppers are just tender. Serve immediately.

Curried Stuffed Peppers Energy 267kcal/1116kJ; Protein 13.9g; Carbohydrate 26.1g, of which sugars 15.3g; Fat 12.5g, of which saturates 4.7g; Cholesterol 37mg; Calcium 81mg; Fibre 4.4g; Sodium 84mg.
Curried Parsnip Pie Energy 411kcal/1721kJ; Protein 5.9g; Carbohydrate 47.4g, of which sugars 24.8g; Fat 23.4g, of which saturates 13.9g; Cholesterol 117mg; Calcium 96mg; Fibre 1.7g; Sodium 106mg.

Potato with Spicy Cottage Cheese

Always choose a variety of potato recommended for baking for this recipe, as the texture of the potato should not be too dry. This dish makes an excellent low-fat snack at any time of the day.

Serves 4

4 medium baking potatoes
225g/8oz/1 cup low-fat
  cottage cheese
10ml/2 tsp tomato
  purée (paste)
2.5ml/½ tsp ground cumin

2.5ml/½ tsp ground coriander
2.5ml/½ tsp chilli powder
2.5ml/½ tsp salt
15ml/1 tbsp corn or
  sunflower oil
2.5ml/½ tsp mixed onion and
  mustard seeds
3 curry leaves
30ml/2 tbsp water

For the garnish

mixed salad leaves
fresh coriander (cilantro) sprigs
lemon wedges
2 tomatoes, quartered

1 Preheat the oven to 180°C/350°F/Gas 4. Wash, pat dry and make a slit in the middle of each potato. Prick the potatoes a few times, then wrap in foil. Bake for about 1 hour until soft. Put the cottage cheese into a heatproof dish and set aside.

2 In a separate bowl, mix together the tomato purée, ground cumin, ground coriander, chilli powder and salt.

3 Heat the oil in a small pan for about 1 minute. Add the mixed onion and mustard seeds and the curry leaves. When the leaves turn a shade darker and release their aroma, pour the spice mixture into the pan and lower the heat.

4 Add the water and mix well. Cook for a further 1 minute, then pour the spicy tomato mixture on to the cottage cheese and blend everything together well.

5 Check that the potatoes are cooked right through by inserting a metal skewer. Unwrap the potatoes and divide the cottage cheese mixture equally between the four potatoes. Garnish the potatoes with the mixed salad leaves, fresh coriander sprigs, lemon wedges and tomato quarters.

Curry Fried Noodles

On its own, tofu has a fairly bland flavour, but it is very good at taking on the flavours of the other ingredients it is cooked with. This delicious curry takes advantage of that by cooking the tofu with traditional spice paste.

Serves 4

60ml/4 tbsp vegetable oil
30–45ml/2–3 tbsp curry paste
225g/8oz smoked tofu, cut into
  2.5cm/1in cubes

225g/8oz green beans, cut into
  2.5cm/1in lengths
1 red (bell) pepper, seeded and
  cut into fine strips
350g/12oz rice vermicelli, soaked
  in warm water until soft
15ml/1 tbsp soy sauce
salt and ground black pepper
2 spring onions (scallions),
  finely sliced, 2 red chillies,
  seeded and cut into thin slices,
  and 1 lime, cut into wedges,
  to garnish

1 Heat half the oil in a wok or large frying pan. Add the curry paste to the pan and stir-fry for a few minutes until it releases all the fragrant aromas.

2 Add the tofu to the pan and fry until golden brown all over. Using a slotted spoon remove the tofu cubes from the pan and set aside until required.

3 Add the remaining oil to the wok or pan. When the oil is hot, add the green beans and red pepper strips. Stir-fry for about 4–5 minutes until the vegetables are cooked. You may need to moisten them with a little water.

4 Drain the soaked noodles thoroughly and then add them to the wok or frying pan.

5 Continue to stir-fry until the noodles are heated through, then return the curried tofu to the wok or pan. Season with soy sauce, salt and black pepper.

6 Transfer the mixture to a warmed serving dish. Sprinkle with the sliced spring onions and chillies and serve immediately with the lime wedges on the side.

Baked Potato Energy 256kcal/1086kJ; Protein 12.4g; Carbohydrate 43.8g, of which sugars 5.4g; Fat 4.8g, of which saturates 1.1g; Cholesterol 3mg; Calcium 64mg; Fibre 2.6g; Sodium 249mg.
Curry Noodles Energy 479kcal/1996kJ; Protein 13.8g; Carbohydrate 73.7g, of which sugars 4.3g; Fat 14.2g, of which saturates 1.7g; Cholesterol 0mg; Calcium 332mg; Fibre 2g; Sodium 11mg.

Cauliflower and Coconut Milk Curry

This delicious vegetable curry combines rich coconut milk with spices, and is perfect as a vegetarian main course or as part of a buffet.

Serves 4
1 cauliflower
2 medium tomatoes
1 onion, chopped
2 garlic cloves, crushed

1 fresh green chilli, seeded and
   roughly chopped
2.5ml/½ tsp ground turmeric
30ml/2 tbsp sunflower oil
400ml/14fl oz/1⅔ cups
   coconut milk
250ml/8fl oz/1 cup water
5ml/1 tsp sugar
5ml/1 tsp tamarind pulp,
   soaked in 45ml/3 tbsp
   warm water
salt

1 Trim the stalk from the cauliflower and divide into small florets. Peel the tomatoes if you like, then chop them into even pieces, roughly 1–2.5cm/½–1in long.

2 Grind the chopped onion, garlic, green chilli and ground turmeric to a paste in a food processor.

3 Heat the oil in a karahi, wok or large frying pan and stir-fry the spice paste until the aromatic flavours are released, without allowing it to brown or burn.

4 Add the cauliflower florets to the pan and toss well to coat in the spice mixture. Stir in the coconut milk, water and sugar, and add salt to taste. Simmer for about 5 minutes. Strain the tamarind, discard the pulp and reserve the juice.

5 Add the tamarind juice and chopped tomatoes to the pan then cook for 2–3 minutes only. Taste and adjust the seasoning if necessary, then serve immediately.

> **Cook's Tip**
> *Always be careful when preparing fresh or dried chillies as they can irritate sensitive skin. Wear plastic gloves or ensure you wash your hands thoroughly after preparation.*

Okra in Chilli Yogurt

This tangy vegetable curry can be served as an accompaniment, but also makes an excellent vegetarian meal served with tarka dhal and chapatis or other Indian breads. The secret of cooking okra is not to overcook it, as the resulting sticky juices can be somewhat unpleasant.

Serves 4
450g/1lb okra
30ml/2 tbsp vegetable oil

2.5ml/½ tsp onion seeds
3 fresh red or green chillies,
   seeded and chopped
1 onion, sliced
1.5ml/¼ tsp ground turmeric
10ml/2 tsp desiccated
   (dry unsweetened
   shredded) coconut
2.5ml/½ tsp salt
15ml/1 tbsp natural
   (plain) yogurt
2 tomatoes, quartered
15ml/1 tbsp chopped fresh
   coriander (cilantro)

1 Wash and trim the okra. Cut each one into pieces roughly 1cm/½in long and set aside.

2 Heat the vegetable oil in a wok, karahi or large frying pan. Add the onion seeds, red or green chillies and onion, and cook for about 5 minutes, stirring frequently.

3 When the onion is golden brown, lower the heat and add the turmeric, desiccated coconut and salt. Fry for about 1 minute, stirring all the time.

4 Add the okra to the pan. Increase the heat to medium-high and cook briskly for a few minutes, stirring all the time until the okra has turned lightly golden. Take care not to overcook the okra as it will begin to release its glutinous juices.

5 Add the yogurt, tomatoes and fresh coriander to the pan. Stir well to ensure all the ingredients are well combined.

6 Cook the curry for a further 4–5 minutes until everything is warmed through. Transfer to a warmed serving dish and serve immediately as a side dish or as a main course accompanied by dhal and Indian bread.

Cauliflower Curry Energy 122kcal/504kJ; Protein 3.7g; Carbohydrate 7.4g, of which sugars 3.3g; Fat 8.8g, of which saturates 1.2g; Cholesterol 0mg; Calcium 34mg; Fibre 1.4g; Sodium 41mg.
Okra in Chilli Yogurt Energy 211kcal/873kJ; Protein 5g; Carbohydrate 6.3g, of which sugars 5.2g; Fat 18.7g, of which saturates 7.1g; Cholesterol 0mg; Calcium 246mg; Fibre 7.6g; Sodium 15mg.

Hot Masala Okra with Coriander

Okra, or 'ladies' fingers', are a popular Indian vegetable. In this recipe they are stir-fried with a dry masala spice mixture to make a delicious side dish.

Serves 4
450g/1lb okra
2.5ml/½ tsp ground turmeric
5ml/1 tsp chilli powder
15ml/1 tbsp ground cumin
15ml/1 tbsp ground coriander
1.5ml/¼ tsp salt
1.5ml/¼ tsp sugar
15ml/1 tbsp lemon juice
15ml/1 tbsp desiccated (dry
    unsweetened shredded) coconut
30ml/2 tbsp chopped fresh
    coriander (cilantro)
45ml/3 tbsp vegetable oil
2.5ml/½ tsp cumin seeds
2.5ml/½ tsp black mustard seeds
chopped fresh tomatoes,
    to garnish
poppadums, to serve

1 Wash, pat dry and trim the the ends of the okra. In a mixing bowl, mix together the turmeric, chilli powder, cumin, ground coriander, salt, sugar, lemon juice, desiccated coconut and the chopped fresh coriander. Mix well to combine.

2 Heat the vegetable oil in a wok or large, heavy frying pan that has a tight-fitting lid. Add the cumin seeds and mustard seeds to the pan and fry, stirring constantly, for about 2–3 minutes, or until the seeds begin to splutter and release their aromatic fragrances.

3 Add the spice mixture to the pan and continue to cook, stirring constantly, for 2 minutes.

4 Add the okra to the pan, cover, and cook over a low heat for about 10 minutes, or until the okra is tender.

5 Transfer to a serving dish and garnish with the chopped fresh tomatoes. Serve immediately with poppadums.

Cook's Tip
Poppadums are wafer-thin crisp breads from India. Buy them in Asian stores and look out for the versions with added spices.

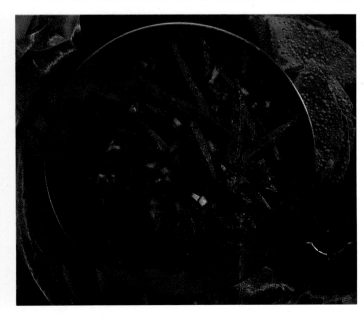

Corn and Pea Chilli Curry

Tender corn on the cob is cooked in a spicy tomato sauce. Indian breads, such as chapatis, make the perfect accompaniment to this curry.

Serves 4
6 pieces of fresh corn on the cob
45ml/3 tbsp vegetable oil
2.5ml/½ tsp cumin seeds
1 onion, finely chopped
2 garlic cloves, crushed
1 green chilli, finely chopped
15ml/1 tbsp curry paste
5ml/1 tsp ground coriander
5ml/1 tsp ground cumin
1.5ml/¼ tsp ground turmeric
2.5ml/½ tsp salt
2.5ml/½ tsp sugar
400g/14oz can
    chopped tomatoes
15ml/1 tbsp tomato
    purée (paste)
150ml/¼ pint/⅔ cup water
115g/4oz frozen peas, thawed
30ml/2 tbsp chopped fresh
    coriander (cilantro)
chapatis, to serve (optional)

1 With a sharp knife, cut each piece of corn in half crossways to make 12 equal pieces in total. Bring a large pan of water to the boil and cook the corn cob pieces for about 10–12 minutes. Drain well.

2 Heat the oil in a pan and fry the cumin seeds for 2 minutes, or until they begin to splutter. Add the chopped onion, garlic and chilli and fry for 5–6 minutes until the onion is golden.

3 Add the curry paste and fry for 2 minutes. Stir in the remaining spices, salt and sugar and fry for 2–3 minutes.

4 Add the tomatoes and tomato purée with the water and simmer for 5 minutes. Add the peas and cook for 5 minutes.

5 Add the pieces of corn and fresh coriander and cook for a further 6–8 minutes, or until the corn and peas are tender. Serve with chapatis, for mopping up the rich sauce, if you like.

Cook's Tip
If corn on the cob is out of season, this curry can also be made with the frozen variety of sliced corn cobs.

Masala Okra Energy 211kcal/873kJ; Protein 5g; Carbohydrate 6.3g, of which sugars 5.2g; Fat 18.7g, of which saturates 7.1g; Cholesterol 0mg; Calcium 246mg; Fibre 7.6g; Sodium 15mg.
Corn Curry Energy 260kcal/1089kJ; Protein 8.6g; Carbohydrate 29.7g, of which sugars 7.1g; Fat 12.9g, of which saturates 1.7g; Cholesterol 0mg; Calcium 68mg; Fibre 5.6g; Sodium 46mg.

Spiced Root Vegetable Gratin

This subtly gratin makes a fine supper dish. It also makes a good accompaniment to a vegetable or bean curry

Serves 4

2 large potatoes, total weight about 450g/1lb
2 sweet potatoes, total weight about 275g/10oz
175g/6oz celeriac
15ml/1 tbsp unsalted butter
5ml/1 tsp curry powder
5ml/1 tsp ground turmeric
2.5ml/½ tsp ground coriander
5ml/1 tsp mild chilli powder
3 shallots, chopped
150ml/¼ pint/⅔ cup single (light) cream
150ml/¼ pint/⅔ cup semi-skimmed (low-fat) milk
salt and ground black pepper
chopped fresh flat leaf parsley, to garnish

1 Thinly slice the potatoes, sweet potatoes and celeriac, using a sharp knife or the slicing attachment on a food processor. Immediately place the vegetables in a bowl of cold water to prevent them discolouring.

2 Preheat the oven to 180°C/350°F/Gas 4. Heat half the butter in a heavy pan, add the curry powder, turmeric and coriander and half the chilli powder. Cook for 2 minutes, then set aside to cool slightly.

3 Drain the vegetables, then pat dry with kitchen paper. Place in a bowl, add the spice mixture and the shallots and mix well.

4 Arrange the vegetables in a lightly greased gratin dish, seasoning between the layers with salt and pepper.

5 Mix together the cream and milk, pour the mixture over the vegetables, then sprinkle the remaining chilli powder on top.

6 Cover the dish with a sheet of baking parchment and bake in the preheated oven for about 45 minutes.

7 Remove the baking parchment, dot the gratin with the remaining butter and bake for a further 50 minutes. Serve immediately, garnished with chopped fresh parsley.

Cauliflower, Pea and Potato Curry

This highly spiced vegetable curry is often prepared for religious festivals and other special occasions in India. It also makes a delicious light lunch.

Serves 4

500g/1¼lb potatoes
1 small cauliflower or 350g/12oz cauliflower florets, with outer stalks removed
45ml/3 tbsp sunflower oil or olive oil
1 large onion, finely sliced
5ml/1 tsp ginger purée
5ml/1 tsp garlic purée
2 green chillies, chopped, seeded if preferred
2.5ml/½ tsp ground turmeric
5ml/1 tsp ground coriander
175g/6oz fresh tomatoes, chopped
5ml/1 tsp salt, or to taste
115g/4oz frozen garden peas
15ml/1 tbsp chopped fresh coriander (cilantro), to garnish

1 Halve or quarter the potatoes – the pieces should be quite chunky so that they do not fall apart during cooking.

2 Divide the cauliflower into 2.5cm/1in florets, then blanch them briefly and plunge them in cold water.

3 Heat the oil in a large, non-stick pan over a medium to high heat and brown the potatoes in two to three batches until they are well browned and form a crust on the surface – they will look a little like roast potatoes. Drain them thoroughly on absorbent kitchen paper.

4 In the same oil, fry the onion, ginger, garlic and chillies over a low to medium heat, stirring regularly, for 6–8 minutes or until the mixture begins to brown.

5 Add the ground turmeric and coriander, cook for 1 minute and then add the tomatoes, fried potatoes and salt. Pour in 400ml/14fl oz/1⅔ cups warm water. Bring this to the boil, reduce the heat to low, then cover and cook for 15 minutes.

6 Drain the cauliflower and add to the pan with the coated potato mixture. Add the peas, cook for 5 minutes. Remove from the heat and serve, garnished with coriander.

Root Vegetable Gratin Energy 268kcal/1129kJ; Protein 5.8g; Carbohydrate 37.7g, of which sugars 9.8g; Fat 11.6g, of which saturates 7.1g; Cholesterol 31mg; Calcium 127mg; Fibre 3.6g; Sodium 117mg.
Cauliflower Curry Energy 276kcal/1153kJ; Protein 9.7g; Carbohydrate 37g, of which sugars 11.6g; Fat 10.9g, of which saturates 1.5g; Cholesterol 0mg; Calcium 89mg; Fibre 6.5g; Sodium 33.8mg.

Potato Curry with Yogurt

Variations of this simple Indian curry are popular in Singapore, where fusion dishes like this one cater for a community that includes people from all over Asia, as well as from Europe and the Americas.

Serves 4

6 garlic cloves, chopped
25g/1oz fresh root ginger, peeled and chopped
30ml/2 tbsp ghee, or 15ml/1 tbsp oil and 15g/½oz/1 tbsp butter
6 shallots, halved lengthways and sliced along the grain
2 fresh green chillies, seeded and finely sliced
10ml/2 tsp sugar
a handful of fresh or dried curry leaves
2 cinnamon sticks
5–10ml/1–2 tsp ground turmeric
15ml/1 tbsp garam masala
500g/1¼lb waxy potatoes, cut into bitesize pieces
2 tomatoes, peeled, seeded and quartered
250ml/8fl oz/1 cup Greek (US strained plain) yogurt
salt and ground black pepper
5ml/1 tsp red chilli powder, and fresh coriander (cilantro) and mint leaves, finely chopped, to garnish
1 lemon, cut into quarters, to serve

1 Using a mortar and pestle or a food processor, grind the garlic and ginger to a coarse paste.

2 Heat the ghee or oil and butter in a heavy pan and stir in the shallots and chillies, until fragrant. Add the garlic and ginger paste with the sugar, and stir until the mixture begins to colour. Stir in the curry leaves, cinnamon sticks, turmeric and garam masala, and toss in the potatoes, making sure they are well coated in the spice mixture.

3 Pour just enough cold water into the pan to cover the potatoes. Bring to the boil, then reduce the heat and simmer until the potatoes are just cooked – they should still have a bite to them rather than being mushy.

4 Season with salt and pepper to taste. Gently toss in the tomatoes to heat them through. Fold in the yogurt so that it is streaky. Sprinkle with the chilli powder, coriander and mint. Serve immediately from the pan, with lemon to squeeze over.

Cheese with Mushrooms and Peas

An Indian cheese, known as paneer, is used in both sweet and savoury dishes. In India this cheese is often made at home, although in recent years it has become available commercially. It is a useful source of protein for the many vegetarians living in India.

Serves 4–6

90ml/6 tbsp ghee or vegetable oil
225g/8oz paneer, cubed
1 onion, finely chopped
a few fresh mint leaves, chopped, plus extra sprigs to garnish
50g/2oz chopped fresh coriander (cilantro)
3 fresh green chillies, chopped
3 garlic cloves
2.5cm/1in piece fresh root ginger, sliced
5ml/1 tsp ground turmeric
5ml/1 tsp chilli powder (optional)
5ml/1 tsp garam masala
225g/8oz/3 cups tiny button (white) mushrooms, washed
225g/8oz/2 cups frozen peas, thawed
175ml/6fl oz/¾ cup natural (plain) yogurt, mixed with 5ml/1 tsp cornflour (cornstarch)
salt

1 Heat the ghee or oil in a wok, karahi or large pan, and fry the paneer cubes until they are golden brown on all sides. Remove, drain on kitchen paper, and keep to one side.

2 Grind the onion, mint, coriander, chillies, garlic and ginger with a mortar and pestle or in a food processor or blender to a fairly smooth paste.

3 Remove to a bowl and mix in the turmeric, chilli powder, if using, and garam masala, and season with salt to taste.

4 Remove excess ghee or oil from the pan, leaving about 15ml/1 tbsp. Heat and fry the paste over a medium heat for 8–10 minutes, or until the oil separates.

5 Add the mushrooms, thawed peas and paneer, and mix well. Cool the mixture slightly and gradually fold in the yogurt.

6 Simmer for about 10 minutes, until the vegetables are tender and the flavours well mixed. Remove to a serving dish, garnish with sprigs of fresh mint and serve immediately.

Cheese with Mushrooms Energy 294kcal/1217kJ; Protein 14.4g; Carbohydrate 14g, of which sugars 7.3g; Fat 20.3g, of which saturates 3.7g; Cholesterol 10mg; Calcium 174mg; Fibre 3.5g; Sodium 210mg.
Potato Curry Energy 231kcal/967kJ; Protein 6.7g; Carbohydrate 26.2g, of which sugars 7.4g; Fat 12.4g, of which saturates 4.1g; Cholesterol 0mg; Calcium 110mg; Fibre 2g; Sodium 63mg.

Spicy Courgette Curry

This is an excellent way to spice up an everyday vegetable. The courgettes are thickly sliced and then combined with authentic Indian spices for a delicious, colourful vegetable curry.

Serves 4
675g/1½lb courgettes (zucchini)
45ml/3 tbsp vegetable oil
2.5ml/½ tsp cumin seeds
2.5ml/½ tsp mustard seeds
1 onion, thinly sliced

2 garlic cloves, crushed
1.5ml/¼ tsp ground turmeric
1.5ml/¼ tsp chilli powder
5ml/1 tsp ground coriander
5ml/1 tsp ground cumin
2.5ml/½ tsp salt
15ml/1 tbsp tomato
   purée (paste)
400g/14oz can
   chopped tomatoes
150ml/¼ pint/⅔ cup water
15ml/1 tbsp chopped fresh
   coriander (cilantro)
5ml/1 tsp garam masala

1 Trim the ends from the courgettes and discard, then cut them into slices, about 1cm/½in thick.

2 Heat the oil in a wok or large frying pan and fry the cumin with the mustard seeds for about 2 minutes until they begin to splutter and release their aromatic fragrances.

3 Add the onion and garlic to the pan and fry for about 5–6 minutes until the onion begins to soften.

4 Add the ground turmeric, chilli powder, coriander, cumin and salt and fry for about 2–3 minutes, stirring constantly.

5 Add the sliced courgettes to the pan all at once, and cook for about 5–7 minutes until just tender.

6 Mix together the tomato purée and chopped tomatoes in a bowl and add to the pan with the water. Mix well until all the ingredients are well combined. Cover the pan and simmer for 10 minutes until the sauce thickens.

7 Stir in the fresh coriander and the garam masala, then cook for 5 minutes or until heated through. Transfer to a serving dish and serve immediately.

Spicy Bitter Gourds

Bitter gourds are widely used in Indian cooking, both on their own as a side dish and combined with other vegetables in a curry.

Serves 4
675g/1½lb bitter gourds
60ml/4 tbsp vegetable oil
2.5ml/½ tsp cumin seeds
6 spring onions (scallions), chopped
5 tomatoes, finely chopped
2.5cm/1in piece root ginger,
   finely chopped

2 garlic cloves, crushed
2 fresh green chillies, seeded and
   finely chopped
2.5ml/½ tsp salt, plus extra
   to taste
2.5ml/½ tsp chilli powder
5ml/1 tsp ground coriander
5ml/1 tsp ground cumin
45ml/3 tbsp peanuts, crushed
45ml/3 tbsp soft dark
   brown sugar
15ml/1 tbsp gram flour
fresh coriander (cilantro) sprigs,
   to garnish

1 Bring a large pan of lightly salted water to the boil. Peel the bitter gourds using a small sharp knife and halve them. Discard the seeds. Cut into 2cm/¾in pieces, then cook in the water for about 10–15 minutes, or until they are tender. Drain well and set aside while you prepare the other ingredients.

2 Heat the oil in a large pan and fry the cumin seeds for about 2 minutes until they begin to splutter. Add the spring onions and fry for 3–4 minutes. Add the tomatoes, ginger, garlic and chillies and cook for 5 minutes.

3 Add the salt, remaining spices, the peanuts and sugar and cook for about 2–3 minutes, stirring constantly.

4 Add the bitter gourds and mix well. Sprinkle over the gram flour. Cover and simmer over a low heat for 5–8 minutes, or until all of the gram flour has been absorbed into the sauce. Serve garnished with fresh coriander sprigs.

> **Cook's Tip**
> For a quick and easy way to crush peanuts, put into a food processor or blender and process for about 20–30 seconds.

Spicy Bitter Gourds Energy 304kcal/1268kJ; Protein 8.9g; Carbohydrate 27g, of which sugars 19.6g; Fat 18.6g, of which saturates 2.8g; Cholesterol 0mg; Calcium 89mg; Fibre 3.8g; Sodium 19mg.
Courgette Curry Energy 161kcal/666kJ; Protein 5.8g; Carbohydrate 11g, of which sugars 6.5g; Fat 10.9g, of which saturates 1.5g; Cholesterol 0mg; Calcium 73mg; Fibre 2.6g; Sodium 24mg.

Cabbage with Chilli and Cumin

This cabbage dish is only lightly spiced. It makes a good accompaniment to many other dishes, or a great main dish for a vegetarian lunch or a mid-week dinner.

Serves 4
15ml/1 tbsp corn oil
50g/2oz/4 tbsp butter
2.5ml/½ tsp coriander
  seeds, crushed
2.5ml/½ tsp white cumin seeds
6 dried red chillies
1 small Savoy cabbage,
  finely shredded
12 mangetouts (snow peas)
3 fresh red chillies, seeded
  and sliced
12 baby corn cobs
salt
25g/1oz/¼ cup flaked (sliced)
  almonds, toasted, and
  5ml/1 tbsp chopped fresh
  coriander (cilantro), to garnish

1 Heat the oil and butter in a wok or a large, heavy frying pan and add the crushed coriander seeds, white cumin seeds and dried red chillies. Fry for about 1–2 minutes, stirring constantly, until the spices release their fragrances.

2 Add the shredded cabbage and the mangetouts to the pan and fry, stirring constantly, for about 5 minutes, until the vegetables are just tender.

3 Finally add the fresh red chillies, baby corn cobs and salt to the pan, and fry for a further 3 minutes.

4 Remove the pan from the heat and toss the ingredients together. Garnish with the toasted almonds and chopped fresh coriander, and serve immediately.

> **Variations**
> • Many other vegetables will work equally well in this dish. If mangetouts are out of season, you could replace them with any other green beans. You can also try adding some (bell) peppers in place of the baby corn cobs.
> • If you prefer a little more heat, you can keep the seeds in the chillies or increase the amount of chillies used.

Mushroom and Okra Curry

The sliced okra not only flavours this unusual curry, but thickens it, too.

Serves 4
4 garlic cloves, roughly chopped
2.5cm/1in piece fresh root ginger,
  roughly chopped
1 or 2 fresh red chillies, seeded
  and chopped
175ml/6fl oz/¾ cup cold water
15ml/1 tbsp sunflower oil
5ml/1 tsp coriander seeds
5ml/1 tsp cumin seeds
5ml/1 tsp ground cumin
seeds from 2 green cardamom
  pods, ground
pinch of ground turmeric
400g/14oz can chopped
  tomatoes
450g/1lb/6 cups mushrooms,
  quartered if large
225g/8oz okra, trimmed
  and sliced
30ml/2 tbsp chopped fresh
  coriander (cilantro)
plain boiled basmati rice,
  to serve

For the mango relish
1 large ripe mango, about
  500g/1¼lb
1 small garlic clove, crushed
1 small onion, finely chopped
10ml/2 tsp grated fresh
  root ginger
1 fresh red chilli, seeded and
  finely chopped
a pinch each of salt and sugar

1 To make the mango relish, peel the mango, cut the flesh off the stone (pit) and chop it finely. Place the mango pieces in a bowl and mash with a fork. Add the garlic, onion, ginger, chilli, salt and sugar and mix well. Set aside.

2 Put the garlic, ginger, chillies and 45ml/3 tbsp of the water in a blender or food processor and blend to a smooth paste.

3 Heat the oil in a large pan. Add the coriander and cumin seeds, and the ground cumin, ground cardamom and turmeric, and cook for 1 minute, until aromatic. Scrape in the garlic paste, then add the tomatoes, mushrooms and okra. Pour in the remaining water. Stir to mix well, and bring to the boil. Reduce the heat, cover and simmer the curry for 5 minutes.

4 Remove the lid, increase the heat slightly and cook for 5–10 minutes more, until the okra is tender. Stir in the fresh coriander and serve with the rice and the mango relish.

Cabbage with Chilli Energy 230kcal/952kJ; Protein 6.2g; Carbohydrate 11.3g, of which sugars 7.1g; Fat 18.2g, of which saturates 7.3g; Cholesterol 27mg; Calcium 104mg; Fibre 3.8g; Sodium 416mg.
Mushroom and Okra Curry Energy 152kcal/645kJ; Protein 5.9g; Carbohydrate 24.2g, of which sugars 22.7g; Fat 4.4g, of which saturates 0.7g; Cholesterol 0mg; Calcium 143mg; Fibre 8g; Sodium 55mg.

Mushroom Curry with Garam Masala

This is a delicious way of cooking mushrooms. It goes well with meat dishes, but is also great served on its own as a vegetarian main course.

Serves 4

30ml/2 tbsp vegetable oil
2.5ml/½ tsp cumin seeds
1.5ml/¼ tsp black peppercorns
4 green cardamom pods
1.5ml/¼ tsp ground turmeric
1 onion, finely chopped
5ml/1 tsp ground cumin

5ml/1 tsp ground coriander
2.5ml/½ tsp garam masala
1 fresh green chilli, finely chopped
2 garlic cloves, crushed
2.5cm/1in piece fresh root ginger, grated
400g/14oz can chopped tomatoes
1.5ml/¼ tsp salt
450g/1lb/6 cups button (white) mushrooms, halved
chopped fresh coriander (cilantro), to garnish

1 Heat the oil in a large, heavy pan and fry the cumin seeds, peppercorns, cardamom pods and turmeric for 2–3 minutes.

2 Add the onion and fry for about 5 minutes until golden. Stir in the cumin, ground coriander and garam masala and fry for a further 2 minutes.

3 Add the chilli, garlic and ginger and fry for 2–3 minutes, stirring all the time. Add the tomatoes and salt. Bring to the boil and simmer for 5 minutes.

4 Add the mushrooms. Cover and simmer over a low heat for 10 minutes. Garnish with chopped coriander before serving.

Cook's Tip
The distinctive flavour of mushrooms goes well with this mixture of spices. If you don't want to use button (white) mushrooms, you can substitute any other mushrooms. Dried mushrooms can be added, if you like. Soak dried mushrooms before using, and add them to the recipe with the tomatoes.

Aromatic Vegetable Curry with Mushrooms and Beans

Here the aim is to produce a subtle curry rather than an assault on the senses.

Serves 4

50g/2oz/¼ cup butter
2 onions, sliced
2 garlic cloves, crushed
2.5cm/1in piece fresh root ginger, grated
5ml/1 tsp ground cumin
15ml/1 tbsp ground coriander
6 cardamom pods
5cm/2in piece of cinnamon stick
5ml/1 tsp ground turmeric
1 fresh red chilli, seeded and finely chopped

1 potato, peeled and cut into 2.5cm/1in cubes
1 small aubergine (eggplant), chopped
115g/4oz/1½ cups mushrooms, thickly sliced
175ml/6fl oz/¾ cup water
115g/4oz green beans, cut into 2.5cm/1in lengths
60ml/4 tbsp natural (plain) yogurt
150ml/¼ pint/⅔ cup double (heavy) cream
5ml/1 tsp garam masala
salt and ground black pepper
fresh coriander (cilantro) sprigs, to garnish
plain boiled rice, to serve

1 Melt the butter in a heavy pan. Add the onions and cook for 5 minutes until soft. Add the garlic and ginger and cook for 2 minutes, then stir in the cumin, coriander, cardamom pods, cinnamon stick, turmeric and finely chopped chilli. Cook, stirring constantly, for 30 seconds.

2 Add the potato cubes, aubergine and mushrooms and the water. Cover the pan, bring to the boil, then lower the heat and simmer for 15 minutes.

3 Add the beans to the pan and cook, uncovered, for about 5 minutes. With a slotted spoon, remove the vegetables to a warmed serving dish and keep hot.

4 Allow the cooking liquid to bubble up until it has reduced a little. Season with salt and pepper to taste, then stir in the yogurt, double cream and garam masala. Pour the sauce over the vegetables and garnish with fresh coriander. Serve the curry immediately with plain boiled rice.

Mushroom Curry Energy 110kcal/459kJ; Protein 4.2g; Carbohydrate 7.1g, of which sugars 3.3g; Fat 7.7g, of which saturates 1.1g; Cholesterol 0mg; Calcium 32mg; Fibre 2.2g; Sodium 18mg.
Aromatic Curry Energy 183kcal/766kJ; Protein 7g; Carbohydrate 22.7g, of which sugars 10.5g; Fat 7.9g, of which saturates 1.1g; Cholesterol 0mg; Calcium 82mg; Fibre 6.6g; Sodium 253mg.

Punjab Roasted Aubergines with Spring Onions

This classic dish, made of roasted and mashed aubergines cooked with spring onions, is known as bharta in the Punjab region. Traditionally, the aubergine is roasted over charcoal, but a hot electric or gas oven will produce similar results, although the smoky flavour will be missing.

Serves 4

2 large aubergines (eggplants)
45ml/3 tbsp vegetable oil
2.5ml/½ tsp black mustard seeds
1 bunch spring onions (scallions), finely chopped
115g/4oz/1½ cups button (white) mushrooms, halved
2 garlic cloves, crushed
1 fresh red chilli, finely chopped
2.5ml/½ tsp chilli powder
5ml/1 tsp ground cumin
5ml/1 tsp ground coriander
1.5ml/¼ tsp ground turmeric
5ml/1 tsp salt
400g/14oz can chopped tomatoes
15ml/1 tbsp chopped fresh coriander (cilantro), plus a few extra sprigs to garnish

1 Preheat the oven to 200°C/400°F/Gas 6. Place the aubergines in a baking dish, brush with 15ml/1 tbsp of the oil and prick with a fork. Bake for 30–35 minutes until soft.

2 Meanwhile, heat the remaining oil in a large pan and fry the black mustard seeds for about 2 minutes until they splutter.

3 Add the spring onions, mushrooms, garlic and chilli to the pan, and fry for about 5 minutes more.

4 Stir in the chilli powder, cumin, coriander, turmeric and salt and fry for 4 minutes. Add the tomatoes and cook for 5 minutes.

5 Cut the aubergines in half lengthwise and scoop out the soft flesh into a large mixing bowl. Mash the flesh to a coarse texture, using a fork or potato masher.

6 Add the aubergines to the pan with the coriander. Bring to the boil and simmer for 5 minutes until the sauce thickens. Serve garnished with the fresh coriander.

Spiced Potato Curry with Chilli and Paprika

This spicy potato curry is an Andean stew called ajiaco. It gets its name from aji, a generic word for hot pepper. The dish combines potatoes, fresh cheese and chilli: there are many variations but these three main ingredients are always included. It can be served with rice and vegetables, or with roasted or grilled meats. It is substantial and flexible – choose your own assortment of vegetables, such as pumpkin, butternut squash, winter melon, yams, aubergines or beans.

Serves 6

1kg/2¼lb floury potatoes, such as King Edward
60ml/4 tbsp vegetable oil
6 spring onions (scallions), chopped
5ml/1 tsp grated garlic
30ml/2 tbsp chilli sauce
5ml/1 tsp paprika
250ml/8fl oz/1 cup evaporated milk
120ml/4fl oz/½ cup water
150g/5oz feta cheese
4 hard-boiled eggs, roughly chopped
salt and ground black pepper

1 Boil the potatoes in their skins in lightly salted water for 20 minutes, until tender.

2 Peel the potatoes and crush them lightly (they do not need to be mashed to a purée). Set aside.

3 Heat the oil in a heavy frying pan over a medium heat and fry the spring onions and garlic for about 8 minutes, stirring frequently, until browned.

4 Add the chilli sauce and paprika, season with salt and pepper, then stir in the potatoes, milk and water.

5 Mash the cheese with a fork and add to the potato mixture with the chopped eggs.

6 Stir with a wooden spoon and leave the mixture to simmer for 5 minutes before serving.

Punjab Aubergines Energy 136kcal/363kJ; Protein 3.6g; Carbohydrate 8.4g, of which sugars 5.5g; Fat 10.2g, of which saturates 0.7g; Cholesterol 0mg; Calcium 57mg; Fibre 4g; Sodium 19mg.
Spiced Potato Curry Energy 306kcal/1281kJ; Protein 11.6g; Carbohydrate 28.7g, of which sugars 2.8g; Fat 17.1g, of which saturates 5.5g; Cholesterol 144mg; Calcium 129mg; Fibre 1.8g; Sodium 427mg.

Stuffed Aubergines with Tamarind

The traditional way of cooking with tamarind is in a terracotta dish, which brings out the full fruity tartness of the tamarind. This spicy aubergine dish will add a refreshing tang to any meal.

Serves 4
12 baby aubergines (eggplants)
30ml/2 tbsp vegetable oil
1 small onion, chopped
10ml/2 tsp grated fresh
   root ginger
10ml/2 tsp crushed garlic

5ml/1 tsp coriander seeds
5ml/1 tsp cumin seeds
10ml/2 tsp white poppy seeds
10ml/2 tsp sesame seeds
10ml/2 tsp desiccated
   (dry unsweetened
   shredded) coconut
15ml/1 tbsp dry-roasted
   skinned peanuts
2.5–5ml/½–1 tsp chilli powder
5ml/1 tsp salt
6–8 curry leaves
1–2 dried red chillies, seeded
   and chopped
2.5ml/½ tsp concentrated
   tamarind paste

1 Make three deep slits lengthwise on each aubergine, without cutting through, then soak in salted water for 20 minutes.

2 Heat half the oil in a pan and fry the onion for 3–4 minutes. Add the ginger and garlic and cook for 30 seconds.

3 Add the coriander and cumin seeds and fry for 30 seconds, then add the poppy seeds, sesame seeds and coconut. Fry for 1 minute, stirring constantly. Allow to cool slightly, then grind the spices in a food processor, adding 105ml/7 tbsp warm water.

4 Mix the peanuts, chilli powder and salt into the spice paste. Drain the aubergines and dry on kitchen paper. Stuff each of the slits with the spice paste and reserve any remaining paste.

5 Heat the remaining oil in a large pan over a medium heat and add the curry leaves and chillies. Let the chillies blacken, then add the aubergines and the tamarind blended with 105ml/7 tbsp hot water. Stir in any remaining paste.

6 Cover the pan and simmer gently for 15–20 minutes or until the aubergines are tender. Serve immediately.

Vegetable Korma

Korma-style cooking was originally used for meat and poultry dishes, but it proved so popular that vegetarian recipes were created. This colourful curry is a combination of vegetables coated in a luxurious almond sauce, exotically spiced with cardamom and coriander.

Serves 4
115g/4oz fine green beans, cut
   into 5cm/2in pieces
375g/13oz cauliflower, divided
   into 1cm/½in florets
115g/4oz carrots, cut into batons

375g/13oz potatoes, boiled in
   their skins and cooled
50g/2oz blanched almonds,
   soaked in 150ml/5fl oz/⅔ cup
   boiling water for 20 minutes
60ml/4 tbsp sunflower oil or
   olive oil
2 medium onions, finely chopped
2 green chillies, seeded and
   finely chopped
10ml/2 tsp ginger purée
15ml/1 tbsp ground coriander
1.5ml/¼ tsp ground turmeric
2.5ml/½ tsp chilli powder
5ml/1 tsp salt, or to taste
2.5ml/½ tsp sugar
120ml/4fl oz/½ cup double
   (heavy) cream

1 Blanch all the vegetables separately – the beans for about 3 minutes, the cauliflower for 3 minutes and the carrots for 5 minutes – then plunge them immediately into cold water. Cut the cooked potatoes into 2.5cm/1in cubes.

2 Purée the blanched almonds in a blender or food processor with the water in which they were soaked, and set aside.

3 In a heavy frying pan, heat the oil over a medium heat and add the onions, green chillies and ginger purée. Fry them for 10–12 minutes, stirring regularly, until they turn a light brown colour and the onions have softened.

4 Add the coriander, turmeric and chilli powder. Reduce the heat to a low temperature and fry for 1 minute.

5 Add the vegetables, salt and sugar. Add 150ml/5fl oz/⅔ cup warm water, stir once and then bring to the boil. Reduce the heat to low, add the cream and cook for 2–3 minutes to heat through, then serve immediately.

Stuffed Aubergines Energy 132kcal/549kJ; Protein 2.9g; Carbohydrate 4.7g, of which sugars 3.8g; Fat 11.5g, of which saturates 3.3g; Cholesterol 0mg; Calcium 36mg; Fibre 3.7g; Sodium 5mg.
Vegetable Korma Energy 381kcal/1577kJ; Protein 5.1g; Carbohydrate 20.9g, of which sugars 9.9g; Fat 31.4g, of which saturates 19.3g; Cholesterol 78mg; Calcium 95mg; Fibre 3.9g; Sodium 108mg.

Fried Hard-boiled Eggs in Red Sauce

A popular snack at street stalls in Malaysia and Singapore, this spicy egg dish originally comes from Indonesia. It is usually served wrapped in a banana leaf and eaten with plain steamed rice, sliced chillies, onion and fresh coriander, and it is ideal for a quick, tasty meal.

Serves 4
vegetable oil, for deep-frying
8 eggs, hard-boiled and shelled
1 lemon grass stalk, trimmed,
  quartered and crushed
2 large tomatoes, skinned,
  seeded and chopped to a pulp
5–10ml/1–2 tsp sugar
30ml/2 tbsp dark soy sauce
juice of 1 lime
fresh coriander (cilantro) and mint
  leaves, coarsely chopped,
  to garnish

For the spice paste
4–6 fresh red chillies, seeded
  and chopped
4 shallots, chopped
2 garlic cloves, peeled
  and chopped
2.5ml/½ tsp vegetable paste
  or mam roi

1 Using a mortar and pestle or a food processor, grind together the ingredients for the spice paste until smooth. Set aside while you prepare the other ingredients.

2 Heat enough oil for deep-frying in a wok or heavy pan and deep-fry the whole boiled eggs until they are golden brown. Lift them out and drain.

3 Reserve about 15ml/1 tbsp of the oil in the wok or pan and discard the rest. Heat the oil in the wok or heavy pan and stir in the spice paste. Cook, stirring frequently, for 2–3 minutes or until it becomes fragrant but not browned.

4 Add the lemon grass to the pan, followed by the chopped tomatoes and sugar. Cook over a medium heat for 2–3 minutes, until it forms a thick paste.

5 Reduce the heat and stir in the soy sauce and lime juice. Add 30ml/2 tbsp water to thin the sauce. Toss in the eggs, making sure they are thoroughly coated, and serve hot, garnished with chopped coriander and mint leaves.

Egg and Lentil Curry

Eggs are an excellent addition to vegetarian curries and, combined with lentils, make a substantial and extremely tasty curry.

Serves 4
75g/3oz/½ cup green lentils
750ml/1¼ pints/3 cups stock
6 eggs
30ml/2 tbsp vegetable oil
3 cloves
1.5ml/¼ tsp black peppercorns
1 onion, finely chopped
2 green chillies, finely chopped
2 garlic cloves, crushed
2.5cm/1in piece of fresh root
  ginger, peeled and
  finely chopped
30ml/2 tbsp curry paste
400g/14oz can chopped
  tomatoes
2.5ml/½ tsp sugar
2.5ml/½ tsp garam masala

1 Wash the lentils under cold running water, checking for small stones. Put the lentils in a large pan with the stock. Cover and simmer for 15 minutes or until soft. Drain and set aside.

2 Cook the eggs in boiling water for 10 minutes. Remove from the boiling water and set aside to cool slightly. When cool enough to handle, peel and cut in half lengthways.

3 Heat the oil in a large pan and fry the cloves and peppercorns for about 2 minutes. Add the onion, chillies, garlic and ginger to the pan and fry the mixture for a further 5–6 minutes, stirring frequently.

4 Stir the curry paste into the pan and fry for about 2 minutes, stirring constantly, until the aromatic fragrances are released.

5 Add the tomatoes and sugar and stir in 175ml/6fl oz/¾ cup water. Simmer for about 5 minutes until the sauce thickens, stirring occasionally. Add the eggs, drained lentils and garam masala. Cover and simmer for 10 minutes, then serve.

> **Variation**
> You can substitute red lentils for the green. Red lentils tend to disintegrate more when cooking, resulting in a smoother curry.

Fried Eggs Energy 271kcal/1125kJ; Protein 13.3g; Carbohydrate 5.5g, of which sugars 5g; Fat 22.3g, of which saturates 4.4g; Cholesterol 381mg; Calcium 67mg; Fibre 0.7g; Sodium 679mg.
Egg and Lentil Curry Energy 238kcal/997kJ; Protein 14.6g; Carbohydrate 14.2g, of which sugars 4.1g; Fat 14.4g, of which saturates 3.1g; Cholesterol 285mg; Calcium 60mg; Fibre 1.9g; Sodium 121mg.

Eggs Baked on Chipsticks

This is an unusual and
delicious way of combining
eggs with potato sticks.
The potato sticks are
cooked with spices to form
a pancake. Eggs are then
placed on top of the potato
pancake and gently cooked.

Serves 4–6
225g/8oz salted chipsticks
2 fresh green chillies, seeded and
  finely chopped
a few coriander (cilantro)
  sprigs, chopped
1.5ml/¼ tsp ground turmeric
60ml/4 tbsp vegetable oil or
  sunflower oil
75ml/5 tbsp water
6 eggs
3 spring onions (scallions),
  finely chopped
salt and ground black pepper
warm chapatis and a simple
  mixed green salad,
  to serve (optional)

1 In a large mixing bowl, mix together the salted chipsticks,
chopped chillies, coriander and turmeric.

2 Heat 30ml/2 tbsp of the oil in a heavy frying pan. Add the
chipstick mixture and water. Cook until the chipsticks turn soft,
and then crisp up again.

3 Place a dinner plate or chopping board over the frying pan,
and hold it firmly in place as you turn the pan over and carefully
transfer the chipstick pancake on to the plate or board.

4 Heat the remaining oil in the pan and slide the pancake back
into the frying pan to brown the other side.

5 Gently break the eggs over the pancake, cover the frying pan
and allow the eggs to set over a low heat. Season well and
sprinkle with spring onions. Cook until the base is crisp. Serve
immediately for breakfast, or with warm chapatis and a simple
salad for a light lunch or supper.

Cook's Tip
*There are a number of crisp (US potato chip) producers who
make chipsticks. Look for them in supermarkets.*

Spicy Omelette

This irresistible omelette is
classic Parsi food, which
originated along the shores
of the Caspian Sea, and
the cuisine offers some
unique flavours, which
appeal to both Eastern
and Western palates. Serve
at any time of day, whether
for breakfast, a light lunch
or a quick supper.

Serves 4–6
30ml/2 tbsp vegetable oil
1 onion, finely chopped
2.5ml/½ tsp ground cumin
1 garlic clove, crushed
1 or 2 fresh green chillies, seeded
  and finely chopped
a few coriander (cilantro) sprigs,
  chopped, plus a little extra,
  to garnish
1 firm tomato, chopped
1 small potato, cubed and boiled
  until just tender
25g/1oz/¼ cup cooked peas
25g/1oz/¼ cup cooked corn, or
  canned corn, drained
2 eggs, beaten
25g/1oz/¼ cup grated cheese
salt and ground black pepper

1 Heat the vegetable oil in a wok, karahi or large pan, and fry
the onion for 5 minutes until beginning to soften.

2 Add the next eight ingredients to the pan and cook until
they are well blended but the potato and tomato are still firm.
Season to taste with salt and ground black pepper.

3 Increase the heat and pour in the beaten eggs. Reduce the
heat, cover and cook until the bottom layer has browned.

4 Turn the omelette over and sprinkle with the grated cheese.
Place under a hot grill (broiler) and cook until the egg sets and
the cheese has melted and browned slightly.

5 Garnish the omelette with sprigs of coriander and serve with
salad for a light lunch. If you prefer, serve it for a tasty breakfast.

Variation
*You can use any vegetable with the potatoes. Try thickly sliced
button (white) mushrooms, added in step 1.*

Eggs on Chipsticks Energy 276kcal/1153kJ; Protein 8.7g; Carbohydrate 20.4g, of which sugars 0.6g; Fat 18.5g, of which saturates 6.8g; Cholesterol 190mg; Calcium 58mg; Fibre 2.5g; Sodium 373mg.
Spicy Omelette Energy 93kcal/388kJ; Protein 4g; Carbohydrate 3.7g, of which sugars 1.2g; Fat 7.1g, of which saturates 1.9g; Cholesterol 67mg; Calcium 46mg; Fibre 0.6g; Sodium 104mg.

Purée of Spiced Lentils with Eggs

This unusual dish of brown lentils spiced with fresh coriander and mint makes an excellent supper or light lunch or an unusual breakfast dish. For a nuttier flavour you could add a 400g/14oz can of unsweetened chestnut purée to the lentil mixture.

Serves 4
450g/1lb/2 cups washed
 brown lentils
3 leeks, thinly sliced
10ml/2 tsp coriander seeds,
 crushed
15ml/1 tbsp chopped fresh
 coriander (cilantro)
30ml/2 tbsp chopped fresh
 mint leaves
15ml/1 tbsp red wine vinegar
1 litre/1¾ pints/4 cups
 vegetable stock
4 eggs
salt and ground black pepper
generous handful of fresh
 parsley, stalks removed,
 roughly chopped, to garnish

1 Put the lentils in a deep pan. Add the leeks, coriander seeds, fresh coriander, mint, vinegar and vegetable stock and stir until the ingredients are well combined.

2 Bring the mixture to the boil, then lower the heat and simmer for 30–40 minutes, until the lentils are cooked and have absorbed the liquid. Preheat the oven to 180°C/350°F/Gas 4.

3 Season the lentils with salt and pepper, and mix well. Spread them out in four lightly greased baking dishes.

4 Using the back of a spoon, make a hollow in the lentil mixture in each dish. Break an egg into each hollow.

5 Cover the dishes with foil and bake for 15–20 minutes, or until the egg whites are set and the yolks are still soft. Sprinkle with plenty of parsley and serve immediately.

> **Cook's Tip**
> If you prefer, the lentil mixture can be put into a large dish. Make four indentations in the mixture to hold the eggs.

Creamy Black Lentils

Black lentils, or urad dhal, are available whole, split, and skinned and split. Generally, both split, and skinned and split versions are used in west and south Indian cooking, whereas whole black lentils are a typical ingredient in the north.

Serves 4–6
175g/6oz/¾ cup black
 lentils, soaked overnight
50g/2oz/¼ cup red split lentils
120ml/4fl oz/½ cup double (heavy)
 cream, plus extra to serve
120ml/4fl oz/½ cup natural
 (plain) yogurt
5ml/1 tsp cornflour (cornstarch)
45ml/3 tbsp ghee or vegetable oil
1 onion, finely chopped
5cm/2in piece fresh root
 ginger, crushed
4 fresh green chillies, chopped
1 tomato, chopped
2.5ml/½ tsp chilli powder
2.5ml/½ tsp ground turmeric
2.5ml/½ tsp ground cumin
2 garlic cloves, sliced
salt
coriander (cilantro) sprigs and
 sliced red chilli, to garnish

1 Drain the black lentils and place in a large pan with the red lentils. Cover with water and bring to the boil. Reduce the heat, cover the pan and simmer until tender. Mash the lentils with a spoon or fork, and set aside to cool.

2 In a large bowl, mix together the cream, yogurt and cornflour, and stir into the lentils in the pan.

3 Heat 15ml/1 tbsp of the ghee or oil in a wok, karahi or large pan, and fry the onion, ginger, two green chillies and the tomato until the onion is soft. Add the ground spices and salt and fry for a further 2 minutes. Stir into the lentil mixture and mix well to combine. Reheat, then transfer to a heatproof serving dish and keep warm.

4 Heat the remaining ghee or oil in a frying pan over a low heat and fry the garlic slices and remaining chillies until the garlic slices are golden brown.

5 Pour the garlic and chillies over the lentils and fold in just before serving. Place extra cream on the table for the diners to add more to their helping if they wish.

Purée of Lentils Energy 470kcal/1990kJ; Protein 35.9g; Carbohydrate 68.4g, of which sugars 6g; Fat 7.9g, of which saturates 1.9g; Cholesterol 190mg; Calcium 148mg; Fibre 8.8g; Sodium 116mg.
Creamy Black Lentils Energy 309kcal/1289kJ; Protein 11g; Carbohydrate 26.2g, of which sugars 3.8g; Fat 18.6g, of which saturates 10.1g; Cholesterol 28mg; Calcium 77mg; Fibre 2.2g; Sodium 38mg.

Boiled Egg Curry

This spicy Indian dish is usually served with a biryani or pilau rice, but it is equally good served with some Indian bread such as naan or chapati.

Serves 4–6
10ml/2 tsp white poppy seeds
10ml/2 tsp white sesame seeds
10ml/2 tsp whole coriander seeds
10ml/2 tbsp desiccated
  (dry unsweetened
  shredded) coconut

350ml/12fl oz/1½ cups
  tomato juice
10ml/2 tsp gram flour
5ml/1 tsp grated fresh root ginger
5ml/1 tsp chilli powder
1.5ml/¼ tsp asafoetida
5ml/1 tsp sugar
6 hard-boiled eggs, halved
10ml/2 tbsp sesame oil
5ml/1 tsp cumin seeds
4 whole dried red chillies
6–8 curry leaves
4 garlic cloves, finely sliced
salt

1 Heat a frying pan and dry-fry the poppy, sesame and coriander seeds for 3–4 minutes until they release their aromatic fragrances and begin to splutter.

2 Add the coconut and dry-fry until it browns. Cool and grind the ingredients together using a mortar and pestle or a food processor or blender.

3 Pour a little of the tomato juice into a small bowl and mix with the gram flour to form a smooth paste.

4 Add the ginger, chilli powder, asafoetida, salt and sugar and the ground spices to the paste. Mix well until combined.

5 Add the remaining tomato juice to the bowl and mix well. Transfer the contents of the bowl into a heavy pan and simmer gently for 10 minutes.

6 Add the hard-boiled eggs to the pan and cover with the sauce. Heat the oil in a separate frying pan and fry the remaining ingredients until the chillies turn dark brown.

7 Pour the spices and oil over the egg curry, mix gently together and reheat for a minute. Serve immediately.

Balti Vegetables with Cashew Nuts

This quick and versatile stir-fry will accommodate most other combinations of vegetables – you do not have to use the selection suggested here.

Serves 4
2 medium carrots
1 medium red (bell)
  pepper, seeded
1 medium green (bell)
  pepper, seeded

2 courgettes (zucchini)
115g/4oz green beans
1 medium bunch spring
  onions (scallions)
15ml/1 tbsp vegetable oil
4–6 curry leaves
2.5ml/½ tsp cumin seeds
4 dried red chillies
10–12 cashew nuts
5ml/1 tsp salt
30ml/2 tbsp lemon juice
fresh mint leaves, to garnish

1 Prepare the vegetables: cut the carrots, peppers and courgettes into matchsticks, halve the beans and finely chop the spring onions. Set aside while you prepare the other ingredients.

2 Heat the vegetable oil in a karahi, wok or large heavy frying pan and fry the curry leaves, cumin seeds and dried red chillies for about 1 minute, stirring constantly.

3 Add the vegetables and nuts to the pan, and stir them in gently. Add the salt and lemon juice. Continue to stir and cook for about 3–5 minutes.

4 When all the ingredients are warmed through, transfer the vegetables to a warmed serving dish, garnish with the fresh mint leaves and serve immediately.

Variation
Small florets of broccoli or cauliflower are delicious cooked in a stir-fry like this. The florets should be cooked until they are only just tender so that they retain their crunch. You could use them instead of the courgettes (zucchini) in the recipe. Alternatively, use button (white) mushrooms, mangetouts (snow peas) and a handful of beansprouts.

Boiled Egg Curry Energy 229kcal/953kJ; Protein 10.7g; Carbohydrate 4.6g, of which sugars 3.7g; Fat 19g, of which saturates 6.7g; Cholesterol 254mg; Calcium 81mg; Fibre 1.7g; Sodium 276mg.
Balti Vegetables Energy 105kcal/436kJ; Protein 4.2g; Carbohydrate 11.2g, of which sugars 10.1g; Fat 5.1g, of which saturates 0.9g; Cholesterol 0mg; Calcium 56mg; Fibre 3.9g; Sodium 510mg.

Indian-spiced Vegetable Curry

This is a very delicately spiced vegetable dish that makes a light meal when served with rice and bread. It is also a good partner to a heavily spiced meat curry.

Serves 4
350g/12oz mixed vegetables:
  beans, peas, potatoes,
  cauliflower, carrots, cabbage,
  mangetouts (snow peas) and
  button (white) mushrooms
30ml/2 tbsp vegetable oil
5ml/1 tsp cumin seeds, roasted
2.5ml/½ tsp mustard seeds
2.5ml/½ tsp onion seeds
5ml/1 tsp ground turmeric
2 garlic cloves, crushed
6–8 curry leaves
1 whole dried red chilli
5ml/1 tsp sugar
150ml/¼ pint/⅔ cup natural
  (plain) yogurt, mixed with
  5ml/1 tsp cornflour (cornstarch)
salt
boiled plain basmati rice and
  warm Indian breads,
  to serve

1 Prepare all the vegetables you have chosen: string the beans; thaw the peas, if frozen; cube the potatoes; cut the cauliflower into florets; dice the carrots; shred the cabbage; top and tail the mangetouts; wash the mushrooms and leave whole.

2 Heat a wok or large pan with enough water to cook all the vegetables and bring to the boil. First add the potatoes and carrots and cook until nearly tender, then add all the other vegetables and cook until still firm. All the vegetables should be crunchy except the potatoes. Drain well.

3 Heat the oil in a frying pan and add the cumin, mustard and onion seeds. Fry gently for 1–2 minutes, stirring constantly until the seeds begin to splutter.

4 Add the turmeric, garlic, curry leaves and dried red chilli to the pan. Fry gently until the garlic is golden brown and the chilli nearly burnt. Reduce the heat.

5 Fold in the drained vegetables, add the sugar and season with salt. Gradually add the yogurt mixed with the cornflour and stir well. Heat the curry until bubbling and serve immediately with rice and Indian breads.

Spicy Spinach Dhal

There are many different types of dhals eaten in India, with each region having its own speciality. This is a delicious, lightly spiced dish with a mild nutty flavour from the lentils, which combine beautifully with the spinach. Serve as a main meal with rice and breads or with a meat dish.

Serves 4
175g/6oz/1 cup chana dhal (yellow
  lentils) or yellow split peas
175ml/6fl oz/¾ cup water
30ml/2 tbsp vegetable oil
1.5ml/¼ tsp black mustard seeds
1 onion, thinly sliced
2 garlic cloves, crushed
2.5cm/1in piece fresh root
  ginger, grated
1 red chilli, seeded and
  finely chopped
275g/10oz frozen
  spinach, thawed
1.5ml/¼ tsp chilli powder
2.5ml/½ tsp ground coriander
2.5ml/½ tsp garam masala
2.5ml/½ tsp salt

1 Wash the chana dhal or split peas in several changes of cold water, carefully picking through it to remove any stones or bits of grit. Place in a large bowl and cover with plenty of cold water. Leave to soak for 30 minutes.

2 Drain the chana dhal or split peas and place in a large pan with the measured water. Bring to the boil, cover the pan, reduce the heat and simmer for about 20–25 minutes, or until the dhal or peas are soft and tender.

3 Meanwhile, heat the oil in a wok or large frying pan and fry the mustard seeds for 2 minutes until they begin to splutter.

4 Add the onion, garlic, ginger and chilli to the pan and fry for 5–6 minutes, stirring constantly. Add the spinach to the pan and cook for about 10–12 minutes, or until the spinach is dry and the liquid has evaporated.

5 Stir in the chilli powder, coriander, garam masala and salt and cook for a further 2–3 minutes.

6 Drain the chana dhal or split peas, add to the spinach mixture and cook for about 5 minutes. Serve immediately.

Indian-spiced Curry Energy 92kcal/384kJ; Protein 3.1g; Carbohydrate 10.2g, of which sugars 3.4g; Fat 4.7g, of which saturates 0.7g; Cholesterol 0mg; Calcium 99mg; Fibre 0.9g; Sodium 61mg.
Spicy Dhal Energy 226kcal/949kJ; Protein 13.3g; Carbohydrate 28.7g, of which sugars 2.9g; Fat 7.3g, of which saturates 0.9g; Cholesterol 0mg; Calcium 152mg; Fibre 3.8g; Sodium 114mg.

Kidney Bean Curry

This Punjabi dish is a fine example of the area's hearty, robust cuisine. It is widely eaten all over the state, and is even sold by street vendors. Boiled rice makes a good accompaniment.

Serves 4

225g/8oz/1¼ cups dried red
   kidney beans
30ml/2 tbsp vegetable oil
2.5ml/½ tsp cumin seeds
1 onion, thinly sliced
1 fresh green chilli, seeded
   and finely chopped
2 garlic cloves, crushed
2.5cm/1in piece fresh root
   ginger, grated
30ml/2 tbsp curry paste
5ml/1 tsp ground cumin
5ml/1 tsp ground coriander
2.5ml/½ tsp chilli powder
2.5ml/½ tsp salt
400g/14oz can
   chopped tomatoes
30ml/2 tbsp chopped fresh
   coriander (cilantro)

1 Place the kidney beans in a large bowl of cold water and then leave them to soak overnight.

2 Drain the beans and place in a large pan with double the volume of water. Boil vigorously for 10 minutes. Drain, rinse and return the beans to the pan. Add double the volume of water and bring to the boil. Reduce the heat, then cover and cook for 1–1½ hours, or until the beans are soft. This process is essential in order to remove the toxins from the dried kidney beans.

3 Meanwhile, heat the oil in a wok, karahi or large pan and fry the cumin seeds for 2 minutes. Add the onion, chilli, garlic and ginger and fry for 5 minutes. Stir in the curry paste, cumin, coriander, chilli powder and salt, and cook for 5 minutes.

4 Add the tomatoes and simmer for 5 minutes. Add the beans and fresh coriander, reserving a little for the garnish. Cover and cook for 15 minutes adding a little water if necessary. Serve garnished with the reserved coriander.

> **Cook's Tip**
> *Drained and rinsed canned beans can be used instead of dried.*

Fried Spiced Lentils

This simple and spicy supper dish is perfect for a gathering of family or friends. It uses traditional Indian lentils and peas, which can be found in large supermarkets or Asian markets and stores.

Serves 4–6

115g/4oz/½ cup red gram
   (pigeon peas) or green lentils
50g/2oz/¼ cup Bengal gram
4 fresh green chillies
5ml/1 tsp ground turmeric
1 large onion, sliced
400g/14oz can
   chopped tomatoes
60ml/4 tbsp vegetable oil
   or sunflower oil
2.5ml/½ tsp mustard seeds
2.5ml/½ tsp cumin seeds
1 garlic clove, crushed
6 curry leaves
2 dried red chillies
salt
a few curry leaves, to garnish

1 Place the red gram or lentils and bengal gram in a heavy pan and pour in 350ml/12fl oz/1½ cups water. Add the chillies, turmeric and onion slices to the pan and slowly bring to the boil. Reduce the heat and simmer gently, covered, until the gram and lentils are soft and the water has evaporated.

2 Mash the mixture with the back of a spoon. When nearly smooth, add the tomatoes and salt to taste, and mix well. If necessary, thin with a little hot water.

3 Heat the vegetable or sunflower oil in a frying pan. Fry the remaining ingredients until the garlic just begins to brown. Pour the oil and spices over the mixture and cover. After 5 minutes, mix well, garnish, and serve immediately.

> **Cook's Tips**
> • *Red gram, or pigeon peas, are the fruit of a small shrub but are used as a vegetable. They form a staple food in India as well as Africa and the Caribbean, and you will find them in Asian and Caribbean stores and markets.*
> • *Bengal gram, or chana, is a small variety of chickpea, which is commonly used in Indian cuisine.*

Kidney Bean Curry Energy 156kcal/653kJ; Protein 6.4g; Carbohydrate 17g, of which sugars 5.4g; Fat 7.6g, of which saturates 1g; Cholesterol 0mg; Calcium 90mg; Fibre 5.1g; Sodium 236mg.
Fried Spiced Lentils Energy 262kcal/1095kJ; Protein 10.3g; Carbohydrate 26.9g, of which sugars 4.6g; Fat 13.3g, of which saturates 6.2g; Cholesterol 0mg; Calcium 36mg; Fibre 3.1g; Sodium 84mg.

Tarka Dhal

Tarka is a hot oil seasoning that is folded into a dish before serving. Dhal is cooked every day in an Indian household, and a much simpler version is made for most family meals. Tarka dhal is commonly found in Bengal, Assam and Bangladesh and it is the combination of spices that gives away its origin.

Serves 4–6

115g/4oz/½ cup red split lentils, washed
50g/2oz/¼ cup chana dhal (yellow lentils) or yellow split peas, washed
600ml/1 pint/2½ cups water
5ml/1 tsp grated fresh root ginger
5ml/1 tsp crushed garlic
2.5ml/½ tsp ground turmeric
2 fresh green chillies, seeded and chopped
7.5ml/1½ tsp salt

For the tarka

30ml/2 tbsp vegetable oil
1 onion, sliced
2.5ml/½ tsp mixed mustard and onion seeds
4 dried red chillies
1 tomato, sliced

To garnish

15ml/1 tbsp chopped fresh coriander (cilantro), 1–2 fresh green chillies, seeded and sliced, and 15ml/1 tbsp chopped mint

1 Pick over the washed lentils and chana dhal or yellow split peas and remove any stones, then place in a large pan.

2 Add the measured water with the ginger, garlic, turmeric and chopped green chillies, bring to the boil, lower the heat and simmer for about 15–20 minutes or until the lentils are soft.

3 Mash the lentils with the back of a spoon until they are of the same consistency as a thick soup. Add the salt. If the mixture looks too dry, add a little more water.

4 To prepare the tarka, heat the oil in another pan and fry the onion with the mustard and onion seeds, dried red chillies and sliced tomato for about 2 minutes.

5 Pour the tarka over the dhal in the pan and garnish with the chopped fresh coriander, fresh green chillies and chopped mint. Serve immediately.

Chilli Lentils and Spiced Vegetables

This deliciously spicy curry is often served for breakfast with Indian pancakes or rice dumplings, but can also be eaten as a main course.

Serves 4–6

60ml/4 tbsp vegetable oil
2.5ml/½ tsp mustard seeds
2.5ml/½ tsp cumin seeds
2 whole dried red chillies
1.5ml/¼ tsp asafoetida
6–8 curry leaves
2 garlic cloves, crushed
30ml/2 tbsp desiccated (dry unsweetened shredded) coconut
225g/8oz red split lentils, picked, washed and drained
10ml/2 tsp sambhar masala
2.5ml/½ tsp ground turmeric
450ml/¾ pint/scant 2 cups water
450g/1lb mixed vegetables (okra, courgettes/zucchini, cauliflower, shallots and sweet peppers)
15ml/1 tbsp tamarind pulp mixed with 45ml/3 tbsp water, strained, and pulp and seeds discarded
4 firm tomatoes, quartered
60ml/4 tbsp vegetable oil or sunflower oil
2 garlic cloves, finely sliced
a handful coriander (cilantro) leaves, chopped

1 Heat the vegetable oil in a large frying pan. Add the mustard seeds and cumin seeds and fry for 1–2 minutes until they are fragrant and beginning to splutter.

2 Add the chillies, asafoetida, curry leaves, garlic and desiccated coconut to the pan. Cook the mixture over a medium heat, stirring constantly, for about 4–5 minutes until the coconut begins to brown, taking care to avoid it burning.

3 Stir the lentils into the pan, mixing well until combined. Add the sambhar masala and ground turmeric and mix. Pour in the measured water and bring the mixture to the boil.

4 Reduce the heat and simmer gently until the lentils are tender and mushy. Add all the vegetables, tamarind juice and tomatoes to the pan. Bring to the boil, then reduce the heat and simmer gently for about 10–15 minutes, until the vegetables are just tender. They should still retain a little crunch.

5 Transfer the mixture to a large bowl. Fry the garlic slices and coriander. Sprinkle over the lentils and vegetables and serve.

Tarka Dhal Energy 213kcal/898kJ; Protein 11.3g; Carbohydrate 28.2g, of which sugars 2.7g; Fat 7.1g, of which saturates 0.9g; Cholesterol 0mg; Calcium 42mg; Fibre 2.5g; Sodium 18mg.
Chilli Lentils Energy 229kcal/963kJ; Protein 11.5g; Carbohydrate 27.5g, of which sugars 5.4g; Fat 9g, of which saturates 1.2g; Cholesterol 0mg; Calcium 54mg; Fibre 3.2g; Sodium 23mg.

Red Lentil and Tomato Dhal

This is Indian comfort food at its best – there's nothing like a bowl of dhal spiced with mustard seeds, cumin and coriander to clear away the blues.

Serves 4
30ml/2 tbsp sunflower oil
1 green chilli, halved
2 red onions, halved and
   thinly sliced
10ml/2 tsp finely grated garlic
10ml/2 tsp finely grated fresh
   root ginger
10ml/2 tsp black mustard seeds
15ml/1 tbsp cumin seeds
10ml/2 tsp crushed coriander seeds
10 curry leaves
250g/9oz/generous 1 cup red
   split lentils, rinsed and drained
2.5ml/1/2 tsp turmeric
2 plum tomatoes, roughly chopped
salt
coriander (cilantro) leaves
   and crispy fried onion,
   to garnish (optional)
natural (plain) yogurt, poppadums
   and griddled flatbread or
   naans, to serve

1 Heat a wok or large pan over a medium heat and add the sunflower oil. When hot add the green chilli and onions, lower the heat and cook gently for 10–12 minutes, until softened.

2 Increase the heat slightly and add the garlic, ginger, mustard seeds, cumin seeds, coriander seeds and curry leaves to the pan. Cook for 2–3 minutes, stirring frequently.

3 Add the lentils to the pan with about 700ml/1 pint 2fl oz/ scant 3 cups water, the turmeric and tomatoes and season with plenty of salt. Stir well and bring the mixture to the boil, cover the pan, reduce the heat and cook very gently for about 25–30 minutes, stirring occasionally.

4 Check the seasoning, then garnish with coriander leaves and crispy fried onion, if you like, and serve with yogurt, poppadums and flatbread or naans.

Variation
Use yellow split peas in place of the lentils. Like red lentils, they do not need to be soaked before cooking.

Richly Spiced Dhal

Flavoured with spices, coconut milk and tomatoes, this lentil dish makes a filling supper or an excellent side dish to go alongside a dry curry for an Indian banquet. However, warm naan bread and yogurt are all that are needed as accompaniments for a tasty meal.

Serves 4
30ml/2 tbsp vegetable oil
1 large onion, finely chopped
3 garlic cloves, chopped
1 carrot, diced
10ml/2 tsp cumin seeds
10ml/2 tsp yellow mustard seeds
2.5cm/1in piece fresh root
   ginger, grated
10ml/2 tsp ground turmeric
5ml/1 tsp mild chilli powder
5ml/1 tsp garam masala
225g/8oz/1 cup red split lentils
400ml/14fl oz/1²/₃ cups water
400ml/14fl oz/1²/₃ cups
   coconut milk
5 tomatoes, seeded and chopped
juice of 2 limes
60ml/4 tbsp chopped fresh
   coriander (cilantro)
salt and ground black pepper
25g/1oz/1/4 cup flaked (sliced)
   almonds, toasted, to garnish

1 Heat the oil in a large heavy pan. Fry the onion for about 5 minutes until softened, stirring occasionally. Stir the garlic, carrot, cumin and mustard seeds, and ginger into the pan. Cook for about 5 minutes, stirring, until the seeds begin to pop and the carrot has softened slightly.

2 Stir in the ground turmeric, chilli powder and garam masala, and cook for 1 minute or until the flavours begin to mingle, stirring to prevent the spices burning.

3 Add the lentils, water, coconut milk and tomatoes, and season well with salt and black pepper. Bring to the boil, then reduce the heat and simmer, covered, for about 45 minutes, stirring occasionally to prevent the lentils sticking.

4 Stir the lime juice and 45ml/3 tbsp of the fresh coriander into the pan, then check the seasoning.

5 Cook for a further 15 minutes until the lentils soften and become tender. Sprinkle with the remaining coriander and the flaked almonds and serve immediately.

Red Lentil Dhal Energy 295kcal/1242kJ; Protein 16.1g; Carbohydrate 43.7g, of which sugars 8.5g; Fat 7.6g, of which saturates 1g; Cholesterol 0mg; Calcium 71mg; Fibre 4.7g; Sodium 30mg.
Richly Spiced Dhal Energy 295kcal/1242kJ; Protein 16.1g; Carbohydrate 43.7g, of which sugars 8.5g; Fat 7.6g, of which saturates 1g; Cholesterol 0mg; Calcium 71mg; Fibre 4.7g; Sodium 30mg.

Lentil, Tomato and Aubergine Curry

This curry goes equally well with boiled basmati rice or crusty white bread. Pigeon peas are available from most Asian stores, but green lentils also work well.

Serves 4

225g/8oz/1 cup red gram (pigeon peas) or green lentils
2.5ml/½ tsp ground turmeric
1 large aubergine (eggplant)
7.5ml/1½ tsp salt, or to taste
15ml/1 tbsp coriander seeds
5ml/1 tsp cumin seeds
1–4 dried red chillies, roughly broken up
2.5ml/½ tsp black peppercorns
2.5ml/½ tsp black mustard seeds
225g/8oz fresh tomatoes, chopped
30ml/2 tbsp tamarind juice, made with 15ml/1tbsp tamarind pulp and 15ml/1tbsp water, strained and the pulp discarded, or the juice of 1 lime
30ml/2 tbsp fresh coriander (cilantro) leaves and stalks, finely chopped

1 Put the pigeon peas or lentils in a pan and add the turmeric and 1.2 litres/2 pints/5 cups water. Bring the water to the boil, then reduce the heat to medium and cook the lentils for about 3–4 minutes or until all the foam subsides.

2 Reduce the heat to low, cover the pan with a tight-fitting lid and simmer gently for about 20 minutes.

3 Add the aubergine and salt to the pan, re-cover and continue to cook for a further 8–10 minutes or until the aubergine is tender when prodded with a fork.

4 Meanwhile, preheat a small heavy pan over a medium heat. Reduce the heat to low and add the coriander seeds, cumin seeds, chillies, peppercorns and mustard seeds. Stir and roast them for about 30–60 seconds until they begin to splutter and release their aromatic fragrances.

5 Remove them from the pan and leave to cool, then grind finely in a spice grinder, food processor or blender.

6 Add the spice mix to the pigeon peas or lentils, followed by the tomatoes and tamarind or lime juice. Simmer for 2–3 minutes. Add the chopped coriander, remove from the heat and serve.

Spicy Parsnip and Chickpea Stew

The sweet flavour of parsnips goes very well with the spices in this Indian-style vegetable stew.

Serves 4

200g/7oz dried chickpeas, soaked overnight in cold water, then drained
7 garlic cloves, finely chopped
1 small onion, chopped
5cm/2in piece fresh root ginger, chopped
2 green chillies, seeded and chopped
450ml/¾ pint/scant 2 cups plus 75ml/5 tbsp water
60ml/4 tbsp groundnut (peanut) oil
5ml/1 tsp cumin seeds
10ml/2 tsp ground coriander seeds
5ml/1 tsp ground turmeric
2.5–5ml/½–1 tsp chilli powder
50g/2oz cashew nuts, toasted and ground
250g/9oz tomatoes, peeled and chopped
900g/2lb parsnips, cut into chunks
5ml/1 tsp ground roasted cumin seeds
juice of 1 lime, to taste
salt and ground black pepper

To serve
fresh coriander leaves
a few cashew nuts, toasted

1 Put the chickpeas in a pan, cover with cold water and bring to the boil. Boil vigorously for 10 minutes, then reduce the heat to medium and cook for 1–1½ hours, or until tender. Drain.

2 Set 10ml/2 tsp of the garlic aside, then place the remainder in a food processor or blender with the onion, ginger and half the chillies. Add the 75ml/5 tbsp water and process to a paste.

3 Heat the oil in a large frying pan and cook the cumin seeds for 30 seconds. Stir in the coriander seeds, turmeric, chilli powder and the ground cashew nuts. Add the ginger and chilli paste and cook until the liquid begins to evaporate. Add the tomatoes and cook until the mixture turns red-brown in colour.

4 Mix in the chickpeas and parsnips with the remaining water, 5ml/1 tsp salt and plenty of pepper. Bring to the boil, stir, then simmer, uncovered, for 15–20 minutes.

5 Add the ground cumin with more salt and lime juice to taste. Stir in the reserved garlic and green chilli, and cook briefly. Serve immediately, garnished with the coriander and cashew nuts.

Lentil Curry Energy 215kcal/914kJ; Protein 15.5g; Carbohydrate 36.2g, of which sugars 3.1g; Fat 2.1g, of which saturates 0.3g; Cholesterol 0mg; Calcium 69.8mg; Fibre 4.8g; Sodium 28mg.
Parsnips and Chickpeas Energy 495kcal/2079kJ; Protein 17.9g; Carbohydrate 58.4g, of which sugars 17.6g; Fat 22.8g, of which saturates 4.1g; Cholesterol 0mg; Calcium 185mg; Fibre 16.9g; Sodium 84mg.

Toor Dhal with Chilli and Cherry Tomatoes

Toor dhal has a wonderfully rich texture, which is best appreciated if served with plain boiled rice. Fresh fenugreek leaves, which are available from Asian grocers, impart a stunning aroma.

Serves 4

115g/4oz toor dhal
45ml/3 tbsp corn oil
1.5ml/¼ tsp onion seeds
1 medium bunch spring onions
  (scallions), roughly chopped
5ml/1 tsp crushed garlic
1.5ml/¼ tsp ground turmeric
7.5ml/1½ tsp crushed ginger
5ml/1 tsp chilli powder
30ml/2 tbsp fresh
  fenugreek leaves
5ml/1 tsp salt
150ml/¼ pint/⅔ cup water
6–8 cherry tomatoes
30ml/2 tbsp fresh coriander
  (cilantro) leaves
½ green (bell) pepper, seeded
  and sliced
15ml/1 tbsp lemon juice
shredded spring onion (scallion)
  tops and fresh coriander
  (cilantro) leaves, to garnish

1 Cook the toor dhal or lentils in a large pan of boiling water until it is soft and mushy. Set aside.

2 Heat the oil with the onion seeds in a non-stick wok or frying pan for a few seconds until hot. Add the dhal to the wok or frying pan and stir-fry for about 3 minutes.

3 Add the spring onions to the pan followed by the garlic, turmeric, ginger, chilli powder, fenugreek leaves and salt and continue to stir-fry for 5–7 minutes.

4 Pour in enough water to loosen the mixture. Add the cherry tomatoes, coriander, green pepper and lemon juice. Serve garnished with shredded onion tops and coriander leaves.

Cook's Tip
Any remaining fresh fenugreek leaves can be frozen in a plastic bag. Use spinach if you cannot get fenugreek.

Courgettes with Dhal and Aromatic Spices

The nutty flavour of split peas goes particularly well with courgettes and tomatoes, perked up with a selection of aromatic spices. Serve with plain rice or bread for a filling and tasty supper.

Serves 4–6

225g/8oz courgettes
  (zucchini)
1 large onion
2 garlic cloves
2 fresh green chillies
175g/6oz/⅔ cup mung dhal
  or yellow split peas
2.5ml/½ tsp ground turmeric
60ml/4 tbsp vegetable oil
2.5ml/½ tsp mustard seeds
2.5ml/½ tsp cumin seeds
1.5ml/¼ tsp asafoetida
a few fresh coriander (cilantro)
  and mint leaves, chopped
6–8 curry leaves
2.5ml/½ tsp sugar
200g/7oz can chopped
  tomatoes
60ml/4 tbsp lemon juice
salt

1 Cut the courgettes into wedges. Finely slice the onion and crush the garlic. Chop the green chillies.

2 In a large pan, simmer the dhal or peas and turmeric in 300ml/½ pint/1¼ cups water, until cooked but not mushy. Drain the cooked lentils, retaining the cooking liquid, and set aside while you cook the vegetables.

3 Heat the oil in a frying pan and add the courgette wedges, sliced onion, crushed garlic and chopped chillies. Add the mustard and cumin seeds, asafoetida, fresh coriander and mint, and stir in the curry leaves and sugar. Fry the ingredients together, stirring occasionally, and then add the chopped tomatoes. Mix well and add salt to taste.

4 Cover the pan and cook until the courgettes are nearly tender but still have a little crunch.

5 Fold in the drained dhal or peas and the lemon juice. If the dish is too dry, add some of the reserved cooking water. Reheat thoroughly and serve immediately.

Toor Dhal Energy 192kcal/806kJ; Protein 8.2g; Carbohydrate 20.2g, of which sugars 3.3g; Fat 9.4g, of which saturates 1.4g; Cholesterol 0mg; Calcium 34mg; Fibre 2.3g; Sodium 16mg.
Courgettes with Dhal Energy 196kcal/823kJ; Protein 9.7g; Carbohydrate 24g, of which sugars 4.7g; Fat 7.7g, of which saturates 1g; Cholesterol 0mg; Calcium 72mg; Fibre 3.2g; Sodium 23mg.

Madras Sambal with Chilli and Spices

There are many variations of this dish but it is regularly cooked in one form or another in many Indian homes and served as part of a meal. You can use any combination of vegetables that are in season.

Serves 4

225g/8 oz/1 cup toor dhal or
   yellow split lentils
600ml/1 pint/2½ cups water
2.5ml/½ tsp ground turmeric
2 large potatoes, cut into
   2.5cm/1in chunks

30ml/2 tbsp vegetable oil
2.5ml/½ tsp black
   mustard seeds
1.5ml/¼ tsp fenugreek seeds
4 curry leaves
1 onion, thinly sliced
115g/4oz green beans, cut into
   2.5cm/1in lengths
5ml/1 tsp salt
2.5ml/½ tsp chilli powder
15ml/1 tbsp lemon juice
60ml/4 tbsp desiccated
   (dry unsweetened
   shredded) coconut
toasted coconut pieces,
   to garnish

1 Wash the toor dhal or lentils in several changes of water, picking through to remove any stones. Place in a heavy pan with the measured water and the turmeric. Cover and simmer for about 30–35 minutes, until the lentils are soft.

2 Par-boil the potatoes in a large pan of boiling water for about 10 minutes until they are just tender. Drain well and set aside.

3 Heat the oil in a large frying pan and fry the mustard seeds, fenugreek seeds and curry leaves for 2–3 minutes, stirring constantly, until the seeds begin to splutter.

4 Add the onion and the green beans to the pan and fry for 7–8 minutes. Add the potatoes to the pan and cook, stirring, for a further 2–3 minutes.

5 Stir in the toor dhal or lentils with the salt, chilli powder and lemon juice and simmer for 2 minutes. Stir in the coconut and simmer for about 5 minutes, until the vegetables are tender. Garnish with toasted coconut and serve immediately.

Spicy Mung Bean and Potato Curry

Mung beans are one of the beans that do not require soaking. In this recipe they are cooked with potatoes and traditional Indian spices to give a tasty, healthy curry.

Serves 4

175g/6oz/1 cup mung beans
750ml/1¼ pints/3 cups water
225g/8oz potatoes, cut into
   2cm/¾in chunks
30ml/2 tbsp vegetable oil
2.5ml/½ tsp cumin seeds

1 green chilli, finely chopped
1 garlic clove, crushed
2.5cm/1in piece fresh root ginger,
   finely chopped
1.5ml/¼ tsp ground turmeric
2.5ml/½ tsp chilli powder
5ml/1 tsp salt
5ml/1 tsp sugar
4 curry leaves
5 tomatoes, skinned and diced
15ml/1 tbsp tomato purée (paste)
curry leaves, to garnish
plain boiled basmati rice,
   to serve

1 Wash the beans. Bring to the boil in a large pan with the measured water. Cover the pan, reduce the heat and simmer for about 30 minutes, until the beans are soft.

2 In a separate pan, par-boil the potatoes for about 10 minutes until just tender, then drain well.

3 Heat the oil in a wok or frying pan and fry the cumin seeds until they start to splutter.

4 Add the chilli, garlic and ginger to the pan and fry, stirring constantly, for 3–4 minutes until fragrant. Be careful not to let the garlic burn or it will taste bitter.

5 Add the turmeric, chilli powder, salt and sugar to the pan and cook for about 2 minutes, stirring constantly.

6 Add the curry leaves, tomatoes and tomato purée to the pan, mix well and simmer for 5 minutes until the sauce thickens. Add the tomato sauce and potatoes to the mung beans and mix together. Serve immediately with plain boiled rice, and garnish with the curry leaves.

Madras Sambal Energy 401kcal/1687kJ; Protein 16.7g; Carbohydrate 50.8g, of which sugars 5.1g; Fat 16g, of which saturates 8.9g; Cholesterol 0mg; Calcium 52mg; Fibre 6.7g; Sodium 36mg.
Spicy Mung Beans Energy 265kcal/1118kJ; Protein 13.8g; Carbohydrate 37.4g, of which sugars 5.7g; Fat 7.9g, of which saturates 1.1g; Cholesterol 0mg; Calcium 58mg; Fibre 5.8g; Sodium 34mg.

Black-eyed Bean and Potato Curry

Nutty-flavoured black-eyed beans make a nutritious dish. This hot and spicy combination is ideal for an autumn evening.

Serves 4–6
2 potatoes
225g/8oz/1¼ cups black-eyed beans (peas), soaked overnight and drained
1.5ml/¼ tsp bicarbonate of soda (baking soda)
5ml/1 tsp five-spice powder
1.5ml/¼ tsp asafoetida
2 onions, finely chopped
2.5cm/1in piece fresh root ginger, crushed

a few fresh mint leaves
450ml/¾ pint/scant 2 cups water
60ml/4 tbsp vegetable oil
2.5ml/½ tsp each ground cumin, ground coriander, ground turmeric and chilli powder
4 fresh green chillies, seeded and chopped
75ml/5 tbsp tamarind juice made with 15ml/1 tbsp tamarind pulp mixed with 60ml/4 tbsp water, strained, and pulp and seeds discarded
115g/4oz/4 cups fresh coriander (cilantro), chopped
2 firm tomatoes, chopped
salt

1 Cut the potatoes into bitesize cubes and boil in a large pan of lightly salted water until tender.

2 Place the drained black-eyed beans in a heavy pan and add the bicarbonate of soda, five-spice powder and asafoetida. Add the chopped onions, crushed root ginger, mint leaves and the measured water. Simmer until the beans are soft. Drain and reserve the liquid.

3 Heat the vegetable oil in a frying pan. Gently fry the ground cumin and coriander, the turmeric and chilli powder with the green chillies and tamarind juice, until they are well blended and releasing their fragrances.

4 Pour the spice mixture over the black-eyed beans in the pan and mix well until all the ingredients are well combined.

5 Add the potatoes, fresh coriander, tomatoes and salt. Mix well, and, if necessary, thin with a little reserved water. Reheat for a minute and serve immediately.

Spicy Chickpeas with Potato Cakes and Green Chillies

The potato cakes in this recipe are given a slightly sour-sweet flavour by the addition of amchur, a powder that is made from unripe or green mangoes.

Serves 10–12
30ml/2 tbsp vegetable oil
30ml/2 tbsp ground coriander
30ml/2 tbsp ground cumin
2.5ml/½ tsp ground turmeric
2.5ml/½ tsp salt
2.5ml/½ tsp sugar
30ml/2 tbsp flour, mixed to a paste with a little water
450g/1lb boiled chickpeas, well drained

2 fresh green chillies, chopped
5cm/2in piece fresh root ginger, finely crushed
75g/3oz fresh coriander (cilantro) leaves, chopped
2 firm tomatoes, chopped

For the potato cakes
450g/1lb potatoes, boiled and coarsely mashed
4 green chillies, finely chopped
50g/2oz coriander (cilantro) leaves, finely chopped
7.5ml/1½ tsp ground cumin
5ml/1 tsp amchur (dry mango powder)
salt
vegetable oil, for shallow-frying

1 Make the spicy chickpeas. Heat the oil in a pan and fry the coriander, cumin, turmeric, salt, sugar and flour paste until the water has evaporated and the oil separated.

2 Add the chickpeas, chillies, ginger, fresh coriander and tomatoes to the pan. Mix well and simmer for 5 minutes. Transfer to a serving dish and keep warm.

3 To make the potato cakes, mix the mashed potato in a large mixing bowl with the green chillies, coriander, ground cumin, amchur and salt, to taste. Mix well until all the ingredients in the bowl are thoroughly blended.

4 Using your hands, shape the potato mixture into little cakes. Heat the oil in a shallow frying pan or griddle and fry them on both sides until golden brown. Transfer to a warmed serving dish and serve immediately with the spicy chickpeas.

Black-eyed Bean Curry Energy 266kcal/1118kJ; Protein 11.8g; Carbohydrate 36.8g, of which sugars 8.5g; Fat 9g, of which saturates 1.1g; Cholesterol 0mg; Calcium 110mg; Fibre 8.8g; Sodium 28mg.
Spicy Chickpeas Energy 163kcal/684kJ; Protein 5.2g; Carbohydrate 17.3g, of which sugars 1.6g; Fat 8.8g, of which saturates 1.1g; Cholesterol 0mg; Calcium 68mg; Fibre 3g; Sodium 96mg.

Masala Chana

Chickpeas are cooked in a variety of ways all over India. Tamarind adds a sharp, tangy flavour to this slowly simmered curry.

Serves 4
225g/8oz/1¼ cups dried
   chickpeas, soaked overnight
   and drained
50g/2oz tamarind pulp
120ml/4fl oz/½ cup boiling water
30ml/2 tbsp vegetable oil
2.5ml/½ tsp cumin seeds

1 onion, finely chopped
2 garlic cloves, crushed
2.5cm/1in piece fresh root
   ginger, grated
1 fresh green chilli, finely chopped
5ml/1 tsp ground cumin
5ml/1 tsp ground coriander
1.5ml/¼ tsp ground turmeric
2.5ml/½ tsp salt
225g/8oz tomatoes, peeled and
   finely chopped
2.5ml/½ tsp garam masala
chopped fresh chillies and
   chopped onion, to garnish

1 Place the chickpeas in a large pan with double the volume of cold water. Bring to the boil and boil vigorously for about 10 minutes. Skim off any scum that has risen to the surface of the liquid, using a slotted spoon. Lower the heat, cover the pan with a tight-fitting lid and simmer for about 1½–2 hours or until the chickpeas are tender.

2 Meanwhile, break up the tamarind and soak in the boiling water for about 15–20 minutes. Rub the tamarind through a sieve (strainer) into a bowl, discarding any stones and fibre that is left behind in the sieve.

3 Heat the oil in a large, heavy pan and fry the cumin seeds for 2 minutes until they splutter. Add the onion, garlic, ginger and chilli, and fry for 5 minutes.

4 Stir in the cumin and coriander, with the turmeric and salt, and fry for 3–4 minutes. Add the chopped tomatoes. Bring to the boil and then simmer for 5 minutes.

5 Drain the chickpeas and add to the tomato mixture together with the garam masala and tamarind pulp. Cover and simmer gently for about 25–30 minutes. Garnish with the chopped chillies and onion before serving.

Curried Spinach and Potato with Mixed Chillies

This delicious curry, suitable for vegetarians, is mildly spiced with a warming flavour from the fresh and dried chillies.

Serves 4–6
225g/8oz potatoes
60ml/4 tbsp vegetable oil
2.5cm/1in piece fresh root
   ginger, crushed
4 garlic cloves, crushed

1 onion, coarsely chopped
2 green chillies, chopped
2 whole dried red chillies,
   coarsely broken
5ml/1 tsp cumin seeds
225g/8oz fresh spinach, trimmed,
   washed and chopped or
225g/8oz frozen spinach,
   thawed and drained
salt
2 firm tomatoes, coarsely
   chopped, to garnish

1 Wash the potatoes and cut them into quarters. If using small new potatoes, leave them whole. Heat the vegetable oil in a frying pan and fry the potatoes until evenly brown on all sides. Remove from the pan and set aside.

2 Remove the excess oil leaving 15ml/1 tbsp in the pan. Fry the ginger, garlic, onion, green chillies, dried chillies and cumin seeds until the onion is golden brown.

3 Add the potatoes and salt to the pan and stir well. Cover the pan and cook gently until the potatoes are tender and can be easily pierced with a sharp knife.

4 Add the spinach and stir well. Cook with the pan uncovered until the spinach is tender and all the excess fluids in the pan have evaporated. Transfer the curry to a serving plate, garnish with the chopped tomatoes and serve immediately.

> **Cook's Tip**
> India is blessed with over 18 varieties of spinach. If you have access to an Indian or Chinese market or grocer, look out for some of the more unusual varieties.

Masala Chana Energy 256kcal/1075kJ; Protein 13.1g; Carbohydrate 32.2g, of which sugars 4.1g; Fat 9.2g, of which saturates 1.1g; Cholesterol 0mg; Calcium 105mg; Fibre 6.8g; Sodium 285mg.
Curried Spinach Energy 135kcal/560kJ; Protein 3g; Carbohydrate 13.5g, of which sugars 5.9g; Fat 8g, of which saturates 1g; Cholesterol 0mg; Calcium 86mg; Fibre 2.6g; Sodium 62mg.

Potato, Cauliflower and Broad Bean Curry

This is a hot and spicy vegetable curry, loaded with potatoes, cauliflower and broad beans, and is especially tasty when served with rice, a few poppadums and a raita.

Serves 4

2 garlic cloves, chopped
2.5cm/1in piece fresh root ginger
1 fresh green chilli, seeded
  and chopped
30ml/2 tbsp vegetable oil

1 onion, sliced
1 large potato, chopped
15ml/1 tbsp curry powder
1 cauliflower, cut into small florets
600ml/1 pint/2½ cups
  vegetable stock
275g/10oz can broad
  (fava) beans
juice of ½ lemon (optional)
salt and ground black pepper
fresh coriander (cilantro) sprig,
  to garnish
plain boiled rice, to serve

1 Blend the chopped garlic, ginger and chopped chilli with 15ml/1 tbsp of the oil in a food processor or blender until the mixture forms a smooth paste.

2 In a large, heavy pan, fry the sliced onion and chopped potato in the remaining oil for 5 minutes, until the onion is soft and the potato is starting to brown, then stir in the spice paste and curry powder. Cook for another minute.

3 Add the cauliflower florets to the onion and potato and stir well until thoroughly combined with the spicy mixture, then pour in the stock and bring to the boil over a high heat.

4 Season well with salt and black pepper, cover and simmer for 10 minutes. Add the beans with the liquid from the can and cook, uncovered, for a further 10 minutes.

5 Check the seasoning and adjust if necessary. Add a good squeeze of lemon juice, if using, and give the curry a final stir.

6 Serve immediately, on warmed plates, garnished with fresh coriander sprigs and accompanied by plain boiled rice.

Chickpea, Sweet Potato and Aubergine Chilli Dhal

Spicy and delicious – this is a great dish to serve when you want a meal that is nutritious and aromatic.

Serves 3–4

45ml/3 tbsp olive oil
1 red onion, chopped
3 garlic cloves, crushed
115g/4oz sweet potatoes, peeled
  and diced
3 garden eggs or 1 large
  aubergine (eggplant), diced
425g/15oz can chickpeas, drained
5ml/1 tsp dried tarragon

2.5ml/½ tsp dried thyme
5ml/1 tsp ground cumin
5ml/1 tsp ground turmeric
2.5ml/½ tsp ground allspice
5 canned plum tomatoes,
  chopped with 60ml/4 tbsp
  reserved juice
6 ready-to-eat dried apricots
600ml/1 pint/2½ cups
  well-flavoured vegetable stock
1 green chilli, seeded and
  finely chopped
30ml/2 tbsp chopped fresh
  coriander (cilantro)
salt and ground black pepper

1 Heat the olive oil in a large pan. Add the onion, garlic and potatoes and cook until the onion has softened.

2 Stir in the garden eggs or aubergine, then add the chickpeas and the herbs and spices. Stir well to mix and cook over a low heat for a few minutes.

3 Add the tomatoes and their juice, the apricots, stock, chilli and seasoning. Stir well, bring to the boil and cook for 15 minutes.

4 When the sweet potatoes are tender, add the coriander, stir, taste, and adjust the seasoning if necessary. Serve immediately.

Cook's Tip
Garden egg is a small variety of aubergine used in West Africa. It is round and white, which may explain its other name – eggplant. You can peel the aubergine for this dish, if you prefer, but it is not necessary. Either white or orange sweet potatoes can be used and you can add less chickpeas, if you wish.

Broad Bean Curry Energy 194kcal/813kJ; Protein 11.5g; Carbohydrate 20.9g, of which sugars 4.8g; Fat 7.7g, of which saturates 1g; Cholesterol 0mg; Calcium 96mg; Fibre 8.1g; Sodium 40mg.
Chickpea Dhal Energy 322kcal/1356kJ; Protein 12g; Carbohydrate 41.6g, of which sugars 16.6g; Fat 13.5g, of which saturates 1.7g; Cholesterol 0mg; Calcium 107mg; Fibre 9.3g; Sodium 260mg.

Balti Potatoes with Aubergines and Pepper

Choose the smaller variety of aubergines for this curry as they are tastier than the large ones, which contain a lot of water and little flavour. Buy small aubergines from specialist grocers or larger supermarkets.

Serves 4
10–12 baby potatoes
6 small aubergines (eggplants)
1 medium red (bell) pepper
15ml/1 tbsp vegetable oil
2 medium onions, sliced
4–6 curry leaves
2.5ml/½ tsp onion seeds
5ml/1 tsp crushed coriander seeds
2.5ml/½ tsp cumin seeds
5ml/1 tsp grated fresh root ginger
5ml/1 tsp crushed garlic
5ml/1 tsp crushed dried red chillies
15ml/1 tbsp chopped fresh
   fenugreek leaves
5ml/1 tsp chopped fresh
   coriander (cilantro)
15ml/1 tbsp natural (plain)
   low-fat yogurt
fresh coriander (cilantro) leaves,
   to garnish

1 Cook the unpeeled potatoes in a pan of boiling water until they are just tender, but still whole.

2 Cut the aubergines into quarters if very small, or eighths if using slightly larger aubergines.

3 Cut the pepper in half, remove the seeds and ribs and discard, then slice the flesh into thin even strips.

4 Heat the oil in a karahi, wok or large heavy frying pan and fry the sliced onions, curry leaves, onion seeds, crushed coriander seeds and cumin seeds until the onion slices are soft and golden brown, stirring constantly.

5 Add the ginger, garlic, crushed chillies and fenugreek to the pan, followed by the aubergines and potatoes. Stir everything together and cover the pan with a lid. Lower the heat and cook the vegetables for about 5–7 minutes.

6 Remove the lid, add the fresh coriander followed by the yogurt and stir well. Serve garnished with coriander leaves.

Vegetable Curry with Ginger and Chilli

This is a delicious vegetable curry, in which fresh mixed vegetables are cooked in a spicy, aromatic yogurt sauce.

Serves 4
10ml/2 tsp cumin seeds
8 black peppercorns
2 green cardamom pods, seeds only
5cm/2in cinnamon stick
2.5ml/½ tsp grated nutmeg
45ml/3 tbsp vegetable oil
1 green chilli, chopped
2.5cm/1in piece fresh root
   ginger, grated
5ml/1 tsp chilli powder
2.5ml/½ tsp salt
2 large potatoes, cut into
   2.5cm/1in chunks
225g/8oz cauliflower, broken
   into florets
225g/8oz okra, thickly sliced
150ml/¼ pint/⅔ cup natural
   (plain) yogurt
150ml/¼ pint/⅔ cup
   vegetable stock
toasted flaked (sliced) almonds
   and fresh coriander (cilantro)
   sprigs, to garnish

1 Grind the cumin seeds, peppercorns, cardamom seeds, cinnamon stick and nutmeg to a fine powder using a food processor, blender or a mortar and pestle.

2 Heat the oil in a large pan and fry the chopped chilli and ginger for about 2 minutes, stirring all the time.

3 Add the chilli powder, salt and ground spice mixture to the pan and fry for about 2–3 minutes, stirring all the time to prevent the spices from sticking to the pan and burning.

4 Stir the potatoes into the pan, cover, and cook for about 10 minutes over a low heat, stirring occasionally.

5 Add the cauliflower and okra to the pan and mix well to combine the ingredients. Cook for about 5 minutes.

6 Add the yogurt and stock to the pan. Bring to the boil, then reduce the heat. Cover with a lid and simmer for 20 minutes, or until all the vegetables are tender. Garnish with toasted almonds and coriander sprigs, and serve immediately.

Toor Dhal Energy 273kcal/1142kJ; Protein 6.6g; Carbohydrate 34.9g, of which sugars 23.7g; Fat 13.2g, of which saturates 1.5g; Cholesterol 0mg; Calcium 183mg; Fibre 8.4g; Sodium 114mg.
Courgettes with Dhal Energy 238kcal/996kJ; Protein 9.1g; Carbohydrate 26.7g, of which sugars 6.9g; Fat 11.6g, of which saturates 1.8g; Cholesterol 1mg; Calcium 202mg; Fibre 4.3g; Sodium 56mg.

Basmati and Nut Pilaff

Vegetarians will love this simple spicy pilaff. You can add a selection of wild or cultivated mushrooms, if you like.

Serves 4

15–30ml/1–2 tbsp sunflower oil
  or vegetable oil
1 onion, chopped
1 garlic clove, crushed
1 large carrot, coarsely grated
225g/8oz/generous 1 cup
  basmati rice, soaked for 1 hour

5ml/1 tsp cumin seeds
10ml/2 tsp ground coriander
10ml/2 tsp black mustard
  seeds (optional)
4 green cardamom pods
450ml/³⁄₄ pint/scant 2 cups
  vegetable stock or water
1 bay leaf
75g/3oz/³⁄₄ cup unsalted walnuts
  and cashew nuts
salt and ground black pepper
fresh parsley or coriander
  (cilantro) sprigs, to garnish

1 Heat the oil in a large pan and gently fry the onion, garlic and carrot for 3–4 minutes. Drain the rice and then add to the pan with the spices. Cook for 1–2 minutes more, stirring to coat the grains in oil.

2 Pour in the stock or water, add the bay leaf and season well. Bring to the boil, lower the heat, cover the pan with a lid and simmer very gently for 10–12 minutes.

3 Remove the pan from the heat without lifting the lid. Leave to stand for about 5 minutes, then check the rice. If it is cooked, there will be small steam holes on the surface of the rice. Remove and discard the bay leaf and the cardamom pods.

4 Stir in the nuts and check the seasoning. Spoon on to a warmed serving platter, garnish with the fresh parsley or coriander sprigs and serve immediately.

> **Cook's Tip**
> *Use whichever nuts you prefer in this dish – even unsalted peanuts taste good, although almonds, cashew nuts or pistachios are more exotic.*

Spicy Courgettes with Tomato Rice and Fresh Herbs

This slow-cooked rice dish is first simmered on the stove and then finished off in the oven.

Serves 4–8

1kg/2¼lb courgettes (zucchini)
60ml/4 tbsp olive oil
3 onions, finely chopped
3 garlic cloves, crushed
5ml/1 tsp chilli powder
400g/14oz can chopped tomatoes

200g/7oz/1 cup risotto or
  short grain rice
600–750ml/1–1¼ pints/
  2½–3 cups vegetable or
  chicken stock
30ml/2 tbsp chopped
  fresh parsley
30ml/2 tbsp chopped fresh dill
salt and ground white pepper
sprigs of dill and olives, to garnish
thick natural (plain) yogurt,
  to serve

1 Preheat the oven to 190°C/375°F/Gas 5. Top and tail the courgettes and slice into large chunks.

2 Heat half the oil in a large pan and cook the onions and garlic until just soft. Stir in the chilli powder and tomatoes and simmer for about 5 minutes.

3 Add the courgettes and salt to taste. Cook over a low to medium heat for 10–15 minutes, before adding the rice.

4 Add the stock to the pan, cover and simmer for 25 minutes, or until the rice is tender. Stir the mixture occasionally.

5 Season with pepper, and stir in the parsley and dill. Transfer to an ovenproof dish and bake in the oven for about 45 minutes.

6 Halfway through cooking, brush the remaining oil over the courgette mixture. Garnish with the dill and olives, then serve.

> **Cook's Tip**
> *Add extra liquid, as necessary, while simmering the rice on the stove to prevent the mixture from sticking to the pan.*

Basmati and Nut Pilaff Energy 376kcal/1562kJ; Protein 7.5g; Carbohydrate 50g, of which sugars 4g; Fat 16g, of which saturates 1.4g; Cholesterol 0mg; Calcium 42mg; Fibre 1.6g; Sodium 7mg.
Spicy Courgettes Energy 201kcal/837kJ; Protein 5.6g; Carbohydrate 30.1g, of which sugars 8g; Fat 6.6g, of which saturates 1g; Cholesterol 0mg; Calcium 72mg; Fibre 3g; Sodium 10mg.

Vegetable Curry with Lemon Rice

Fragrant jasmine rice, subtly flavoured with lemon grass and cardamom, is the perfect partner for this richly spiced vegetable curry.

Serves 4
10ml/2 tsp vegetable oil
400ml/14fl oz/1⅔ cups coconut milk
300ml/½ pint/1¼ cups vegetable stock
225g/8oz new potatoes, halved
8 baby corn cobs
5ml/1 tsp golden caster (superfine) sugar
185g/6½oz broccoli florets
1 red (bell) pepper, seeded and sliced lengthways
115g/4oz spinach, tough stalks removed, leaves shredded
30ml/2 tbsp chopped fresh coriander (cilantro)
salt and ground black pepper

For the spice paste
1 red chilli, seeded and chopped
3 green chillies, seeded and chopped
1 lemon grass stalk, outer leaves removed and lower 5cm/2in finely chopped
2 shallots, chopped
finely grated rind of 1 lime
2 garlic cloves, chopped
5ml/1 tsp ground coriander
2.5ml/½ tsp ground cumin
1cm/½in piece fresh galangal, finely chopped
30ml/2 tbsp chopped fresh coriander (cilantro)

For the rice
225g/8oz/1¼ cups fragrant jasmine rice
6 cardamom pods, bruised
1 lemon grass stalk, outer leaves removed, cut into 3 pieces
475ml/16fl oz/2 cups water

1 Make the spice paste. Place all the ingredients in a food processor and blend to a coarse paste. Heat the oil in a large, heavy pan. Stir-fry the paste over a medium heat for 1–2 minutes. Pour in the coconut milk and stock and bring to the boil. Reduce the heat, add the potatoes and simmer for 15 minutes.

2 Meanwhile, put the rice, cardamom pods, lemon grass and water in a pan. Bring to the boil, reduce the heat, cover, and cook for 10–15 minutes. Remove the cardamom and lemon grass.

3 Add the corn to the curry, season and cook for 2 minutes. Add the sugar, broccoli and pepper, and cook for 5 minutes. Stir in the spinach and half the coriander. Cook for 2 minutes, then serve with the rice and garnished with the remaining coriander.

Spiced Indian Rice with Spinach, Tomatoes and Cashew Nuts

This all-in-one rice dish is simple to prepare in a slow cooker and makes a delicious, nutritious meal for all the family. It can also be served as a tasty accompaniment to a spicy meat curry.

Serves 4
30ml/2 tbsp sunflower oil
15ml/1 tbsp ghee or unsalted butter
1 onion, finely chopped
2 garlic cloves, crushed
3 tomatoes, peeled, seeded and chopped
275g/10oz/1½ cups easy-cook (converted) brown rice
5ml/1 tsp each ground coriander and ground cumin, or 10ml/2 tsp dhana jeera powder
2 carrots, coarsely grated
750ml/1¼ pints/3 cups boiling vegetable stock
175g/6oz baby spinach leaves, washed
salt and ground black pepper
50g/2oz/½ cup unsalted cashew nuts, toasted, to garnish

1 Heat the oil and ghee or butter in a heavy pan, add the onion and fry gently for 6–7 minutes, until soft. Add the garlic and chopped tomatoes and cook for a further 2 minutes.

2 Rinse the rice in a sieve (strainer) under cold running water, drain well and transfer to the pan. Add the ground coriander and cumin or dhana jeera powder and stir for a few seconds. Turn off the heat and transfer the mixture from the pan to a slow cooker.

3 Stir the carrots into the cooking pot, then pour in the stock, season with salt and pepper, and stir to mix. Switch the slow cooker on to high. Cover and cook for 1 hour.

4 Lay the spinach on the surface of the rice, replace the lid and cook for a further 30–40 minutes, or until the spinach has wilted and the rice is cooked and tender.

5 Stir the spinach into the rice in the pot and check the seasoning, adding a little more salt and pepper, if necessary. Sprinkle the cashew nuts over the rice and serve immediately.

Vegetable Curry Energy 279kcal/1161kJ; Protein 9.8g; Carbohydrate 17.4g, of which sugars 13.3g; Fat 19.4g, of which saturates 3.6g; Cholesterol 5mg; Calcium 99mg; Fibre 3.3g; Sodium 824mg.
Spiced Rice Energy 473kcal/1989kJ; Protein 10.1g; Carbohydrate 72.1g, of which sugars 9.2g; Fat 18g, of which saturates 4.5g; Cholesterol 8mg; Calcium 111mg; Fibre 4.8g; Sodium 349mg.

Sweet Rice with Spiced Chickpeas

This delicious rice dish combines the sweet flavour of the rice with the hot and sour taste of the chickpeas.

Serves 6
350g/12oz/1²/₃ cups dried chickpeas, soaked overnight
60ml/4 tbsp vegetable oil
1 large onion, very finely chopped
225g/8oz tomatoes, peeled and finely chopped
15ml/1 tbsp ground coriander
15ml/1 tbsp ground cumin
5ml/1 tsp ground fenugreek
5ml/1 tsp ground cinnamon
1–2 fresh hot green chillies, seeded and finely sliced

2.5cm/1in piece of fresh root ginger, grated
60ml/4 tbsp lemon juice
salt and ground black pepper
15ml/1 tbsp chopped fresh coriander (cilantro), to garnish

For the rice
40g/1¹/₂oz/3 tbsp ghee or butter
4 green cardamom pods
4 cloves
650ml/22fl oz/2³/₄ cups boiling water
350g/12oz/1³/₄ cups basmati rice, soaked and drained
5–10ml/1–2 tsp sugar
5–6 saffron strands, soaked in warm water

1 Drain the chickpeas and place in a large pan. Pour in water to cover and bring to the boil. Simmer, covered, for 1–1¼ hours until tender. Drain the chickpeas, reserving the cooking liquid.

2 Heat the oil in a pan. Reserve 30ml/2 tbsp of the onion and add the remainder to the pan. Fry for 4–5 minutes, stirring frequently. Add the tomatoes. Cook for 5–6 minutes, until soft.

3 Stir in the coriander, cumin, fenugreek and cinnamon. Cook for 30 seconds, then add the chickpeas and 350ml/12fl oz/1½ cups of the reserved cooking liquid. Season with salt, then cover and simmer for 15–20 minutes, stirring occasionally.

4 Meanwhile, melt the ghee or butter in a pan and fry the cardamom pods and cloves for 2 minutes. Pour in the boiling water and stir in the rice. Cover and cook for 10 minutes.

5 Add the sugar and saffron liquid to the rice. Mix the reserved onion with the chillies, ginger and lemon juice, and add to the chickpeas. Garnish with the coriander and serve with the rice.

Aubergine Pilaff with Cinnamon

This North African rice dish varies from region to region, but all recipes include meaty chunks of aubergine.

Serves 4–6
2 large aubergines (eggplants)
30–45ml/2–3 tbsp olive oil
30–45ml/2–3 tbsp pine nuts
1 large onion, finely chopped
5ml/1 tsp coriander seeds
30ml/2 tbsp currants, soaked for 5–10 minutes and drained
10–15ml/2–3 tsp sugar

15–30ml/1–2 tbsp ground cinnamon
15–30ml/1–2 tbsp dried mint
1 small bunch of fresh dill, finely chopped
3 tomatoes, skinned, seeded and finely chopped
350g/12oz/generous 1³/₄ cups long or short grain rice, well rinsed and drained
sunflower oil, for deep-frying
juice of ¹/₂ lemon
salt and ground black pepper
fresh mint and lemon, to garnish

1 Quarter the aubergines lengthways, then slice each quarter into chunks and place in a large bowl of salted water. Leave to soak for at least 30 minutes.

2 Meanwhile, heat the olive oil in a heavy pan, stir in the pine nuts and cook until they turn golden. Add the onion and cook until soft, then stir in the coriander seeds and currants. Add the sugar, cinnamon, mint and dill and stir in the tomatoes.

3 Add the rice, stirring until well coated, then pour in 900ml/1½ pints/3¾ cups water, season with salt and pepper and bring to the boil. Lower the heat, partially cover the pan, and simmer for 10–12 minutes, until almost all the liquid has been absorbed. Turn off the heat, cover with a dish towel and the lid and leave the rice to steam for about 15 minutes.

4 Heat enough oil for deep-frying in a wok. Drain the aubergines and squeeze them dry, then deep-fry them in batches until golden brown. Lift out and drain on kitchen paper.

5 Transfer the rice into a warmed serving bowl and toss the aubergine chunks through it with the lemon juice. Garnish with the fresh mint and serve the pilaff either warm or cold, with lemon wedges for squeezing over.

Sweet Rice Energy 834kcal/3491kJ; Protein 27.3g; Carbohydrate 126.9g, of which sugars 12.3g; Fat 25.2g, of which saturates 7.1g; Cholesterol 21mg; Calcium 196mg; Fibre 11.3g; Sodium 104mg.
Aubergine Pilaff Energy 369kcal/1539kJ; Protein 6.1g; Carbohydrate 52.2g, of which sugars 11g; Fat 15.2g, of which saturates 1.8g; Cholesterol 0mg; Calcium 38mg; Fibre 2.7g; Sodium 8mg.

Pumpkin Stuffed with Apricot Pilaff

This oven-baked pumpkin filled with a fruity pilaff makes a great centrepiece.

Serves 4–6

1 pumpkin, weighing about
  1.2kg/2¹/₂lb
225g/8oz/generous 1 cup long
  grain rice, well rinsed
30–45ml/2–3 tbsp olive oil
15ml/1 tbsp butter
a few saffron threads
5ml/1 tsp coriander seeds
2–3 strips of orange peel, pith
  removed and finely sliced

45–60ml/3–4 tbsp shelled
  pistachio nuts
30–45ml/2–3 tbsp dried
  cranberries, soaked in boiling
  water for 5 minutes and drained
175g/6oz/³/₄ cup ready-to-eat
  dried apricots, sliced
  or chopped
1 bunch of fresh basil, leaves torn
1 bunch each of fresh coriander
  (cilantro), mint and flat leaf
  parsley, coarsely chopped
salt and ground black pepper
lemon wedges and thick natural
  (plain) yogurt, to serve

1 Preheat the oven to 200°C/400°F/Gas 6. Wash the pumpkin and cut off the stalk end to use as a lid. Scoop all the seeds out of the middle with a spoon, and pull out the stringy fibres. Replace the lid, put the pumpkin on a baking tray and bake for 1 hour.

2 Meanwhile, put the rice in a pan and pour in enough water to cover. Add a pinch of salt and bring to the boil, then partially cover the pan and simmer for 10–12 minutes, until the water has been absorbed and the rice is cooked but still has a bite.

3 Heat the oil and butter in a heavy pan. Stir in the saffron, coriander seeds, orange peel, pistachios, cranberries and apricots, then stir in the cooked rice. Season with salt and pepper. Turn off the heat, cover the pan with a dish towel, followed by the lid, and leave the pilaff to steam for 10 minutes, then toss in the herbs.

4 Spoon the pilaff into the cavity in the pumpkin. Put the lid back on and bake in the oven for a further 20 minutes.

5 To serve, remove the lid and slice a round off the top of the pumpkin. Place the ring on a plate and spoon some pilaff in the middle. Prepare the rest in the same way. Serve with lemon wedges and a bowl of yogurt.

Vegetarian Kedgeree

This spicy lentil and rice dish is a delicious variation of the original Indian version of kedgeree, known as kitchiri. You can serve it as it is, or topped with quartered hard-boiled eggs. It is also good with grilled mushrooms.

Serves 4

50g/2oz/¹/₄ cup red split
  lentils, rinsed
1 bay leaf
225g/8oz/1 cup basmati
  rice, rinsed
4 cloves
50g/2oz/4 tbsp butter
5ml/1 tsp curry powder
2.5ml/¹/₂ tsp mild chilli powder
30ml/2 tbsp chopped fresh flat
  leaf parsley
salt and ground black pepper
4 hard-boiled eggs, quartered, to
  serve (optional)

1 Put the lentils in a pan, add the bay leaf and cover with cold water. Bring to the boil, skim off any foam, then reduce the heat. Cover and simmer for 25–30 minutes, until tender. Drain, then discard the bay leaf.

2 Meanwhile, place the rice in a pan and cover with about 475ml/16fl oz/2 cups boiling water. Add the cloves and a pinch of salt. Cook, covered, for 10–15 minutes, until all the water is absorbed and the rice is tender. Discard the cloves.

3 Melt the butter over a gentle heat in a large frying pan, then add the curry and chilli powders and cook for 1 minute.

4 Stir the lentils and rice into the pan and mix well until they are coated in the spiced butter.

5 Season with salt and pepper and cook for 1–2 minutes until heated through. Stir in the fresh parsley and serve immediately with the hard-boiled eggs, if using.

> **Cook's Tip**
> *Rice is a high-carbohydrate food that provides sustained amounts of energy, making it a perfect food to start the day. Rice can also help to ease diarrhoea and stomach upsets.*

Pumpkin Energy 345kcal/1443kJ; Protein 9.9g; Carbohydrate 50.1g, of which sugars 18.6g; Fat 12g, of which saturates 2.6g; Cholesterol 5mg; Calcium 299mg; Fibre 9.6g; Sodium 93mg.
Vegetarian Kedgeree Energy 481kcal/2015kJ; Protein 14.8g; Carbohydrate 72.6g, of which sugars 4.1g; Fat 15.2g, of which saturates 3.5g; Cholesterol 0mg; Calcium 65mg; Fibre 2.8g; Sodium 82mg.

Tomato Biryani

Although generally served as an accompaniment to meat, poultry or fish dishes, this tasty rice dish can also be eaten as a complete meal on its own.

Serves 4
400g/14oz/2 cups basmati rice
15ml/1 tbsp vegetable oil
2.5ml/½ tsp onion seeds
1 medium onion, sliced

2 medium tomatoes, sliced
1 orange or yellow (bell) pepper, seeded and sliced
5ml/1 tsp grated fresh root ginger
5ml/1 tsp crushed garlic
5ml/1 tsp chilli powder
30ml/2 tbsp chopped fresh coriander (cilantro)
1 medium potato, diced
7.5ml/1½ tsp salt
50g/2oz/½ cup frozen peas
750ml/1¼ pints/3 cups water

1 Wash the rice well under cold running water and leave it to soak in water for about 30 minutes.

2 Heat the oil in a heavy pan and fry the onion seeds for about 1 minute. Add the sliced onion to the pan and fry for about 5–7 minutes, stirring occasionally to prevent the slices from sticking to the pan and burning.

3 Add the sliced tomatoes and pepper, ginger, garlic and chilli powder. Stir-fry for 2 minutes.

4 Add the fresh coriander, potato, salt and peas and stir-fry over a medium heat for a further 5 minutes.

5 Transfer the rice to a colander and drain. Add it to the spiced tomato and potato mixture and stir-fry for 1–2 minutes.

6 Pour in the water and bring to the boil, then lower the heat to medium. Cover and cook the rice for 12–15 minutes. Leave to stand for 5 minutes and then serve.

Cook's Tip
Plain rice can look a bit dull; it is greatly enhanced by adding colourful ingredients such as tomatoes, peppers and peas.

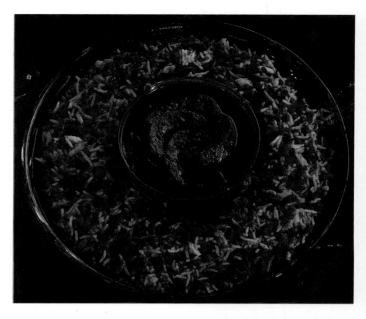

Rice Layered with Bengal Gram

This rice and lentil dish is served with a gourd curry, or palida, which is prominently flavoured with fenugreek and soured with dried mangosteen.

Serves 4–6
175g/6oz/⅔ cup Bengal gram or lentils of your choice
600ml/1 pint/2½ cups water
2.5ml/½ tsp ground turmeric
50g/2oz deep-fried onions, crushed
45ml/3 tbsp green masala paste
a few fresh mint and coriander (cilantro) leaves, chopped
350g/12oz/1¾ cups basmati rice, cooked
30ml/2 tbsp ghee
salt

For the curry
60ml/4 tbsp vegetable oil
1.5ml/¼ tsp fenugreek seeds
15g/½oz dried fenugreek leaves
2 garlic cloves, crushed
5ml/1 tsp ground coriander
5ml/1 tsp cumin seeds
5ml/1 tsp chilli powder
60ml/4 tbsp gram flour mixed with 60ml/4 tbsp water
450g/1lb bottle gourd, peeled, pith and seeds removed and cut into bitesize pieces, or marrow (large zucchini) or firm courgettes (zucchini) prepared in the same way
175ml/6fl oz/¾ cup tomato juice
juice of 3 lemons
salt

1 For the rice, boil the Bengal gram in the water with the turmeric, for 15 minutes or until the grains are soft. Drain and reserve the water. Toss the Bengal gram gently with the deep-fried onions, masala paste, mint and coriander. Add salt to taste.

2 Grease a heavy pan and place a layer of rice in the bottom. Add the Bengal gram mixture and another layer of the remaining rice. Place small knobs (pats) of ghee on top, sprinkle with a little water and heat until steam rises from the mixture. Keep warm.

3 To make the curry, heat the oil in a pan and fry the fenugreek seeds and leaves and the garlic until the garlic turns golden.

4 Mix the ground coriander, cumin and chilli powder to a paste with a little water. Add to the pan and simmer until all the water has evaporated. Add the gram-flour paste, gourd, marrow or courgettes and the tomato juice. Add the lemon juice and salt. Cook until the gourd is soft. Serve immediately with the rice.

Tomato Biryani Energy 475kcal/1990kJ; Protein 11.5g; Carbohydrate 102.9g, of which sugars 9g; Fat 1.9g, of which saturates 0.3g; Cholesterol 0mg; Calcium 47mg; Fibre 3.5g; Sodium 18mg.
Rice with Bengal Gram Energy 326kcal/1367kJ; Protein 11.3g; Carbohydrate 39.6g, of which sugars 2.9g; Fat 14.8g, of which saturates 3.7g; Cholesterol 0mg; Calcium 62mg; Fibre 2.3g; Sodium 82mg.

Vegetable Biryani

This is a good-tempered dish made from everyday ingredients, and thus indispensable for the cook catering for an unexpected vegetarian guest.

Serves 4–6

175g/6oz/scant 1 cup long-grain rice, rinsed
2 whole cloves
seeds from 2 cardamom pods
450ml/¾ pint/scant 2 cups vegetable stock
2 garlic cloves
1 small onion, roughly chopped
5ml/1 tsp cumin seeds
5ml/1 tsp ground coriander
2.5ml/½ tsp ground turmeric
2.5ml/½ tsp chilli powder
1 large potato, cut into 2.5cm/1in cubes
2 carrots, sliced
½ cauliflower, broken into bitesize florets
50g/2oz green beans, cut into 2.5cm/1in lengths
30ml/2 tbsp chopped fresh coriander (cilantro), plus extra to garnish
30ml/2 tbsp lime juice
salt and ground black pepper

1 Put the rice, cloves and cardamom seeds into a large, heavy pan. Pour over the vegetable stock and bring to the boil. Reduce the heat, cover the pan and simmer for 20 minutes or until all the stock has been absorbed.

2 Meanwhile, put the garlic cloves, onion, cumin seeds, ground coriander, turmeric, chilli powder and seasoning into a blender or food processor together with about 30ml/2 tbsp water. Blend until a smooth paste forms. Scrape the paste into a large flameproof casserole.

3 Preheat the oven to 180°C/350°F/Gas 4. Cook the spicy paste in the casserole over a low heat for 2 minutes, stirring occasionally. Add the potato cubes, carrots, cauliflower, beans and 90ml/6 tbsp water. Cover and cook over a low heat for 12 minutes, stirring occasionally. Add the chopped fresh coriander.

4 Remove the cloves from the rice. Spoon the rice over the vegetables. Sprinkle with the lime juice. Cover and cook in the oven for 25 minutes or until the vegetables are tender. Fluff up the rice with a fork before serving, garnished with the extra chopped fresh coriander.

Prawn Pilau

This pilau from Goa combines tasty prawns with a very simple preparation method. A flavoursome meal in itself, the dish also fits easily into a spread that includes meat, poultry and vegetable dishes as well.

Serves 4

275g/10oz/1⅓ cups basmati rice
60ml/4 tbsp sunflower oil or olive oil
5cm/2in piece of cinnamon stick, halved
6 green cardamom pods, bruised
4 cloves
2 bay leaves, crumpled
1 large onion, finely sliced
10ml/2 tsp ginger purée
1 green chilli, finely chopped, and seeded if preferred
5ml/½ tsp ground turmeric
5ml/1 tsp salt, or to taste
15ml/1 tbsp chopped fresh coriander (cilantro)
250g/9oz cooked and peeled prawns (shrimp)

1 Wash the rice in several changes of cold water and soak for 20 minutes. Leave to drain.

2 In a heavy pan, heat the oil over a low heat and add the cinnamon, cardamom, cloves and bay leaves. Stir-fry the ingredients gently for 25–30 seconds and then add the onion. Increase the heat to medium, and fry until the onion is beginning to brown, around 7–8 minutes, stirring regularly to prevent the spices from burning.

3 Add the ginger purée and chilli to the pan and continue to fry until the onion is well browned.

4 Add the turmeric, salt, chopped coriander, prawns and rice to the pan. Stir gently to mix the ingredients. Stir-fry for about 2–3 minutes, then pour in 475ml/16fl oz/2 cups hot water. Bring the mixture to the boil and let it cook, uncovered, for 2–3 minutes. Reduce the heat to low, cover the pan tightly and cook for a further 7–8 minutes.

5 Remove from the heat and leave to stand for 5–6 minutes to absorb the flavour. Fluff up the pilau with a fork and transfer it to a serving dish.

Vegetable Biryani Energy 260kcal/1089kJ; Protein 5.7g; Carbohydrate 50.4g, of which sugars 11.3g; Fat 4.1g, of which saturates 0.6g; Cholesterol 0mg; Calcium 49mg; Fibre 3g; Sodium 27mg.
Prawn Pilau Energy 440kcal/1835kJ; Protein 17.9g; Carbohydrate 64.1g, of which sugars 5.6g; Fat 12.4g, of which saturates 1.3g; Cholesterol 122mg; Calcium 94mg; Fibre 1.4g; Sodium 123mg.

Lamb Curry with Cashew Rice

The lamb and rice in this simple and tasty curry are slowly cooked together in a clay pot.

Serves 4

1 large onion, quartered
2 garlic cloves
1 green chilli, halved and seeded
5cm/2in piece fresh root ginger
15ml/1 tbsp ghee or butter
15ml/1 tbsp vegetable oil
675g/1½lb boned shoulder or leg
   of lamb, cut into chunks
15ml/1 tbsp ground coriander
10ml/2 tsp ground cumin
1 cinnamon stick, in 3 pieces
150ml/¼ pint/⅔ cup thick natural
   (plain) yogurt
150ml/¼ pint/⅔ cup water
75g/3oz/⅓ cup ready-to-eat dried
   apricots, cut into chunks
salt and ground black pepper
1 onion, sliced and fried, and sprigs
   of coriander (cilantro), to garnish

For the rice

250g/9oz/1¼ cups basmati rice
6 cardamom pods, split open
25g/1oz/2 tbsp butter
45ml/3 tbsp toasted cashew nuts
   or flaked (sliced) almonds

1 Soak a large clay pot in cold water for 20 minutes, then drain. Place the onion, garlic, chilli and ginger in a food processor or blender and process with about 15ml/1 tbsp water until a smooth paste forms.

2 Heat the ghee and oil in a pan. Fry the lamb in batches until brown. Remove from the pan, using a slotted spoon, and set aside. Add the paste to the pan, stir in the coriander and cumin, add the cinnamon stick and fry for 1–2 minutes. Return the meat to the pan. Stir in the yogurt and the water, and season. Transfer to the clay pot, cover and place in an unheated oven. Set the oven to 180°C/350°F/Gas 4 and cook for 45 minutes.

3 Meanwhile, place the rice in a bowl, cover with cold water and soak for 20 minutes. Drain and cook in a pan of boiling salted water for 10 minutes. Drain and stir in the cardamom pods.

4 Stir the apricots into the clay pot. Pile the rice on top and dot with the butter. Drizzle over 60ml/4 tbsp water, then sprinkle the cashew nuts or almonds on top. Cover, reduce the oven to 150°C/300°F/Gas 2 and cook for 30 minutes. Fluff up the rice with a fork. Serve with fried onion slices and coriander.

Spicy Lamb and Vegetable Pilau

Tender lamb is served in this dish with basmati rice and a colourful selection of vegetables and cashew nuts. The dish is presented in cabbage leaf 'bowls'.

Serves 4

450g/1lb boned shoulder of
   lamb, cubed
2.5ml/½ tsp dried thyme
2.5ml/½ tsp paprika
5ml/1 tsp garam masala
1 garlic clove, crushed
25ml/1½ tbsp vegetable oil
900ml/1½ pints/3¾ cups stock
large Savoy cabbage leaves,
   to serve

For the rice

25g/1oz/2 tbsp butter
1 onion, chopped
1 medium potato, diced
1 carrot, sliced
½ red (bell) pepper, chopped
1 green chilli, seeded
   and chopped
115g/4oz/1 cup sliced cabbage
60ml/4 tbsp natural (plain) yogurt
2.5ml/½ tsp ground cumin
5 green cardamom pods
2 garlic cloves, crushed
225g/8oz/generous 1 cup
   basmati rice, soaked
   and drained
50g/2oz/½ cup cashew nuts
salt and ground black pepper

1 Put the lamb cubes in a large bowl and add the thyme, paprika, garam masala and garlic, with plenty of salt and pepper. Stir, cover, and leave in a cool place for 2–3 hours.

2 Heat the oil in a pan and brown the lamb, in batches, over a medium heat for 5–6 minutes. Stir in the stock, cover, and cook for 35–40 minutes. Using a slotted spoon, transfer the lamb to a bowl. Pour the liquid into a measuring jug (cup), topping it up with water if necessary to make 600ml/1 pint/2½ cups.

3 Melt the butter in a separate pan and fry the onion, potato and carrot for 5 minutes. Add the red pepper and chilli and fry for 3 minutes more, then stir in the cabbage, yogurt, spices, garlic and the reserved lamb stock. Stir well, cover, then simmer gently for 5–10 minutes, until the cabbage has wilted.

4 Stir the rice into the stew with the lamb. Cover and simmer over a low heat for 20 minutes or until the rice is cooked. Sprinkle in the cashew nuts and season to taste with salt and pepper. Serve hot, cupped in cabbage leaves.

Lamb Curry Energy 769kcal/3208kJ; Protein 43.6g; Carbohydrate 67.6g, of which sugars 14.5g; Fat 36.2g, of which saturates 15g; Cholesterol 142mg; Calcium 134mg; Fibre 2.6g; Sodium 252mg.
Lamb Pilau Energy 751kcal/3135kJ; Protein 33.7g; Carbohydrate 86.3g, of which sugars 7.3g; Fat 30.1g, of which saturates 11.6g; Cholesterol 102mg; Calcium 88mg; Fibre 2.3g; Sodium 200mg.

Lamb Biryani

Serves 4–5
675g/1½lb leg of lamb, cubed
50g/2oz/¼ cup natural (plain) yogurt
5ml/1 tsp salt
75g/3oz ghee
2 large onions, finely sliced
10ml/2 tsp ginger purée
10ml/2 tsp garlic purée

For the ground spice mix
10ml/2 tsp coriander seeds, ground
5ml/1 tsp cumin seeds, ground
2.5cm/1in cinnamon stick, ground
4 cardamom pods, finely ground
4 cloves, finely ground

15ml/1 tbsp poppy seeds, ground
¼ of a whole nutmeg, grated

For the rice
2.5ml/½ tsp saffron, pounded
30ml/2 tbsp hot milk
350g/12oz/1¾ cups basmati
    rice, washed and drained
2.5cm/1in cinnamon stick
4 cardamom pods, bruised
4 cloves
2 star anise
2 whole bay leaves
10ml/2 tsp salt, or to taste
15ml/1 tbsp ghee, melted

1 Put the lamb in a large bowl. Add the yogurt and salt. Mix, and set aside for 20–30 minutes.

2 Melt the ghee over a medium heat and fry the onions. Drain on kitchen paper. Return the pan to the heat and add the ginger and garlic, and fry for 1 minute. Add the ground spice mix and stir-fry for 1–2 minutes. Add the lamb. Stir and cook over a medium heat for 2–3 minutes, then remove from the heat.

3 For the rice, soak the saffron in hot milk and set aside. Preheat the oven to 160°C/ 325°F/Gas Mark 3. Parboil the rice for 5 minutes in 1.5 litres/2½ pints/6¼ cups water and add the remaining ingredients except the ghee. Boil for 3 minutes, then drain, reserving the spices.

4 Spread the lamb evenly in a heavy, ovenproof pan. Top with half the fried onions and pile the rice on top, with the whole spices. Sprinkle the saffron milk and melted ghee over the top.

5 Seal the pan with a double thickness of foil and cover with the lid. Cook in the oven for 1 hour. Leave to stand for 30 minutes. Stir the biryani with a metal spoon to mix the rice and meat. Transfer to a serving dish and garnish with fried onion.

Beef Biryani

Moguls brought this spicy dry curry to central India.

Serves 4
2 large onions
2 garlic cloves, chopped
2.5cm/1in root ginger, chopped
1 green chilli, seeded and chopped
bunch of fresh coriander (cilantro)
60ml/4 tbsp flaked (sliced) almonds
30–45ml/2–3 tbsp water
15ml/1 tbsp butter, plus 30ml/2
    tbsp butter, for the rice
45ml/3 tbsp sunflower oil

30ml/2 tbsp sultanas (golden raisins)
500g/1¼lb braising steak, cubed
5ml/1 tsp ground coriander
15ml/1 tbsp ground cumin
2.5ml/½ tsp ground turmeric
2.5ml/½ tsp ground fenugreek
good pinch of ground cinnamon
175ml/6fl oz/¾ cup natural
    (plain) yogurt
275g/10oz/1½ cups basmati rice
1.2 litres/2 pints/5 cups stock
salt and ground black pepper
2 hard-boiled eggs, chopped, to
    garnish

1 Chop 1 onion. Place in a food processor with the garlic, ginger, chilli, coriander, half the almonds and water and process to a paste. Slice the remaining onion into rings. Heat half the butter and oil in a flameproof casserole and fry the onion for 10–15 minutes. Transfer to a plate. Fry the rest of the almonds and set aside, then fry the sultanas until they swell. Transfer to the plate.

2 Heat the remaining butter in the casserole with 15ml/1 tbsp of the oil. Fry the meat, in batches, until brown and set aside. Heat the remaining oil and pour in the spice paste. Stir-fry for 2–3 minutes. Stir in all the spices, season and cook for 1 minute. Lower the heat, then stir in the yogurt. Add the meat. Stir to coat, cover tightly and simmer for 45 minutes until the meat is tender.

3 Soak the rice in a bowl of cold water for 15 minutes. Preheat the oven to 160°C/325°F/Gas 3. Drain the rice, place in a pan and add the stock. Bring to the boil, cover and cook for 6 minutes. Drain the rice and mound on top of the meat in the casserole.

4 Using a spoon handle, make a hole through the rice and meat mixture, to the bottom. Sprinkle with fried onions, almonds and sultanas and dot with butter. Cover with a lid. Cook in the oven for 30–40 minutes. To serve, place on a warmed serving plate and garnish with the eggs. Serve immediately.

Lamb Biryani Energy 769kcal/3208kJ; Protein 43.6g; Carbohydrate 67.6g, of which sugars 14.5g; Fat 36.2g, of which saturates 15g; Cholesterol 142mg; Calcium 134mg; Fibre 2.6g; Sodium 252mg.
Beef Biryani Energy 778kcal/3240kJ; Protein 40g; Carbohydrate 70.4g, of which sugars 13.4g; Fat 37.4g, of which saturates 11.8g; Cholesterol 94mg; Calcium 164mg; Fibre 2.3g; Sodium 183mg.

Steamed Rice

Good quality rice should have a visible sheen, and the grains will be free from scratches and blemishes.

Serves 4
400g/14oz/2 cups short grain white rice or pudding rice
a drop of sunflower oil

1 Rinse and drain the rice in cold water four or five times. Place the rice in a heavy pan and add cold water to about 5mm/¼in above the level of the rice.

2 Add one drop of sunflower oil to give the rice a lustrous shine, and then cover with a lid and bring to the boil.

3 Lower the heat and leave the rice to steam. Do not remove the lid during the cooking process.

4 After 12–15 minutes turn off the heat and leave the rice, still covered, to steam for a further 5 minutes.

Bamboo-steamed Sticky Rice

Sticky rice is available in Chinese and Asian stores.

Serves 4
350g/12oz/1¾ cups sticky rice

1 Put the rice into a large bowl and fill the bowl with cold water. Leave the rice to soak for at least 6 hours, then drain, rinse thoroughly, and drain again.

2 Fill a wok or heavy pan one-third full with water. Place a bamboo steamer, with the lid on, over the wok or pan and bring the water to the boil.

3 Uncover the steamer and place a damp piece of muslin (cheesecloth) over the rack. Spread the rice out in the middle.

4 Fold the muslin over the rice, cover and steam for about 25 minutes until the rice is tender but firm. The measured quantity of rice grains doubles when cooked.

Five-grain Rice

The extra ingredients in this rice give more of a crunch to the dish's texture, and impart exotic combinations of flavours.

Serves 4
40g/1½oz/generous ¼ cup dried black beans

50g/2oz/¼ cup barley
50g/2oz/¼ cup millet
50g/2oz/¼ cup brown rice
50g/2oz/¼ cup sorghum or lentils
200g/7oz/1 cup short grain white rice
salt

1 Soak the beans, barley, millet, brown rice and sorghum or lentils in cold water for 24 hours.

2 Add the white rice to the soaked grains and black beans. Drain and rinse well in cold running water.

3 Place the rice in a heavy pan and add water to about 5mm/¼in above the level of the rice.

4 Add a generous pinch of salt to the rice, then cover the pan with a lid and bring to the boil.

5 Lower the heat and leave to steam. Do not remove the lid during cooking. After 12–15 minutes turn off the heat and leave the grains, still covered, to steam for a further 5 minutes.

Variations
Other ingredients can be added in place of the grains or beans. Soya beansprouts and chestnuts are popular.

Cook's Tip
Any leftover rice can be stored in the refrigerator. Ensure it is well wrapped with clear film (plastic wrap) to help preserve the moisture. Don't keep rice in the refrigerator for more than two days, reheat thoroughly, and don't reheat more than once.

Steamed Rice Energy 202kcal/845kJ; Protein 4.2g; Carbohydrate 44.9g, of which sugars 0g; Fat 0.3g, of which saturates 0g; Cholesterol 0mg; Calcium 11mg; Fibre 0g; Sodium 0mg.
Sticky Rice Energy 314kcal/1314kJ; Protein 7g; Carbohydrate 66g, of which sugars 0g; Fat 1g, of which saturates 0g; Cholesterol 0mg; Calcium 14mg; Fibre 0g; Sodium 0mg.
Five-grain Rice Energy 299kcal/1252kJ; Protein 6.9g; Carbohydrate 65.2g, of which sugars 9.9g; Fat 1g, of which saturates 0.2g; Cholesterol 0mg; Calcium 34mg; Fibre 2.4g; Sodium 348mg.

Garlic and Ginger Rice

This rice dish goes well with vegetable or meat curries.

Serves 4–6
15ml/1 tbsp vegetable oil
2–3 garlic cloves, finely chopped
25g/1oz fresh root ginger, finely chopped
225g/8oz/generous 1 cup long grain rice, rinsed in several bowls of water and drained
900ml/1½ pints/3¾ cups chicken stock
a bunch of fresh coriander (cilantro) leaves, finely chopped

1 Heat the oil in a heavy pan. Stir in the garlic and ginger and fry until golden. Stir in the rice and allow it to absorb the flavours for 1–2 minutes. Pour in the stock and stir well. Bring the stock to the boil, then reduce the heat.

2 Sprinkle the coriander over the surface of the stock, cover the pan, and leave to cook gently for 20–25 minutes, until the rice has absorbed all the liquid. Turn off the heat and fluff up the rice, cover and leave for 10 minutes before serving.

Fragrant Coconut Rice

The addition of coconut milk makes this rice deliciously creamy.

Serves 4
1 litre/1¾ pints/4 cups coconut milk
450g/1lb/2¼ cups short grain rice, thoroughly washed and drained
1 pandanus (screwpine) leaf, tied in a loose knot
salt

1 Heat the coconut milk in a heavy pan and stir in the rice with a little salt. Add the pandanus leaf and bring to the boil. Reduce the heat and simmer for about 15 minutes or until the liquid has been absorbed.

2 Remove from the heat and cover the pan with a dish towel and the lid. Leave the rice to steam for a further 15–20 minutes, then fluff it up with a fork and serve.

Brown Rice with Lime

It is unusual to find brown rice in Chinese recipes, but the nutty flavour of the grains is enhanced by the fragrance of limes, coriander and lemon grass in this delicious dish.

Serves 4
2 limes
1 lemon grass stalk
225g/8oz/generous 1 cup brown long grain rice
15ml/1 tbsp olive oil
1 onion, chopped
2.5cm/1in piece fresh root ginger, peeled and finely chopped
7.5ml/1½ tsp coriander seeds
7.5ml/1½ tsp cumin seeds
750ml/1¼ pints/3 cups vegetable stock
60ml/4 tbsp chopped fresh coriander (cilantro)
spring onion (scallion) green and toasted coconut strips, to garnish
1 lime cut into 4 wedges, to serve

1 Pare the limes, using a cannelle knife (zester) or fine grater, taking care to avoid cutting into the bitter pith. Set the rind aside. Finely chop the lower bulbous portion of the lemon grass stalk and set it aside.

2 Rinse the rice in plenty of cold running water until the water runs clear. Transfer it into a sieve (strainer) and drain thoroughly.

3 Heat the oil in a large pan. Add the onion, ginger, coriander and cumin seeds, lemon grass and lime rind to the pan and cook over low heat for 2–3 minutes.

4 Add the rice to the pan and cook, stirring constantly, for 1 minute, then pour in the stock and bring to the boil. Reduce the heat to very low and cover the pan.

5 Cook gently for 30 minutes, then check the rice. If it is still crunchy, cover the pan and cook for a further 3–5 minutes. Remove the pan from the heat.

6 Stir in the fresh coriander, fluff up the rice grains with a fork, cover the pan and leave to stand for 10 minutes. Transfer to a warmed dish, garnish with spring onion green and toasted coconut strips, and serve with lime wedges.

Garlic and Ginger Rice Energy 151kcal/632kJ; Protein 3g; Carbohydrate 30g, of which sugars 0g; Fat 2g, of which saturates 0.3g; Cholesterol 0mg; Calcium 9mg; Fibre 0.1g; Sodium 124mg.
Fragrant Coconut Rice Energy 459kcal/1927kJ; Protein 9.1g; Carbohydrate 102g, of which sugars 12.3g; Fat 1.3g, of which saturates 0.5g; Cholesterol 0mg; Calcium 94mg; Fibre 0g; Sodium 275mg.
Brown Rice with Lime Energy 235kcal/996kJ; Protein 4.3g; Carbohydrate 47.3g, of which sugars 1.9g; Fat 4.5g, of which saturates 0.8g; Cholesterol 0mg; Calcium 35mg; Fibre 1.9g; Sodium 6mg.

Pilau Rice with Whole Spices

This fragrant rice dish makes an excellent accompaniment to any curry meal.

Serves 4

generous pinch of saffron strands
600ml/1 pint/2 ½ cups hot
  chicken stock
50g/2oz/¼ cup butter
1 onion, chopped
1 garlic clove, crushed
½ cinnamon stick
6 green cardamom pods
1 bay leaf
250g/9oz/1 ⅓ cups
  basmati rice
50g/2oz/⅓ cup sultanas
  (golden raisins)
15ml/1 tbsp sunflower oil or
  vegetable oil
50g/2oz/½ cup cashew nuts

1 Add the saffron strands to a jug (pitcher) containing the hot chicken stock. Stir well to release the colour of the saffron, and set aside while cooking the other ingredients.

2 Heat the butter in a pan and fry the chopped onion and crushed garlic for 5 minutes. Stir in the cinnamon stick, cardamoms and bay leaf and cook for a further 2 minutes.

3 Add the rice and cook, stirring, for 2 minutes more. Pour in the saffron-flavoured stock and add the sultanas.

4 Bring to the boil, stir, then lower the heat, cover with a tight-fitting lid and cook gently for about 8 minutes or until the rice is tender and all the liquid has been absorbed.

5 Meanwhile, heat the oil in a frying pan and fry the cashew nuts until browned. Drain on kitchen paper. Sprinkle the browned cashew nuts evenly over the rice and serve.

> **Cook's Tip**
> Don't be tempted to use black cardamoms in this dish. They are coarser and more strongly flavoured than green cardamoms and are only used in highly spiced dishes that are cooked for a long time. When using cardamoms of any colour, make sure they are fresh or the dish will taste musty.

Saffron Rice with Cardamoms

The addition of aromatic green cardamom pods, cloves, milk and saffron gives this dish both a delicate flavour and colour. It is the perfect dish to accompany a simple chicken or lamb curry and would also go well with a spicy vegetable dish or dhal.

Serves 6

450g/1lb/2 ⅓ cups basmati rice
750ml/1 ¼ pints/3 cups water
3 green cardamom pods
2 cloves
5ml/1 tsp salt
45ml/3 tbsp semi-skimmed
  (low-fat) milk
2.5ml/½ tsp saffron strands,
  crushed

1 Wash the rice under cold water and leave to soak in water for 20 minutes. Drain the rice well and place it in a pan. Pour the measured water into the pan.

2 Add the cardamoms, cloves and salt. Stir, then bring to the boil. Lower the heat, cover the pan tightly and simmer the rice for about 5 minutes so that it starts to cook.

3 Meanwhile, place the milk in a small heavy pan. Add the saffron strands and heat gently.

4 Add the saffron milk to the rice and stir. Cover again and continue cooking over low heat for 5–6 minutes. Remove the pan from the heat without lifting the lid. Leave the rice to stand for about 5 minutes before serving.

> **Cook's Tips**
> • The saffron milk can be heated in the microwave. Mix the milk and saffron strands in a suitable jug (pitcher) or bowl and warm them for 1 minute on Low.
> • The rice can be coloured and flavoured with a generous pinch of ground turmeric instead of saffron. The effect will not be as subtle, but the results will still be very satisfactory.
> • Just before serving the rice, remove the cardamom pods and whole cloves, or warn guests to look out for them.

Pilau Rice Energy 302kcal/1258kJ; Protein 5.8g; Carbohydrate 46.4g, of which sugars 1g; Fat 10.1g, of which saturates 1.1g; Cholesterol 0mg; Calcium 49mg; Fibre 0.8g; Sodium 2mg.
Saffron Rice Energy 348kcal/1452kJ; Protein 6.7g; Carbohydrate 71g, of which sugars 0.9g; Fat 3.6g, of which saturates 2g; Cholesterol 8mg; Calcium 21mg; Fibre 0.2g; Sodium 515mg.

Persian Rice with Fried Onions

Persian cuisine is exotic and delicious, with intense flavours. This dish forms a lovely crust on the bottom.

Serves 6–8

450g/1lb/2⅓ cups basmati rice, soaked and drained
150ml/¼ pint/⅔ cup sunflower oil
2 garlic cloves, crushed
2 onions, 1 chopped, 1 sliced
600ml/1 pint/2½ cups stock
150g/5oz/⅔ cup green lentils, soaked
50g/2oz/⅓ cup raisins
10ml/2 tsp ground coriander
45ml/3 tbsp tomato purée (paste)
1 egg yolk, beaten
10ml/2 tsp natural (plain) yogurt
75g/3oz/6 tbsp melted butter
a few saffron strands, soaked in a little hot water
salt and ground black pepper

1 Cook the rice in boiling salted water for 10–12 minutes. Drain. Heat 30ml/2 tbsp of the oil in a large pan and fry the garlic and chopped onion for 5 minutes. Stir in the stock, lentils, raisins, coriander and tomato purée. Bring to the boil, lower the heat, cover and simmer for 20 minutes.

2 Mix the egg yolk and yogurt in a bowl. Spoon in about 120ml/4 fl oz/½ cup of the cooked rice and mix thoroughly. Season. Heat about two-thirds of the remaining oil in a large pan and sprinkle the egg and yogurt rice over the bottom.

3 Place a layer of rice in the pan, then a layer of lentils. Build up the layers in a pyramid shape away from the sides. Finish with a layer of plain rice. With a wooden spoon handle, make three holes down to the bottom of the pan; drizzle over the melted butter. Bring to a high heat, then wrap the pan lid in a wet dish towel and place on top. When the rice is steaming well, lower the heat and cook slowly for about 30 minutes.

4 Fry the onion slices in the remaining oil until browned and crisp. Drain. Remove the rice pan from the heat, and dip the base into cold water to loosen the crust. Strain the saffron water into a bowl and stir in a few spoons of cooked rice. Toss the rice and lentils together in the pan and spoon on to a serving dish. Sprinkle the saffron rice on top. Break up the crust and place around the mound. Top with the onions and serve.

Malay Yellow Rice

This is a delicately flavoured rice dish, made with long grain rice that is coloured yellow by vibrant turmeric powder. This simple rice curry is cooked in the same way as plain steamed rice, using the quick and easy absorption method.

Serves 4

30ml/2 tbsp vegetable oil or sesame oil
3 shallots, finely chopped
2 garlic cloves, peeled and finely chopped
450g/1lb/generous 2 cups long grain rice, thoroughly washed and drained
400ml/14fl oz/1⅔ cups coconut milk
10ml/2 tsp ground turmeric
4 fresh curry leaves
2.5ml/½ tsp salt
ground black pepper
2 red chillies, seeded and finely sliced, to garnish

1 Heat the vegetable or sesame oil in a heavy pan and stir in the shallots and garlic. Just as they begin to colour, stir in the rice until the grains are coated in the oil.

2 Pour the coconut milk into the pan, along with about 450ml/¾ pint/scant 2 cups water, the ground turmeric, curry leaves, salt and ground black pepper.

3 Bring the mixture to the boil, then turn down the heat and cover the pan tightly with a lid. Cook gently for 15–20 minutes, until all the liquid has been absorbed.

4 Turn off the heat and leave the rice to steam in the pan for 10 minutes. Fluff up the rice with a fork and serve immediately garnished with the sliced red chillies.

> **Cook's Tip**
> • Regular long grain rice, or other types such as jasmine rice, short grain or sticky rice, can all be used for this recipe.
> • This rice is often served at Malay festivals. It is also one of the popular dishes at Malay and Indonesian stalls, where it is served with a variety of meat and vegetable dishes.

Persian Rice Energy 398kcal/1658kJ; Protein 6.5g; Carbohydrate 69.9g, of which sugars 0.1g; Fat 9.7g, of which saturates 5.9g; Cholesterol 24mg; Calcium 19mg; Fibre 0g; Sodium 559mg.
Malay Yellow Rice Energy 481kcal/2011kJ; Protein 8.8g; Carbohydrate 95.9g, of which sugars 5.8g; Fat 6.4g, of which saturates 0.9g; Cholesterol 0mg; Calcium 54mg; Fibre 0.2g; Sodium 356mg.

Wild Rice Pilaff

Wild rice isn't a rice at all, but is actually a type of wild grass. Call it what you will, it has a wonderful nutty flavour and combines well with long grain rice in this fruity mixture. Serve as a side dish.

Serves 6
200g/7oz/1 cup wild rice
40g/1½oz/3 tbsp butter

½ onion, finely chopped
200g/7oz/1 cup long grain rice
475ml/16fl oz/2 cups
   chicken stock
75g/3oz/¾ cup flaked
   (sliced) almonds
115g/4oz/⅔ cup sultanas
   (golden raisins)
30ml/2 tbsp chopped fresh
   parsley
salt and ground black pepper

1 Bring a large pan of water to the boil. Add the wild rice and 5ml/1 tsp salt. Lower the heat, cover and simmer gently for 45–60 minutes, until the rice is tender. Drain well.

2 Meanwhile, melt 15g/½oz/1 tbsp of the butter in another pan. Add the onion and cook over medium heat for about 5 minutes until it is just softened. Stir in the long grain rice and cook for 1 minute more.

3 Stir in the stock and bring to the boil. Cover the pan with a lid and simmer gently for 30–40 minutes, until the rice is tender and the liquid has been absorbed.

4 Melt the remaining butter in a small pan. Add the almonds and cook until they are just golden. Set aside.

5 Put the rice mixture in a bowl and add the almonds, sultanas and half the parsley. Stir to mix. Taste and adjust the seasoning if necessary. Transfer to a warmed serving dish, sprinkle with the remaining parsley and serve immediately.

Saigon Chilli Rice

Although plain steamed rice is served at almost every meal in Vietnam, many families like to sneak in a little spice too. A burst of chilli for fire, turmeric for colour, and coriander for its cooling flavour, are all that's needed.

Serves 4
15ml/1 tbsp vegetable oil
2–3 green or red Thai chillies,
   seeded and finely chopped
2 garlic cloves, finely chopped

2.5cm/1in fresh root
   ginger, chopped
5ml/1 tsp sugar
10–15ml/2–3 tsp
   ground turmeric
225g/8oz/generous 1 cup long
   grain rice
30ml/2 tbsp nuoc cham
   (Vietnamese fish sauce)
600ml/1 pint/2½ cups water
   or stock
1 bunch of fresh coriander
   (cilantro), stalks removed, leaves
   finely chopped
salt and ground black pepper

1 Heat the oil in a heavy pan. Stir in the chillies, garlic and ginger with the sugar. As they begin to colour, stir in the turmeric. Add the rice, coating it well, then pour in the nuoc mam and the water or stock – the liquid should sit about 2.5cm/1in above the rice.

2 Season with salt and ground black pepper and bring the liquid to the boil. Reduce the heat, cover and simmer for about 25 minutes, or until the water has been absorbed.

3 Remove from the heat and leave the rice to steam for a further 10 minutes before serving.

4 Transfer the rice on to a serving dish. Add some of the coriander and lightly toss together using a fork. Garnish with the remaining fresh coriander.

> **Cook's Tip**
> A well-flavoured stock will make a big difference to the end result. If you haven't time to make your own stock, use a carton or can of good quality stock.

> **Cook's Tip**
> This rice goes well with grilled and stir-fried fish and shellfish dishes, but you can serve it as an alternative to plain rice. Add extra chillies, if you like it hotter.

Saigon Chilli Rice Energy 252kcal/1066kJ; Protein 5g; Carbohydrate 51g, of which sugars 1g; Fat 5g, of which saturates 1g; Cholesterol 0mg; Calcium 24mg; Fibre 0.3g; Sodium 500mg.
Wild Rice Pilaff Energy 424kcal/1769kJ; Protein 8.4g; Carbohydrate 68.3g, of which sugars 14.5g; Fat 13g, of which saturates 4g; Cholesterol 14mg; Calcium 69mg; Fibre 1.7g; Sodium 48mg.

Pineapple Fried Rice

This dish is ideal to prepare for a special occasion meal. Served in the pineapple skin shells, it is sure to be the talking point of the dinner.

Serves 4–6
1 pineapple
30ml/2 tbsp vegetable oil
1 small onion, finely chopped
2 fresh green chillies, seeded and chopped
225g/8oz lean pork, cut into strips
115g/4oz cooked, peeled prawns (shrimp)
675–900g/1½–2lb/3–4 cups plain boiled rice, cooked and completely cold
50g/2oz/⅓ cup roasted cashew nuts
2 spring onions (scallions), chopped
30ml/2 tbsp fish sauce
15ml/1 tbsp soy sauce
2 fresh red chillies, sliced, and 10–12 fresh mint leaves, to garnish

1 Using a sharp knife, cut the pineapple in half. Remove the flesh from both halves by cutting around inside the skin. Reserve the pineapple skin shells for serving the rice.

2 Slice the pineapple flesh and chop it into small even cubes. You will need about 115g/4oz of pineapple in total. Any remaining fruit can be reserved for use in a dessert.

3 Heat the oil in a wok or large pan. Add the onion and chillies and fry for about 3–5 minutes until softened. Add the strips of pork and cook until they have browned on all sides.

4 Stir in the prawns and rice and toss them well together. Continue to stir-fry until the rice is thoroughly heated.

5 Add the chopped pineapple, cashew nuts and spring onions. Season to taste with fish sauce and soy sauce. Spoon into the pineapple shells and garnish with the chillies and mint leaves.

> **Cook's Tip**
> *When buying a pineapple, look for a sweet-smelling fruit with an even brownish/yellow skin. Tap the base – a dull sound means the fruit is ripe. It should also give slightly when pressed.*

Lemon-laced Rice

Lemon-laced rice is very popular all over India – its mildly acidic flavour is a perfect backdrop for any spicy curry. The dish also looks beautiful, with a pale yellow background for black mustard seeds, curry leaves and roasted cashew nuts. If you don't eat nuts, try adding a handful of toasted sunflower or pumpkin seeds instead.

Serves 4
225g/8oz/1¼ cups basmati rice
30ml/2 tbsp sunflower oil or olive oil
2.5ml/½ tsp black mustard seeds
10–12 curry leaves, preferably fresh
25g/1oz cashew nuts, broken
2.5ml/½ tsp ground turmeric
5ml/1 tsp salt, or to taste
30ml/2 tbsp lemon juice

1 Wash and rinse the rice two or three times in cold water, or until the water runs clear. Soak it for 15–20 minutes, rinse and drain it in a colander.

2 Heat the oil in a non-stick pan over a medium heat. When it is hot, but not smoking, add the mustard seeds, curry leaves and cashew nuts. Let them sizzle for 15–20 seconds.

3 Add the rice, turmeric and salt to the pan. Stir-fry the rice for 2–3 minutes, then add 475ml/16fl oz/2 cups hot water and the lemon juice.

4 Stir the pan once, bring to the boil and continue to boil for about 2 minutes. Cover the pan tightly, reduce the heat and simmer gently for an additional 7–8 minutes.

5 Remove the pan from the heat and leave to stand, undisturbed, for 6–7 minutes. Fork through the rice, and serve immediately as an accompaniment to curry.

> **Variation**
> *Replace the lemon juice with 15ml/1 tbsp lime juice and add 50g/2oz/⅓ cup raisins for a fruity variation on this theme.*

Lemon-laced Rice Energy 345kcal/1440kJ; Protein 6.9g; Carbohydrate 57.4g, of which sugars 0.4g; Fat 9.5g, of which saturates 1.4g; Cholesterol 0mg; Calcium 22mg; Fibre 0.2g; Sodium 20mg.
Pineapple Fried Rice Energy 176kcal/738kJ; Protein 4.4g; Carbohydrate 21.6g, of which sugars 5.2g; Fat 8.4g, of which saturates 1.4g; Cholesterol 8mg; Calcium 32mg; Fibre 1.5g; Sodium 344mg.

Rice with Seeds and Spices

Toasted sunflower and sesame seeds impart a rich, nutty flavour to rice spiced with turmeric, cardamom and coriander, for this delicious change from plain boiled rice, and a colourful accompaniment to serve with spicy curries.

Serves 4
5ml/1 tsp sunflower oil
2.5ml/½ tsp ground turmeric
6 cardamom pods, lightly crushed
5ml/1 tsp coriander seeds, lightly crushed
1 garlic clove, crushed
200g/7oz/1 cup basmati rice
400ml/14fl oz/1⅔ cups vegetable stock
115g/4oz/½ cup natural (plain) yogurt
15ml/1 tbsp toasted sunflower seeds
15ml/1 tbsp toasted sesame seeds
salt and ground black pepper
coriander (cilantro) leaves, to garnish

1 Heat the oil in a non-stick frying pan or wok and fry the turmeric, cardamom pods, coriander seeds and garlic for about 1 minute, stirring constantly.

2 Add the rice and stock, bring to the boil, then cover and simmer for 15 minutes, or until just tender.

3 Stir in the yogurt and the toasted sunflower and sesame seeds. Season with salt and ground black pepper and serve immediately, garnished with coriander leaves.

Cook's Tip
Seeds are particularly rich in minerals, so they are a good addition to all kinds of dishes. Light toasting in a frying pan or oven will improve their fine flavour.

Variation
Basmati rice gives the best texture and flavour for this dish, but you can also use ordinary long grain rice in place of the basmati rice, if you prefer.

Rice with Cinnamon and Star Anise

Originating from China, this thick rice porridge or 'congee', known as bubur in Malaysia and Indonesia, has become popular all over South-east Asia. The basic recipe is nourishing but rather bland, and the joy of the dish is derived from the ingredients that are added.

Serves 4–6
25g/1oz fresh root ginger, peeled and sliced
1 cinnamon stick
2 star anise
2.5ml/½ tsp salt
115g/4oz/½ cup short grain rice, thoroughly washed and drained

1 Bring 1.2 litres/2 pints/5 cups water to the boil in a heavy pan. Stir in the spices, the salt and the rice.

2 Reduce the heat, cover the pan, and simmer gently for 1 hour, or longer if you prefer a thicker, smoother consistency. Serve the rice while piping hot.

Variations
With the addition of pickles, strips of omelette and braised dishes, this cinnamon and star anise rice dish is popular for supper in Singapore. In Malaysia, it is enjoyed for breakfast with fried or grilled fish, chicken and beef, as well as with pickles. Often flavoured with ginger, cinnamon and star anise, it is usually cooked until it is thick but the grains are still visible, whereas some of the Chinese versions are cooked for longer, so that the rice breaks down completely and the texture is quite smooth. The consistency varies from family to family: some people like it soupy and eat it with a spoon.

Cook's Tip
This dish is often eaten for breakfast, in Malaysia, and some domestic rice cookers have a 'congee' setting, which allows the dish to be prepared the night before and slowly cooked overnight, in order to be ready in the morning.

Rice with Seeds Energy 310kcal/1294kJ; Protein 8.3g; Carbohydrate 53.5g, of which sugars 2.8g; Fat 6.7g, of which saturates 0.9g; Cholesterol 0mg; Calcium 117mg; Fibre 0.7g; Sodium 31mg.
Rice with Cinnamon Energy 235kcal/996kJ; Protein 4.3g; Carbohydrate 47.3g, of which sugars 1.9g; Fat 4.5g, of which saturates 0.8g; Cholesterol 0mg; Calcium 35mg; Fibre 1.9g; Sodium 6mg.

Basmati Rice and Peas

This is a very simple rice dish, but it is full of flavour and can make a useful quick main course.

Serves 4

300g/11oz/1½ cups basmati rice
15ml/1 tbsp vegetable oil
6–8 curry leaves
1.5ml/¼ tsp mustard seeds
1.5ml/¼ tsp onion seeds
30ml/2 tbsp fresh
 fenugreek leaves
5ml/1 tsp crushed garlic
5ml/1 tsp grated fresh root ginger
5ml/1 tsp salt
115g/4oz/1 cup frozen peas
475ml/16fl oz/2 cups water

1 Wash the rice well under cold running water and leave it to soak in a bowl of water for 30 minutes.

2 Heat the oil in a heavy pan and add the curry leaves, mustard seeds, onion seeds, fenugreek leaves, garlic, ginger and salt and stir-fry for 2–3 minutes.

3 Drain the rice thoroughly, and add it to the pan with the other ingredients. Stir gently to combine.

4 Add the frozen peas and water and bring to the boil. Lower the heat, cover with a lid and cook for 15–20 minutes. Remove from the heat and leave to stand, still covered, for 10 minutes.

5 When ready to serve, fluff up the rice with a fork. Spoon the mixture on to serving plates and serve immediately.

Colourful Pilau Rice

This lightly spiced rice makes an extremely attractive accompaniment to many balti dishes, and is easily made.

Serves 4–6

450g/1lb/2¼ cups
 basmati rice
75g/3oz/6 tbsp unsalted butter
4 cloves
4 green cardamom pods
1 bay leaf
5ml/1 tsp salt
1 litre/1¾ pints/4 cups water
a few drops each of yellow,
 green and red food
 colouring

1 Wash the basmati rice twice under cold running water, drain well and set aside in a sieve (strainer).

2 Melt the butter in a medium pan, and add the cloves, cardamoms, bay leaf and salt. Lower the heat and add the rice. Fry for about 1 minute, stirring constantly.

3 Add the water to the rice and spices and bring to the boil. As soon as it has boiled, cover the pan and reduce the heat. Cook for 10–15 minutes. Taste a grain of rice after 10 minutes; it should be slightly *al dente* (soft but with a bite in the centre).

4 Just before you are ready to serve the rice, pour a few drops of each colouring at different sides of the pan. Leave to stand for 5 minutes so that the colours can 'bleed' into the rice. Mix gently with a fork and serve immediately.

Pea and Mushroom Pilau

Tiny white button mushrooms and sweet petits pois, or baby peas, add an attractive splash of colour and flavour to this delectable rice dish.

Serves 6

450g/1lb/2¼ cups basmati rice
15ml/1 tbsp vegetable oil or
 sunflower oil
2.5ml/½ tsp cumin seeds
2 black cardamom pods
2 cinnamon sticks
3 garlic cloves, sliced
5ml/1 tsp salt
1 medium tomato, sliced
50g/2oz/⅔ cup button (white)
 mushrooms
75g/3oz/¾ cup petits pois
 (baby peas)
750ml/1¼ pints/3 cups water

1 Wash the rice well under cold running water and leave it to soak in water for 30 minutes.

2 In a medium, heavy pan or wok, heat the vegetable or sunflower oil and add the cumin seeds, cardamom pods, cinnamon sticks, garlic and salt.

3 Add the tomato and mushrooms to the pan and cook for about 2–3 minutes, stirring constantly.

4 Transfer the rice to a sieve (strainer) and drain it thoroughly. Add it to the pan with the peas. Stir gently, making sure that you do not break up the grains of rice.

5 Add the water to the pan and bring it to the boil. Lower the heat, cover tightly and continue to cook for about 15–20 minutes. Just before serving, remove the lid from the pan and fluff up the rice with a fork. Spoon into a warmed serving dish and serve immediately.

> **Cook's Tip**
> *Petits pois are small green peas, picked when very young. The tender, sweet peas inside the immature pods are ideal for this delicately flavoured rice dish. However, if you can't find petits pois, garden peas can be used instead.*

Basmati Rice and Peas Energy 329kcal/1373kJ; Protein 8.1g; Carbohydrate 64.4g, of which sugars 0.7g; Fat 4.1g, of which saturates 0.5g; Cholesterol 0mg; Calcium 27mg; Fibre 1.4g; Sodium 493mg.
Colourful Rice Energy 362kcal/1509kJ; Protein 5.6g; Carbohydrate 59.9g, of which sugars 0.1g; Fat 10.7g, of which saturates 6.5g; Cholesterol 27mg; Calcium 17mg; Fibre 0g; Sodium 403mg.
Pea and Mushroom Pilau Energy 304kcal/1272kJ; Protein 6.9g; Carbohydrate 62.2g, of which sugars 0.3g; Fat 2.8g, of which saturates 0.3g; Cholesterol 0mg; Calcium 22mg; Fibre 0.7g; Sodium 1mg.

Aromatic Indian Rice with Peas

This versatile rice dish is often served at elaborate meals for Indian festivals, which include meat and vegetable curries, a yogurt dish, and chutneys.

Serves 4

350g/12oz/1¾ cups basmati rice
45ml/3 tbsp ghee or 30ml/2 tbsp vegetable oil and a small amount of butter
1 cinnamon stick
6–8 cardamom pods, crushed
4 cloves
1 onion, halved lengthways and sliced
25g/1oz fresh root ginger, peeled and grated
5ml/1 tsp sugar
130g/4½oz fresh peas, shelled, or frozen peas
5ml/1 tsp salt

1 Rinse the rice and put it in a bowl. Cover with plenty of water and leave to soak for 30 minutes. Drain thoroughly.

2 Heat the ghee, or oil and butter, in a heavy pan. Stir in the cinnamon stick, cardamom and cloves.

3 Add the onion, ginger and sugar to the pan, and fry until golden, stirring frequently. Add the peas, followed by the rice, and stir for 1 minute to coat the rice in ghee.

4 Pour in 600ml/1 pint/2½ cups water. Add the salt, stir once and bring the liquid to the boil. Reduce the heat and allow to simmer for 15–20 minutes, until the liquid has been absorbed.

5 Turn off the heat, cover the pan with a clean dish towel and the lid, and leave the rice to steam for a further 10 minutes. Spoon the rice on to a serving dish.

> **Variations**
> • This dish also works with diced carrot or beetroot (beet), or chickpeas. You can also add a little tomato purée (paste) to give the rice a red tinge.
> • Sprinkle the rice with chopped fresh mint and coriander (cilantro), if you like, or with roasted chilli and coconut.

Mushroom Pilau

This dish is simplicity itself. Serve with any Indian dish or with roast lamb or chicken.

Serves 4

30ml/2 tbsp vegetable oil
2 shallots, finely chopped
1 garlic clove, crushed
3 green cardamom pods
25g/1oz/2 tbsp ghee or butter
175g/6oz/2½ cups button (white) mushrooms, sliced
225g/8oz/generous 1 cup basmati rice, soaked
5ml/1 tsp grated fresh root ginger
good pinch of garam masala
450ml/¾ pint/scant 2 cups water
15ml/1 tbsp chopped fresh coriander (cilantro)
salt

1 Heat the vegetable oil in a flameproof casserole and fry the shallots, garlic and cardamom pods over medium heat for about 3–4 minutes, stirring frequently, until the shallots have softened and are beginning to brown.

2 Add the ghee or butter. When it has melted, add the mushrooms and fry for 2–3 minutes more.

3 Add the rice, ginger and garam masala. Cook over low heat for 2–3 minutes, stirring constantly, then stir in the water and a little salt. Bring to the boil, then cover tightly and simmer over very low heat for 10 minutes.

4 Remove the casserole from the heat. Leave to stand, covered, for 5 minutes. Add the chopped fresh coriander and fork it through the rice. Spoon the rice into a warmed serving bowl and serve immediately.

> **Variation**
> For a nuttier pilau, fry 1.5ml/¼ tsp cumin seeds with the cardamom pods at step 1. When the rice has almost cooked, drain it and gently stir in a pinch of saffron threads and 15ml/1 tbsp ground almonds. Leave the rice to stand for a few minutes before serving. Alternatively, you could stir in a handful of toasted cashew nuts when the rice is ready.

Mushroom Pilau Energy 309kcal/1286kJ; Protein 5.2g; Carbohydrate 46.3g, of which sugars 1g; Fat 11.2g, of which saturates 4g; Cholesterol 13mg; Calcium 18mg; Fibre 0.7g; Sodium 41mg.
Aromatic Rice Energy 451kcal/1880kJ; Protein 8.9g; Carbohydrate 75.7g, of which sugars 2.6g; Fat 12.2g, of which saturates 5.4g; Cholesterol 0mg; Calcium 28mg; Fibre 1.8g; Sodium 328mg.

Sweet and Sour Rice

This popular Middle Eastern rice dish is flavoured with fruit and spices. Zereshk are small dried berries – use cranberries as a substitute.

Serves 4
50g/2oz/½ cup zereshk or
   fresh cranberries
45g/1½oz/3 tbsp butter
50g/2oz/⅓ cup raisins
50g/2oz/¼ cup sugar
5ml/1 tsp ground cinnamon
5ml/1 tsp ground cumin
350g/12oz/1¾ cups basmati
   rice, soaked
2–3 saffron strands, soaked in
   15ml/1 tbsp boiling water
pinch of salt

1 Thoroughly wash the zereshk or cranberries in cold water at least four or five times to rinse off any bits of grit. Drain well. Melt 15g/½oz/1 tbsp of the butter in a heavy frying pan and fry the raisins for 1–2 minutes.

2 Add the zereshk or cranberries, fry for a few seconds, and then add the sugar, with half of the cinnamon and cumin. Cook briefly and then set aside.

3 Drain the rice, then put it in a pan with plenty of boiling, lightly salted water. Bring back to the boil, reduce the heat and simmer for 4 minutes. Drain and rinse once again.

4 Melt half the remaining butter in the cleaned rice pan, add 15ml/1 tbsp water and stir in half the rice. Sprinkle with half the raisin mixture and top with all but 45ml/3 tbsp of the rice. Sprinkle over the remaining raisin mixture.

5 Mix the remaining cinnamon and cumin with the reserved rice, and sprinkle this mixture evenly over the layered mixture. Melt the remaining butter, drizzle it over the surface, then cover the pan with a clean dish towel. Cover with a tight-fitting lid, lifting the corners of the cloth back over the lid. Steam the rice over a very low heat for 20–30 minutes.

6 Just before serving, mix 45ml/3 tbsp of the rice with the saffron water. Spoon the sweet and sour rice on to a large, flat serving dish and sprinkle the saffron rice over the top, to garnish.

Tanzanian Vegetable Rice

Serve this tasty dish with baked chicken or fish. Add the vegetables near the end of cooking so that they remain crisp.

Serves 4
350g/12oz/1¾ cups basmati rice
45ml/3 tbsp vegetable oil
1 onion, chopped
2 garlic cloves, crushed
750ml/1¼ pints/3 cups vegetable
   stock or water
115g/4oz/⅔ cup fresh or drained
   canned corn kernels
½ red or green (bell) pepper,
   seeded and chopped
1 large carrot, grated
fresh chervil sprigs,
   to garnish

1 Rinse the rice in a sieve (strainer) under cold running water until the water runs clear. Set it aside in the sieve to drain thoroughly for about 15 minutes.

2 Heat the oil in a large pan or wok and fry the chopped onion for a few minutes over a medium heat, stirring frequently, until it starts to soften.

3 Add the rice to the pan and fry for about 10 minutes, stirring constantly to prevent the rice sticking to the bottom of the pan. Then stir in the crushed garlic.

4 Pour the stock or water into the pan and stir well. Bring to the boil, then lower the heat, cover the pan with a tight-fitting lid and simmer for 10 minutes.

5 Sprinkle the corn kernels over the rice, then spread the chopped pepper on top. Sprinkle over the grated carrot.

6 Cover the pan tightly. Steam over a low heat for about 15 minutes or until the rice is tender, then mix with a fork, pile on to a platter and garnish with chervil. Serve immediately.

> **Variation**
> You can replace the corn with the same quantity of fresh or frozen peas, if you prefer.

Sweet and Sour Rice Energy 465kcal/1943kJ; Protein 7g; Carbohydrate 87g, of which sugars 17.2g; Fat 9.8g, of which saturates 5.9g; Cholesterol 24mg; Calcium 32mg; Fibre 0.6g; Sodium 77mg.
Tanzanian Rice Energy 552kcal/2305kJ; Protein 12.7g; Carbohydrate 108.3g; of which sugars 4.8g; Fat 7g; of which saturates 1g; Cholesterol 0mg; Calcium 43mg; Fibre 3g; Sodium 10mg.

Chillies with Green Gram and Rice

The whole spices in this tasty dish are edible, although it is advisable to warn the diners about them to avoid any unexpected surprises.

Serves 4–6
60ml/4 tbsp ghee
1 onion, finely chopped
2 garlic cloves, crushed
2.5cm/1in piece fresh root
    ginger, grated

4 green chillies, chopped
4 whole cloves
2.5cm/1in cinnamon stick
4 whole green cardamoms
5ml/1 tsp turmeric
350g/12oz patna rice, washed
    and soaked for 20 minutes
175g/6oz split green gram,
    washed and soaked for
    20 minutes
600ml/1 pint/2½ cups water
salt

1 Gently heat the ghee in a large heavy pan with a tight-fitting lid. Fry the onion, garlic, ginger, chillies, cloves, cinnamon, cardamoms, turmeric and salt until the onion is beginning to turn soft and translucent.

2 Drain the rice and the green gram, and then add them to the spices in the pan and fry for 2–3 minutes.

3 Add the water to the pan and bring to the boil. Reduce the heat, cover and simmer for about 20–25 minutes, or until all the water has been absorbed.

4 Take the pan off the heat and leave to rest for 5 minutes. Gently toss the mixture together until the ingredients are well combined and serve immediately.

Cook's Tip
Ghee is a clarified unsalted butter widely used in Indian cooking. It has a nutty, caramel flavour and aroma and is made by simmering the butter until all water has boiled off and the milk solids have settled to the bottom. The lack of water and solids mean that it has a longer life and a higher smoking point than normal butter.

Red Fried Rice

This vibrant rice dish owes its appeal as much to the bright colours of its ingredients – red onion, red pepper and cherry tomatoes – as it does to their flavours.

Serves 2
130g/4½oz/¾ cup
    basmati rice

30ml/2 tbsp vegetable oil
1 small red onion, finely
    chopped
1 red (bell) pepper, seeded
    and chopped
225g/8oz cherry tomatoes,
    cut into halves
2 eggs, beaten
salt and ground black pepper
chopped fresh coriander (cilantro),
    to garnish

1 Wash the rice several times under cold running water until the water runs clear. Drain well and set aside.

2 Bring a large pan of water to the boil. Add the basmati rice and cook for 10–12 minutes.

3 Meanwhile, heat the oil in a wok or large, heavy pan until it is very hot. Add the onion and red pepper to the pan and stir-fry for about 2–3 minutes.

4 Add the cherry tomatoes to the pan and continue cooking for 2 minutes more, stirring frequently.

5 Pour the beaten eggs into the pan all at once. Cook for about 30 seconds without stirring, then stir to break up the egg as it just begins to set.

6 Drain the cooked rice thoroughly. Add to the pan and toss it over the heat with the vegetables and egg mixture for about 3 minutes. Season with salt and ground black pepper to taste, sprinkle with the coriander and serve immediately.

Variation
To add even more colour to this bright dish, you could replace the red (bell) pepper with an orange or green variety.

Chillies with Rice Energy 397kcal/1662kJ; Protein 11.6g; Carbohydrate 63.8g, of which sugars 1.3g; Fat 10.7g, of which saturates 4.8g; Cholesterol 0mg; Calcium 31mg; Fibre 1.6g; Sodium 12mg.
Red Fried Rice Energy 437kcal/1821kJ; Protein 12.6g; Carbohydrate 57.4g, of which sugars 10.5g; Fat 17.6g, of which saturates 3.1g; Cholesterol 190mg; Calcium 62mg; Fibre 3g; Sodium 85mg.

Basmati Rice with Potato

Rice is eaten at all meals in Indian and Pakistani homes. There are several ways of cooking rice, and mostly whole spices are used. Always choose a good-quality basmati rice.

Serves 4

300g/11oz/1½ cups basmati rice
15ml/1 tbsp vegetable oil
1 small cinnamon stick
1 bay leaf
1.5ml/¼ tsp black cumin seeds
3 green cardamom pods
1 medium onion, sliced
5ml/1 tsp grated fresh root ginger
5ml/1 tsp crushed garlic
1.5ml/¼ tsp ground turmeric
7.5ml/1½ tsp salt
1 large potato, roughly diced
475ml/16fl oz/2 cups water
15ml/1 tbsp chopped fresh
    coriander (cilantro)

1 Wash the rice well under cold running water and leave it to soak in water for 20 minutes.

2 Heat the oil in a heavy pan, add the cinnamon, bay leaf, black cumin seeds, cardamom pods and onion and cook for about 2 minutes, stirring constantly.

3 Add the ginger, garlic, turmeric, salt and potato to the pan, and cook for a further 1 minute.

4 Drain the rice thoroughly. Add it to the potato and spices in the pan and stir well to combine the ingredients.

5 Pour the water into the pan and then stir in the coriander. Cover the pan with a lid and cook for 15–20 minutes.

6 Remove the pan from the heat and leave to stand, still covered, for 5–10 minutes before serving.

Cook's Tip
It is important to observe the full standing time for this dish before serving. Use a slotted spoon to serve the rice and potato mixture and handle it carefully to avoid breaking or damaging the delicate grains of rice.

Tricolour Pilau Rice

Most Indian restaurants in the West serve this popular vegetable pilau, which has three different vegetables. The effect is easily achieved with canned or frozen vegetables, but for entertaining or a special occasion dinner, you may prefer to use fresh produce.

Serves 4–6

30ml/2 tbsp vegetable oil
2.5ml/½ tsp cumin seeds
2 dried bay leaves
4 green cardamom pods
4 cloves
1 onion, finely chopped
1 carrot, finely diced
225g/8oz/1 cup basmati rice,
    rinsed and soaked for
    30 minutes
50g/2oz/½ cup frozen
    peas, thawed
50g/2oz/⅓ cup frozen
    corn, thawed
25g/1oz/¼ cup cashew nuts,
    lightly fried
475ml/16fl oz/2 cups water
1.5ml/¼ tsp ground cumin
salt

1 Heat the oil in a wok, karahi or large pan over medium heat, and fry the cumin seeds for 2 minutes.

2 Add the bay leaves, cardamoms and cloves to the pan, and fry gently for about 2 minutes more, stirring the spices from time to time so they do not catch on the pan base.

3 Add the chopped onion to the pan and fry for about 5–6 minutes until lightly browned. Stir in the diced carrot and cook, stirring, for a further 3–4 minutes.

4 Drain the soaked basmati rice and add to the contents of the pan. Stir well to combine the ingredients. Add the peas, corn and fried cashew nuts.

5 Pour the measured water into the pan and add the ground cumin. Season with salt to taste. Bring to the boil, cover with a lid and simmer for 15 minutes over low heat until all the water is absorbed.

6 Leave the rice to stand, still covered, for 10 minutes. Transfer to a warmed serving dish and serve.

Basmati Rice with Potato Energy 355kcal/1483kJ; Protein 7.2g; Carbohydrate 70.5g, of which sugars 1.5g; Fat 4.8g, of which saturates 0.6g; Cholesterol 0mg; Calcium 28mg; Fibre 0.7g; Sodium 745mg.
Tricolour Pilau Rice Energy 221kcal/922kJ; Protein 4.9g; Carbohydrate 35.5g, of which sugars 1.8g; Fat 6.5g, of which saturates 0.9g; Cholesterol 0mg; Calcium 18mg; Fibre 0.8g; Sodium 36mg.

Naan

Probably the most popular bread enjoyed with an Indian curry is naan, which was introduced from Persia. Traditionally, naan is not rolled, but patted and stretched until the teardrop shape is achieved. You can, of course, roll it out to a circle, then gently pull the lower end, which will give you the traditional shape.

Makes 3

225g/8oz/2 cups unbleached strong white bread flour
2.5ml/½ tsp salt
15g/½ oz fresh yeast
60ml/4 tbsp milk, heated until lukewarm
15ml/1 tbsp vegetable oil
30ml/2 tbsp natural (plain) yogurt
1 egg, beaten
30–45ml/2–3 tbsp melted ghee or butter, for brushing

1 Sift the flour and salt together into a large bowl. In a smaller bowl, cream the yeast with the milk. Set aside for 15 minutes.

2 Add the yeast and milk mixture, vegetable oil, yogurt and egg to the flour. Combine the mixture using your hands until it forms a soft dough. Add a little lukewarm water if the dough is too dry.

3 Turn the dough out on to a lightly floured surface and knead for about 10 minutes, or until it feels smooth. Return the dough to the bowl, cover and leave in a warm place for about 1 hour, or until it has doubled in size. Preheat the oven to its highest setting – it should not be any lower than 230°C/450°F/Gas 8.

4 Turn out the dough back on to the floured surface and knead for a further 2 minutes. Divide into three equal pieces, shape into balls and roll out into teardrop shapes 25cm/10in long, 13cm/5in wide and 5mm–8mm/¼–⅓in thick.

5 Preheat the grill (broiler) to its highest setting. Meanwhile, place the naan on preheated baking sheets and bake for 3–4 minutes, or until puffed up.

6 Place under the hot grill for a few seconds until the tops brown. Brush with ghee or butter and serve warm.

Garlic and Coriander Naan

Traditionally cooked in a very hot clay oven known as a tandoor, naan are usually eaten with dry meat or vegetable dishes.

Makes 3

275g/10oz/2½ cups unbleached strong white bread flour
5ml/1 tsp salt
5ml/1 tsp dried yeast
60ml/4 tbsp natural (plain) yogurt
15ml/1 tbsp melted butter or ghee, plus 30–45ml/2–3 tbsp for brushing
1 garlic clove, finely chopped
5ml/1 tsp black onion seeds
15ml/1 tbsp chopped fresh coriander (cilantro)
10ml/2 tsp clear honey, warmed

1 Sift the flour and salt together into a large bowl. In a smaller bowl, cream the yeast with the yogurt. Set aside for 15 minutes. Add the yeast mixture to the flour with the smaller quantity of melted butter or ghee, and add the chopped garlic, black onion seeds and chopped coriander, mixing to a soft dough.

2 Transfer the dough on to a lightly floured surface and knead for about 10 minutes until smooth and elastic. Place in a lightly oiled bowl, cover with lightly oiled clear film (plastic wrap) and leave to rise in a warm place for about 45 minutes, or until the dough has doubled in bulk.

3 Preheat the oven to 230°C/450°F/Gas 8. Place three heavy baking sheets in the oven to heat. Turn the dough out on to a lightly floured surface and knock back (punch down). Divide into three equal pieces and shape each into a ball.

4 Cover two of the balls of dough with oiled clear film and roll out the third into a teardrop shape about 25cm/10in long, 13cm/5in wide and about 5mm–8mm/¼–⅓in thick. Preheat the grill (broiler) to its highest setting. Place the single naan on a hot baking sheet and bake for about 3–4 minutes, or until it has puffed up.

5 Remove the naan from the oven, brush with honey and grill for a few seconds or until browned slightly. Wrap in a clean dish towel to keep warm while you roll out and cook the remaining naan. Brush with melted butter or ghee and serve warm.

Naan Energy 315kcal/1334kJ; Protein 9.4g; Carbohydrate 58.5g, of which sugars 1.5g; Fat 6.5g, of which saturates 1.1g; Cholesterol 63mg; Calcium 123mg; Fibre 2.3g; Sodium 356mg.
Garlic Naan Energy 374kcal/1585kJ; Protein 10.4g; Carbohydrate 74.2g, of which sugars 2.9g; Fat 6.1g, of which saturates 3g; Cholesterol 11mg; Calcium 176mg; Fibre 2.8g; Sodium 706mg.

Spiced Naan

Another excellent recipe for naan bread, this time it features the aromatic fennel seeds, onion seeds and cumin seeds.

Makes 6

450g/1lb/4 cups strong white
  bread flour
5ml/1 tsp baking powder
2.5ml/½ tsp salt
1 sachet easy-blend (rapid-rise)
  dried yeast
5ml/1 tsp caster
  (superfine) sugar
5ml/1 tsp fennel seeds
10ml/2 tsp onion seeds
5ml/1 tsp cumin seeds
150ml/¼ pint/⅔ cup
  hand-hot milk
30ml/2 tbsp vegetable oil,
  plus extra for brushing
150ml/¼ pint/⅔ cup natural
  (plain) yogurt
1 egg, beaten

1 Sift the flour, baking powder and salt into a mixing bowl. Stir in the yeast, sugar, fennel seeds, onion seeds and cumin seeds. Make a well in the centre. Stir the hand-hot milk into the flour mixture, then add the oil, yogurt and beaten egg. Mix to form a ball of dough.

2 Transfer the dough on to a lightly floured surface and knead it for 10 minutes until smooth. Return to the clean, lightly oiled bowl and roll the dough to coat it with oil. Cover the bowl with clear film (plastic wrap) and set aside in a warm place until the dough has doubled in bulk.

3 Put a heavy baking sheet in the oven and preheat the oven to 240°C/475°F/Gas 9. Also preheat the grill (broiler). Knead the dough again lightly and divide it into six pieces. Keep five pieces covered while working with the sixth. Quickly roll the piece of dough out to a teardrop shape, brush lightly with oil and slap the naan on to the hot baking sheet. Repeat with the remaining dough.

4 Bake the naan in the preheated oven for about 3 minutes or until they have puffed up, then place the baking sheets under the grill for about 30 seconds or until the naan are lightly browned. Serve hot or warm as an accompaniment to an Indian curry.

Chapatis

A chapati is an unleavened bread that is made from chapati flour, a wholemeal flour known as atta, which is finer than the Western equivalent. An equal quantity of standard wholemeal flour and plain flour will also produce satisfactory results, although chapati flour is widely available from Indian grocers.

This is the everyday bread of the Indian home.

Makes 8–10

225g/8oz/2 cups chapati flour
  or an equal quantity of
  wholemeal (whole-wheat) flour
  and plain (all-purpose) flour
2.5ml/½ tsp salt
175ml/6fl oz/¾ cup water

1 Sift the flour and salt into a large mixing bowl. Make a well in the centre and gradually stir in the water, mixing it well with your fingers.

2 Form a supple dough and knead for 7–10 minutes. Ideally, cover with clear film (plastic wrap) and leave to one side for 15–20 minutes to rest.

3 Divide the dough into eight to ten equal portions. Roll out each piece to a circle on a well-floured surface.

4 Place a tava (chapati griddle) or heavy frying pan over high heat. When steam rises from it, lower the heat to medium and add the first chapati to the pan.

5 When the chapati begins to bubble, carefully turn it over. Press down with a clean dish towel or a flat spoon and turn the chapati over once again.

6 Remove the cooked chapati from the pan and keep warm in a piece of foil lined with kitchen paper while you cook the other chapatis.

7 Repeat the process until all the dough has been used up. Serve immediately.

Spiced Naan Energy 311kcal/1319kJ; Protein 11g; Carbohydrate 63.8g, of which sugars 4.9g; Fat 3.2g, of which saturates 0.9g; Cholesterol 34mg; Calcium 197mg; Fibre 2.3g; Sodium 211mg.
Chapatis Energy 99kcal/421kJ; Protein 3.7g; Carbohydrate 19.9g, of which sugars 0.5g; Fat 1.1g, of which saturates 0.2g; Cholesterol 0mg; Calcium 38mg; Fibre 1.9g; Sodium 165mg.

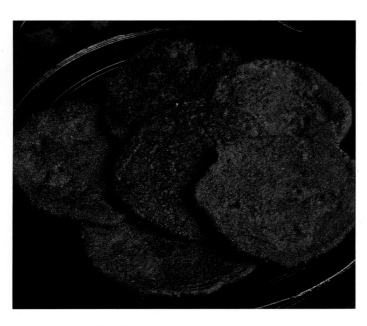

Red Lentil Pancakes

This is a type of *dosa*, which is essentially a pancake from southern India, but it is used in a similar fashion to north Indian bread.

Makes 6
150g/5oz/¾ cup long
   grain rice
50g/2oz/¼ cup red split lentils
250ml/8fl oz/1 cup warm water
5ml/1 tsp salt
2.5ml/½ tsp ground turmeric
2.5ml/½ tsp ground black pepper
30ml/2 tbsp chopped fresh
   coriander (cilantro)
vegetable oil, for frying
   and drizzling

1 Place the rice and lentils in a large bowl, cover with the warm water, cover and soak for at least 8 hours or overnight.

2 Drain off the water and reserve. Place the rice and lentils in a food processor or blender and blend until smooth. Blend in the reserved soaking water. Scrape into a bowl, cover tightly with clear film (plastic wrap) and leave in a warm place to ferment for about 24 hours.

3 Stir the salt, turmeric, black pepper and coriander into the rice mixture. Heat a heavy frying pan over medium heat for a few minutes until hot. Smear the pan with oil and add about 30–45ml/2–3 tbsp of the batter mixture.

4 Using the rounded base of a soup spoon, gently spread the batter out, using a circular motion, to make a pancake that is about 15cm/6in in diameter.

5 Cook in the pan for 1½–2 minutes, or until set. Drizzle a little oil over the pancake and around the edges. Turn over and cook for about 1 minute, or until golden brown. Keep the cooked pancakes warm in a low oven or on a plate over simmering water while cooking the remaining pancakes. Serve warm.

> **Variation**
> Add 60ml/4 tbsp grated coconut to the batter just before cooking to create a richer flavour.

Parathas

Making paratha is similar to making flaky pastry, although paratha can be handled freely, unlike flaky pastry.

Makes 12–15
350g/12oz/3 cups chapati flour
   or an equal quantity of
   wholemeal (whole-wheat) flour
   and plain (all-purpose) flour
50g/2oz/½ cup plain
   (all-purpose) flour for dusting
   work surfaces
50g/2oz/½ cup plain
   (all-purpose) flour
5ml/1 tsp salt
40g/1½oz/3 tbsp ghee or
   unsalted butter

1 Sift the flours and salt into a bowl. Make a well in the centre and add 10ml/2 tsp melted ghee or butter. Fold it into the flour to make a crumbly texture.

2 Gradually add water to the flour and ghee or butter in the bowl to make a soft, pliable dough. Knead until the dough is smooth. Cover and leave to rest for 30 minutes.

3 Heat the remaining ghee or butter in a small heavy pan over low heat until fully melted. Divide the dough into about 12–15 equal portions and keep covered.

4 Take one portion at a time and roll out on a lightly floured surface or chopping board to about 10cm/4in in diameter.

5 Brush the dough with a little of the melted ghee or butter and sprinkle with flour.

6 With a sharp knife, make a straight cut from the centre to the edge of the dough, then lift a cut edge and roll the dough into a cone shape. Lift it and flatten it again into a ball.

7 Roll the dough out again on a lightly floured surface or chopping board until it is about 18cm/7in wide.

8 Heat a griddle and cook one paratha at a time, placing a little of the remaining ghee along the edges. Cook on each side until golden brown. Serve immediately while hot.

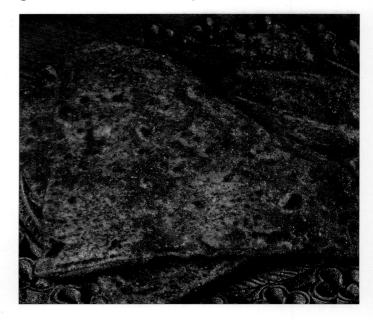

Red Lentil Pancakes Energy 153kcal/641kJ; Protein 4.1g; Carbohydrate 25.1g, of which sugars 0.3g; Fat 4.1g, of which saturates 0.4g; Cholesterol 0mg; Calcium 21mg; Fibre 0.7g; Sodium 333mg.
Parathas Energy 108kcal/456kJ; Protein 2.3g; Carbohydrate 19.2g, of which sugars 0.4g; Fat 3g, of which saturates 1.3g; Cholesterol 0mg; Calcium 35mg; Fibre 0.8g; Sodium 132mg.

Missi Rotis

These delicious unleavened breads are a speciality from Punjab in India. Gram flour, also known as besan, is made from ground chickpeas and is combined here with the traditional wheat flour.

Makes 4
115g/4oz/1 cup gram flour
115g/4oz/1 cup wholemeal
  (whole-wheat) flour
1 fresh green chilli, seeded
  and chopped
½ onion, finely chopped
15ml/1 tbsp chopped fresh
  coriander (cilantro)
2.5ml/½ tsp ground turmeric
2.5ml/½ tsp salt
15ml/1 tbsp vegetable oil or
  melted butter
120–150ml/4–5fl oz/½– ⅔ cup
  lukewarm water
30–45ml/2–3 tbsp melted
  unsalted butter or ghee

1 Mix the two types of flour, chilli, onion, coriander, turmeric and salt together in a large mixing bowl. Stir in the 15ml/1 tbsp vegetable oil or melted butter.

2 Mix sufficient water into the mixture to make a pliable soft dough. Turn out the dough on to a lightly floured surface and knead with your hands until smooth.

3 Place in a lightly oiled bowl, cover with lightly oiled clear film (plastic wrap) and leave to rest for 30 minutes.

4 Turn the dough out on to a lightly floured surface. Divide the dough into four equal pieces and shape into balls in the palms of your hands. Roll out each ball into a thick round about 15–18cm/6–7in in diameter.

5 Heat a griddle or heavy frying pan over medium heat for a few minutes until hot. Brush both sides of one roti with some melted butter or ghee. Add it to the griddle or frying pan and cook for about 2 minutes, turning after 1 minute.

6 Brush the cooked roti lightly with melted butter or ghee again, slide it on to a plate and keep warm in a low oven while cooking the remaining rotis in the same way. Serve the rotis immediately while still warm.

Tandoori Rotis

Roti means bread, and it is the most common food in central and northern India. For generations, roti has been made with just wholemeal flour, salt and water, although the art of making rotis is generally more refined these days.

Makes 6
350g/12oz/3 cups chapati
  flour or wholemeal
  (whole-wheat) flour
5ml/1 tsp salt
250ml/8fl oz/1 cup water
30–45ml/2–3 tbsp melted ghee
  or unsalted butter,
  for brushing

1 Sift the flour and salt into a large mixing bowl. Add the water to the bowl and mix it with your hands or a wooden spoon until a soft, pliable dough forms.

2 Knead the dough on a lightly floured work surface for about 3–4 minutes until smooth.

3 Place the dough in a lightly oiled bowl, cover with lightly oiled clear film (plastic wrap) and leave to rest for 1 hour.

4 Turn out the dough on to a lightly floured surface. Divide the dough into six even pieces and shape each into a ball with your hands. Press out into a larger round with the palm of your hand, cover with a piece of lightly oiled clear film and leave to rest for about 10 minutes.

5 Meanwhile, preheat the oven to 230°C/450°F/Gas 8. Place three baking sheets in the oven to heat.

6 Roll the rotis into 15cm/6in rounds, place two on each baking sheet and bake for 8–10 minutes. Brush with melted ghee or butter and serve warm.

Cook's Tip
Tandoori rotis are traditionally baked in a tandoor, or clay oven, but they can also be made successfully in an electric or gas oven set at the highest setting.

Missi Rotis Energy 298kcal/1267kJ; Protein 8.5g; Carbohydrate 65.8g, of which sugars 1.6g; Fat 2g, of which saturates 0.3g; Cholesterol 0mg; Calcium 114mg; Fibre 3.2g; Sodium 3mg.
Tandoori Rotis Energy 244kcal/1030kJ; Protein 5.5g; Carbohydrate 45.3g, of which sugars 0.9g; Fat 5.8g, of which saturates 2.5g; Cholesterol 0mg; Calcium 82mg; Fibre 1.8g; Sodium 329mg.

Pooris

These delicious little deep-fried breads, shaped into discs, make it very easy to overindulge.

Makes 12

115g/4oz/1 cup unbleached plain (all-purpose) flour
115g/4oz/1 cup wholemeal (whole-wheat) flour
2.5ml/½ tsp salt
2.5ml/½ tsp chilli powder
30ml/2 tbsp vegetable oil
100–120ml/3½–4fl oz/ scant ⅓ – ½ cup water
vegetable oil, for frying

1 Sift the flours, salt and chilli powder, if using, into a mixing bowl. Add the vegetable oil then add sufficient water to mix to a dough. Turn out on to a lightly floured surface and knead for 8–10 minutes until smooth. Place in an oiled bowl and cover with oiled clear film (plastic wrap). Leave for 30 minutes.

2 Turn out on to the floured surface. Divide the dough into 12 equal pieces. Keeping the rest of the dough covered, roll one piece into a 13cm/5in round. Repeat with the remaining dough. Stack the pooris, layered between sheets of lightly oiled clear film, to keep them moist.

3 Pour the oil for frying to a depth of 2.5cm/1in in a deep frying pan and heat it to 180°C/350°F. Lift one poori and gently slide it into the oil; it will sink but will then return to the surface and begin to sizzle. Gently press the poori into the oil. It will puff up. Turn the poori over after a few seconds and allow it to cook for a further 20–30 seconds.

4 Remove the poori from the pan and pat dry with kitchen paper. Place the cooked poori on a large baking tray, in a single layer, and keep warm in a low oven while you cook the remaining pooris. Serve immediately while warm.

> **Variation**
> For spinach-flavoured pooris, thaw 50g/2oz frozen spinach, drain, and add to the dough with a little grated fresh root ginger and 2.5ml/½ tsp ground cumin.

Bhaturas

These leavened and deep-fried breads are from Punjab, where the local people enjoy them with a bowl of chickpea curry.

Makes 10

15g/½oz fresh yeast
5ml/1 tsp sugar
120ml/4fl oz/½ cup lukewarm water
200g/7oz/1¾ cups plain (all-purpose) flour
50g/2oz/½ cup semolina
2.5ml/½ tsp salt
15g/½oz/1 tbsp ghee or butter
30ml/2 tbsp natural (plain) yogurt
vegetable oil, for frying

1 Mix the yeast with the sugar and water in a jug (pitcher). Sift the flour into a large mixing bowl and stir in the semolina and salt. Rub in the ghee or butter.

2 Add the yeast mixture and yogurt to the bowl and mix to a dough. Turn out on to a lightly floured surface and knead for about 10 minutes until smooth and elastic.

3 Place the dough in an oiled bowl, cover with oiled clear film (plastic wrap) and leave to rise, in a warm place, for about 1 hour, or until doubled in size.

4 Turn out on to a lightly floured surface and knock back (punch down). Divide into ten equal pieces and shape each into a ball. Flatten into discs with the palm of your hand. Roll out on a lightly floured surface into 13cm/5in rounds.

5 Heat oil to a depth of 1cm/½in in a deep frying pan and slide in one bhatura. Fry for 1 minute, turning over after 30 seconds, then drain on kitchen paper. Keep warm in a low oven while frying the remaining bhaturas. Serve immediately, while hot.

> **Cook's Tip**
> Ghee is available from Indian stores and some supermarkets but is easy to make at home. Melt unsalted butter over low heat. Simmer gently until the residue becomes light golden, then leave to cool. Strain through muslin (cheesecloth).

Pooris Energy 120kcal/501kJ; Protein 2.1g; Carbohydrate 13.5g, of which sugars 0.3g; Fat 6.7g, of which saturates 0.8g; Cholesterol 0mg; Calcium 17mg; Fibre 1.2g; Sodium 164mg.
Bhaturas Energy 141kcal/590kJ; Protein 2.6g; Carbohydrate 19.7g, of which sugars 0.5g; Fat 6.3g, of which saturates 1.3g; Cholesterol 0mg; Calcium 35mg; Fibre 0.7g; Sodium 102mg.

Thin and Crispy Flat Bread

Thin and crispy, this flat bread is universally eaten throughout the Middle East. It's ideal for serving with soups and appetizers.

Makes 10

275g/10oz/2½ cups unbleached
  strong white bread flour
175g/6oz/1½ cups wholemeal
  (whole-wheat) flour
5ml/1 tsp salt
15g/½oz fresh yeast
250ml/8fl oz/1 cup lukewarm
  water
60ml/4 tbsp natural (plain) yogurt
  or milk

1 Sift the flours and salt together into a large bowl and make a well in the centre. Mix the yeast with half the lukewarm water until creamy, then stir in the remaining water.

2 Add the yeast mixture and yogurt or milk to the centre of the flour and mix to a soft dough. Turn out on to a lightly floured surface and knead for 8–10 minutes until smooth and elastic. Place in a lightly oiled bowl, cover with lightly oiled clear film (plastic wrap) and leave to rise, in a warm place, for about 1 hour, or until doubled in bulk. Knock back (punch down) the dough, re-cover and leave to rise for 30 minutes.

3 Turn the dough back out on to a lightly floured surface. Knock back gently and divide into ten equal pieces. Shape into balls, then flatten into discs with the palm of your hand. Cover and leave it to rest for 5 minutes.

4 Meanwhile, preheat the oven to the maximum temperature – it should be at least 230°C/450°F/Gas 8. Place three or four baking sheets in the oven to heat.

5 Roll the dough as thinly as possible, then lift it over the backs of your hands and stretch and turn the dough. Leave to rest in between rolling for a few minutes if necessary to avoid tearing.

6 Place four on the baking sheets and bake for 6–8 minutes, or until starting to brown. Stack the remaining rolled dough, layered between clear film to keep moist. Transfer to a wire rack to cool and cook the remaining breads. Serve hot.

Syrian Onion Bread

The basic Arab breads of the Levant and Gulf have traditionally been made with a finely ground wholemeal flour similar to chapati flour, but now are being made with white flour as well. This Syrian version has a tasty, aromatic topping.

Makes 8

450g/1lb/4 cups unbleached
  strong white bread flour
5ml/1 tsp salt
20g/¾oz fresh yeast
280ml/9fl oz/scant 1¼ cups
  lukewarm water

For the topping
60ml/4 tbsp finely
  chopped onion
5ml/1 tsp ground cumin
10ml/2 tsp ground coriander
10ml/2 tsp chopped
  fresh mint
30ml/2 tbsp olive oil

1 Lightly flour two baking sheets. Sift the flour and salt together into a large mixing bowl and make a well in the centre. Cream the yeast with a little of the water in a small bowl, then mix in the remaining yeast until well combined.

2 Add the yeast mixture to the centre of the flour and mix to a firm dough. Turn out on to a lightly floured surface and knead for 8–10 minutes until smooth and elastic.

3 Place the dough in a lightly oiled bowl, cover with lightly oiled clear film (plastic wrap) and leave to rise, in a warm place, for about 1 hour, or until doubled in size.

4 Knock back (punch down) the dough and turn out on to a lightly floured work surface. Divide the dough into eight equal pieces and roll into 13–15cm/5–6in rounds. Make them slightly concave. Prick all over with a fork and space well apart on the baking sheets. Cover with lightly oiled clear film and leave to rise for about 15–20 minutes.

5 Meanwhile, preheat the oven to 200°C/400°F/Gas 6. Mix the chopped onion, ground cumin, ground coriander and chopped mint in a bowl. Brush the breads with the olive oil for the topping, sprinkle them evenly with the spicy onion mixture and bake for 15–20 minutes. Serve the onion breads warm.

Flat Bread Energy 108kcal/456kJ; Protein 2.3g; Carbohydrate 19.2g, of which sugars 0.4g; Fat 3g, of which saturates 1.3g; Cholesterol 0mg; Calcium 35mg; Fibre 0.8g; Sodium 132mg.
Syrian Bread Energy 220kcal/932kJ; Protein 5.5g; Carbohydrate 44.4g, of which sugars 1.3g; Fat 3.5g, of which saturates 0.5g; Cholesterol 0mg; Calcium 85mg; Fibre 1.9g; Sodium 248mg.

Winter Melon Pachadi

In India, there are a variety of pachadi and raita dishes designed to cool the palate and aid digestion when eating spicy food. These are made with yogurt and cooling vegetables and herbs, such as winter melon, okra, courgette, spinach, pumpkin, and cucumber with mint.

Serves 4

225g/8oz winter melon, peeled, seeded and diced
5ml/1 tsp ground turmeric
5ml/1 tsp red chilli powder
300ml/½ pint/1¼ cups Greek (US strained plain) yogurt
2.5ml/½ tsp salt
2.5ml/½ tsp sugar
15g/½oz fresh root ginger, peeled and grated
1 green chilli, seeded and finely chopped
15ml/1 tbsp vegetable oil
1.5ml/¼ tsp ground asafoetida
5ml/1 tsp brown mustard seeds
8–10 dried curry leaves
1 dried red chilli, seeded and roughly chopped

1 Put the winter melon in a heavy pan with the turmeric and chilli powder and pour in enough water to just cover. Bring to the boil and cook gently, uncovered, until the winter melon is tender and all the water has evaporated.

2 In a bowl, beat the yogurt with the salt and sugar until smooth and creamy. Add the ginger and green chilli, and fold in the warm winter melon.

3 Heat the oil in small heavy pan. Stir in the asafoetida and the mustard seeds. As soon as the mustard seeds pop, stir in the curry leaves and dried chilli. When the chilli darkens, add the spices to the yogurt and mix well. Serve at room temperature.

Cook's Tip
In Malaysia and Singapore cooling Indian dishes like pachadi are often served at the Indian and Malay stalls and coffee shops to balance the hot curries and spicy grilled dishes. In many Indian households, the pachadi is made a day or two in advance, so that the flavours mingle.

Cucumber and Pineapple Sambal

Sambals are the little side dishes served at almost every Malay meal. In poorer societies, a main meal may simply be a bowl of rice and a sambal made from pounded shrimp paste, chillies and lime juice: the sambal is poured over the rice to give it flavour. This recipe is known as sambal nanas. Use sparingly, as it is quite fiery.

Serves 8–10

1 small or ½ large fresh ripe pineapple
½ cucumber, halved lengthways
50g/2oz dried shrimps
1 large fresh red chilli, seeded and roughly chopped
1cm/½in cube shrimp paste, prepared
juice of 1 large lemon or lime
soft light brown sugar, to taste (optional)
salt

1 Cut off the top and the bottom of the pineapple. Stand it upright on a board, then slice off the skin from top to bottom, cutting out the spines. Slice the pineapple, removing the central core. Cut into thin slices and set aside.

2 Trim the ends from the cucumber and slice thinly. Sprinkle with salt and set aside. Place the dried shrimps in a food processor and chop finely. Add the chopped red chilli, prepared shrimp paste and lemon or lime juice, and process again until a coarse paste has formed.

3 Rinse the cucumber, drain and dry on kitchen paper. Mix with the pineapple and chill. Just before serving, spoon in the spice mixture with sugar to taste, if liked. Mix well and serve.

Cook's Tip
The pungent shrimp paste, also called blachan and terasi, is popular in many South-east Asian countries, and is available in Asian food markets. Since it can taste a bit raw in a sambal, dry-fry it by wrapping it in foil and heating it in a frying pan over a low heat for 5 minutes, turning from time to time. If the shrimp paste is to be fried with other spices, this preliminary cooking can be eliminated.

Melon Pachadi Energy 127kcal/527kJ; Protein 5.1g; Carbohydrate 5.3g, of which sugars 5.3g; Fat 10.5g, of which saturates 4.2g; Cholesterol 0mg; Calcium 120mg; Fibre 0.2g; Sodium 316mg.
Cucumber Sambal Energy 105kcal/446kJ; Protein 13.3g; Carbohydrate 11.9g, of which sugars 11.9g; Fat 0.8g, of which saturates 0.1g; Cholesterol 114mg; Calcium 298mg; Fibre 1.5g; Sodium 1715mg.

Chilli and Mustard Pineapple

Pineapple is cooked with coconut milk and a blend of spices in this South Indian dish, which could be served with any meat, fish or vegetable curry. The chilli adds heat, and the mustard seeds lend a nutty flavour that complements the sweet pineapple.

Serves 4
1 pineapple
50ml/2fl oz/¼ cup water
150ml/¼ pint/⅔ cup
   coconut milk
2.5ml/½ tsp ground turmeric
2.5ml/½ tsp crushed dried
   red chillies
5ml/1 tsp salt
10ml/2 tsp sugar
15ml/1 tbsp groundnut
   (peanut) oil or vegetable oil
2.5ml/½ tsp mustard seeds
2.5ml/½ tsp cumin seeds
1 small onion or ½ large onion,
   finely chopped
1–2 dried red chillies, seeded
   and broken up
6–8 curry leaves

1 Halve the pineapple lengthways and cut each half into two, so that you end up with four boat-shaped pieces. Peel them and remove the eyes and the central core and discard. Cut the flesh into bitesize pieces.

2 Put the pineapple in a wok, karahi or large pan and add the measured water, with the coconut milk, turmeric and crushed chillies. Bring to a slow simmer over a low heat, and cook, covered, for 10–12 minutes, or until the pineapple is just soft, but do not let it go mushy.

3 Add the salt and sugar to the pineapple, and cook, uncovered, until the sauce thickens.

4 Heat the oil in a second pan, and add the mustard seeds. As soon as they begin to pop, add the cumin seeds and the onion. Fry for 6–7 minutes, stirring regularly, until the onion is soft.

5 Add the broken up dried red chillies and the curry leaves to the pan. Fry for about 1–2 minutes and pour the entire contents over the pineapple. Stir well, then remove from the heat. Serve hot or cold, but not chilled.

Sweet-and-sour Pineapple

This may sound like a Chinese recipe, but it is a traditional Bengali dish. The predominant flavour is ginger, and the pieces of golden pineapple, dotted with plump, juicy raisins, have plenty of visual appeal with a taste to match.

Serves 4
800g/1¾lb pineapple rings or
   chunks in natural juice
15ml/1 tbsp vegetable oil or
   sunflower oil
2.5ml/½ tsp black mustard seeds
2.5ml/½ tsp cumin seeds
2.5ml/½ tsp onion seeds
10ml/2 tsp grated fresh
   root ginger
5ml/1 tsp crushed dried chillies,
   seeds removed (optional)
50g/2oz/⅓ cup seedless raisins
115g/4oz/generous ½ cup sugar
7.5ml/1½ tsp salt

1 Drain the pineapple in a sieve (strainer) and reserve the juice. Chop the pineapple rings or chunks finely (you should have approximately 500g/1¼lb).

2 Heat the vegetable oil in a wok, karahi or large pan over a medium heat and immediately add the mustard seeds. As soon as they pop, add the cumin seeds, then the onion seeds. Add the ginger and chillies and stir-fry the spices briskly for 30 seconds until they release their flavours.

3 Add the pineapple, raisins, sugar and salt to the pan. Pour in about 300ml/½ pint/1¼ cups of the juice (make up with cold water if necessary) and add to the pineapple.

4 Bring the mixture to the boil, reduce the heat to medium and cook, uncovered, for 20–25 minutes. Serve hot.

Variation
Two or three mangoes can be used for this dish instead of the pineapple, if you prefer. Choose ripe fruits that will be full of flavour. To prepare, cut off both sides of the fruit, keeping close to the stone (pit), then peel off the skin and chop the flesh into chunks. Canned mangoes in natural juice could also be used.

Sweet-and-sour Pineapple Energy 215kcal/915kJ; Protein 1.2g; Carbohydrate 55.7g, of which sugars 55.6g; Fat 0.1g, of which saturates 0g; Cholesterol 0mg; Calcium 38mg; Fibre 1.4g; Sodium 5mg.
Chilli Pineapple Energy 138kcal/584kJ; Protein 1.5g; Carbohydrate 26.7g, of which sugars 25.5g; Fat 3.6g, of which saturates 0.5g; Cholesterol 0mg; Calcium 57mg; Fibre 2.6g; Sodium 47mg.

Stuffed Indian Bananas with Coriander and Cumin

Bananas are cooked with spices including coriander and cumin in many different ways in India. Green bananas are available from Indian stores or use plantains or unripe eating bananas.

Serves 4

4 green bananas or plantains
30ml/2 tbsp ground coriander
15ml/1 tbsp ground cumin
5ml/1 tsp chilli powder
2.5ml/½ tsp salt
1.5ml/¼ tsp ground turmeric
5ml/1 tsp sugar
15ml/1 tbsp gram flour
45ml/3 tbsp chopped fresh
   coriander (cilantro), plus extra
   sprigs to garnish
90ml/6 tbsp vegetable oil
1.5ml/¼ tsp cumin seeds
1.5ml/¼ tsp black mustard seeds
warm chapatis, to serve

1 Trim the bananas or plantains and cut each crossways into three pieces, leaving the skin on. Make a lengthwise slit along each piece, without cutting all the way through the flesh.

2 On a plate, mix together the ground coriander, cumin, chilli powder, salt, turmeric, sugar, gram flour, chopped fresh coriander and 15ml/1 tbsp of the oil. Use your fingers to combine well. Carefully stuff each piece of banana with the spice mixture, taking care not to break the bananas in half.

3 Heat the remaining oil in a wok, karahi or large pan, and fry the cumin and mustard seeds for 2 minutes or until they begin to splutter and release their fragrances.

4 Add the bananas and toss gently in the oil. Cover and simmer over a low heat for 15 minutes, stirring from time to time, until the bananas are soft but not mushy. Garnish with the fresh coriander sprigs, and serve with warm chapatis, if you like.

Variation
Baby courgettes (zucchini) would make a delicious alternative to bananas in this dish.

Stuffed Okra with Ginger, Cumin and Chilli

The Gujarati community excels in the art of vegetarian cooking. Stuffed okra is easy to make.

Serves 4–6

225g/8oz large okra
15ml/1 tbsp amchur (dry
   mango powder)
2.5ml/½ tsp ground ginger
2.5ml/½ tsp ground cumin
2.5ml/½ tsp hot chilli
   powder (optional)
2.5ml/½ tsp ground turmeric
vegetable oil or groundnut
   (peanut) oil, for frying
   and mixing
30ml/2 tbsp cornflour
   (cornstarch), placed in a
   plastic bag
salt

1 Wash the okra, and trim off the tips and discard. Make a slit lengthwise in the centre of each okra, taking care not to cut all the way through the pod.

2 In a bowl, mix the amchur, ginger, cumin, chilli, if using, turmeric and salt with a few drops of vegetable oil. Leave the mixture to rest for 1–2 hours or refrigerate overnight.

3 Using your fingers, part the slit of each okra carefully without opening it all the way and, using a small spoon, fill each with as much filling as possible. Put all the okra into the plastic bag with the cornflour, hold the top closed and shake the bag carefully to cover all the okra evenly.

4 Fill a wok, karahi or large pan with enough oil to sit 2.5cm/1in deep. Heat the oil and fry the okra in small batches for 5–8 minutes or until they are brown and slightly crisp. Serve hot with any meat, poultry or fish curry.

Cook's Tip
When buying okra, choose pods without any blemishes or damage. Wash them thoroughly, rubbing each one gently with a soft vegetable brush or your fingertips.

Stuffed Indian Bananas Energy 268kcal/1122kJ; Protein 3.1g; Carbohydrate 39.6g, of which sugars 26.3g; Fat 11.9g, of which saturates 1.5g; Cholesterol 0mg; Calcium 30mg; Fibre 1.8g; Sodium 3mg.
Stuffed Okra Energy 176kcal/734kJ; Protein 1.7g; Carbohydrate 15.5g, of which sugars 1.4g; Fat 12.4g, of which saturates 1.6g; Cholesterol 0mg; Calcium 92mg; Fibre 2.3g; Sodium 12mg.

Indian Spiced Okra with Almonds and Paprika

Okra pods have a ridged skin and a tapered, oblong shape. Firm, brightly coloured pods are well suited to cooking with spices.

Serves 2–4
225g/8oz okra
50g/2oz/½ cup blanched almonds, chopped
25g/1oz/2 tbsp butter
15ml/1 tbsp sunflower oil or vegetable oil
2 garlic cloves, crushed
2.5cm/1in piece fresh root ginger, grated
5ml/1 tsp cumin seeds
5ml/1 tsp ground coriander
5ml/1 tsp paprika
salt and ground black pepper

1 Trim just the tops of the okra stems and around the edges of the stalks. They have a sticky liquid which oozes out if prepared too far ahead, so only trim them immediately before they will be cooked.

2 In a large pan, fry the almonds in the butter until they are lightly golden, then remove.

3 Add the sunflower or vegetable oil to the pan and fry the okra, stirring constantly, for 2 minutes.

4 Add the garlic and ginger and fry for a minute, then add the spices and cook for another minute or so, stirring all the time.

5 Pour in about 300ml/½ pint/1¼ cups water. Season well with salt and ground black pepper, cover the pan with a lid and simmer for about 5 minutes or so until the okra feel just tender. Finally, mix in the fried almonds and serve hot.

> **Variation**
> Try okra sliced, fried in garlic and spices, then stirred into a pilaff of basmati rice with cauliflower florets and carrots. This makes a colourful and delicious dish – especially when topped with crushed grilled poppadums.

Okra with Green Mango and Lentils

If you like okra, you'll love this spicy and tangy dish. The green mango adds a delicious tartness that is a perfect complement to the nuttiness of the lentils and the kick from the red chillies and chilli powder.

Serves 4
115g/4oz/⅔ cup chana dhal (yellow lentils)
45ml/3 tbsp corn oil
2.5ml/½ tsp onion seeds
2 medium onions, sliced
2.5ml/½ tsp ground fenugreek
5ml/1 tsp grated fresh root ginger
5ml/1 tsp crushed garlic
7.5ml/1½ tsp chilli powder
1.5ml/¼ tsp turmeric
5ml/1 tsp ground coriander
1 green (unripe) mango, peeled and sliced
450g/1lb okra, cut into 1cm/½in pieces
7.5ml/1½ tsp salt
2 fresh red chillies, seeded and sliced
30ml/2 tbsp chopped fresh coriander (cilantro)
1 tomato, sliced

1 Wash the lentils thoroughly and put in a pan with enough water to cover. Bring to the boil and cook for about 15 minutes or until soft but not mushy. Drain and set to one side.

2 Heat the oil in a wok, deep frying pan or a karahi and fry the onion seeds until they begin to pop.

3 Add the onions to the pan and fry over a medium heat for 5–7 minutes until golden brown.

4 Lower the heat and add the ground fenugreek, ginger, garlic, chilli powder, turmeric and ground coriander to the pan. Cook for 1–2 minutes, stirring frequently.

5 Add the mango slices and the okra. Stir well and add the salt, red chillies and fresh coriander. Stir-fry for about 3 minutes or until the okra is well cooked.

6 Finally, add the cooked lentils and sliced tomato and cook for a further 3 minutes. Serve hot.

Indian Spiced Okra Energy 211kcal/873kJ; Protein 5g; Carbohydrate 6.3g, of which sugars 5.2g; Fat 18.7g, of which saturates 7.1g; Cholesterol 0mg; Calcium 246mg; Fibre 7.6g; Sodium 15mg.
Okra with Mango Energy 253kcal/1063kJ; Protein 11.3g; Carbohydrate 31.6g, of which sugars 13.7g; Fat 10.1g, of which saturates 1.4g; Cholesterol 0mg; Calcium 220mg; Fibre 8.2g; Sodium 25mg.

Spicy Glazed Pumpkin with Coconut Sauce

Pumpkins, butternut squash and winter melons can all be cooked in this way. Throughout Vietnam and Cambodia, variations of this sweet, mellow dish are often served as an accompaniment to rice or a spicy curry.

Serves 4
200mll/7fl oz/scant 1 cup
  coconut milk
15ml/1 tbsp nuoc mam or
  tuk trey
30ml/2 tbsp palm sugar (jaggery)
30ml/2 tbsp groundnut
  (peanut) oil
4 garlic cloves, finely chopped
25g/1oz fresh root ginger, peeled
  and finely shredded
675g/1½lb pumpkin flesh, cubed
ground black pepper
a handful of curry or basil leaves,
  to garnish
chilli oil, for drizzling
fried onion rings, to garnish
plain boiled or coconut rice,
  to serve

1 In a bowl, beat the coconut milk and the nuoc mam or tuk trey with the sugar, until it has dissolved. Set aside.

2 Heat the oil in a wok or heavy pan and stir in the garlic and ginger. Stir-fry until they begin to colour, then stir in the pumpkin cubes, mixing well to combine.

3 Pour in the coconut milk and mix well. Reduce the heat, cover and simmer for about 20 minutes, until the pumpkin is tender and the sauce has reduced.

4 Season with pepper and garnish with curry or basil leaves and fried onion rings. Serve hot with plain or coconut rice, drizzled with a little chilli oil.

> ### Cook's Tip
> *Nuoc mam is a fish sauce popular in Vietnam and Cambodia. It is made from salted and fermented small fish. Tuk trey is another fish sauce from the region featuring other ingredients such as vinegar, lime juice, sugar and garlic.*

Malay Pak Choi in Spiced Coconut Milk

The abundant vegetables of Malaysia are often cooked in coconut milk. The style of this dish is sweet and rich, with plentiful use of shrimp paste, which is a key ingredient. For this dish, you could use green beans, curly kale, or any type of cabbage, all of which are delicious served with steamed, braised or spicy fish dishes.

Serves 4
4 shallots, chopped
2 garlic cloves, peeled and
  finely chopped
1 lemon grass stalk, trimmed
  and chopped
25g/1oz fresh root ginger, peeled
  and chopped
2 red chillies, seeded and
  finely chopped
5ml/1 tsp shrimp paste
5ml/1 tsp ground turmeric
5ml/1 tsp palm sugar (jaggery)
15ml/1 tbsp sesame or groundnut
  (peanut) oil
400ml/14fl oz/1⅔ cups
  coconut milk
450g/1lb pak choi (bok choy),
  separated into leaves
salt and ground black pepper

1 Using a mortar and pestle or food processor, grind the shallots, garlic, lemon grass, ginger and chillies to a paste. Beat in the shrimp paste, turmeric and sugar.

2 Heat the oil in a wok or heavy pan, and stir in the spice paste. Cook for 2 minutes until fragrant and beginning to colour.

3 Pour in the coconut milk, mix well, and let it bubble away over a medium to high heat until it thickens.

4 Drop in the cabbage leaves, coating them in the coconut milk, and cook for a minute or two until wilted. Season to taste with salt and pepper and serve immediately.

> ### Variation
> *Make the dish using Chinese leaves (Chinese cabbage) or kale, cut into thick ribbons, or a mixture of the two.*

Glazed Pumpkin Energy 114kcal/477kJ; Protein 1.5g; Carbohydrate 14g, of which sugars 13.4g; Fat 6g, of which saturates 1g; Cholesterol 0mg; Calcium 68mg; Fibre 1.7g; Sodium 323mg.
Malay Pak Choi Energy 112kcal/469kJ; Protein 2.1g; Carbohydrate 13g, of which sugars 12.6g; Fat 6.1g, of which saturates 1g; Cholesterol 0mg; Calcium 89mg; Fibre 2.6g; Sodium 119mg.

Mixed Vegetables in a Spicy Coconut Broth

There are many ways to make a vegetable curry, but this recipe, in which the vegetables are simmered in coconut milk, is typical of South India. This cross between a soup and stew is perfect for a vegetarian lunch, with warm naan bread or soft chapatis as an accompaniment.

Serves 4

225g/8oz potatoes, cut into
   5cm/2in cubes
125g/4oz/¾ cup green beans
150g/5oz carrots, cut into chunks
500ml/17fl oz/2¼ cups
   vegetable stock or water
1 small aubergine (eggplant),
   about 225g/8oz,
   quartered lengthwise
75g/3oz coconut milk powder
5ml/1 tsp salt, or to taste
30ml/2 tbsp vegetable oil
6–8 fresh or 8–10 dried
   curry leaves
1–2 dried red chillies, chopped
   into small pieces
5ml/1 tsp ground cumin
5ml/1 tsp ground coriander
2.5ml/½ tsp ground turmeric

1 Put the potatoes, beans and carrots in a large pan and add 300ml/½ pint/1¼ cups of the stock or water. Bring to the boil. Reduce the heat a little, cover the pan and cook for 5 minutes.

2 Cut the aubergine quarters into pieces about 5cm/2in thick and add them to the pan.

3 Blend the coconut milk powder with the remaining hot water and add it to the soup with the salt. Bring to a slow simmer, cover and cook for 6–7 minutes.

4 In a small pan, heat the vegetable oil over a medium heat and add the curry leaves and the chillies. Immediately follow with the cumin, coriander and turmeric. Cook the spices for about 30–40 seconds, stirring frequently.

5 Pour the entire contents of the pan over the vegetables. Stir to distribute the spices evenly and remove the pan from the heat. Ladle the soup into warmed bowls and serve piping hot, with any naan bread or soft chapatis.

Masala Beans with Fenugreek and Coriander

The term masala refers to the blending of several spices to achieve a distinctive taste, with different spice-combinations being used to complement specific ingredients.

Serves 4

1 onion
5ml/1 tsp ground cumin
5ml/1 tsp ground coriander
5ml/1 tsp sesame seeds
5ml/1 tsp chilli powder
2.5ml/½ tsp crushed garlic
1.5ml/¼ tsp ground turmeric
5ml/1 tsp salt
30ml/2 tbsp vegetable oil
1 tomato, quartered
225g/8oz/1½ cups green
   beans, blanched
1 bunch fresh fenugreek leaves,
   stems discarded
60ml/4 tbsp chopped fresh
   coriander (cilantro)
15ml/1 tbsp lemon juice

1 Roughly chop the onion. Mix together the cumin and coriander, sesame seeds, chilli powder, garlic, turmeric and salt.

2 Put the chopped onion and spice mixture into a food processor or blender, and process for about 30–45 seconds until you have a rough paste.

3 In a wok, karahi or large pan, heat the oil over a medium heat and fry the spice paste for 5 minutes, stirring occasionally.

4 Add the tomato quarters, blanched green beans, fresh fenugreek and chopped coriander.

5 Stir-fry the contents of the pan for about 5 minutes, then sprinkle in the lemon juice and serve.

> **Variation**
> Instead of fresh fenugreek, you can also use 15ml/1 tbsp dried fenugreek for this recipe. Dried fenugreek is readily available from Indian stores and markets. It may be sold by its Indian name, kasuri methi.

Vegetables in Coconut Energy 80kcal/335kJ; Protein 1.2g; Carbohydrate 5.6g, of which sugars 5.3g; Fat 6.1g, of which saturates 0.9g; Cholesterol 0mg; Calcium 29mg; Fibre 2.3g; Sodium 71mg.
Masala Beans Energy 72kcal/295kJ; Protein 1.6g; Carbohydrate 2.9g, of which sugars 2.4g; Fat 6g, of which saturates 0.9g; Cholesterol 0mg; Calcium 47mg; Fibre 2.1g; Sodium 6mg.

Fiery Bean Stew with Chillies and Coconut Milk

This curry is from the Philippines, which is well renowned for its fiery food. In typical style, this rich, pungent dish is hot, and it is served with extra chillies to chew on.

Serves 3–4

30–45ml/2–3 tbsp coconut or groundnut (peanut) oil
1 onion, finely chopped
2–3 garlic cloves, finely chopped
40g/1½oz fresh root ginger, finely chopped
1 lemon grass stalk, finely chopped
4–5 red chillies, seeded and finely chopped

15–30ml/1–2 tbsp bagoong or 15ml/1 tbsp shrimp paste
15–30ml/1–2 tbsp tamarind paste
15–30ml/1–2 tbsp palm sugar (jaggery)
2 x 400g/14oz cans unsweetened coconut milk
4 kaffir lime leaves
500g/1¼lb yard-long beans
salt and ground black pepper
1 bunch of fresh coriander (cilantro) leaves, roughly chopped, to garnish

To serve

cooked rice
raw chillies

1 Heat the oil in a wok or large, heavy frying pan that has a lid. Stir in the onion, garlic, ginger, lemon grass and chillies and fry until fragrant and beginning to colour. Add the bagoong or shrimp paste, tamarind paste and sugar to the pan and stir in the coconut milk and lime leaves.

2 Bring the mixture to the boil, reduce the heat and toss in the whole beans. Partially cover the pan and cook the beans gently for 6–8 minutes until tender. Season the stew with salt and pepper to taste and sprinkle with chopped coriander to garnish. Serve with rice and extra chillies to chew on.

Cook's Tip
If you prefer, you can reduce the quantity of chillies used in the recipe to suit your taste buds and you do not have to serve the stew with extra chillies if you don't want to.

Stir-fried Crispy Tofu with Asparagus

Asparagus is not only elegant but also delicious. This fabulous Thai dish is the perfect side dish to serve at a dinner party.

Serves 2

250g/9oz deep-fried tofu cubes
30ml/2 tbsp groundnut (peanut) oil
15ml/1 tbsp Thai green curry paste

30ml/2 tbsp light soy sauce
2 kaffir lime leaves, rolled into cylinders and then thinly sliced
30ml/2 tbsp sugar
150ml/¼ pint/⅔ cup vegetable stock
250g/9oz Asian asparagus, trimmed and sliced into 5cm/2in lengths
30ml/2 tbsp roasted peanuts, finely chopped

1 Preheat the grill (broiler) to medium. Place the tofu cubes in a grill pan and grill (broil) for 2–3 minutes, then turn them over and continue to cook until they are crisp and golden brown all over. Watch them carefully; they must not be allowed to burn.

2 Heat the oil in a wok or heavy frying pan. Add the green curry paste and cook over a medium heat, stirring constantly, for 1–2 minutes, until it gives off its aroma.

3 Stir the soy sauce, lime leaves, sugar and vegetable stock into the wok or pan and mix well. Bring to the boil, then reduce the heat to low so that the mixture is just simmering.

4 Add the asparagus and simmer gently for 5 minutes. Meanwhile, chop each piece of tofu into four pieces, then add to the pan along with the peanuts.

5 Toss to coat all the ingredients in the sauce, then spoon into a warmed dish and serve immediately.

Variation
Substitute slim carrot batons, baby leeks or small broccoli florets for the Asian asparagus, if you like.

Fiery Bean Stew Energy 200kcal/840kJ; Protein 5.5g; Carbohydrate 24.4g, of which sugars 22.9g; Fat 9.7g, of which saturates 1.5g; Cholesterol 19mg; Calcium 158mg; Fibre 3.4g; Sodium 384mg.
Stir-fried Tofu Energy 287kcal/1195kJ; Protein 14.3g; Carbohydrate 20.3g, of which sugars 19.5g; Fat 17g, of which saturates 2.1g; Cholesterol 0mg; Calcium 682mg; Fibre 2.2g; Sodium 1075mg.

Corn on the Cob in Onion Curry Sauce

Corn is grown extensively in the Punjab region, where it is used in many delicacies. Here, corn is cooked in a thick rich onion sauce in this classic Punjabi dish. It is excellent served with naan bread or other Indian breads on the side.

Serves 4–6
4 corn cobs, thawed if frozen
vegetable oil, for frying
1 large onion, finely chopped
2 cloves garlic, crushed
5cm/2in piece fresh root ginger, crushed
2.5ml/1/2 tsp ground turmeric
2.5ml/1/2 tsp onion seeds
2.5ml/1/2 tsp cumin seeds
2.5ml/1/2 tsp five-spice powder
6–8 curry leaves
2.5ml/1/2 tsp sugar
200ml/7fl oz/scant 1 cup natural (plain) yogurt
chilli powder, to taste

1 Cut each corn cob in half, using a heavy knife or cleaver to make clean cuts. Heat the oil in a wok, karahi or large pan and fry the corn until golden brown, stirring occasionally. Remove the corn from the pan and keep warm.

2 Remove any excess oil, leaving about 30ml/2 tbsp in the wok. Grind the onion, garlic and ginger to a paste using a mortar and pestle, a food processor or a blender.

3 Transfer the onion paste to a bowl and add the spices, chilli powder, curry leaves and sugar. Mix well to ensure all the ingredients are combined.

4 Heat the oil gently and fry the onion paste mixture for about 8–10 minutes until all the spices have blended well and the oil separates from the sauce.

5 Set aside the mixture to cool a little and then fold in the yogurt. Mix to a smooth sauce.

6 Reheat the sauce over a low heat for about 10–12 minutes. Place the corn in a warmed serving dish and pour the sauce over it. Serve immediately while hot.

Southern Thai Curried Vegetables with Coconut

Rich curry flavours are found in the food of Thailand, where many dishes are made with coconut milk and spiced with turmeric.

Serves 4
90g/3 1/2oz Chinese leaves (Chinese cabbage), shredded
90g/3 1/2oz beansprouts
90g/3 1/2oz/scant 1 cup green beans, trimmed
100g/3 1/2oz broccoli florets
15ml/1 tbsp sesame seeds, toasted

For the sauce
60ml/4 tbsp coconut cream
5ml/1 tsp Thai red curry paste
90g/3 1/2oz/1 1/4 cups oyster mushrooms or field (portabello) mushrooms, sliced
60ml/4 tbsp coconut milk
5ml/1 tsp ground turmeric
5ml/1 tsp thick tamarind juice, made by mixing tamarind paste with a little warm water
juice of 1/2 lemon
60ml/4 tbsp light soy sauce
5ml/1 tsp palm sugar (jaggery) or light muscovado (brown) sugar

1 Blanch the shredded Chinese leaves, beansprouts, green beans and broccoli in boiling water for 1 minute per batch. Drain, place in a bowl and leave to cool.

2 To make the sauce, pour the coconut cream into a wok or frying pan and heat gently for 2–3 minutes, until it separates. Stir in the red curry paste. Cook over a low heat for 30 seconds.

3 Increase the heat, add the mushrooms and cook for a further 2–3 minutes. Pour in the coconut milk and stir in the turmeric, tamarind juice, lemon juice, soy sauce and sugar.

4 Pour the mixture over the prepared vegetables and toss well to combine. Sprinkle with the toasted sesame seeds and serve.

Cook's Tip
To make coconut cream use a carton or can of coconut milk. Skim the cream off the top and cook 60ml/4 tbsp of it before adding the paste. Add the measured milk later, as in the recipe.

Corn on the Cob Energy 164kcal/689kJ; Protein 4.2g; Carbohydrate 20.1g, of which sugars 4g; Fat 8g, of which saturates 1.1g; Cholesterol 0mg; Calcium 19mg; Fibre 2g; Sodium 44mg.
Southern Thai Vegetables Energy 162kcal/672kJ; Protein 5g; Carbohydrate 6.3g, of which sugars 5.4g; Fat 13.2g, of which saturates 9.4g; Cholesterol 0mg; Calcium 75mg; Fibre 2.5g; Sodium 1096mg.

Spiced Aubergine with Chilli Sauce and Sesame Seeds

Chunks of aubergine are coated in a rich sauce and sprinkled with sesame seeds to make an unusual side dish that is quick to cook. This straightforward yet versatile vegetarian dish can be served hot, warm or cold, as the occasion demands.

Serves 4–6
2 aubergines, total weight about 600g/1lb 6oz, cut into large chunks

15ml/1 tbsp salt
5ml/1 tsp chilli powder, or to taste
75–90ml/5–6 tbsp sunflower oil or vegetable oil
15ml/1 tbsp rice wine or medium-dry sherry
100ml/3 1/2fl oz/scant 1/2 cup water
75ml/5 tbsp chilli bean sauce (see Cook's Tip)
salt and ground black pepper
a few toasted sesame seeds, to garnish

1 Place the aubergine chunks on a plate, sprinkle them with the salt and leave to stand for 15–20 minutes. Rinse well, drain and pat dry thoroughly with kitchen paper. Toss the aubergine cubes in the chilli powder.

2 Heat a wok or large frying pan and add the sunflower or vegetable oil. When the oil is hot, add the aubergine chunks, with the rice wine or sherry. Stir constantly until the aubergine chunks start to turn a little brown.

3 Stir the measured water into the pan, cover with a lid and steam for 2–3 minutes. Add the chilli bean sauce and cook for 2 minutes. Season to taste, then spoon on to a serving dish, sprinkle with sesame seeds and serve.

Cook's Tip
If you can't get hold of chilli bean sauce, use 15–30ml/ 1–2 tbsp chilli paste mixed with 2 crushed garlic cloves, 15ml/1 tbsp each dark soy sauce and rice vinegar, and 10ml/2 tsp light soy sauce.

Roasted Root Vegetables with Spices

These spiced vegetables can be roasted alongside a joint of meat or a whole chicken. They will virtually look after themselves and make a delicious side dish.

Serves 4
3 parsnips, peeled
3 potatoes, peeled
3 carrots, peeled

3 sweet potatoes, peeled
60ml/4 tbsp olive oil
8 shallots, peeled
2 garlic cloves, sliced
10ml/2 tsp white mustard seeds
10ml/2 tsp coriander seeds, lightly crushed
5ml/1 tsp cumin seeds
2 bay leaves
salt and ground black pepper

1 Preheat the oven to 190°C/375°F/Gas 5. Bring a pan of lightly salted water to the boil. Cut the parsnips, potatoes, carrots and sweet potatoes into chunks.

2 Add the mixed vegetable chunks to the pan and bring the water back to the boil. Boil for about 2–3 minutes, then drain the vegetables thoroughly.

3 Pour the olive oil into a large, heavy roasting pan and place over a medium heat. When the oil is hot add the drained vegetables together with the whole shallots and garlic. Fry, tossing the vegetables over the heat, until they have turned pale golden at the edges.

4 Add the mustard, coriander and cumin seeds and the bay leaves. Cook for 1 minute, then season with salt and pepper.

5 Transfer the roasting pan to the oven and roast for about 45 minutes, turning the vegetables occasionally, until they are crisp and golden and cooked through. Serve immediately.

Variation
You can vary the selection of vegetables according to what is available. Try using swede (rutabaga) or pumpkin instead of, or as well as, the vegetables suggested.

Spiced Aubergine Energy 173kcal/719kJ; Protein 6g; Carbohydrate 10.6g, of which sugars 6.6g; Fat 12.4g, of which saturates 2g; Cholesterol 95mg; Calcium 62mg; Fibre 3.2g; Sodium 44mg.
Roasted Vegetables Energy 290kcal/1213kJ; Protein 11.5g; Carbohydrate 32.5g, of which sugars 13.3g; Fat 13.6g, of which saturates 1.6g; Cholesterol 0mg; Calcium 175mg; Fibre 9.1g; Sodium 271mg.

Spiced Coconut Mushrooms

Here is a simple and delicious way to cook mushrooms. They can be served with almost any Indian meal as well as with traditional grilled or roasted meats and poultry.

Serves 4
30ml/2 tbsp groundnut (peanut) oil
2 garlic cloves, finely chopped
2 fresh red chillies, seeded and sliced into rings
3 shallots or 1 small onion, finely chopped
225g/8oz/3 cups brown cap (cremini) mushrooms, thickly sliced
150ml/¼ pint/⅔ cup coconut milk
30ml/2 tbsp chopped fresh coriander (cilantro)
salt and ground black pepper

1 Heat a karahi, wok or heavy frying pan until hot, add the groundnut oil and swirl it around. Add the garlic and chillies, then stir-fry for a few seconds.

2 Add the chopped shallots or onion and cook them for about 2–3 minutes, stirring constantly, until softened. Add the mushrooms and stir-fry for 3 minutes.

3 Pour the coconut milk into the pan and bring to the boil. Boil rapidly over high heat until the liquid has reduced by about half and has thickened to coat the mushrooms. Season to taste with salt and black pepper.

4 Sprinkle over the chopped fresh coriander and toss the mushrooms gently to mix. Serve immediately.

> **Variations**
> • You can use chopped fresh chives instead of chopped fresh coriander (cilantro), if you wish.
> • White (button) mushrooms or field (portabello) mushrooms would also work well in this dish instead of the brown cap (cremini) mushrooms.
> • Sprinkle some chopped toasted cashew nuts over the mushrooms before serving, if you like.

Spiced Pumpkin Wedges and Sautéed Spinach

Warmly spiced roasted pumpkin, combined with creamy spinach and the fire of chilli, makes a lovely accompaniment for curries, grills and roasts.

Serves 4–6
10ml/2 tsp coriander seeds
5ml/1 tsp cumin seeds
5ml/1 tsp fennel seeds
5–10ml/1–2 tsp cinnamon
2 dried red chillies, chopped
coarse salt
2 garlic cloves
30ml/2 tbsp olive oil
1 medium pumpkin, halved, seeded, cut into 6–8 wedges

For the sautéed spinach
30–45ml/2–3 tbsp pine nuts
30–45ml/2–3 tbsp olive oil
1 red onion, halved and sliced
1–2 dried red chillies, finely sliced
1 apple, peeled, cored and sliced
2 garlic cloves, crushed
5–10ml/1–2 tsp ground roasted cumin
10ml/2 tsp clear honey
450g/1lb spinach, steamed and roughly chopped
60–75ml/4–5 tbsp double (heavy) cream
salt and ground black pepper
a handful of fresh spinach leaves, to garnish

1 Preheat the oven to 200°C/400°F/Gas 6. Grind the coriander, cumin and fennel seeds, cinnamon and chillies with a little coarse salt in a mortar with a pestle. Add the garlic and a little of the olive oil and pound to form a paste. Rub the spice mixture over the pumpkin segments and place them, skin side down, in an ovenproof dish or roasting pan. Bake the spiced pumpkin for 35–40 minutes, or until tender.

2 To make the spinach, roast the pine nuts in a dry frying pan until golden, then transfer on to a plate. Add the olive oil to the pan. Sauté the onion with the chilli until soft, then stir in the apple and garlic. Once the apple begins to colour, stir in most of the pine nuts, most of the cumin and the honey.

3 Toss in the spinach and, once it has heated through, stir in most of the cream. Season to taste and remove from the heat. Swirl the last of the cream on top, sprinkle with the reserved pine nuts and roasted cumin, and spinach leaves. Serve hot.

Pumpkin Energy 456kcal/1897kJ; Protein 18.9g; Carbohydrate 22.1g, of which sugars 17.1g; Fat 31.9g, of which saturates 13.2g; Cholesterol 45mg; Calcium 635mg; Fibre 10g; Sodium 337mg.
Spiced Mushrooms Energy 76kcal/313kJ; Protein 2g; Carbohydrate 3.4g, of which sugars 3g; Fat 6.1g, of which saturates 0.8g; Cholesterol 0mg; Calcium 26mg; Fibre 0.8g; Sodium 46mg.

Courgettes with Mushrooms in a Spicy Sauce

When cream and mushrooms are cooked together they complement each other beautifully. Though this dish sounds very rich, by using single cream and very little oil you can keep the fat content to a minimum.

Serves 4

30ml/2 tbsp vegetable oil
1 medium onion, roughly chopped
5ml/1 tsp ground coriander
5ml/1 tsp ground cumin
5ml/1 tsp salt
2.5ml/½ tsp chilli powder
225g/8oz/3 cups mushrooms, thickly sliced
2 medium courgettes (zucchini), thickly sliced
45ml/3 tbsp single (light) cream
15ml/1 tbsp chopped fresh coriander (cilantro), to garnish (optional)

1 Heat the oil in a large frying pan and fry the chopped onion for 6–8 minutes until golden brown.

2 Lower the heat to medium, add the ground coriander, cumin, salt and chilli powder to the pan and stir together well.

3 Once the onions and the spices are well blended, add the mushrooms and courgettes and cook gently, stirring frequently, for about 5 minutes until soft. If the mixture seems too dry just add a little water to loosen.

4 Finally pour the cream into the pan and mix in well to combine with the vegetables. Garnish with fresh chopped coriander, if you wish, and serve immediately.

> **Cook's Tip**
> Choose whichever mushrooms are available for this dish. White (button) mushrooms, field (portabello) mushrooms and brown cap (cremini) mushrooms all work well. More exotic mushrooms such as chanterelles, oyster mushrooms and morel mushrooms will also be delicious cooked in this way.

Stir-fried Vegetable Florets with Hazelnuts

A rich hazelnut dressing turns crunchy cauliflower and broccoli into a very special vegetable dish. It works well as a side dish to a vegetarian or meat curry but can equally be eaten on its own with some freshly baked Indian breads.

Serves 4

175g/6oz/1½ cups bitesize cauliflower florets
175g/6oz/1½ cups bitesize broccoli florets
15ml/1 tbsp sunflower oil
50g/2oz/½ cup hazelnuts, finely chopped
¼ red chilli, finely chopped, or 5ml/1 tsp chilli powder (optional)
60ml/4 tbsp crème fraîche or fromage frais
salt and ground black pepper
chilli powder, to garnish

1 Make sure the cauliflower and broccoli florets are all of an even size so that they cook at the same time. Heat the sunflower oil in a pan or wok and toss the florets over a high heat for about 1 minute.

2 Reduce the heat and continue cooking the vegetables for another 5 minutes, stirring frequently.

3 Add the chopped hazelnuts and fresh chilli or chilli powder, if using, to the pan. Stir well to combine the ingredients. Season with salt and ground black pepper.

4 When the cauliflower is crisp and nearly tender, stir in the crème fraîche or fromage frais. Continue to cook for about 2 minutes until heated through. Serve immediately, sprinkled with a little chilli powder.

> **Cook's Tip**
> The crisper these florets are the better, so cook them just long enough to make them piping hot, and give them time to absorb all the flavours.

Courgettes with Mushrooms Energy 90kcal/374kJ; Protein 5g; Carbohydrate 7.5g, of which sugars 3.4g; Fat 4.9g, of which saturates 0.7g; Cholesterol 0mg; Calcium 69mg; Fibre 1.7g; Sodium 16mg.
Stir-fried Florets Energy 205kcal/849kJ; Protein 3.9g; Carbohydrate 20.1g, of which sugars 17.4g; Fat 12.5g, of which saturates 2.1g; Cholesterol 0mg; Calcium 61mg; Fibre 5.8g; Sodium 93mg.

Balti Corn with Cauliflower and Chilli

This quick, tasty and nutritious vegetable dish is a great side dish to serve with a more substantial curry. It will also make a delicious main course if served with plain boiled rice, a dhal-based dish or simply with some Indian bread such as naan, chapati or paratha.

Serves 4

30ml/2 tbsp corn oil
4 curry leaves
1.5ml/¼ tsp onion seeds
2 medium onions, diced
1 red chilli, seeded and chopped
175g/6oz frozen corn
½ small cauliflower, cut into small florets
3–7 mint leaves

1 Heat the corn oil in a wok or large frying pan. Add the curry leaves and the onion seeds and cook, stirring constantly, for about 30 seconds.

2 Add the diced onions to the pan and fry them for about 5–8 minutes until golden brown.

3 Add the chilli, corn and cauliflower to the pan and cook, stirring frequently, for 5–8 minutes.

4 Finally, add the mint leaves and heat for 2–3 minutes until the vegetables are tender. Serve immediately.

> **Variation**
> Using frozen corn means this dish is very quick and simple to prepare, but, if you prefer, use fresh corn that has been sliced from a couple of cooked cobs.

> **Cook's Tip**
> It is best to cook this dish just before you are ready to serve, as the flavours tend to diminish if it is kept warm for too long.

Balti Mushrooms in a Garlic and Chilli Sauce

This is a simple and delicious Balti recipe which could be accompanied by bread or one of the rice side dishes from this book.

Serves 4

350g/12oz/4½ cups button (white) mushrooms
15ml/1 tbsp vegetable oil
1 bay leaf
3 garlic cloves, roughly chopped
2 fresh green chillies, seeded and chopped
225g/8oz/1 cup low-fat fromage frais or ricotta cheese
15ml/1 tbsp chopped fresh mint
15ml/1 tbsp chopped fresh coriander (cilantro)
5ml/1 tsp salt
fresh mint and coriander (cilantro) leaves, to garnish

1 Cut the button mushrooms in half if small, or in quarters if they are large, and set aside.

2 Heat the oil in a karahi, wok or large, heavy frying pan, then add the bay leaf, chopped garlic and chillies, and quickly cook for about 1 minute, stirring frequently.

3 Add the chopped mushrooms to the pan. Cook for about 2 minutes, stirring frequently.

4 Remove from the heat and stir in the fromage frais or ricotta cheese, followed by the mint, coriander and salt.

5 Return the pan to the heat and stir-fry for 2–3 minutes, then transfer to a warmed serving dish and garnish with the fresh mint and coriander leaves before serving.

> **Cook's Tip**
> Balti curries have their origins in Baltistan, the area that is now North Pakistan. They are traditionally aromatic but not heavily flavoured with chilli, and Indian bread is usually used to scoop up the food rather than utensils. However, plain boiled or steamed rice also goes well with all the dishes.

Balti Corn Energy 124kcal/519kJ; Protein 4.g; Carbohydrate 19g, of which sugars 4g; Fat 4g, of which saturates 1g; Cholesterol 0mg; Fibre 3g; Sodium 120mg.
Balti Mushrooms Energy 153kcal/633kJ; Protein 5.4g; Carbohydrate 3.1g, of which sugars 2.8g; Fat 13.3g, of which saturates 4.4g; Cholesterol 5mg; Calcium 90mg; Fibre 1.5g; Sodium 28mg.

Spinach and Mushroom Curry

A tasty vegetable that is often overlooked, spinach is highly nutritious. Cooked in this way it tastes wonderful. Serve with chapatis.

Serves 4

450g/1lb fresh or frozen
   spinach, thawed
30ml/2 tbsp vegetable oil
2 medium onions, diced
6–8 curry leaves
1.5ml/¼ tsp onion seeds

5ml/1 tsp crushed garlic
5ml/1 tsp grated fresh root ginger
5ml/1 tsp chilli powder
5ml/1 tsp salt
7.5ml/1½ tsp ground coriander
1 large red (bell) pepper, seeded
   and sliced
115g/4oz/1½ cups mushrooms,
   roughly chopped
225g/8oz/1 cup low-fat fromage
   frais or ricotta cheese
30ml/2 tbsp fresh coriander
   (cilantro) leaves

1 If using fresh spinach, blanch it briefly in a pan of boiling water and drain thoroughly. If using frozen spinach, drain well. Set aside while you cook the other ingredients.

2 Heat the oil in a karahi, wok or heavy pan and fry the onions with the curry leaves and the onion seeds for 1–2 minutes. Add the garlic, ginger, chilli powder, salt and ground coriander. Stir-fry for a further 2–3 minutes.

3 Add half the red pepper slices and all the mushrooms and continue to stir-fry for 2–3 minutes.

4 Add the spinach and stir-fry for 4–6 minutes, then add the fromage frais or ricotta and half the fresh coriander, followed by the remaining red pepper slices. Cook for 2–3 minutes before serving, garnished with the remaining coriander.

Cook's Tip
Whether you use fresh or frozen spinach, make sure it is well drained, otherwise the stir-fried mixture will be too wet when you add the fromage frais or ricotta. Transfer the spinach into a colander, and press it against the sides of the colander with a wooden spoon to extract as much liquid as possible.

Vegetables with Almonds and Indian Spices

Natural yogurt is added to the vegetables towards the end of the cooking time, which not only gives this dish a tangy note but also makes it creamy.

Serves 4

30ml/2 tbsp vegetable oil
2 medium onions, sliced
5cm/2in piece fresh root
   ginger, grated
5ml/1 tsp black peppercorns,
   roughly crushed
1 bay leaf
1.5ml/¼ tsp turmeric

5ml/1 tsp ground coriander
5ml/1 tsp salt
2.5ml/½ tsp garam masala
175g/6oz/2½ cups mushrooms,
   thickly sliced
1 medium courgette (zucchini),
   thickly sliced
50g/2oz green beans, sliced into
   2.5cm/1in pieces
15ml/1 tbsp roughly chopped
   fresh mint
150ml/¼ pint/⅔ cup water
30ml/2 tbsp natural (plain)
   low-fat yogurt
25g/1oz/¼ cup flaked
   (sliced) almonds, to garnish

1 In a wok or deep frying pan, heat the vegetable oil and fry the sliced onions with the ginger, crushed black peppercorns and bay leaf for 3–5 minutes.

2 Lower the heat and add the turmeric, ground coriander, salt and garam masala, stirring occasionally.

3 Gradually add the mushrooms, courgette, green beans and the mint. Stir gently so that the vegetables retain their shapes.

4 Pour the measured water into the pan and bring to the boil, then lower the heat and simmer gently until all the water has evaporated.

5 In a bowl, beat the yogurt with a fork, then pour on to the vegetables and mix together well.

6 Cook the vegetables for a further 2–3 minutes until everything is warmed through, stirring occasionally. Serve immediately garnished with the flaked almonds.

Spinach and Mushroom Energy 225kcal/933kJ; Protein 10.8g; Carbohydrate 10g, of which sugars 6.2g; Fat 16.2g, of which saturates 6.1g; Cholesterol 24mg; Calcium 215mg; Fibre 3.4g; Sodium 164mg.
Vegetables with Almonds Energy 182kcal/754kJ; Protein 6.7g; Carbohydrate 14.7g, of which sugars 7.7g; Fat 11.4g, of which saturates 1.3g; Cholesterol 0mg; Calcium 97mg; Fibre 3.1g; Sodium 17mg.

Curried Winter Vegetables

A mixture of chunky mashed root vegetables, such as carrots, parsnips and turnips or swedes, makes a wonderfully warming winter side dish.

Serves 4–6
225g/8oz carrots, chopped
225g/8oz parsnips, chopped
1 small swede (rutabaga), chopped
25g/1oz/2 tbsp butter
10ml/2 tsp mild curry paste
115g/4oz/½ cup fromage frais or ricotta cheese
15ml/1 tbsp fresh chives, finely chopped
salt and ground black pepper

1 Boil the carrots, parsnips and swede in a large pan with plenty of lightly salted water for about 6–8 minutes, or until they are just tender but not soft.

2 Drain the vegetables then return them to the pan with the butter, curry paste and seasoning.

3 Mash the vegetables lightly with a fork or potato masher so that you end up with a chunky purée; you want to retain a good coarse texture with plenty of chunks.

4 Stir the fromage frais or ricotta cheese and chopped chives into the pan. Check the seasoning, adding more if needed, and serve immediately while hot. This is a good dish to prepare in advance and reheat when required.

Cook's Tip
Vegetable purées are a popular accompaniment with any dish which could be a little on the dry side, providing a good contrast of textures and colours.

Variation
Other vegetables work well in this dish: try pumpkin, sweet potatoes, potatoes, peas, broccoli or leeks.

Balti Baby Vegetables with Chilli and Chickpeas

There is a wonderful selection of baby vegetables available these days, and this simple recipe does full justice to their delicate flavour and attractive appearance. Serve as part of a main meal or even as a light appetizer.

Serves 4–6
10 new potatoes, halved
12–14 baby carrots
12–14 baby courgettes (zucchini)
30ml/2 tbsp corn oil
15 baby onions
30ml/2 tbsp chilli sauce
5ml/1 tsp crushed garlic
5ml/1 tsp grated fresh root ginger
5ml/1 tsp salt
400g/14oz/scant 3 cups drained canned chickpeas
10 cherry tomatoes
5ml/1 tsp crushed dried red chillies, seeds removed
30ml/2 tbsp sesame seeds

1 Bring a medium pan of salted water to the boil and add the new potatoes and baby carrots. Cook for 12–15 minutes.

2 Add the courgettes, and boil for a further 5 minutes or until all the vegetables are just tender. Take care not to overcook the vegetables, as there will be additional cooking time later. Drain the vegetables well and put them in a bowl. Set aside.

3 Heat the corn oil in a karahi, wok or deep frying pan and add the baby onions. Fry over a medium heat until the onions turn golden brown, stirring frequently.

4 Lower the heat and add the chilli sauce, garlic, ginger and salt, taking care not to burn the mixture.

5 Stir in the chickpeas and stir-fry over a medium heat until the moisture has evaporated.

6 Add the cooked vegetables and cherry tomatoes, and stir over the heat with a slotted spoon for about 2 minutes.

7 Sprinkle the crushed red chillies and sesame seeds evenly over the vegetable mixture and serve.

Curried Vegetables Energy 268kcal/1129kJ; Protein 5.8g; Carbohydrate 37.8g, of which sugars 9.8g; Fat 11.6g, of which saturates 7.1g; Cholesterol 31mg; Calcium 127mg; Fibre 3.6g; Sodium 117mg.
Balti Baby Vegetables Energy 221kcal/929kJ; Protein 9g; Carbohydrate 32.5g, of which sugars 11g; Fat 7.1g, of which saturates 0.9g; Cholesterol 0mg; Calcium 90mg; Fibre 6.5g; Sodium 174mg.

Middle Eastern Vegetable Stew

A spiced dish of mixed vegetables makes a delicious and filling vegetarian side dish. Children may prefer less chilli.

Serves 4–6
45ml/3 tbsp vegetable stock
I green (bell) pepper, seeded
  and sliced
2 medium courgettes
  (zucchini), sliced
2 medium carrots, sliced
2 celery sticks, sliced
2 medium potatoes, diced
400g/14oz can
  chopped tomatoes
5ml/1 tsp chilli powder
30ml/2 tbsp chopped fresh mint
15ml/1 tbsp ground cumin
400g/14oz can cooked
  chickpeas, drained
salt and black pepper
mint sprigs, to garnish

I Heat the vegetable stock in a large flameproof casserole until boiling, then add the sliced pepper, courgettes, carrots, and celery. Stir over a high heat for 2–3 minutes, until the vegetables are just beginning to soften.

2 Add the potatoes, tomatoes, chilli powder, mint, and cumin. Add the chickpeas and bring to the boil.

3 Reduce the heat, cover the casserole, and simmer for about 30 minutes, or until all the vegetables are tender. Season to taste with salt and black pepper and serve immediately while hot, garnished with the mint sprigs.

Cook's Tip
Chickpeas are traditional in this type of Middle Eastern dish. If you prefer you can use dried chickpeas, which need to be soaked and cooked, instead of the pre-cooked canned variety.

Variation
Other vegetables can be substituted for those in the recipe, if you prefer, just use whatever you have to hand – try swede (rutabaga), sweet potato or parsnips.

Gujarati Stuffed Vegetables with a Spicy Tomato Sauce

In this fabulous recipe from Gujarat in India, two different vegetables are stuffed with an irresistible blend of spices and peanuts.

Serves 4
12 small potatoes
8 baby aubergines (eggplants)
single (light) cream, to
  garnish (optional)

For the stuffing
15ml/1 tbsp sesame seeds
30ml/2 tbsp ground coriander
30ml/2 tbsp ground cumin
2.5ml/½ tsp salt
1.5ml/¼ tsp chilli powder
2.5ml/½ tsp ground turmeric

10ml/2 tsp sugar
1.5ml/¼ tsp garam masala
15ml/1 tbsp peanuts,
  roughly crushed
15ml/1 tbsp gram flour
2 garlic cloves, crushed
15ml/1 tbsp lemon juice
30ml/2 tbsp chopped fresh
  coriander (cilantro)

For the sauce
30ml/2 tbsp vegetable oil
2.5ml/½ tsp black
  mustard seeds
400g/14oz can
  chopped tomatoes
30ml/2 tbsp chopped fresh
  coriander (cilantro)
150ml/¼ pint/⅔ cup water

I Preheat the oven to 200°C/400°F/Gas 6. Make slits in the potatoes and aubergines, without cutting right through.

2 Mix all the ingredients for the stuffing together in a bowl. Using a small spoon, carefully stuff the potatoes and aubergines with the spice mixture. Place the stuffed vegetables, evenly spaced, in a greased ovenproof dish.

3 Heat the oil in a pan and fry the mustard seeds for 2 minutes until they begin to splutter, then add the tomatoes, coriander and any leftover stuffing, together with the water. Simmer for 5 minutes until the sauce thickens.

4 Pour the sauce over the potatoes and aubergines. Cover and bake for 25–30 minutes until the vegetables are soft. Garnish with single cream, if using. Serve with any Indian bread or with a meat or chicken curry of your choice.

Middle Eastern Stew Energy 149kcal/630kJ; Protein 7.8g; Carbohydrate 24.9g, of which sugars 6.8g; Fat 2.7g, of which saturates 0.4g; Cholesterol 0mg; Calcium 66mg; Fibre 5.7g; Sodium 172mg.
Gujarati Vegetables Energy 302kcal/1260kJ; Protein 7.2g; Carbohydrate 35.2g, of which sugars 9.6g; Fat 14.9g, of which saturates 3g; Cholesterol 9mg; Calcium 75mg; Fibre 2.3g; Sodium 191mg.

Vegetables and Beans with Curry Leaves

This spicy mix of vegetables and beans is quite a dry curry, so it is ideal to serve alongside a saucy meat curry or dhal. It is quite a hot dish, so feel free to reduce the amount of dried red chillies to suit your taste.

Serves 4
30ml/2 tbsp vegetable oil
6 curry leaves
3 garlic cloves, sliced
3 dried red chillies
1.5ml/¼ tsp onion seeds

1.5ml/¼ tsp fenugreek seeds
3 fresh green chillies, seeded and chopped
10ml/2 tsp desiccated (dry unsweetened shredded) coconut, plus extra to garnish (optional)
115g/4oz/½ cup canned red kidney beans, drained
1 medium carrot, cut into strips
50g/2oz green beans, diagonally sliced
1 medium red (bell) pepper, cut into strips
5ml/1 tsp salt
30ml/2 tbsp lemon juice

1 Heat the vegetable oil in a wok, karahi or deep frying pan. Add the curry leaves, garlic cloves, dried chillies, and onion and fenugreek seeds and cook over a medium heat for about 5–6 minutes, stirring frequently.

2 When the spices in the pan turn a shade darker, add the remaining ingredients and stir well to combine.

3 Lower the heat, cover the pan with a lid and cook for about 5 minutes, stirring occasionally.

4 Transfer the curry to a warmed serving dish and serve garnished with extra coconut, if you wish.

Cook's Tip
Fresh curry leaves are extremely aromatic and there really is no substitute for them. Fresh curry leaves also freeze well, but if necessary you can use dried ones.

Vegetable Chilli

This spicy chilli is packed with healthy vegetables and is sure to go down a treat with the whole family.

Serves 8
50ml/2fl oz/¼ cup olive oil or vegetable oil
2 onions, chopped
75g/3oz celery, finely sliced
2 carrots, cut in 1cm/½in cubes
2 garlic cloves, crushed
2.5ml/½ tsp celery seeds
1.5ml/¼ tsp cayenne
5ml/1 tsp ground cumin

45ml/3 tbsp chilli powder
400g/14oz canned chopped plum tomatoes with their juice
250ml/8fl oz/1 cup vegetable stock or water
2.5ml/½ tsp fresh or dried thyme
1 bay leaf
350g/12oz cauliflower florets
3 courgettes (zucchini), cut into 1cm/½in cubes
300g/11oz can corn, drained
400g/14oz can kidney or pinto beans, drained
hot pepper sauce (optional)
salt

1 Heat the oil in a large flameproof casserole or heavy pan and add the onions, celery, carrots, and garlic. Cover the casserole and cook over a low heat for 8–10 minutes stirring from time to time, until the onions are softened.

2 Stir in the celery seeds, cayenne, cumin, and chilli powder. Mix well. Add the tomatoes, stock or water, salt, thyme and bay leaf. Stir. Cook for 15 minutes, uncovered.

3 Add the cauliflower and courgettes to the pan. Cover and cook for a further 10 minutes.

4 Add the corn and kidney or pinto beans, stir well, and cook for 10 minutes more, uncovered. Check the seasoning, and add a dash of hot pepper sauce if desired. Serve with freshly boiled rice or baked potatoes, if you like.

Variation
This dish is a great way to use up any left over vegetables in the kitchen cupboard – try broccoli, aubergines (eggplants), butternut squash or sweet potato.

Vegetables and Beans Energy 86kcal/358kJ; Protein 3.3g; Carbohydrate 10.6g, of which sugars 4.9g; Fat 3.7g, of which saturates 0.5g; Cholesterol 0mg; Calcium 38mg; Fibre 3.1g; Sodium 118mg.
Vegetable Chilli Energy 149kcal/629kJ; Protein 5.2g; Carbohydrate 21.4g, of which sugars 9g; Fat 5.3g, of which saturates 0.8g; Cholesterol 0mg; Calcium 58mg; Fibre 5g; Sodium 614mg.

Spicy Tamarind Chickpeas

Chickpeas make a good base for many vegetarian curries cooked in a slow cooker. Here, they are tossed with sharp tamarind and spices to make a light lunch or side dish.

Serves 4
225g/8oz/1¼ cups dried chickpeas
50g/2oz tamarind pulp
45ml/3 tbsp vegetable oil
2.5ml/½ tsp cumin seeds

1 onion, very finely chopped
2 garlic cloves, crushed
2.5cm/1in piece of fresh root
   ginger, peeled and grated
5ml/1 tsp ground cumin
5ml/1 tsp ground coriander
1.5ml/¼ tsp ground turmeric
1 fresh green chilli, finely chopped
2.5ml/½ tsp salt
225g/8oz tomatoes, chopped
2.5ml/½ tsp garam masala
chopped fresh chillies and
   chopped red onion, to garnish

1 Put the chickpeas in a large bowl and pour over cold water to cover. Leave to soak for at least 8 hours, or overnight.

2 Drain the chickpeas and put in a pan with at least double the volume of cold water. Bring the water to the boil and boil vigorously for at least 10 minutes. Skim off any scum, then drain the chickpeas and transfer into a slow cooker.

3 Pour 750ml/1¼ pints/3 cups of near-boiling water over the chickpeas and switch the slow cooker to high. Cover with the lid and cook for 4–5 hours, or until the chickpeas are just tender.

4 Meanwhile, break up the tamarind with a fork. Pour over 120ml/4fl oz/½ cup of boiling water and leave to soak for 15 minutes. Transfer into a sieve (strainer) and discard the water. Rub the pulp through, discarding any stones and fibre.

5 Heat the oil in a large pan, add the cumin seeds and fry for 2 minutes, until they splutter. Add the onion, garlic and ginger and fry for 5 minutes. Add the cumin, coriander, turmeric, chilli and salt and fry for 3–4 minutes. Add the tomatoes, garam masala and tamarind pulp and bring to the boil.

6 Stir the tamarind mixture into the chickpeas, cover and cook for a further 1 hour. Serve garnished with the chilli and onion.

Spinach with Spicy Chickpeas

This richly flavoured side dish makes an excellent accompaniment to a dry curry or a rice-based stir-fry. It is particularly good served drizzled with a little plain yogurt – the sharp, creamy flavour complements the complex spices perfectly.

Serves 4
200g/7oz dried chickpeas
30ml/2 tbsp sunflower oil
2 onions, halved and
   thinly sliced
10ml/2 tsp ground coriander

10ml/2 tsp ground cumin
5ml/1 tsp hot chilli powder
2.5ml/½ tsp ground turmeric
15ml/1 tbsp medium or hot
   curry powder
400g/14oz can
   chopped tomatoes
5ml/1 tsp caster
   (superfine) sugar
30ml/2 tbsp chopped fresh
   mint leaves
115g/4oz baby leaf spinach
salt and ground black pepper

1 Soak the chickpeas in cold water overnight. Drain, rinse and place in a large pan. Cover with water and bring to the boil. Reduce the heat and simmer for 45 minutes to 1¼ hours, or until just tender. Drain and set aside.

2 Heat the oil in a wok or frying pan, add the onions and cook over a low heat for 15 minutes, until lightly golden.

3 Add the ground coriander and cumin, chilli powder, turmeric and curry powder to the onions in the pan and cook for about 2–3 minutes, stirring frequently.

4 Add the tomatoes, sugar and 105ml/7 tbsp water to the pan and bring to the boil. Cover, reduce the heat and simmer gently for 15 minutes, stirring occasionally.

5 Add the chickpeas to the pan, season well and cook gently for 8–10 minutes. Stir in the chopped mint.

6 Divide the spinach leaves between shallow bowls, top with the chickpea mixture and serve immediately with a main course of curry or stir-fry.

Spicy Chickpeas Energy 277kcal/1164kJ; Protein 12.8g; Carbohydrate 32.6g, of which sugars 5.3g; Fat 11.5g, of which saturates 1.3g; Cholesterol 0mg; Calcium 103mg; Fibre 7.1g; Sodium 274mg.
Spinach with Chickpeas Energy 267kcal/1122kJ; Protein 13.3g; Carbohydrate 35.5g, of which sugars 10.2g; Fat 9g, of which saturates 1.1g; Cholesterol 0mg; Calcium 170mg; Fibre 8.2g; Sodium 83mg.

Aloo Saag

Traditional Indian spices – mustard seed, ginger and chilli – give a really good kick to potatoes and spinach in this delicious, authentic curry.

Serves 4
450g/1lb spinach
30ml/2 tbsp vegetable oil

5ml/1 tsp black mustard seeds
1 onion, thinly sliced
2 garlic cloves, crushed
2.5cm/1in piece fresh root ginger, finely chopped
675g/1½lb firm potatoes, cut into 2.5cm/1in chunks
5ml/1 tsp chilli powder
5ml/1 tsp salt
120ml/4fl oz/½ cup water

1 Wash the spinach in several changes of water then blanch it in a little boiling water for 3–4 minutes.

2 Drain the spinach thoroughly and set aside to cool slightly. When it is cool enough to handle, use your hands to squeeze out all the remaining liquid.

3 Heat the oil in a large pan and fry the mustard seeds for 2 minutes, stirring, until they begin to splutter.

4 Add the onion, garlic and ginger to the pan and cook for 5 minutes, stirring frequently.

5 Stir in the potatoes, chilli powder, salt and water and cook for about 8 minutes, stirring occasionally.

6 Finally, add the spinach to the pan. Cover and simmer for 10–15 minutes until the spinach is very soft and the potatoes are tender. Serve immediately while hot.

Cook's Tip
To make certain that the spinach is dry before adding it to the potatoes, put it in a clean dish towel, roll up tightly and squeeze gently to remove any excess liquid. Choose a firm waxy variety of potato or a baby salad potato so the pieces do not break up during cooking.

Masala Mashed Potatoes

This delightfully simple variation on the popular Western side dish can be used as an accompaniment to just about any main course dish, not just Indian spicy dishes and curries.

Serves 4
3 medium potatoes
15ml/1 tbsp chopped fresh mint and coriander (cilantro), mixed

5ml/1 tsp mango powder (amchur)
5ml/1 tsp salt
5ml/1 tsp crushed black peppercorns
1 fresh red chilli, seeded and chopped
1 fresh green chilli, seeded and chopped
50g/2oz/¼ cup butter

1 Put the potatoes in a large pan. Add enough water to cover and bring to the boil, then simmer for about 15 minutes, or until the potatoes are tender, but do not allow them to get too soft.

2 Drain thoroughly and leave to cool slightly, then mash them down using a masher or potato ricer.

3 Stir all the remaining ingredients together in a small mixing bowl until well combined.

4 Stir the herb and spice mixture into the mashed potatoes. Mix together thoroughly with a fork and transfer to a warmed serving dish. Serve immediately.

Cook's Tip
Mango powder, also known as amchur, is the unripe green fruit of the mango tree ground to a powder. The sour mangoes are sliced and dried in the sun, turning a light brown, before they are ground. Mango powder adds a fruity sharpness and a slightly resinous bouquet to a dish. It is widely used with vegetables and is usually added towards the end of the cooking time. If mango powder is unavailable, the nearest substitute is lemon or lime juice, but it will not taste quite the same.

Aloo Saag Energy 201kcal/845kJ; Protein 6.2g; Carbohydrate 30.2g, of which sugars 4.7g; Fat 6.9g, of which saturates 0.9g; Cholesterol 0mg; Calcium 205mg; Fibre 4.3g; Sodium 668mg.
Masala Potatoes Energy 219kcal/919kJ; Protein 3.1g; Carbohydrate 28.9g, of which sugars 3g; Fat 10.9g, of which saturates 6.7g; Cholesterol 27mg; Calcium 13mg; Fibre 1.8g; Sodium 600mg.

Spiced Potatoes and Carrots with Fresh Herbs

Ready prepared 'parisienne' vegetables have recently become available in many supermarkets. These are simply root vegetables that have been peeled and cut into perfectly spherical shapes. This dish looks extremely fresh and appetizing and is equally as delicious.

Serves 4

175g/6oz carrots parisienne
175g/6oz potatoes parisienne
115g/4oz runner (green)
   beans, sliced
75 g/3 oz/6 tbsp butter
15ml/1 tbsp corn oil
1.5ml/¼ tsp onion seeds
1.5ml/¼ tsp fenugreek seeds
4 dried red chillies, seeded and
   roughly chopped
2.5ml/½ tsp mustard seeds
6 curry leaves
1 medium onion, sliced
5ml/1 tsp salt
4 garlic cloves, sliced
4 fresh red chillies, sliced
15ml/1 tbsp chopped fresh
   coriander (cilantro)
15ml/1 tbsp fresh mint leaves,
   finely chopped
mint sprig, to garnish

1 Place the carrots, potatoes and runner beans into a large pan of boiling water, and cook for about 7–8 minutes, or until they are just tender but do not let them become overcooked. Drain thoroughly and set to one side.

2 Heat the butter and oil in a wok, deep frying pan or a large karahi and add the onion seeds, fenugreek seeds, dried red chillies, mustard seeds and curry leaves. Stir-fry over a medium heat for 2 minutes until they release their fragrances.

3 Add the sliced onion to the pan with the spices and fry for about 3–5 minutes, stirring frequently.

4 Add the salt, garlic and fresh chillies to the pan, followed by the cooked vegetables, and cook for about 5 minutes, over a medium heat, stirring gently.

5 Add the fresh coriander and mint to the pan and serve immediately garnished with a sprig of mint.

Cauliflower and Potatoes with Indian Spices

Cauliflower and potatoes are encrusted with Indian spices in this delicious curry. It is a popular side dish or can be served as a main course with other dishes such as a salad, spicy dhal or simply with Indian breads.

Serves 4

450g/1lb potatoes, cut into
   2.5cm/1in chunks
30ml/2 tbsp vegetable oil
5ml/1 tsp cumin seeds
1 green chilli, finely chopped
450g/1lb cauliflower, broken
   into florets
5ml/1 tsp ground coriander
5ml/1 tsp ground cumin
1.5ml/¼ tsp chilli powder
2.5ml/½ tsp ground turmeric
2.5ml/½ tsp salt
chopped fresh coriander (cilantro),
   to garnish
tomato and onion salad and
   pickle, to serve

1 Par-boil the potatoes in a large pan of boiling water for 10 minutes. Drain well and set aside.

2 Heat the oil in a wok or large frying pan and fry the cumin seeds for about 2 minutes, until they begin to splutter and release their fragrance. Add the chilli to the pan and fry, stirring constantly, for a further 1 minute.

3 Add the cauliflower florets to the pan and fry, stirring constantly, for about 5 minutes.

4 Add the potatoes, the ground spices and salt and cook for 7–10 minutes, or until both the vegetables are tender.

5 Garnish with fresh coriander and serve immediately with a tomato and onion salad and pickle.

> **Variation**
> Try using sweet potatoes instead of ordinary potatoes for an alternative curry with a sweeter flavour. The cauliflower could also be replaced with the same amount of broccoli.

Spiced Potatoes Energy 252kcal/1044kJ; Protein 3.5g; Carbohydrate 16.1g, of which sugars 5.7g; Fat 19.9g, of which saturates 10.4g; Cholesterol 40mg; Calcium 72mg; Fibre 3g; Sodium 628mg.
Cauliflower and Potatoes Energy 181kcal/759kJ; Protein 6.7g; Carbohydrate 23.2g, of which sugars 4.3g; Fat 7.5g, of which saturates 1.1g; Cholesterol 0mg; Calcium 40mg; Fibre 3.2g; Sodium 24mg.

Karahi Potatoes with Whole Spices and Mixed Chillies

The potato is transformed into something quite exotic when it is cooked as part of a dish like this.

Serves 4
15ml/1 tbsp vegetable oil
5ml/1 tsp cumin seeds
3 curry leaves
5ml/1 tsp crushed dried red chillies
2.5ml/½ tsp mixed onion, mustard and fenugreek seeds
2.5ml/½ tsp fennel seeds
3 garlic cloves, sliced
2.5cm/1in piece fresh root ginger, grated
2 onions, sliced
6 new potatoes, thinly sliced
15ml/1 tbsp chopped fresh coriander (cilantro)
1 fresh red chilli, seeded and sliced
1 fresh green chilli, seeded and sliced

1 Heat the oil in a karahi, wok or heavy pan. Lower the heat slightly and add the cumin seeds, curry leaves, dried red chillies, mixed onion, mustard and fenugreek seeds, fennel seeds, garlic slices and ginger. Fry for 1 minute.

2 Add the onions to the pan and fry for a further 5 minutes, or until the onions are golden brown.

3 Add the potatoes, fresh coriander and red and green chillies and mix well. Cover the pan tightly with a lid or foil; if using foil, make sure that it does not touch the food. Cook over a very low heat for about 7 minutes or until the potatoes are tender.

4 Remove the pan from the heat, and take off the lid or foil cover. Serve hot straight from the pan.

Cook's Tip
Choose a waxy variety of new potato for this fairly hot vegetable dish; if you use a very soft potato, it will not be possible to cut it into thin slices without it breaking up. Suitable varieties are often labelled 'salad potatoes' when sold at supermarkets. Leave the skin on for a tastier result.

Baby Potatoes with Red Chillies and Coriander

When new potatoes are in season and plentiful, there really is no better way to enjoy them than in this classic spicy side dish. Enjoy it as an accompaniment to a curry main course or simply on its own with some chutneys or pickles.

Serves 4
12–14 baby new potatoes, peeled and halved
30ml/2 tbsp vegetable oil
2.5ml/½ tsp crushed dried red chillies
2.5ml/½ tsp white cumin seeds
2.5ml/½ tsp fennel seeds
2.5ml/½ tsp crushed coriander seeds
15ml/1 tbsp salt
1 medium onion, sliced
1–4 fresh red chillies, chopped
15ml/1 tbsp chopped fresh coriander (cilantro)

1 Cook the baby potatoes in a large pan of boiling water until soft but still firm. Remove the pan from the heat and drain off all the water.

2 In a wok or deep frying pan, heat the vegetable oil, then turn down the heat to medium. Then add the crushed chillies, cumin, fennel and coriander seeds and salt to the pan and fry, stirring frequently, for 30–40 seconds.

3 Add the sliced onion to the pan and fry for 6–7 minutes, stirring frequently, until golden brown. Then add the potatoes, red chillies and fresh coriander.

4 Cover the pan with a lid and cook for a further 5–7 minutes over a very low heat. Serve immediately.

Variation
The quantity of red chillies used here may be too fiery for some palates, particularly children. For a milder version, either seed the chillies, use fewer or substitute them with 1 roughly chopped red (bell) pepper.

Karahi Potatoes Energy 152kcal/641kJ; Protein 3.8g; Carbohydrate 27.5g, of which sugars 6g; Fat 3.9g, of which saturates 0.5g; Cholesterol 0mg; Calcium 46mg; Fibre 2.6g; Sodium 19mg.
Potatoes with Red Chillies Energy 101kcal/421kJ; Protein 1.4g; Carbohydrate 11.4g, of which sugars 1.8g; Fat 5.8g, of which saturates 0.7g; Cholesterol 0mg; Calcium 20mg; Fibre 1.2g; Sodium 501mg.

Indian Potatoes with Poppy Seeds

Poppy seeds are used in Indian cooking as thickening agents, and to lend a nutty taste to sauces. It is the creamy white variety of poppy seed that is used here, rather than the ones with a blue-grey hue that are used for baking.

Serves 4
45ml/3 tbsp white poppy seeds
45–60ml/3–4 tbsp vegetable oil
675g/1½lb potatoes, peeled and
   cut into 1cm/½in cubes

2.5ml/½ tsp black mustard seeds
2.5ml/½ tsp onion seeds
2.5ml/½ tsp cumin seeds
2.5ml/½ tsp fennel seeds
1–2 dried red chillies, chopped or
   broken into small pieces
2.5ml/½ tsp ground turmeric
2.5ml/½ tsp salt
150ml/¼ pint/⅔ cup
   warm water
chopped fresh coriander (cilantro),
   to garnish
pooris and natural (plain) yogurt,
   to serve

1 Preheat a wok, karahi or large pan over a medium heat. When the pan is hot, reduce the heat slightly and add the poppy seeds. Stir them around in the pan until they are just a shade darker. Remove from the pan and allow to cool.

2 In the pan, heat the vegetable oil over a medium heat and fry the cubes of potatoes until they are light brown. Remove them with a slotted spoon and drain on kitchen paper.

3 To the same oil, add the mustard seeds. As soon as they begin to pop, add the onion, cumin and fennel seeds and the chillies. Let the chillies blacken.

4 Stir in the turmeric and follow quickly with the fried potatoes and salt. Stir well and add the warm water. Bring to the boil, cover the pan with the lid and reduce the heat to low. Cook for 8–10 minutes, or until the potatoes are tender.

5 Grind the poppy seeds with a mortar and pestle or in a spice grinder. Stir the ground seeds into the potatoes. They should form a thick paste which clings to the potatoes. If there is too much liquid, continue to stir over medium heat. Transfer to a serving dish. Garnish with coriander and serve with pooris and yogurt.

Bombay Potatoes

This authentic dish is most closely linked to the Gujarati, a totally vegetarian community and the largest population group in the city of Mumbai.

Serves 4–6
2 onions
2 fresh green chillies
50g/2oz/2 cups fresh
   coriander (cilantro)

450g/1lb new potatoes
5ml/1 tsp turmeric
60ml/4 tbsp vegetable oil
2 dried red chillies
6–8 curry leaves
1.5ml/¼ tsp asafoetida
2.5ml/½ tsp each cumin,
   mustard, onion, fennel and
   nigella seeds
lemon juice, to taste
salt

1 Chop the onions and chillies finely, and coarsely chop the coriander. Scrub the potatoes under cold running water and cut them into small pieces.

2 Cook the potatoes in a large pan of boiling water with a little salt and 2.5ml/½ tsp of the turmeric for 10–15 minutes, or until tender. Drain the potatoes well, then mash them with a potato masher and set aside.

3 Heat the vegetable oil in a frying pan and fry the dried chillies and curry leaves over a medium-high heat, stirring frequently, until the chillies are nearly burnt.

4 Add the chopped onions, green chillies, fresh coriander and remaining turmeric to the pan and fry for 2 minutes, until the onions are starting to soften.

5 Add the asafoetida, cumin, mustard, onion, fennel and nigella seeds to the pan. Cook, stirring occasionally, until the onions are soft and translucent but not brown.

6 Fold the potatoes into the pan and add a few drops of water if the mixture is a little dry. Cook over a low heat for about 10–12 minutes, stirring well to ensure the spices are evenly mixed throughout the dish. Stir the lemon juice into the potatoes to taste, and serve immediately.

Indian Potatoes Energy 179kcal/748kJ; Protein 2.6g; Carbohydrate 21.8g, of which sugars 5.9g; Fat 9.7g, of which saturates 1.2g; Cholesterol 0mg; Calcium 27mg; Fibre 2.1g; Sodium 13mg.
Bombay Potatoes Energy 143kcal/595kJ; Protein 2.1g; Carbohydrate 17.4g, of which sugars 4.7g; Fat 7.7g, of which saturates 0.9g; Cholesterol 0mg; Calcium 21mg; Fibre 1.7g; Sodium 10mg.

Potatoes in Chilli Tamarind Sauce

In this favourite potato dish from southern India, the combination of chilli and tamarind awakens the taste buds immediately. This version adapts the classic recipe slightly, to reduce the pungency and enhance the fiery appearance.

Serves 4–6

450g/1lb small new potatoes, washed and dried

25g/1oz whole dried red chillies

7.5ml/1½ tsp cumin seeds

4 garlic cloves

90ml/6 tbsp vegetable oil

60ml/4 tbsp thick tamarind juice, made by mixing tamarind paste with warm water

30ml/2 tbsp tomato purée (paste)

4 curry leaves

5ml/1 tsp sugar

1.5ml/¼ tsp asafoetida

salt

coriander (cilantro) sprigs and lemon wedges, to garnish

1 Cook the potatoes in a large pan of salted water for about 12–15 minutes, or until they are just cooked, ensuring they do not break. To test, insert a thin sharp knife into the potatoes. Drain the potatoes and place in a bowl of iced water to cool them down and prevent further cooking.

2 Soak the chillies for 5 minutes in warm water. Drain and grind with the cumin seeds and garlic to a coarse paste either using a mortar and pestle or in a food processor.

3 Heat the oil in a wok or deep frying pan and fry the spice paste, tamarind juice, tomato purée, curry leaves, salt, sugar and asafoetida until the oil separates from the spice paste.

4 Drain the the potatoes and add to the pan. Reduce the heat to low, cover the pan with a lid and simmer the potatoes for 5 minutes. Garnish with coriander and lemon wedges and serve immediately.

Variation

Chunks of sweet potatoes can be used as an alternative to new potatoes in this dish, if you prefer.

Potatoes in Spicy Yogurt Sauce

Tiny potatoes cooked with their skins on are delicious in this fairly spicy yet tangy yogurt sauce. Serve with any meat or fish dish or just with hot chapatis.

Serves 4

12 small new or salad potatoes, halved

300ml/½ pint/1¼ cups natural (plain) low-fat yogurt

300ml/½ pint/1¼ cups water

1.5ml/¼ tsp turmeric

5ml/1 tsp chilli powder

5ml/1 tsp ground coriander

2.5ml/½ tsp ground cumin

5ml/1 tsp salt

5ml/1 tsp light soft brown sugar

30ml/2 tbsp vegetable oil

5ml/1 tsp white cumin seeds

15ml/1 tbsp chopped fresh coriander (cilantro)

2 fresh green chillies, sliced

1 coriander (cilantro) sprig, to garnish (optional)

1 Cook the potatoes in their skins in boiling salted water until just tender, then drain and set aside.

2 Place the yogurt, water, turmeric, chilli powder, ground coriander, ground cumin, salt and sugar in a bowl. Mix well until all the ingredients are combined. Set aside.

3 Heat the vegetable oil in a medium pan over a medium-high heat and stir in the white cumin seeds.

4 Reduce the heat to medium, and stir the prepared yogurt mixture into the pan. Cook the sauce, stirring continuously, for about 3–5 minutes until heated through and bubbling.

5 Add the fresh coriander, green chillies and potatoes to the sauce. Mix well and cook for 5–7 minutes, stirring occasionally. Transfer to a serving dish, garnish with the coriander sprig, if you wish, and serve immediately.

Cook's Tip

If new or salad potatoes are unavailable, use 450g/1lb large potatoes instead, but choose a waxy not a floury variety. Peel them and cut into large chunks, then cook as described above.

Potatoes in Tamarind Sauce Energy 90kcal/379kJ; Protein 2.7g; Carbohydrate 19.5g, of which sugars 5.7g; Fat 0.7g, of which saturates 0.1g; Cholesterol 0mg; Calcium 30mg; Fibre 1.9g; Sodium 12mg.
Potatoes in Yogurt Sauce Energy 161kcal/677kJ; Protein 5.9g; Carbohydrate 24.7g, of which sugars 7g; Fat 5.1g, of which saturates 1g; Cholesterol 1mg; Calcium 154mg; Fibre 1.1g; Sodium 73mg.

Mango Chutney

No Indian meal would be complete without this classic chutney, which is ideal for making in a slow cooker. Its gloriously sweet, tangy flavour is the perfect complement to warm spices.

Makes 450g/1lb
3 firm mangoes
120ml/4fl oz/½ cup cider vinegar
200g/7oz/scant 1 cup light muscovado (brown) sugar
1 small red finger chilli or jalapeño chilli, split
2.5cm/1in piece fresh root ginger, peeled and finely chopped
1 garlic clove, finely chopped
5 cardamom pods, bruised
1 bay leaf
2.5ml/½ tsp salt

1 Peel the mangoes and cut out the stone (pit), then cut the flesh into small chunks or thin wedges.

2 Put the chopped mangoes in the ceramic cooking pot of the slow cooker. Add the cider vinegar, stir briefly to combine, and cover the slow cooker with the lid. Switch the slow cooker to the high setting and cook for about 2 hours, stirring the chutney halfway through the cooking time.

3 Stir the sugar, chilli, ginger, garlic, bruised cardamom pods, bay leaf and salt into the mango mixture, until the sugar has dissolved completely.

4 Cover and cook for 2 hours, then uncover and let the mixture cook for a further 1 hour, or until the chutney is reduced to a thick consistency and no excess liquid remains. Stir the chutney every 15 minutes during the last hour.

5 Remove and discard the bay leaf and the chilli. Spoon the chutney into hot sterilized jars and seal. Store for 1 week before eating and use within 1 year.

Cook's Tip
To make a more fiery chutney, seed and slice two green chillies and stir into the chutney mixture with the other spices.

Hot Coconut Chutney with Onion

Serve this exotic chutney as an accompaniment for Indian curries or with a raita and other chutneys and poppadums as an interesting start to a meal.

Serves 4–6
200g/7oz fresh coconut, grated
3–4 fresh green chillies, seeded and chopped
20g/¾oz fresh coriander (cilantro), chopped
30ml/2 tbsp chopped fresh mint
30–45ml/2–3 tbsp lime juice
about 2.5ml/½ tsp salt
about 2.5ml/½ tsp caster (superfine) sugar
15–30ml/1–2 tbsp coconut milk (optional)
30ml/2 tbsp groundnut (peanut) oil
5ml/1 tsp kalonji
1 small onion, very finely chopped
fresh coriander (cilantro) sprigs, to garnish

1 Place the coconut, chillies, coriander and fresh mint in a food processor or blender. Add 30ml/2 tbsp of the lime juice, then process until thoroughly chopped.

2 Scrape the mixture into a bowl and add more lime juice to taste. Add salt and sugar to taste. If the mixture is dry, stir in 15–30ml/1–2 tbsp coconut milk.

3 Heat the groundnut oil in a small heavy pan and fry the kalonji until they begin to pop, then reduce the heat and add the onion. Fry, stirring frequently, for about 4–5 minutes, until the onion softens but does not brown.

4 Add the onion mixture to the coconut mixture. Stir well to combine the two and leave to cool. Garnish with fresh coriander sprigs before serving.

Cook's Tips
• *Kalonji are small black seeds which have a slightly bitter, yet pleasant, taste. They are fried to release their flavour.*
• *Use more chillies in step 1 to make the paste if you prefer a chutney with a hotter flavour.*

Mango Chutney Energy 1045kcal/4465kJ; Protein 4.1g; Carbohydrate 272.5g, of which sugars 271.1g; Fat 0.9g, of which saturates 0.5g; Cholesterol 0mg; Calcium 908mg; Fibre 11.7g; Sodium 1002mg.
Coconut Chutney Energy 145kcal/596kJ; Protein 1.6g; Carbohydrate 2.8g, of which sugars 2.5g; Fat 14.2g, of which saturates 9.3g; Cholesterol 0mg; Calcium 40mg; Fibre 3.3g; Sodium 11mg.

Tomato and Fresh Chilli Chutney

This fresh-tasting and invigorating chutney is the perfect partner to liven up a simple curry or dhal.

Makes about 475ml/ 16fl oz/2 cups
1 red (bell) pepper
4 tomatoes, chopped
2 fresh green chillies, chopped
1 garlic clove, crushed
1.5ml/¼ tsp salt
2.5ml/½ tsp sugar
5ml/1 tsp chilli powder
45ml/3 tbsp tomato
   purée (paste)
15ml/1 tbsp chopped fresh
   coriander (cilantro)

1 Halve the red pepper and remove the core and seeds. Roughly chop the red pepper halves into chunks.

2 Process the pepper with the tomatoes, chillies, garlic, salt, sugar, chilli powder, tomato purée and coriander with 30ml/ 2 tbsp water in a food processor until smooth. Transfer to a sterilized jar, cover and chill until needed.

Mint and Coconut Chutney

This chutney is made using fresh mint leaves and desiccated coconut, all bound together with yogurt.

Makes about 350ml/ 12fl oz/1½ cups
50g/2oz fresh mint leaves
90ml/6 tbsp desiccated
   (dry unsweetened
   shredded) coconut
15ml/1 tbsp sesame seeds
1.5ml/¼ tsp salt
175ml/6fl oz/¾ cup natural
   (plain) yogurt

1 Finely chop the fresh mint leaves, using a sharp kitchen knife or a specialist herb chopper.

2 Put the mint with the coconut, sesame seeds, salt and yogurt into a food processor or blender and process until smooth.

3 Transfer the chutney to a sterilized jar, cover and chill in the refrigerator until needed.

Squash, Apricot and Almond Chutney

Coriander seeds and ground turmeric add a deliciously spicy touch to this rich, slow-cooker chutney. It is ideal spooned on to little savoury canapés or with melting cubes of mozzarella cheese; it is also good in sandwiches, helping to spice up a variety of fillings.

Makes about 1.8kg/4lb
1 small butternut squash,
   weighing about 800g/1¾lb
400g/14oz/2 cups golden sugar
300ml/½ pint/1¼ cups
   cider vinegar
2 onions, finely chopped
225g/8oz/1 cup ready-to-eat
   dried apricots, chopped
finely grated rind and juice of
   1 orange
2.5ml/½ tsp turmeric
15ml/1 tbsp coriander seeds
15ml/1 tbsp salt
115g/4oz/1 cup flaked
   (sliced) almonds

1 Halve the butternut squash and scoop out the seeds. Peel off the skin, then cut the flesh into 1cm/½in cubes.

2 Put the sugar and vinegar in the ceramic cooking pot of the cooker and switch to high. Heat for 30 minutes, then stir until the sugar has completely dissolved.

3 Add the butternut squash, onions, apricots, orange rind and juice, turmeric, coriander seeds and salt to the slow cooker pot and stir well until the ingredients are well combined.

4 Cover the slow cooker with the lid and cook for about 5–6 hours, stirring occasionally during that time.

5 After about 5 hours the chutney should be a fairly thick consistency with relatively little liquid. If it is still quite runny at this stage, cook uncovered for the final hour. Stir the flaked almonds into the chutney.

6 Spoon the chutney into warmed sterilized jars, cover and seal. Store in a cool, dark place and allow the chutney to mature for at least 1 month before eating. It should be used within 2 years. Once opened, store jars of the chutney in the refrigerator and use within 2 months.

Tomato and Chilli Chutney Energy 187kcal/794kJ; Protein 9.7g; Carbohydrate 33.2g, of which sugars 30g; Fat 2.5g, of which saturates 0.5g; Cholesterol 0mg; Calcium 175mg; Fibre 7.5g; Sodium 157mg.
Mint and Coconut Chutney Energy 753kcal/3117kJ; Protein 18.6g Carbohydrate 21.7g, of which sugars 18.9g; Fat 66.6g, of which saturates 50.2g; Cholesterol 2mg; Calcium 559mg; Fibre 13.5g Sodium 181mg.
Squash Chutney Energy 2770kcal/11,723kJ; Protein 41.7g; Carbohydrate 532.6g, of which sugars 524.1g; Fat 67.3g, of which saturates 5.9g; Cholesterol 0mg; Calcium 807mg; Fibre 31.6g; Sodium 5967mg.

Sesame Seed and Chilli Chutney

This is an extremely versatile Indian chutney, which doubles as a delicious dip for poppadums, pakora or bhajias. It also makes a tasty sandwich filling with cucumber.

Serves 4
175g/6oz sesame seeds
5ml/1 tsp salt
120–150ml/4–5fl oz/½–⅔
   cup water
2 green chillies, seeded and diced
60ml/4 tbsp chopped fresh
   coriander (cilantro)
15ml/1 tbsp chopped fresh
   mint leaves
15ml/1 tbsp tamarind paste
30ml/2 tbsp sugar
5ml/1 tsp corn oil
1.5ml/¼ tsp onion seeds
4 curry leaves
6 onion rings, 1 green chilli, seeded
   and sliced, 1 red chilli,
   seeded and sliced, and
   15ml/1 tbsp fresh coriander
   (cilantro) leaves, to garnish

1 Dry-roast the sesame seeds and leave to cool. Place them in a spice grinder and grind to a grainy powder, or grind the seeds using a mortar and pestle.

2 Transfer the sesame powder to a bowl. Add the salt, water, diced chillies, coriander, mint, tamarind paste and sugar and, using a fork, mix everything together.

3 Taste and adjust the seasoning if necessary: the mixture should have a sweet-and-sour flavour.

4 Heat the oil in a heavy pan and fry the onion seeds and curry leaves, stirring constantly, for 2–3 minutes until the seeds begin to splutter and release their fragrances.

5 Add the sesame seed paste to the pan and fry the mixture for about 45 seconds, stirring constantly to avoid it sticking to the base of the pan and burning. Transfer the mixture to a warmed serving dish.

6 Garnish the chutney with onion rings, sliced green and red chillies and the fresh coriander leaves. If it is not to be eaten immediately, cover the chutney tightly and store it in the refrigerator until it is required.

Fresh Coriander Relish

Delicious as an accompaniment to kebabs, samosas and bhajias, this relish can also be used as a spread for cucumber or tomato sandwiches.

**Makes about 450g/1lb/
2 cups**
30ml/2 tbsp vegetable oil
1 dried red chilli
1.5ml/¼ tsp each cumin, fennel
   and onion seeds
1.5ml/¼ tsp asafoetida
4 curry leaves
115g/4oz/1⅓ cups desiccated
   (dry unsweetened
   shredded) coconut
10ml/2 tsp sugar
3 fresh green chillies, seeded
   and chopped
175–225g/6–8oz fresh coriander
   (cilantro), chopped
60ml/4 tbsp mint sauce
juice of 3 lemons
salt

1 Heat the oil in a frying pan and add the dried chilli, the cumin, fennel and onion seeds, the asafoetida, curry leaves, desiccated coconut, sugar and salt to taste. Fry, stirring often, until the coconut turns golden brown. Transfer into a bowl and set aside to cool.

2 Grind the spice mixture with the green chillies, fresh coriander and mint sauce in a food processor or blender or with a mortar and pestle. Moisten with lemon juice. Scrape into a bowl and chill before serving.

Cook's Tip
This may seem like a lot of coriander, but it is compacted when it is ground with the spices.

Variation
For Coriander and Walnut Relish, put 90ml/6 tbsp fresh coriander leaves, 2 garlic cloves, 50g/2oz chopped onion and 60ml/4 tbsp sugar into a food processor and grind until thick. Add 50g/2oz/½ cup chopped walnuts and mix well. Add salt and ground black pepper to taste.

Sesame Chutney Energy 303kcal/1256kJ; Protein 8.5g; Carbohydrate 8.6g, of which sugars 8.4g; Fat 26.3g, of which saturates 3.7g; Cholesterol 0mg; Calcium 327mg; Fibre 4.2g; Sodium 506mg.
Fresh Coriander Relish Energy 1121kcal/4640kJ; Protein 17.2g; Carbohydrate 42.7g, of which sugars 36.5g; Fat 98.5g, of which saturates 64.3g; Cholesterol 0mg; Calcium 631mg; Fibre 28.3g; Sodium 534mg.

Tomato Relish

This is a simple relish that can be served with most meals. It provides a contrast to hot curries, with its crunchy texture and refreshing ingredients.

Serves 4–6
2 small fresh green chillies
2 limes
2.5ml/½ tsp sugar, or to taste
2 onions, finely chopped
4 firm tomatoes, seeded and
    finely chopped
½ cucumber, finely chopped
a few fresh coriander (cilantro)
    leaves, chopped
salt and ground black pepper
a few fresh mint leaves,
    to garnish

1 Using a sharp knife, cut both the green chillies in half. Scrape out the seeds and discard, then chop the chillies finely and place them in a small bowl.

2 Squeeze the limes. Pour the juice into a glass bowl and add the sugar, with salt and pepper to taste. Set aside until the sugar and salt have dissolved, stirring the mixture occasionally.

3 Add the chopped chillies to the bowl, with the chopped onions, tomatoes, cucumber and fresh coriander leaves. Mix well to combine the ingredients.

4 Cover the bowl with clear film (plastic wrap) and place in the refrigerator for at least 3 hours, so that the flavours blend. Just before serving, taste the relish and add more salt, pepper or sugar if needed. Garnish with mint and serve.

Cook's Tip
If you find that preparing chillies irritates your skin then wear a pair of kitchen gloves or cover your hands with a plastic bag.

Variation
For a milder-flavoured relish, use just one chilli, or dispense with them altogether and substitute with a green (bell) pepper.

Bombay Duck and Chilli Pickle

The bummalo fish is found off the west coast of India during the monsoon season. It is salted and dried in the sun and is characterized by a strong smell and distinctive piquancy. How this fish acquired the name Bombay duck in the West is far from certain.

Serves 4–6
6–8 pieces bummalo (Bombay
    duck), soaked in water for
    5 minutes
60ml/4 tbsp vegetable oil
2 fresh red chillies, crushed
15ml/1 tbsp sugar
450g/1lb cherry tomatoes, cut
    in half
115g/4oz fried onions

1 Pat the soaked fish dry with kitchen paper. Heat the oil in a frying pan and fry the fish pieces for about 30–45 seconds on both sides until crisp. Be careful not to burn them as they will taste bitter. Drain well on kitchen paper. When cool enough to handle, break the fish into small pieces.

2 To the same oil, add the chillies and fry, stirring constantly, for about 2–3 minutes, until the chillies release their aromas.

3 Add the sugar, cherry tomatoes and fried onions to the pan and mix well to combine the ingredients. Continue to cook, stirring frequently, until the tomatoes become pulpy and the mixture is blended into a fairly thick sauce.

4 Fold the fish pieces into the tomato sauce and cook for a minute until all the ingredients are heated through. Serve immediately if eating hot, or it will be equally delicious if left to cool before eating cold.

Cook's Tip
The origin of the term 'Bombay duck' is uncertain. Some believe that, during the British Raj, the dried fish was often transported on the railway and that the mail carriages of the train (dak means 'mail' in Hindi) would smell of the fish, consequently leading the British to refer to the pungent smell of the fish as the 'Bombay dak', which became 'duck'.

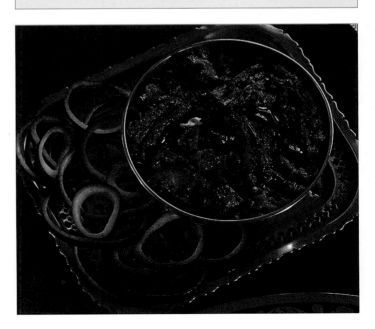

Tomato Relish Energy 530kcal/2262kJ; Protein 3.7g; Carbohydrate 134.1g, of which sugars 134.1g; Fat 1.4g, of which saturates 0.5g; Cholesterol 0mg; Calcium 93mg; Fibre 4.5g; Sodium 2012mg.
Bombay Duck Pickle Energy 156kcal/652kJ; Protein 11.8g; Carbohydrate 5g, of which sugars 4.2g; Fat 10g, of which saturates 1.9g; Cholesterol 22mg; Calcium 22mg; Fibre 1.4g; Sodium 141mg.

Apple and Sultana Chutney

Use wine or cider vinegar for this stovetop chutney to give it a subtle and mellow flavour. The chutney is perfect served with Indian food or cheeses and freshly made bread.

Makes about 900g/2lb

350g/12oz cooking apples
115g/4oz/²/₃ cup sultanas
   (golden raisins)
50g/2oz onion
25g/1oz/¹/₄ cup
   almonds, blanched
5ml/1 tsp white peppercorns
2.5ml/¹/₂ tsp coriander seeds
175g/6oz/scant 1 cup sugar
10ml/2 tsp salt
5ml/1 tsp ground ginger
450ml/³/₄ pint/scant 2 cups cider
   vinegar or wine vinegar
1.5ml/¹/₄ tsp cayenne pepper
red chillies (optional)

1 Peel, core and chop the apples. Chop the sultanas, onion and almonds. Tie the peppercorns and coriander seeds in muslin (cheesecloth), using a long piece of string, and then tie to the handle of a preserving pan or stainless steel pan.

2 Put the sugar, salt, ground ginger and vinegar into the pan, with the cayenne pepper to taste. Heat the mixture gently, stirring, until the sugar has completely dissolved.

3 Add the chopped fruit to the pan. Bring the mixture to the boil and then lower the heat. Simmer for about 1¹/₂–2 hours, or until most of the liquid has evaporated.

4 Spoon the chutney into warmed sterilized jars and place one whole fresh chilli in each jar, if using. Leave until cold, then cover and seal the jars and attach a label to each one.

5 Store in a cool, dark place. The chutney is best left for a month to mature before eating and will keep for at least 6 months, if it is correctly stored.

> **Variation**
> For a mild chutney, add only a little cayenne pepper. For a spicier one, increase the quantity to taste.

Lime Pickle

Sharp lime pickle is one of the best-known Indian relishes. For this recipe, you will need ripe limes, with a yellow tinge on the skin.

**Makes about 900g/2lb/
4 cups**

10–12 limes
15ml/1 tbsp salt
120ml/4fl oz/¹/₂ cup malt vinegar
250ml/8fl oz/1 cup vegetable oil
5ml/1 tsp asafoetida
10–12 garlic cloves, crushed
2.5cm/1in piece of fresh root
   ginger, grated
10–12 curry leaves
30ml/2 tbsp black mustard seeds,
   finely ground
15ml/1 tbsp cumin seeds,
   finely ground
10ml/2 tsp fenugreek seeds,
   finely ground
10ml/2 tsp ground turmeric
10ml/2 tsp chilli powder
10 green chillies, halved
20ml/4 tsp salt
20ml/4 tsp sugar

1 Wash the limes and dry them with a cloth. Trim them, then cut them into quarters. Sprinkle the quarters with the salt and put them in a colander over a bowl. Set aside for 2 hours, then transfer them to another bowl and add the vinegar. Stir until any remaining salt is dissolved and drain in the colander again.

2 Heat the oil in a pan over a medium heat and add the asafoetida, followed by the garlic, ginger and curry leaves. Allow them to brown in the pan slightly.

3 Add the ground seeds, turmeric and chilli powder, and stir-fry for 1 minute, then add the green chillies, salt and sugar. Stir-fry for 1 minute longer before adding the limes. Remove the pan from the heat and allow to cool completely.

4 Store the lime pickle in sterilized, airtight jars. Leave the pickle in the jar for 4–5 weeks to mature before eating. The pickle will keep for 10–12 months.

> **Cook's Tip**
> To sterilize jars for bottling pickles or chutneys, boil them in water for a minimum of 10 minutes.

Apple Chutney Energy 1299kcal/5525kJ; Protein 10.9g; Carbohydrate 299.5g, of which sugars 297.7g; Fat 14.9g, of which saturates 1.1g; Cholesterol 0mg; Calcium 254mg; Fibre 10.4g; Sodium 3.97g.
Lime Pickle Energy 120kcal/492kJ; Protein 0.1g; Carbohydrate 0.3g, of which sugars 0.2g; Fat 13.1g, of which saturates 1.6g; Cholesterol 0mg; Calcium 9mg; Fibre 0.1g; Sodium 436mg.

Green Chilli Pickle

Southern India is the source of some of the hottest curries and pickles. You might imagine that eating them would be a case of going for the burn, but they actually help to cool the body in the heat of the Indian sun.

Makes 450–550g/1–1¼lb/ 2–2½ cups

50g/2oz/4 tbsp yellow mustard seeds, crushed

50g/2oz/4 tbsp freshly ground cumin seeds
25g/1oz/¼ cup ground turmeric
50g/2oz garlic cloves, crushed, plus 20 small garlic cloves, peeled but left whole
150ml/¼ pint/⅔ cup white vinegar
75g/3oz/6 tbsp sugar
10ml/2 tsp salt
150ml/¼ pint/⅔ cup mustard oil
450g/1lb small or medium fresh green chillies

1 Mix together the mustard and cumin seeds, the turmeric, crushed garlic, white vinegar, sugar and salt in a sterilized glass bowl until the ingredients are well blended.

2 Cover the bowl with a clean cloth and leave to rest in a cool place for 24 hours. This enables the spices to infuse (steep) and the sugar and salt to dissolve.

3 Heat the mustard oil in a frying pan and gently fry the spice mixture for about 5 minutes. (Keep a window open while cooking with mustard oil as it is very pungent and the smoke from it may irritate the eyes.)

4 Add the whole, peeled garlic cloves to the pan and fry for a further 5 minutes, stirring frequently.

5 Halve each fresh green chilli, washing your hands carefully afterwards to avoid irritating sensitive skin. Add the chillies and cook gently until tender but still green in colour. This will take about 30 minutes over a low heat.

6 Cool thoroughly, then pour into sterilized jars, ensuring that the oil is evenly distributed if you are using more than one jar. Leave to rest for a week before serving.

Red Hot Relish

Make this tangy, stovetop relish during the summer months when tomatoes and peppers are plentiful.

Makes about 1.3kg/3lb

800g/1¾lb ripe tomatoes, skinned and quartered
450g/1lb red onions, chopped
3 red (bell) peppers, chopped

3 fresh red chillies, seeded and finely sliced
200g/7oz/1 cup sugar
200ml/7fl oz/scant 1 cup red wine vinegar
30ml/2 tbsp mustard seeds
10ml/2 tsp celery seeds
15ml/1 tbsp paprika
5ml/1 tsp salt

1 Put the tomatoes, onions, peppers and chillies in a preserving pan, cover with a lid and simmer over a very low heat for about 10 minutes, stirring once or twice, until the tomato juices run.

2 Add the sugar and vinegar and slowly bring to the boil until the sugar has dissolved completely. Add the mustard seeds, celery seeds, paprika and salt, and stir well to combine.

3 Increase the heat slightly and cook the relish, uncovered, for 30 minutes, or until the mixture has a thick, moist consistency.

4 Spoon the relish into warmed sterilized jars, cover and seal. Store in a cool, dark place and leave for at least 2 weeks before eating. Use the relish within 1 year of making.

Papaya and Lemon Relish

This chunky relish is best made in a slow cooker. Serve with roast meats.

Makes 450g/1lb

1 large unripe papaya
1 onion, very thinly sliced
175ml/6fl oz/generous ¾ cup red wine vinegar

juice of 2 lemons
165g/5½oz/¾ cup golden caster (superfine) sugar
1 cinnamon stick
1 bay leaf
2.5ml/½ tsp hot paprika
2.5ml/½ tsp salt
150g/5oz/1 cup sultanas (golden raisins)

1 Peel the papaya and cut it in half lengthways. Remove the seeds then cut the flesh into small even chunks.

2 Place the papaya chunks in the ceramic cooking pot, add the onion slices and stir in the vinegar. Switch the slow cooker to the high setting, cover with the lid and cook for 2 hours.

3 Add the lemon juice, sugar, cinnamon stick, bay leaf, paprika, salt and sultanas to the ceramic cooking pot. Gently stir the mixture until all of the sugar has completely dissolved.

4 Cook the chutney for a further 1 hour. Leave the cover of the slow cooker off to allow some of the liquid to evaporate and the mixture to reduce. It should be fairly thick and syrupy.

5 Ladle the chutney into hot sterilized jars. Seal and store the chutney for 1 week to allow it to mature. Use within a year but opened jars should be chilled and consumed within 2 weeks.

Green Chilli Pickle Energy 1953kcal/8134kJ; Protein 51.5g; Carbohydrate 176.9g, of which sugars 95.2g; Fat 123.3g, of which saturates 14.7g; Cholesterol 0mg; Calcium 488mg; Fibre 8.2g; Sodium 96mg.
Red Hot Relish Energy 1270kcal/5392kJ; Protein 17.8g; Carbohydrate 306.2g, of which sugars 294.1g; Fat 5.6g, of which saturates 1.4g; Cholesterol 0mg; Calcium 320mg; Fibre 23.5g; Sodium 121mg.
Papaya Relish Energy 1294kcal/5511kJ; Protein 8.4g; Carbohydrate 332.7g, of which sugars 332.7g; Fat 1.4g, of which saturates 0g; Cholesterol 0mg; Calcium 272mg; Fibre 16.1g; Sodium 1111mg.

Onion, Mango and Peanut Chaat

Chaats are spiced relishes of vegetables and nuts served with Indian meals. Amchur adds a deliciously fruity sourness to this mixture of onions and mango.

Serves 4
90g/3½oz/scant 1 cup
   unsalted peanuts
15ml/1 tbsp groundnut
   (peanut) oil
1 onion, chopped
10cm/4in piece cucumber, seeded
   and cut into 5mm/¼in dice
1 mango, peeled, stoned (pitted)
   and diced
1 green chilli, seeded and chopped
30ml/2 tbsp chopped fresh
   coriander (cilantro)
15ml/1 tbsp chopped fresh mint
15ml/1 tbsp lime juice, or to taste
light muscovado (brown) sugar,
   to taste

For the chaat masala
10ml/2 tsp ground toasted
   cumin seeds
2.5ml/½ tsp cayenne pepper
5ml/1 tsp mango
   powder (amchur)
2.5ml/½ tsp garam masala
pinch of ground asafoetida
salt and ground black pepper

1 To make the chaat masala, mix all the spices together, then season with 2.5ml/½ tsp each of salt and pepper.

2 Fry the peanuts in the oil until lightly browned, stirring frequently, then drain on kitchen paper until cool.

3 Put the onion in a mixing bowl with the cucumber, mango, chilli, fresh coriander and mint. Sprinkle in 5ml/1 tsp of the chaat masala and mix well to thoroughly combine.

4 Stir in the peanuts and then add lime juice and/or sugar to taste. Set the mixture aside for 20–30 minutes to give the flavours time to develop. Transfer the mixture into a serving bowl, sprinkle another 5ml/1 tsp of the chaat masala over the top and serve immediately.

> **Cook's Tip**
> *Any remaining chaat masala can be placed in a sealed jar and kept in a cool place for 4–6 weeks.*

Sweet and Hot Dried-fruit Chutney

This rich, thick and slightly sticky preserve of spiced dried fruit is simple to make in the slow cooker. It is a wonderful way to enliven cold roast turkey left over from your Christmas or Thanksgiving dinner.

Makes about 1.5kg/3lb 6oz
350g/12oz/1½ cups ready-to-eat
   dried apricots
225g/8oz/1½ cups dried dates,
   stoned (pitted)
225g/8oz/1⅓ cups dried figs
50g/2oz/⅓ cup glacé (candied)
   citrus peel
150g/5oz/1 cup raisins
50g/2oz/½ cup dried cranberries
75ml/2½fl oz/⅓ cup
   cranberry juice
300ml/½ pint/1¼ cups
   cider vinegar
225g/8oz/1 cup caster
   (superfine) sugar
finely grated rind of 1 lemon
5ml/1 tsp mixed (apple pie) spice
5ml/1 tsp ground coriander
5ml/1 tsp cayenne pepper
5ml/1 tsp salt

1 Chop the apricots, dates, figs and citrus peel, and put all the dried fruit in the ceramic cooking pot. Pour over the cranberry juice, stir, then cover the slow cooker and switch to low. Cook for 1 hour, or until the fruit has absorbed most of the juice.

2 Add the cider vinegar and sugar to the pot. Turn the slow cooker up to high and stir until the sugar has dissolved.

3 Re-cover and cook for 2 more hours, or until the fruit is very soft and the chutney fairly thick (it will thicken further as it cools). Stir in the lemon rind, mixed spice, coriander, cayenne pepper and salt. Cook, uncovered, for about 30 minutes, until little excess liquid remains.

4 Spoon the chutney into warmed sterilized jars, cover and seal. Store in a cool, dark place. Open within 10 months and, once opened, store in the refrigerator and use within 2 months.

> **Variation**
> *Pitted prunes can be substituted for the dates, and dried sour cherries for the dried cranberries.*

Onion Chaat Energy 189kcal/788kJ; Protein 6.9g; Carbohydrate 9.8g, of which sugars 6.6g; Fat 14g, of which saturates 2.4g; Cholesterol 0mg; Calcium 41mg; Fibre 2.4g; Sodium 4mg.
Sweet Chutney Energy 2873kcal/12,248kJ; Protein 32g; Carbohydrate 714.3g, of which sugars 703.5g; Fat 6.8g, of which saturates 0.2g; Cholesterol 0mg; Calcium 1075mg; Fibre 52.1g; Sodium 2358mg.

Pineapple Pickle

This sweet-and-sour pickle is ideal as an accompaniment to curries.

Serves 6–8

15ml/1 tbsp brown mustard seeds
2 dried chillies, soaked in water, seeded, and squeezed dry
15g/½oz fresh root ginger, chopped
1 garlic clove, chopped
5ml/1 tsp ground turmeric
200ml/7fl oz/scant 1 cup white wine vinegar or rice vinegar
15ml/1 tbsp palm sugar (jaggery)
1 pineapple, cored and diced
salt

1 Dry-roast the mustard seeds until they pop. Using a mortar and pestle or food processor, grind the chillies, ginger and garlic to a paste. Stir in the mustard seeds and ground turmeric. Add the vinegar and sugar, stirring until the sugar has dissolved.

2 Put the pineapple in a bowl and pour over the sauce. Add salt to taste. The pickle will keep for 3 days in the refrigerator.

Chilli Strips with Lime

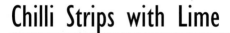

This fresh, tangy relish is made with strips of fresh chilli, lime juice and onion. It is ideal for serving with curries, stews, rice dishes or bean dishes.

Makes about 60ml/4 tbsp

10 fresh green chillies
½ white onion
4 limes
2.5ml/½ tsp dried oregano
salt

1 Roast the chillies in a griddle pan over a medium heat until the skins are charred and blistered but not blackened. Place the chillies in a plastic bag and tie the top. Set aside for 20 minutes.

2 Meanwhile, slice the onion very thinly and put it in a bowl. Squeeze the limes and add the juice to the bowl, with any pulp that gathers. Stir in the oregano.

3 Peel the chillies. Slit them, scrape out the seeds, then cut the chillies into long strips. Add to the onion mixture and season with salt. Cover and chill for 1 day before serving.

Onion Relish

This fiery side dish from Mexico is particularly good served with chicken, turkey or fish dishes.

Makes 1 small jar

2 fresh red fresno chillies
5ml/1 tsp allspice berries
2.5ml/½ tsp black peppercorns
5ml/1 tsp dried oregano
2 white onions
2 garlic cloves, peeled
100ml/3½fl oz/⅓ cup white wine vinegar
200ml/7fl oz/scant 1 cup cider vinegar
salt

1 Spear the fresno chillies on a long-handled metal skewer and roast them over the flame of a gas burner until the skins blister. Take care not to let the flesh burn. Alternatively, dry-fry them in a griddle pan until the skins are scorched. Place the roasted chillies in a strong plastic bag and tie or twist the top. Set aside for 20 minutes.

2 Meanwhile, place the allspice, black peppercorns and oregano in a mortar or food processor. Grind slowly by hand with a pestle or process until coarsely ground.

3 Cut the onions in half and slice them thinly. Put them in a bowl. Dry-roast the garlic in a heavy frying pan until golden, then crush and add to the onions in the bowl.

4 Remove the chillies from the bag and peel off the skins. Slit the chillies, scrape out the seeds, then chop them.

5 Add the ground spices to the onion mixture, followed by the chillies. Stir in both vinegars. Add salt to taste and mix thoroughly. Cover the bowl and chill in the refrigerator for at least 1 day before serving.

> **Cook's Tip**
> *White onions have a pungent flavour and are good in this relish. Spanish (Bermuda) onions can also be used, and shallots also make an excellent pickle.*

Pineapple Pickle Energy 56kcal/238kJ; Protein 0.7g; Carbohydrate 12.5g, of which sugars 12.2g; Fat 0.2g, of which saturates 0g; Cholesterol 0mg; Calcium 20mg; Fibre 1.3g; Sodium 4mg.
Chilli Strips with Lime Energy 49kcal/204kJ; Protein 3.9g; Carbohydrate 7g, of which sugars 5.7g; Fat 0.7g, of which saturates 0g; Cholesterol 0mg; Calcium 52mg; Fibre 0.9g; Sodium 10mg.
Onion Relish: Energy 173kcal/721kJ; Protein 6.3g; Carbohydrate 35.1g, of which sugars 22.4g; Fat 2.1g, of which saturates 0.2g; Cholesterol 0mg; Calcium 118mg; Fibre 5.6g; Sodium 15mg.

Cucumber Raita

Raitas are slightly sour, yogurt-based accompaniments that have a cooling effect on the palate when eaten with spicy foods. They help to balance out the flavours of an Indian meal. This is the cucumber version, which is one of the most popular varieties.

Makes about 600ml/1 pint/ 2½ cups
½ cucumber
1 fresh green chilli, seeded and chopped
300ml/½ pint/1¼ cups natural (plain) yogurt
1.5ml/¼ tsp salt
1.5ml/¼ tsp ground cumin

1 Dice the cucumber finely and place in a large mixing bowl. Sprinkle over the chopped green chilli and mix well to combine it with the cucumber.

2 Place the natural yogurt in a bowl and beat it with a fork until it becomes smooth, then stir it into the cucumber and chilli mixture in the large bowl.

3 Stir the salt and ground cumin into the yogurt mixture. Cover the bowl with clear film (plastic wrap) and chill in the refrigerator for at least 30 minutes before serving.

Cook's Tip
The cucumber can be sprinkled with 5ml/1 tsp salt and left in a sieve (strainer) to release any excess moisture, if you prefer, although this isn't necessary. If you do salt the cucumber, ensure that it is well rinsed and squeezed dry afterwards.

Variations
• Instead of using cucumber in this raita, use two skinned, seeded and chopped tomatoes and about 15ml/1 tbsp chopped fresh coriander (cilantro).
• If you prefer, the cucumber can be grated, rather than diced, before adding to the yogurt.

Fruit Raita

Refreshing yogurt raitas are not just made with vegetables, they can also be made with almost any fruit. For this version, grapes and bananas are used.

Serves 4
350ml/12fl oz/1½ cups natural (plain) yogurt

75g/3oz seedless grapes
50g/2oz shelled walnuts
2 firm bananas, sliced
5ml/1 tsp sugar
5ml/1 tsp freshly ground cumin seeds
salt
1.5ml/¼ tsp freshly roasted cumin seeds, and chilli powder, to garnish

1 Put the yogurt, grapes and walnuts in a large mixing bowl. Fold in the banana slices.

2 Stir in the sugar, ground cumin and salt. Chill and sprinkle on the roasted cumin seeds and chilli powder before serving.

Spiced Yogurt

This refreshing yogurt accompaniment features whole and ground spice seeds as well as a slight kick from the dried red chilli and curry leaves.

Makes 450ml/¾ pint/scant 2 cups
450ml/¾ pint/scant 2 cups natural (plain) yogurt

2.5ml/½ tsp freshly ground fennel seeds
2.5ml/½ tsp sugar
60ml/4 tbsp vegetable oil
1 dried red chilli
1.5ml/¼ tsp mustard seeds
1.5ml/¼ tsp cumin seeds
4–6 curry leaves
a pinch each of asafoetida and ground turmeric
salt

1 Mix together the yogurt, fennel seeds and sugar, and add salt to taste. Chill in the refrigerator.

2 Heat the oil and fry the remaining ingredients. When the chilli turns dark, pour the oil and spices over the yogurt and mix. Cover and chill before serving.

Cucumber Raita Energy 31kcal/131kJ; Protein 2.8g; Carbohydrate 4.2g, of which sugars 4g; Fat 0.6g, of which saturates 0.3g; Cholesterol 1mg; Calcium 104mg; Fibre 0.2g; Sodium 141mg.
Fruit Raita Energy 202kcal/847kJ; Protein 7.2g; Carbohydrate 23.2g, of which sugars 21.5g; Fat 9.8g, of which saturates 1.2g; Cholesterol 1mg; Calcium 186mg; Fibre 1.1g; Sodium 75mg.
Spiced Yogurt Energy 441kcal/1842kJ; Protein 25.2g; Carbohydrate 41.6g, of which sugars 36.4g; Fat 21.5g, of which saturates 4.3g; Cholesterol 6mg; Calcium 884mg; Fibre 0g; Sodium 379mg.

Pickled Onions

The English love of pickled onions is famous, and at the time of the Raj the popular pickle was introduced into India. The onions should be stored in a cool, dark place for at least 6 weeks before being eaten.

Makes 3 or 4 450g/1lb jars
1kg/2¼lb pickling onions
115g/4oz/½ cup salt
750ml/1¼ pints/3 cups
   malt vinegar
15ml/1 tbsp sugar
2 or 3 dried red chillies
5ml/1 tsp brown mustard seeds
15ml/1 tbsp coriander seeds
5ml/1 tsp allspice berries
5ml/1 tsp black peppercorns
5cm/2in piece fresh root
   ginger, sliced
2 or 3 blades of mace
2 or 3 fresh bay leaves

1 Trim off the root end of each onion, but leave the onion layers attached. Cut a thin slice off the top (neck) end of each onion. Place the onions in a bowl, then cover with boiling water. Leave to stand for about 4 minutes, then drain. Peel off the skin from each onion with a small, sharp knife.

2 Place the peeled onions in a bowl and cover with cold water, then drain the water off and pour it into a large pan. Add the salt and heat slightly to dissolve it, then cool before pouring the brine over the onions. Cover the bowl with a plate and weigh it down slightly so that all the onions are submerged in the brine. Leave the onions to stand in the salted water for 24 hours.

3 Pour the vinegar into a large pan. Wrap all the remaining ingredients, except the bay leaves, in a piece of muslin (cheesecloth) or sew them into a filter paper for coffee. Add to the vinegar with the bay leaves. Bring to the boil, simmer for 5 minutes, then remove from the heat. Leave overnight so that the flavours have time to combine.

4 Drain the onions, rinse and pat dry. Pack them into sterilized jars. Add some or all of the spice from the vinegar, but not the ginger slices. The pickle will get hotter if you add the chillies. Pour the vinegar over the onions to cover and add the bay leaves. Cover the jars with non-metallic lids.

Hot Pickled Shallots

Pickling shallots in this way demands some patience while the vinegar and spices work their magic, but the results are worth the wait.

Makes 2–3 jars
5 or 6 small red or green bird's
   eye chillies
500g/1¼lb Thai pink
   shallots, peeled
2 large garlic cloves, peeled,
   halved and any green
   shoots removed

For the vinegar
40g/1½oz/3 tbsp sugar
10ml/2 tsp salt
5cm/2in piece fresh root
   ginger, sliced
15ml/1 tbsp coriander seeds
2 lemon grass stalks, cut in
   half lengthways
4 kaffir lime leaves or pared
   strips of lime rind
600ml/1 pint/2½ cups
   cider vinegar
15ml/1 tbsp chopped fresh
   coriander (cilantro)

1 The chillies can be left whole, or halved and seeded. The pickle will be hotter if you leave the seeds in. If leaving the chillies whole, prick them several times with a cocktail stick (toothpick). Bring a large pan of water to the boil.

2 Add the chillies, shallots and garlic. Blanch for 1–2 minutes, then drain. Rinse all the vegetables under cold water. Drain again.

3 Prepare the vinegar. Put the sugar, salt, ginger, coriander seeds, lemon grass and lime leaves or lime rind in a pan, pour in the vinegar and bring to the boil.

4 Reduce the heat to low and simmer the spiced vinegar for about 3–4 minutes to allow the flavours to mingle. Remove from the heat and set aside to cool.

5 Remove and discard the ginger from the pan, then bring the vinegar back to the boil. Add the fresh coriander, chillies, shallots and garlic, and cook for 1 minute.

6 Pack the shallots into sterilized jars, distributing the lemon grass, lime leaves, chillies and garlic among them. Pour over the hot vinegar. Set aside to cool, then seal and store in a cool, dark place for 2 months before eating.

Hot Pickled Shallots Energy 127kcal/536kJ; Protein 2.3g; Carbohydrate 30.4g, of which sugars 26.5g; Fat 0.4g, of which saturates 0g; Cholesterol 0mg; Calcium 52mg; Fibre 2.7g; Sodium 7mg.
Pickled Onions Energy 109kcal/454kJ; Protein 3.1g; Carbohydrate 24.5g, of which sugars 18.6g; Fat 0.5g, of which saturates 0g; Cholesterol 0mg; Calcium 67mg; Fibre 3.6g; Sodium 8mg.

Pak Choi Salad with Lime Dressing

If you like your food hot and spicy, then this is the dish for you! The fiery flavours pack a punch.

Serves 4
30ml/2 tbsp oil
3 fresh red chillies, cut into
  thin strips
4 garlic cloves, thinly sliced

6 spring onions (scallions),
  sliced diagonally
2 pak choi (bok choy), shredded
15ml/1 tbsp crushed peanuts

For the dressing
30ml/2 tbsp fresh lime juice
15–30ml/1–2 tbsp Thai
  fish sauce
250ml/8fl oz/1 cup coconut milk

1 To make the dressing, put the lime juice and fish sauce in a bowl and mix well, then gradually whisk in the coconut milk until thoroughly combined.

2 Heat the oil in a wok and stir-fry the chillies for 2–3 minutes, until crisp. Transfer to a plate using a slotted spoon. Add the garlic to the wok and stir-fry for 30–60 seconds, until golden brown. Transfer to the plate.

3 Stir-fry the white parts of the spring onions for about 2–3 minutes, then add the green parts and stir-fry for 1 minute more. Transfer to the plate.

4 Bring a large pan of lightly salted water to the boil and add the pak choi. Stir twice, then drain immediately.

5 Place the pak choi in a large mixing bowl, pour over the dressing and toss to mix. Spoon into a large serving bowl and sprinkle with the crushed peanuts and the stir-fried chilli mixture. Serve immediately while still warm.

Cook's Tip
• *Thai fish sauce is traditionally used for this dressing, but if you are cooking for vegetarians, mushroom ketchup is a suitable vegetarian alternative.*
• *If pak choi is unavailable, use Chinese cabbage instead.*

Curried Red Cabbage Slaw

Quick and easy to make, this is a useful dish for a last-minute gathering.

Serves 4–6
½ red cabbage, thinly sliced
1 red (bell) pepper, chopped or
  very thinly sliced
½ red onion, chopped

60ml/4 tbsp red wine vinegar
60ml/4 tbsp sugar, or to taste
120ml/4fl oz/½ cup Greek
  (US strained plain) yogurt
120ml/4fl oz/½ cup mayonnaise,
  preferably home-made
1.5ml/¼ tsp curry powder
2–3 handfuls of raisins
salt and ground black pepper

1 Put the cabbage, red pepper and red onions in a large mixing bowl and toss to combine thoroughly.

2 Heat the red wine vinegar and sugar in a small pan, stirring constantly until the sugar has dissolved, then pour over the vegetables. Leave to cool slightly.

3 Mix together the yogurt and mayonnaise, then stir into the cabbage mixture. Season to taste with curry powder, salt and ground black pepper, then mix in the raisins.

4 Chill the salad in the refrigerator for at least 2 hours before serving. Just before serving, drain off any excess liquid and briefly stir the slaw again.

Spiced Aubergine Salad

The delicate flavours of aubergine, tomatoes and cucumber are lightly spiced with cumin and coriander in this fresh-tasting salad.

Serves 4
2 small aubergines (eggplants) or
  1 large aubergine, sliced
75ml/5 tbsp extra-virgin olive oil
50ml/2fl oz/¼ cup red
  wine vinegar

2 garlic cloves, crushed
15ml/1 tbsp lemon juice
2.5ml/½ tsp ground cumin
2.5ml/½ tsp ground coriander
½ cucumber, thinly sliced
2 well-flavoured tomatoes,
  thinly sliced
30ml/2 tbsp natural
  (plain) yogurt
salt and ground black pepper
chopped fresh flat leaf parsley,
  to garnish

1 Preheat the grill (broiler). Lightly brush the aubergine slices with olive oil and cook under a high heat, turning once, until they are golden and tender.

2 When the aubergine slices are done, transfer them to a chopping board and cut them into quarters.

3 In a bowl, mix together the remaining oil, the vinegar, garlic, lemon juice, cumin and coriander. Season with salt and black pepper to taste and mix thoroughly.

4 Add the warm aubergines to the bowl, stir well and chill in the refrigerator for at least 2 hours. Add the sliced cucumber and tomatoes to the aubergine. Transfer to a serving dish and spoon the yogurt on top. Sprinkle with the chopped fresh parsley and serve immediately.

Pak Choi Salad Energy 104kcal/434kJ; Protein 3.3g; Carbohydrate 5.2g, of which sugars 4.8g; Fat 8g, of which saturates 1.2g; Cholesterol 0mg; Calcium 116mg; Fibre 1.5g; Sodium 408mg.
Curried Cabbage Slaw Energy 286kcal/1194kJ; Protein 3.5g; Carbohydrate 31.6g, of which sugars 31g; Fat 17g, of which saturates 2.6g; Cholesterol 17mg; Calcium 108mg; Fibre 3.1g; Sodium 134mg.
Aubergine Salad Energy 161kcal/669kJ; Protein 2.3g; Carbohydrate 5.8g, of which sugars 5.5g; Fat 14.6g, of which saturates 2.2g; Cholesterol 0mg; Calcium 37mg; Fibre 3.7g; Sodium 15mg.

Lentil and Spinach Salad

This wonderful, earthy salad is great for a curry or with spicy barbecued food.

Serves 6
225g/8oz/1 cup Puy lentils
1 fresh bay leaf
1 celery stick
fresh thyme sprig
30ml/2 tbsp olive oil
1 onion or 3–4 shallots, chopped
10ml/2 tsp crushed toasted
   cumin seeds

400g/14oz young spinach
salt and ground black pepper
30–45ml/2–3 tbsp chopped fresh
   parsley, plus a few extra sprigs
   to garnish

For the dressing
75ml/5 tbsp extra virgin olive oil
5ml/1 tsp Dijon mustard
15–25ml/3–5 tsp red or white
   wine vinegar
1 garlic clove, finely chopped
2.5ml/½ tsp grated lemon rind

1 Rinse the lentils and place them in a large pan. Add plenty of water to cover. Tie the bay leaf, celery and thyme into a bundle and add to the pan, then bring to the boil. Reduce the heat so that the water boils steadily. Cook the lentils for 30–45 minutes, until just tender. Do not add salt at this stage.

2 Meanwhile, to make the dressing, mix the oil, mustard, 15ml/3 tsp vinegar, the garlic and lemon rind, and season well.

3 Thoroughly drain the lentils, discarding the herbs and celery, and transfer them into a large bowl. Add most of the dressing and toss well, then set the lentils aside, stirring occasionally.

4 Heat the oil in a deep frying pan and cook the onion or shallots over low heat for about 4–5 minutes, until they are beginning to soften. Add the cumin and cook for 1 minute. Add the spinach and season to taste, cover and cook for about 2 minutes. Stir, then cook again briefly until wilted.

5 Stir the spinach into the lentils and leave the salad to cool. Bring back to room temperature if necessary. Stir in the remaining dressing and chopped parsley. Adjust the seasoning, adding extra salt and pepper or red wine vinegar if necessary. Turn the salad on to a serving platter and sprinkle over some fresh parsley sprigs before serving.

Curried Potato Salad with Mango

This sweet and spicy salad is a wonderful accompaniment to Indian feasts.

Serves 4–6
900g/2lb new potatoes
15ml/1 tbsp olive oil
1 onion, sliced into rings
1 garlic clove, crushed
5ml/1 tsp ground cumin
5ml/1 tsp ground coriander
1 mango, peeled, stoned (pitted)
   and diced
30ml/2 tbsp demerara
   (raw) sugar
30ml/2 tbsp lime juice
15ml/1 tbsp sesame seeds
salt and ground black pepper
deep fried coriander (cilantro)
   leaves, to garnish (optional)

1 Cut the potatoes in half, then cook them in their skins in boiling salted water until tender. Drain well.

2 Heat the oil in a large frying pan and fry the onion and garlic over a low heat for 8–10 minutes, stirring frequently, until they start to soften and turn brown.

3 Stir the ground cumin and coriander into the pan and fry for a few seconds. Stir in the diced mango and sugar and fry for a further 5 minutes, until soft.

4 Remove the pan from the heat and squeeze in the lime juice. Season with salt and pepper.

5 Place the potatoes in a large serving bowl and spoon the mango dressing over the top. Sprinkle with the sesame seeds and serve while the dressing is still warm. Garnish with the deep-fried coriander leaves, if using.

Cook's Tip
To prepare the mango, cut through the mango lengthwise on either side of the stone (pit) to slice off two sections. Leaving the skin on each section, cross hatch the flesh, then bend it back so that the cubes stand proud of the skin. Slice them off with a small knife. Peel the remaining central section of the mango, then cut off the remaining flesh in chunks and dice.

Lentil Salad Energy 248kcal/1037kJ; Protein 11.2g; Carbohydrate 20.3g, of which sugars 2.1g; Fat 14.1g, of which saturates 2g; Cholesterol 0mg; Calcium 150mg; Fibre 5.1g; Sodium 102mg.
Curried Potato Salad Energy 174kcal/737kJ; Protein 3.3g; Carbohydrate 33.7g, of which sugars 11.2g; Fat 3.8g, of which saturates 0.7g; Cholesterol 0mg; Calcium 34mg; Fibre 2.5g; Sodium 18mg.

Potato Salad with Egg and Coronation Dressing

The connection between this recipe and traditional Indian cooking is tenuous, but coronation dressing is so popular that it would have been churlish to leave it out.

Serves 6

450g/1lb new potatoes
45ml/3 tbsp French dressing
3 spring onions (scallions), chopped
6 eggs, hard-boiled and halved
frilly lettuce leaves
¼ cucumber, cut into thin strips
6 large radishes, sliced
salad cress (optional)
salt and ground black pepper

For the coronation dressing
30ml/2 tbsp olive oil
1 small onion, chopped
15ml/1 tbsp mild curry powder or korma spice mix
10ml/2 tsp tomato purée (paste)
30ml/2 tbsp lemon juice
30ml/2 tbsp sherry
300ml/½ pint/1¼ cups mayonnaise
150ml/¼ pint/⅔ cup natural (plain) yogurt

1 Boil the potatoes in a pan of salted water until tender. Drain them, transfer to a large bowl and toss in the French dressing while they are still warm.

2 Stir the spring onions and the salt and pepper into the bowl with the potatoes, and leave to cool thoroughly.

3 Meanwhile, make the coronation dressing. Heat the oil in a small pan. Fry the onion for 3 minutes, until soft.

4 Stir in the curry powder or spice mix and fry for a further 1 minute, stirring constantly. Remove from the heat and mix in all the other dressing ingredients.

5 Pour the dressing over the potatoes and toss well. Add the eggs, then chill in the refrigerator.

6 Line a serving platter with the lettuce leaves and spoon the salad into the centre. Sprinkle over the cucumber and radishes with the cress, if using. Serve immediately.

Potato and Cellophane Noodle Salad

This tasty salad is an ideal side dish to serve at an Indian banquet or to take on a picnic. The recipe features gram flour, also known as besan, which is made from ground chickpeas.

Serves 4

2 medium potatoes, peeled and cut into eighths
175g/6oz cellophane noodles, soaked in hot water until soft
60ml/4 tbsp vegetable oil
1 onion, finely sliced
5ml/1 tsp ground turmeric
60ml/4 tbsp gram flour
5ml/1 tsp grated lemon rind
60–75ml/4–5 tbsp lemon juice
45ml/3 tbsp fish sauce
4 spring onions (scallions), finely sliced
salt and ground black pepper

1 Place the potatoes in a large pan. Add water to cover, bring to the boil and cook for about 15 minutes or until the potatoes are tender but still have a firmness to them. Drain the potatoes and set them aside to cool.

2 Meanwhile, cook the drained noodles in a pan of boiling water for 3 minutes or according to the packet instructions. Drain and rinse under cold running water. Drain well.

3 Heat the oil in a heavy frying pan. Add the onion and turmeric and fry for about 5–7 minutes until golden brown. Drain the onion, reserving the oil.

4 Heat a small frying pan. Add the gram flour and stir constantly for about 4–5 minutes until it turns light golden brown in colour. Take care to avoid it burning.

5 Mix the potatoes, noodles and fried onion in a large bowl. Add the reserved oil and the toasted gram flour with the lemon rind and juice, fish sauce and spring onions.

6 Mix all the ingredients together well and adjust the seasoning to taste with more salt and ground black pepper, if necessary. Serve the salad immediately.

Potato Salad Energy 590kcal/2443kJ; Protein 10.6g; Carbohydrate 18.1g, of which sugars 5.7g; Fat 51.9g, of which saturates 8.9g; Cholesterol 228mg; Calcium 114mg; Fibre 1.6g; Sodium 403mg.
Potato and Noodle Salad Energy 379kcal/1585kJ; Protein 8.2g; Carbohydrate 60g, of which sugars 3.2g; Fat 11.6g, of which saturates 1.7g; Cholesterol 0mg; Calcium 43mg; Fibre 1.4g; Sodium 558mg.

Curried Chicken Salad with Green Beans and Penne

This mildly spicy sauce goes well with lean chicken.

Serves 4

2 cooked chicken breast portions,
  skinned and boned
175g/6oz green beans
350g/12oz multi-coloured penne
150ml/¼ pint/⅔ cup natural
  (plain) yogurt

5ml/1 tsp mild curry powder
1 garlic clove, crushed
1 fresh green chilli, seeded and
  finely chopped
30ml/2 tbsp chopped fresh
  coriander (cilantro) and a few
  extra leaves to garnish
4 firm ripe tomatoes, skinned and
  seeded, and cut into strips
salt and ground black pepper

1 Cut the chicken into strips. Cut the green beans into 2.5cm/1in lengths and cook in boiling water for 5 minutes. Drain and rinse under cold water.

2 Cook the pasta in a large pan of lightly salted boiling water according to the packet instructions. Drain and rinse thoroughly.

3 To make the sauce, mix the yogurt, curry powder, garlic, chilli and chopped coriander together in a bowl. Stir in the chicken pieces and leave to stand for 30 minutes.

4 Transfer the pasta to a large serving bowl and toss with the beans and tomatoes. Spoon the chicken mixture on top. Garnish with the coriander leaves and serve immediately.

> **Variations**
> • This salad becomes the perfect lunchbox treat, delicious, filling and healthy, if you simply toss the pasta, beans and tomatoes in with the chicken, so that all the ingredients have a light coating of curry sauce. It's also a good way to use up left-over roast chicken – just omit step one.
> • The salad also works well with boiled and sliced waxy salad potatoes or white rice instead of the pasta. Simply add chopped red (bell) pepper for colour.

Rice Vermicelli and Fried Pork Salad

Fragrant pork tossed with beansprouts and fine noodles is a winning dish.

Serves 4

225g/8oz lean pork
2 garlic cloves, finely chopped
2 slices fresh root ginger, peeled
  and finely chopped
30–45ml/2–3 tbsp rice wine
45ml/3 tbsp vegetable oil or
  sunflower oil
2 lemon grass stalks,
  finely chopped

10ml/2 tsp curry powder
175g/6oz/¾ cup beansprouts
225g/8oz rice vermicelli, soaked
  in warm water until soft
  then drained
½ lettuce, finely shredded
30ml/2 tbsp fresh mint leaves
lemon juice and Thai fish sauce,
  to taste
salt and ground black pepper
2 spring onions (scallions),
  chopped, and 25g/1oz/¼ cup
  toasted peanuts, chopped,
  to garnish

1 Cut the pork into thin strips. Place in a shallow dish with half the garlic and ginger. Season with salt and pepper, pour over 30ml/2 tbsp rice wine and set aside to marinate for 1 hour.

2 Heat the oil in a frying pan. Add the remaining garlic and ginger and fry for a few seconds until fragrant. Stir in the pork, with the marinade, and add the lemon grass and curry powder. Fry on a high heat until the pork is golden and cooked through, adding more rice wine if the mixture seems too dry.

3 Place the beansprouts in a sieve (strainer) and lower into a pan of boiling water for 1 minute, then drain and refresh under cold running water. Drain again. Using the same water, cook the rice vermicelli for 3–5 minutes, until tender. Drain and rinse.

4 Drain the vermicelli well and put in a large bowl. Add the beansprouts, shredded lettuce and mint leaves. Season with lemon juice and fish sauce to taste. Toss lightly.

5 Divide the vermicelli mixture between individual serving plates and top with the pork. Garnish with spring onions and peanuts, and serve immediately.

Chicken Salad Energy 430kcal/1828kJ; Protein 32.1g; Carbohydrate 72.5g, of which sugars 9.8g; Fat 3.4g, of which saturates 0.7g; Cholesterol 53mg; Calcium 128mg; Fibre 4.8g; Sodium 94mg.
Fried Pork Salad Energy 409kcal/1705kJ; Protein 20.8g; Carbohydrate 48.7g, of which sugars 2.8g; Fat 14.5g, of which saturates 2.4g; Cholesterol 35mg; Calcium 68mg; Fibre 2.4g; Sodium 60mg.

Korean Cucumber Namul

This sautéed dish retains the natural succulence of the cucumber, while also infusing the recipe with a pleasantly refreshing hint of garlic and fresh chilli.

Serves 2

200g/7oz cucumber
15ml/1 tbsp vegetable oil
5ml/1 tsp spring onion (scallion), finely chopped
1 garlic clove, crushed
5ml/1 tsp sesame oil or groundnut (peanut) oil
sesame seeds, and seeded and shredded red chilli, to garnish
salt

1 Thinly slice the cucumber and place in a colander over a bowl. Sprinkle with about 5ml/1 tsp salt, then leave to stand in a cool place for at least 10 minutes.

2 Drain off any excess liquid from the cucumber slices and transfer them to a clean bowl.

3 Coat a frying pan or wok with the vegetable oil, and heat it over a medium heat. Add the spring onion, garlic and cucumber to the pan, and quickly stir-fry together for about 2–3 minutes.

4 Remove the pan from the heat, add the sesame or groundnut oil and toss lightly to blend all the ingredients. Place the salad in a shallow serving dish and garnish with the sesame seeds and shredded red chilli before serving.

Cook's Tip
Take care when handling chillies that you don't touch other sensitive parts of your body afterwards otherwise the chilli oil from your fingers will cause irritation. Wash your hands well.

Variation
Replace the chilli with thin strips of shredded red (bell) pepper if you prefer a version with less heat.

Green Mango Salad

Green mangoes have light green flesh and go well with prawns (shrimp) or beef.

Serves 4

450g/1lb green mangoes
rind and juice of 2 limes
30ml/2 tbsp sugar
30ml/2 tbsp nuoc cham (Vietnamese fish sauce)
2 green Thai chillies, seeded and finely sliced
1 small bunch fresh coriander (cilantro), stalks removed, finely chopped
salt

1 Peel, halve and stone (pit) the mangoes, then slice into strips.

2 In a bowl, mix together the lime juice and rind, sugar and nuoc cham. Add the mango strips with the chillies and coriander. Add salt to taste and set aside for 20 minutes before serving.

Rocket and Coriander Salad

Rocket leaves have a wonderful, peppery flavour and, mixed with coriander, make a delicious salad. You may need extra spinach to pad this salad out unless you have a big supply of rocket.

Serves 4

115g/4oz or more rocket (arugula) leaves
115g/4oz young spinach leaves
1 large bunch (about 25g/1oz) fresh coriander
2–3 fresh parsley sprigs
1 garlic clove, crushed
45ml/3 tbsp olive oil
10ml/2 tsp white wine vinegar
pinch of paprika
salt
cayenne pepper

1 Wash the rocket and spinach, pat dry, then place in a salad bowl. Chop the herbs and add to the salad.

2 In a small jug (pitcher), blend together the garlic, olive oil, vinegar, paprika, salt and cayenne pepper.

3 Pour the dressing over the salad in the bowl. Toss with your hands to coat the salad in the dressing and serve immediately.

Korean Namul Energy 74kcal/304kJ; Protein 0.8g; Carbohydrate 1.7g, of which sugars 1.6g; Fat 7.1g, of which saturates 0.9g; Cholesterol 0mg; Calcium 20mg; Fibre 0.7g; Sodium 4mg.
Green Mango Salad Energy 92kcal/391kJ; Protein 1g; Carbohydrate 22g, of which sugars 15g; Fat 0g, of which saturates 0g; Cholesterol 0mg; Calcium 32mg; Fibre 33g; Sodium 0.5mg.
Rocket Salad Energy 68kcal/280kJ; Protein 2g; Carbohydrate 1.3g, of which sugars 1.2g; Fat 6.1g, of which saturates 0.9g; Cholesterol 0mg; Calcium 123mg; Fibre 1.8g; Sodium 85mg.

Green Papaya Salad

This salad appears in many guises in South-east Asia. As green papaya is not easy to get hold of, finely grated carrots, cucumber or even crisp green apple can be used instead. Alternatively, use very thinly sliced white cabbage.

Serves 4

1 green papaya
4 garlic cloves, coarsely chopped
15ml/1 tbsp chopped shallots
3–4 fresh red chillies, seeded and sliced
2.5ml/½ tsp salt
2–3 yard-long beans or 6 green beans, cut into 2cm/¾in lengths
2 tomatoes, cut into thin wedges
45ml/3 tbsp Thai fish sauce
15ml/1 tbsp caster (superfine) sugar
juice of 1 lime
30ml/2 tbsp crushed roasted peanuts
sliced fresh red chillies, to garnish

1 Cut the papaya in half lengthways. Scrape out the seeds with a spoon and discard, then peel, using a swivel vegetable peeler or a small sharp knife. Shred the papaya flesh finely in a food processor or by using a grater.

2 Put the garlic, shallots, red chillies and salt in a large mortar and grind to a paste with a pestle.

3 Add the shredded papaya to the mortar, a small amount at a time, pounding with the pestle until it becomes slightly limp.

4 Add the sliced yard-long or green beans and wedges of tomato to the mortar and crush them lightly with the pestle until they are incorporated.

5 Season the mixture with the fish sauce, sugar and lime juice. Transfer to a serving dish and sprinkle with the crushed roasted peanuts. Garnish with the red chillies and serve immediately.

> **Cook's Tip**
> Wen ripe, papayas have a vivid golden-yellow skin and juicy, silky flesh. The seeds are edible, with a peppery taste.

Indonesian Curried Salad

Originally from Indonesia, this salad has been well integrated into the cuisine of Malaysia and Singapore, and there is even an Indian version, made with added hard-boiled eggs, fried tofu, sliced fish cakes and a spicy dressing. As this recipe is so flexible, you can really use any combination of fruit and vegetables, depending on what is available, and make the sauce as pungent and fiery as you like.

Serves 4–6

1 jicama (sweet turnip), peeled and finely sliced
1 small cucumber, partially peeled and finely sliced
1 green mango, peeled and finely sliced
1 star fruit (carambola), finely sliced
4 slices fresh pineapple, cored
half a pomelo, separated into segments, with the membrane removed
a handful of beansprouts, rinsed and drained
fresh mint leaves, to garnish

For the sauce
225g/8oz/2 cups roasted peanuts
4 garlic cloves, chopped
2–4 red chillies, seeded and finely chopped
10ml/2 tsp shrimp paste, dry-roasted in a pan over a high heat
15ml/1 tbsp tamarind paste
30ml/2 tbsp palm sugar (jaggery)
salt

1 First make the sauce. Using a mortar and pestle, food processor or blender, grind the peanuts with the garlic and chillies to a coarse paste. Transfer the paste to a mixing bowl.

2 Beat the roasted shrimp paste, tamarind paste and sugar into the peanut and chilli paste in the bowl. Add enough water to make a thick, pouring sauce, and stir well until the sugar has dissolved. Add salt to taste.

3 Arrange the sliced fruit and vegetables on a plate, with the beansprouts sprinkled over the top.

4 Drizzle the sauce over the salad and garnish with mint leaves. Serve as an accompaniment to grilled meats and spicy dishes, or on its own as a healthy snack.

Green Papaya Salad Energy 63kcal/263kJ; Protein 2.5g; Carbohydrate 6.2g, of which sugars 5.6g; Fat 3.3g, of which saturates 0.6g; Cholesterol 0mg; Calcium 19mg; Fibre 1.8g; Sodium 835mg.
Indonesian Salad Energy 330kcal/1381kJ; Protein 12.9g; Carbohydrate 28g, of which sugars 25.1g; Fat 19.3g, of which saturates 3.4g; Cholesterol 13mg; Calcium 114mg; Fibre 6.3g; Sodium 416mg.

Nutty Bean Salad with Courgettes and Pasta Shells

Serve this delicious salad
as an accompaniment or as
an appetizer.

Serves 4
1 medium onion, cut into 12 rings
115g/4oz/¹/₂ cup canned red
    kidney beans, drained
1 medium green courgette
    (zucchini), sliced
1 medium yellow courgette, sliced
50g/2oz/²/₃ cup pasta
    shells, cooked
50g/2oz/¹/₂ cup cashew nuts
25g/1oz/¹/₄ cup peanuts

For the dressing
120ml/4fl oz/¹/₂ cup fromage
    frais or ricotta cheese
30ml/2 tbsp natural (plain) yogurt
1 fresh green chilli, seeded and
    finely chopped
15ml/1 tbsp chopped fresh
    coriander (cilantro)
2.5ml/¹/₂ tsp salt
2.5ml/¹/₂ tsp crushed black
    peppercorns
2.5ml/¹/₂ tsp crushed dried
    red chillies
15ml/1 tbsp lemon juice
lime wedges, to garnish

1 Arrange the onion rings, red kidney beans, courgette slices
and pasta in a large salad dish and sprinkle the cashew nuts and
peanuts over the top.

2 In a separate bowl, blend together the fromage frais or
ricotta cheese, yogurt, chopped green chilli, fresh coriander and
salt and beat it well using a fork.

3 Sprinkle the black pepper, crushed red chillies and lemon
juice over the dressing in the bowl.

4 Garnish the salad with the lime wedges and serve
immediately with the dressing either in a separate bowl or
poured over the salad and gently tossed to combine.

> **Cook's Tip**
> *If you cannot find a yellow courgette (zucchini), then simply use
> another of the green variety. The salad may not look quite as
> colourful but the flavour will not suffer as a result.*

Sweet Cucumber Salad

This sweet dipping sauce is
good served with Thai bites.

Makes 120ml/4fl oz/¹/₂ cup
¹/₄ small cucumber, thinly sliced
75ml/5 tbsp water

30ml/2 tbsp sugar
2.5ml/¹/₂ tsp salt
15ml/1 tbsp rice or white
    wine vinegar
2 shallots or 1 small red onion,
    thinly sliced

1 With a sharp knife, cut the cucumber slices into quarters.

2 Put the water, sugar, salt and vinegar into a pan, bring to the
boil and simmer until the sugar has dissolved. Leave to cool.
Add the cucumber and shallots or onion. Serve immediately.

Pepper and Cucumber Salad

Fresh herbs transform
familiar ingredients into a
tasty side salad.

Serves 4
1 yellow or red (bell) pepper
1 large cucumber
4–5 tomatoes
1 bunch spring onions (scallions)
30ml/2 tbsp fresh parsley

30ml/2 tbsp fresh mint
30ml/2 tbsp fresh
    coriander (cilantro)
2 pitta breads, to serve

For the dressing
2 garlic cloves, crushed
75ml/5 tbsp olive oil
juice of 2 lemons
salt and ground black pepper

1 Halve, seed and core the pepper, then slice. Roughly chop
the cucumber and tomatoes. Place in a large salad bowl.

2 Slice the spring onions and add to the cucumber, tomatoes
and pepper. Finely chop the fresh herbs and add to the bowl.

3 To make the dressing, blend the garlic with the oil and lemon
juice, then season to taste. Pour over the salad and toss.

4 Toast the pitta breads under a hot grill (broiler) and serve
immediately while hot, alongside the salad.

Nutty Bean Salad Energy 106kcal/444kJ; Protein 5.5g; Carbohydrate 11.9g, of which sugars 3.5g; Fat 4.4g, of which saturates 0.7g; Cholesterol 0mg; Calcium 62mg; Fibre 4.4g; Sodium 228mg..
Sweet Cucumber Salad Energy 147kcal/624kJ; Protein 1.4g; Carbohydrate 37.2g, of which sugars 35.8g; Fat 0.2g, of which saturates 0g; Cholesterol 0mg; Calcium 44mg; Fibre 1.3g; Sodium 6mg.
Pepper Salad Energy 159kcal/656kJ; Protein 1.8g; Carbohydrate 5.8g, of which sugars 5.6g; Fat 14.4g, of which saturates 2.1g; Cholesterol 0mg; Calcium 46mg; Fibre 2.4g; Sodium 13mg.

Sweet Potato and Carrot Salad

This simple salad has a delicious sweet-and-sour taste, and can be served warm as part of a light lunch or supper or eaten in a larger quantity as a main course.

Serves 4
1 medium sweet potato
2 carrots, cut into thick
    diagonal slices
3 medium tomatoes
8–10 iceberg lettuce leaves or
    Little Gem (Bibb) lettuce
75g/3oz/½ cup canned
    chickpeas, drained

For the dressing
15ml/1 tbsp clear honey
90ml/6 tbsp natural (plain)
    low-fat yogurt
2.5ml/½ tsp salt
2.5ml/1 tsp coarsely ground
    black pepper

For the garnish
15ml/1 tbsp walnuts, shelled
    and halved
15ml/1 tbsp sultanas
    (golden raisins)
1 small onion, cut into rings

1 Peel the sweet potato and roughly dice. Boil until soft but not mushy, cover the pan and set aside.

2 Boil the carrots for just a few minutes making sure they remain crunchy. Add the carrots to the sweet potato.

3 Drain all the water from the sweet potato and carrots and place them together in a bowl.

4 Slice the tops off the tomatoes, then scoop out and discard the seeds. Roughly chop the flesh.

5 Line a serving bowl with the lettuce leaves. Mix the sweet potato, carrots, chickpeas and tomatoes together and place in the bowl.

6 In a separate bowl, blend together all the ingredients for the dressing and beat using a fork or small whisk.

7 Garnish the salad with the walnuts, sultanas and onion rings. Pour the dressing over the salad or serve it in a separate bowl.

Mango, Tomato and Red Onion Salad

The firm texture of under-ripe mango blends perfectly with the tomato and gives this salad a delicious tropical touch. Serve this salad as a side dish to an Indian meal or as an appetizer.

Serves 4
1 firm under-ripe mango
2 large tomatoes or 1 beef
    tomato, sliced
½ red onion, sliced into rings
½ cucumber, peeled and
    thinly sliced

For the dressing
30ml/2 tbsp sunflower or
    vegetable oil
15ml/1 tbsp lemon juice
1 garlic clove, crushed
2.5ml/½ tsp hot pepper sauce
salt and ground black pepper
chopped fresh chives,
    to garnish

1 Halve the mango lengthwise, cutting either side of the stone (pit). Cut the flesh into slices and peel the skin away.

2 Arrange the mango slices, tomato, onion and cucumber on a large serving plate or in a shallow salad bowl.

3 To make the dressing, blend the sunflower or vegetable oil, lemon juice, garlic, pepper sauce and seasoning in a blender or food processor, or, if you prefer, place in a small screw-top jar and shake vigorously to combine.

4 Pour the dressing over the salad. Toss well with your hands or salad servers to ensure that the ingredients are all well coated in the dressing. Serve the salad immediately garnished with the chopped fresh chives.

> **Cook's Tip**
> *You can adjust the quantity of hot pepper sauce in the dressing to suit your taste. Be careful as some varieties of hot pepper sauce are much hotter than others so always taste a tiny bit to check the heat levels.*

Mango Salad Energy 89kcal/369kJ; Protein 1.1g; Carbohydrate 8.6g, of which sugars 7.9g; Fat 5.8g, of which saturates 0.8g; Cholesterol 0mg; Calcium 17mg; Fibre 1.9g; Sodium 7mg.
Sweet Potato Salad 153kcal/648kJ; Protein 4.7g; Carbohydrate 26.7g, of which sugars 15.4g; Fat 3.9g, of which saturates 0.6g; Cholesterol 0mg; Calcium 88mg; Fibre 3.9g; Sodium 95mg.

Cucumber and Shallot Salad

In Malaysia and Singapore, this light, refreshing salad is served with Indian food almost as often as the cooling mint-flavoured cucumber raita. The Malays also enjoy this salad with many of their spicy fish and grilled meat dishes. It can be made ahead of time and kept in the refrigerator. Serve it as a salad, or a relish.

Serves 4
1 cucumber, peeled, halved lengthways and seeded
4 shallots, halved lengthways and sliced finely along the grain
1–2 green chillies, seeded and sliced finely lengthways
60ml/4 tbsp coconut milk
5–10ml/1–2 tsp cumin seeds, dry-roasted and ground to a powder
salt
1 lime, quartered, to serve

1 Slice the cucumber halves finely and sprinkle with a little salt. Set aside for about 10–15 minutes to draw out any excess moisture. Rinse well and drain off any excess water.

2 Put the cucumber, shallots and chillies in a salad serving bowl. Pour in the coconut milk and toss well. Sprinkle most of the roasted cumin seeds over the top.

3 Just before serving, toss the salad again, season with salt, and sprinkle the rest of the roasted cumin seeds over the top. Serve with lime wedges to squeeze over the salad.

Orange and Red Onion Salad

Cumin and mint give this refreshing, quick-to-prepare salad a very Middle Eastern flavour. Small, seedless oranges are most suitable, if available.

Serves 6
6 oranges
2 red onions

15ml/1 tbsp cumin seeds
5ml/1 tsp coarsely ground black pepper
15ml/1 tbsp chopped fresh mint
90ml/6 tbsp olive oil
salt
fresh mint sprigs and black olives, to garnish

1 Slice the oranges thinly, catching any juices. Holding each orange slice in turn over a bowl, cut round with scissors to remove the peel and pith. Reserve the juice.

2 Slice the red onions thinly and as evenly as possible. Separate each of the slices into rings.

3 Arrange the orange and onion slices in layers in a shallow dish, sprinkling each layer with cumin seeds, ground black pepper, chopped mint, olive oil and salt to taste. Pour over the reserved orange juice.

4 Leave the salad in a cool place or in the refrigerator for a minimum of 2 hours but no longer than about 4 hours.

5 Sprinkle over the fresh mint sprigs and black olives to garnish, and serve immediately.

Vietnamese Table Salad

The Vietnamese table salad can vary from a bowl of fresh, leafy herbs to a more tropical combination of beansprouts, water chestnuts, mangoes, bananas, star fruit, peanuts and rice noodles. The arrangement of a salad is simple and attractive.

Serves 4–6
1 crunchy lettuce, individual leaves separated
half a cucumber, peeled and thinly sliced

2 carrots, peeled and finely sliced
200g/7oz/scant 1 cup beansprouts
2 unripe star fruit (carambola), finely sliced
2 green bananas, finely sliced
1 firm papaya, cut in half, seeds removed, peeled and finely sliced
1 bunch each fresh mint and basil, stalks removed
1 lime
dipping sauce, to serve

1 Arrange all the ingredients, except the lime and sauce, on a large serving plate, with the lettuce leaves placed on one side so that they can be used as wrappers.

2 Squeeze the lime and pour the juice all over the sliced fruits, particularly the bananas to help them retain their colour and avoid discoloration from contact with the air.

3 Place the salad on the serving plate in the middle of the table. Serve immediately with a dipping sauce in a separate bowl so that diners can help themselves.

Cook's Tip
• When this Vietnamese table salad, known as sa lach dia, is served on its own, the vegetables and fruit are usually folded into little packets using lettuce leaves or rice wrappers, and then dipped in a sauce, or added bit by bit to bowls of plain boiled rice or noodles.
• Choose a lettuce with crisp, crunchy leaves such as iceberg, Little Gem (Bibb), cos or romaine.

Cucumber Salad Energy 17kcal/68kJ; Protein 0.7g; Carbohydrate 3.3g, of which sugars 2.7g; Fat 0.1g, of which saturates 0g; Cholesterol 0mg; Calcium 19mg; Fibre 0.7g; Sodium 15mg.
Orange Salad Energy 199kcal/825kJ; Protein 1.6g; Carbohydrate 11.5g, of which sugars 11.3g; Fat 16.6g, of which saturates 2.4g; Cholesterol 0mg; Calcium 68mg; Fibre 2.3g; Sodium 7mg
Vietnamese Salad Energy 108kcal/455kJ; Protein 4g; Carbohydrate 21g, of which sugars 12g; Fat 1g, of which saturates 0g; Cholesterol 0mg; Calcium 110mg; Fibre 42g; Sodium 20mg.

Fruit and Raw Vegetable Gado-Gado

Banana leaves are often used as wrappers in which to cook small parcels of food, but if you are serving this salad for a special occasion, you could use a large single banana leaf instead of the mixed salad leaves to line the platter.

Serves 6
½ cucumber
2 pears (not too ripe) or 175g/6oz wedge of yam bean
1–2 eating apples
juice of ½ lemon
mixed salad leaves or 1–2 banana leaves
6 tomatoes, seeded and cut into wedges
3 fresh pineapple slices, cored and cut into wedges
3 hard-boiled eggs, quartered
175g/6oz egg noodles, cooked, cooled and chopped
deep-fried onions, to garnish

For the peanut sauce
2–4 fresh red chillies, seeded and ground, or 15ml/1 tbsp hot tomato sambal
300ml/½ pint/1¼ cups coconut milk
350g/12oz/1¼ cups crunchy peanut butter
15ml/1 tbsp dark soy sauce or dark brown sugar
5ml/1 tsp tamarind pulp, soaked in 45ml/3 tbsp warm water
coarsely crushed peanuts
salt

1 Make the peanut sauce. Put the ground chillies or hot tomato sambal in a pan. Pour in the coconut milk, then stir in the peanut butter. Heat gently, stirring, until well blended.

2 Simmer the sauce gently until it begins to thicken, then stir in the soy sauce or sugar. Strain in the tamarind juice, discarding the seeds and pulp, add salt to taste and stir well. Spoon into a bowl and sprinkle with coarsely crushed peanuts.

3 To make the salad, core the cucumber and peel the pears or yam bean. Cut the flesh into fine matchsticks. Finely shred the apples and sprinkle them with the lemon juice. Spread a bed of mixed salad leaves on a flat platter and pile the cucumber, pears or yam bean, apples, tomatoes and pineapple on top.

4 Add the quartered eggs and the noodles and garnish with the deep-fried onions. Serve with the peanut sauce.

Cambodian Soya Beansprout Salad

Unlike mung beansprouts, soya beansprouts are slightly poisonous raw and need to be par-boiled before using. Tossed in a salad and served with noodles and rice they make a perfect light meal.

Serves 4
450g/1lb fresh soya beansprouts
2 spring onions (scallions), finely sliced
1 small bunch fresh coriander (cilantro), stalks removed

For the dressing
15ml/1 tbsp sesame oil
30ml/2 tbsp light soy sauce
15ml/1 tbsp white rice vinegar
10ml/2 tsp palm sugar (jaggery)
1 fresh red chilli, seeded and finely sliced
15g/½oz fresh young root ginger, finely shredded

1 To make the dressing, in a bowl, beat the sesame oil, soy sauce and rice vinegar with the palm sugar, until it dissolves. Stir in the sliced red chilli and ginger and set the bowl aside for about 30 minutes to let the flavours develop.

2 Bring a pan of salted water to the boil. Drop in the beansprouts and blanch for a minute only. Drain and refresh under cold water until cool. Drain again and put them into a clean dish towel. Shake out the excess water.

3 Put the beansprouts into a bowl with the spring onions. Pour over the dressing and toss well. Garnish with the coriander leaves and serve immediately.

Fennel Coleslaw

Another variation on traditional coleslaw in which the flavour of fennel plays a major role in creating this delectable salad.

Serves 4
175g/6oz fennel
2 spring onions (scallions)
175g/6oz white cabbage
115g/4oz celery
175g/6oz carrots
50g/2oz/scant ½ cup sultanas (golden raisins)
2.5ml/½ tsp caraway seeds (optional)
15ml/1 tbsp chopped fresh parsley
45ml/3 tbsp extra-virgin olive oil
5ml/1 tsp lemon juice
strips of spring onion (scallion), to garnish

1 Using a sharp knife, cut the fennel and spring onions into thin slices. Place in a serving bowl.

2 Slice the cabbage and celery finely and cut the carrots into fine strips. Add to the fennel and spring onions in the serving bowl. Add the sultanas and caraway seeds to the bowl, if using, and toss lightly to mix through.

3 Stir the chopped parsley, olive oil and lemon juice into the bowl and mix all the ingredients very thoroughly.

4 Cover the bowl with clear film (plastic wrap) and chill in the refrigerator for about 3 hours to allow all the flavours of the coleslaw to mingle together. Serve the coleslaw immediately, garnished with strips of spring onion.

Fruit Gado-Gado Energy 577kcal/2411kJ; Protein 21.2g; Carbohydrate 46.3g, of which sugars 21g; Fat 35.5g, of which saturates 8.4g; Cholesterol 95mg; Calcium 88mg; Fibre 6.8g; Sodium 482mg.
Cambodian Salad Energy 95kcal/396kJ; Protein 4.5g; Carbohydrate 8.4g, of which sugars 5.6g; Fat 5.6g, of which saturates 0.5g; Cholesterol 3mg; Calcium 54mg; Fibre 2.4g; Sodium 79mg.
Fennel Coleslaw Energy 145kcal/604kJ; Protein 1.9g; Carbohydrate 15.6g, of which sugars 15.3g; Fat 8.7g, of which saturates 1.2g; Cholesterol 0mg; Calcium 70mg; Fibre 3.8g; Sodium 46mg.

Raw Vegetable Yam

In Thai cooking, 'yam' dishes are salads made with raw or lightly cooked vegetables. Serve with a fiery curry to appreciate the cooling effect.

Serves 4

50g/2oz watercress or baby
   spinach, chopped
¹/₂ cucumber, finely diced
2 celery sticks, finely diced
2 carrots, finely diced
1 red (bell) pepper, seeded
   and finely diced
2 tomatoes, seeded and
   finely diced
small bunch fresh mint,
   finely chopped
90g/3¹/₂oz cellophane noodles

For the yam

2 small fresh red chillies, seeded
   and finely chopped
60ml/4 tbsp light soy sauce
45ml/3 tbsp lemon juice
5ml/1 tsp palm sugar (jaggery)
   or light muscovado
   (brown) sugar
60ml/4 tbsp water
1 head pickled garlic, finely
   chopped, plus 15ml/1 tbsp
   vinegar from the jar
50g/2oz/scant ¹/₂ cup peanuts,
   roasted and chopped
90g/3¹/₂oz fried tofu,
   finely chopped
15ml/1 tbsp sesame
   seeds, toasted

1 Place the watercress or spinach, cucumber, celery, carrots, red pepper and tomatoes in a large serving bowl. Add the chopped fresh mint and toss together.

2 Soak the noodles in boiling water for about 3 minutes, or according to the packet instructions, rinse in cold water.

3 Drain the noodles well and snip with a pair of scissors into shorter lengths. Add them to the vegetables in the bowl.

4 To make the yam, put the chopped chillies in a pan and add the soy sauce, lemon juice, sugar and water. Place over a medium heat and stir until the sugar has dissolved.

5 Add the garlic, with the pickling vinegar from the jar, then mix in the chopped nuts, tofu and toasted sesame seeds.

6 Pour the yam over the vegetables and noodles, toss together until well mixed, and serve immediately.

Bamboo Shoot Salad

This hot, sharp-flavoured salad originated in north-eastern Thailand. Serve with noodles and stir-fried vegetables, or as a side dish with a green or red curry.

Serves 4

400g/14oz canned bamboo
   shoots, in large pieces
25g/1oz/about 3 tbsp
   glutinous rice

30ml/2 tbsp chopped shallots
15ml/1 tbsp chopped garlic
45ml/3 tbsp chopped spring
   onions (scallions)
30ml/2 tbsp light soy sauce
30ml/2 tbsp fresh lime juice
5ml/1 tsp sugar
2.5ml/¹/₂ tsp dried chilli flakes
20–25 small fresh mint leaves
15ml/1 tbsp toasted
   sesame seeds

1 Rinse the bamboo shoots under cold running water, then drain them and pat them thoroughly dry with kitchen paper and set them aside.

2 Dry-roast the rice in a frying pan until it is golden brown. Leave to cool slightly, then turn into a mortar and grind to fine crumbs with a pestle.

3 Transfer the rice to a bowl and add the shallots, garlic, spring onions, soy sauce, lime juice, sugar, chillies and half the mint leaves. Mix well.

4 Add the bamboo shoots to the bowl and toss well to ensure they are evenly coated in all the other ingredients.

5 Sprinkle the salad with the toasted sesame seeds and the remaining fresh mint leaves and serve immediately.

> **Cook's Tips**
> • Glutinous rice does not, in fact, contain any gluten – it's just sticky. It is very popular in South-east Asian cooking.
> • This recipe works best with canned whole bamboo shoots, if you can find them – they have more flavour than the more common sliced variety.

Raw Vegetable Yam Energy 276kcal/1152kJ; Protein 12.1g; Carbohydrate 28.8g, of which sugars 9g; Fat 12.4g, of which saturates 1.5g; Cholesterol 0mg; Calcium 415mg; Fibre 3.1g; Sodium 1101mg.
Bamboo Shoot Salad Energy 72kcal/305kJ; Protein 3.9g; Carbohydrate 13g, of which sugars 6.2g; Fat 0.7g, of which saturates 0.1g; Cholesterol 0mg; Calcium 31mg; Fibre 1.9g; Sodium 185mg.

Malay Vegetable Salad

This beansprout salad, known as kerabu, is deliciously crunchy and fresh, packed with crisp vegetables and lots of herbs. It is usually served as a side dish to accompany many of the highly spiced Malay curries.

Serves 4

115g/4oz fresh coconut, grated
30ml/2 tbsp dried prawns (shrimp), soaked in warm water for 1 hour or until soft
225g/8oz beansprouts, rinsed and drained
1 small cucumber, peeled, seeded and cut into julienne strips
2–3 spring onions (scallions), trimmed, cut into 2.5cm/1in pieces and halved lengthways
a handful of young, tender mangetouts (snow peas), halved diagonally
a handful of cooked green beans, halved lengthways
a handful of fresh chives, chopped into 2.5cm/1in pieces
a handful of fresh mint leaves, finely chopped
2–3 fresh red chillies, seeded and sliced finely along the length
juice of 2 limes
10ml/2 tsp sugar
salt and ground black pepper

1 Dry-roast the coconut in a heavy pan until it is lightly browned and emits a nutty aroma.

2 Using a mortar and pestle or a food processor, grind the roasted coconut to a coarse powder. Drain the soaked dried prawns and grind them coarsely too.

3 Put the vegetables, herbs and chillies into a bowl. Mix the lime juice with the sugar and pour it over the salad.

4 Season with salt and black pepper. Sprinkle the ground coconut and dried prawns over the salad, and toss well until thoroughly mixed. Serve immediately.

> **Cook's Tip**
> Try a mixture of other herbs in this salad, depending on what is available. Coriander (cilantro) and parsley both work well.

Prawn and Mint Salad

Use fresh rather than frozen prawns in this mouthwatering salad. Fresh prawns make all the difference to this salad, as cooking them in butter adds to the piquant flavour. Garnish with shavings of fresh coconut for a tropical topping.

Serves 4

12 large raw prawns (shrimp)
15ml/1 tbsp unsalted butter
15ml/1 tbsp Thai fish sauce
juice of 1 lime
45ml/3 tbsp thin coconut milk
5ml/1 tsp caster (superfine) sugar
1 garlic clove, crushed
2.5cm/1in piece fresh root ginger, peeled and grated
2 red chillies, seeded and finely chopped
30ml/2 tbsp fresh mint leaves
225g/8oz light green lettuce leaves
ground black pepper

1 Carefully peel the raw prawns, removing and discarding the heads and outer shells, but leaving the tails intact.

2 Using a sharp knife, carefully remove the dark-coloured vein that runs along the back of each prawn.

3 Melt the butter in a large frying pan. When it begins to foam, add the prawns and toss over a high heat until they turn pink. Remove from the heat; it is important not to cook them for too long so that their tenderness is retained.

4 In a small bowl mix the fish sauce, lime juice, coconut milk, sugar, garlic, ginger and chillies together. Season to taste with freshly ground black pepper.

5 Toss the warm prawns into the sauce with the mint leaves. Arrange the lettuce leaves on a serving plate and place the prawn and mint mixture in the centre.

> **Cook's Tip**
> If you can't find any fresh, raw prawns you could use frozen ones. Completely thaw the prawns, then toss very quickly in the hot butter to make the most of their flavour.

Malay Salad Energy 230kcal/947kJ; Protein 12.6g; Carbohydrate 15.9g, of which sugars 13.9g; Fat 12.9g, of which saturates 10.2g; Cholesterol 0mg; Calcium 151mg; Fibre 7.8g; Sodium 24mg.
Prawn Salad Energy 83kcal/347kJ; Protein 9.8g; Carbohydrate 2.5g, of which sugars 1.7g; Fat 3.8g, of which saturates 2.1g; Cholesterol 106mg; Calcium 86mg; Fibre 0.5g; Sodium 144mg.

Index